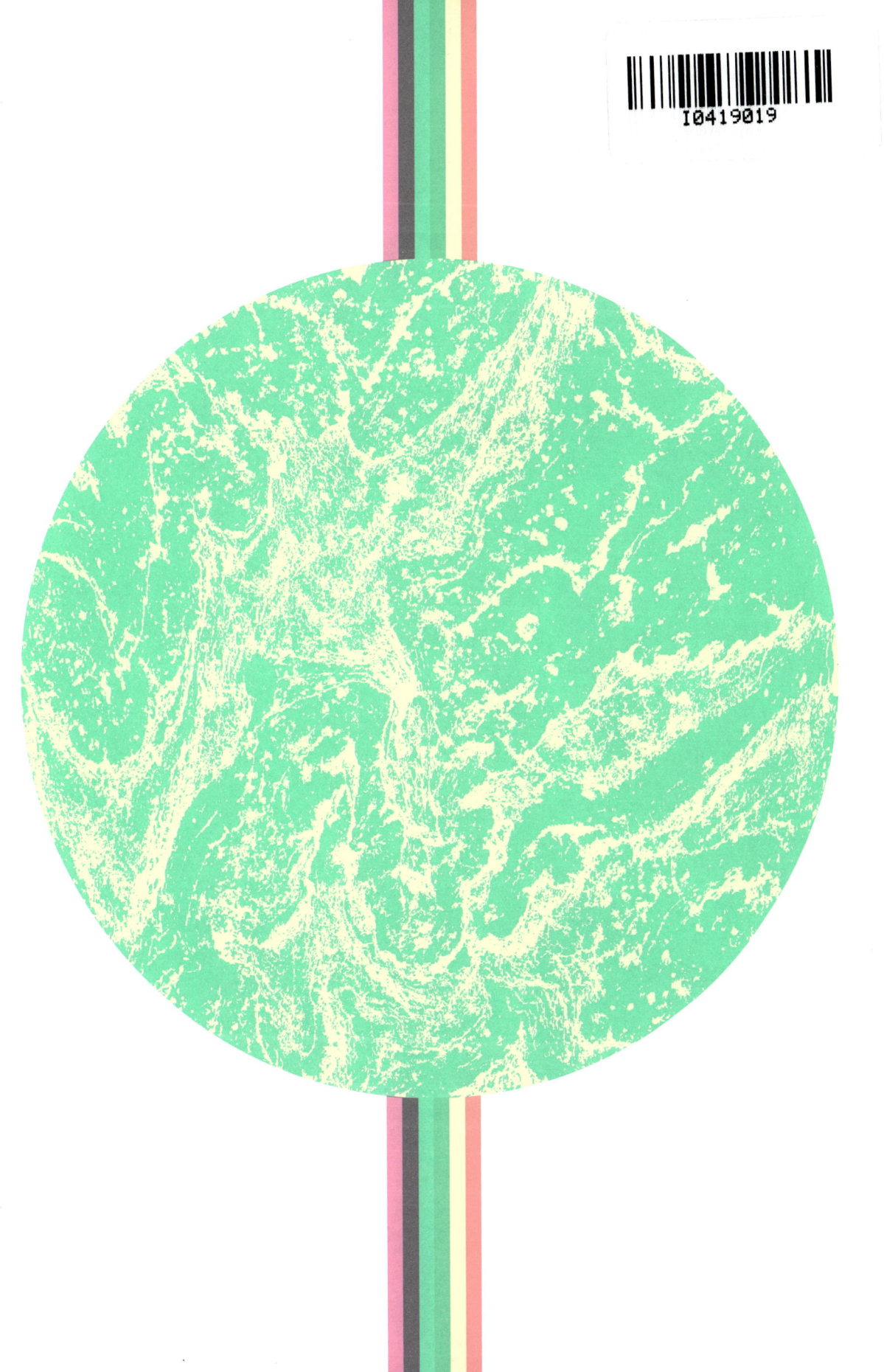

The 36th Ljubljana Biennale of Graphic Arts
International Centre of Graphic Arts

MGLC

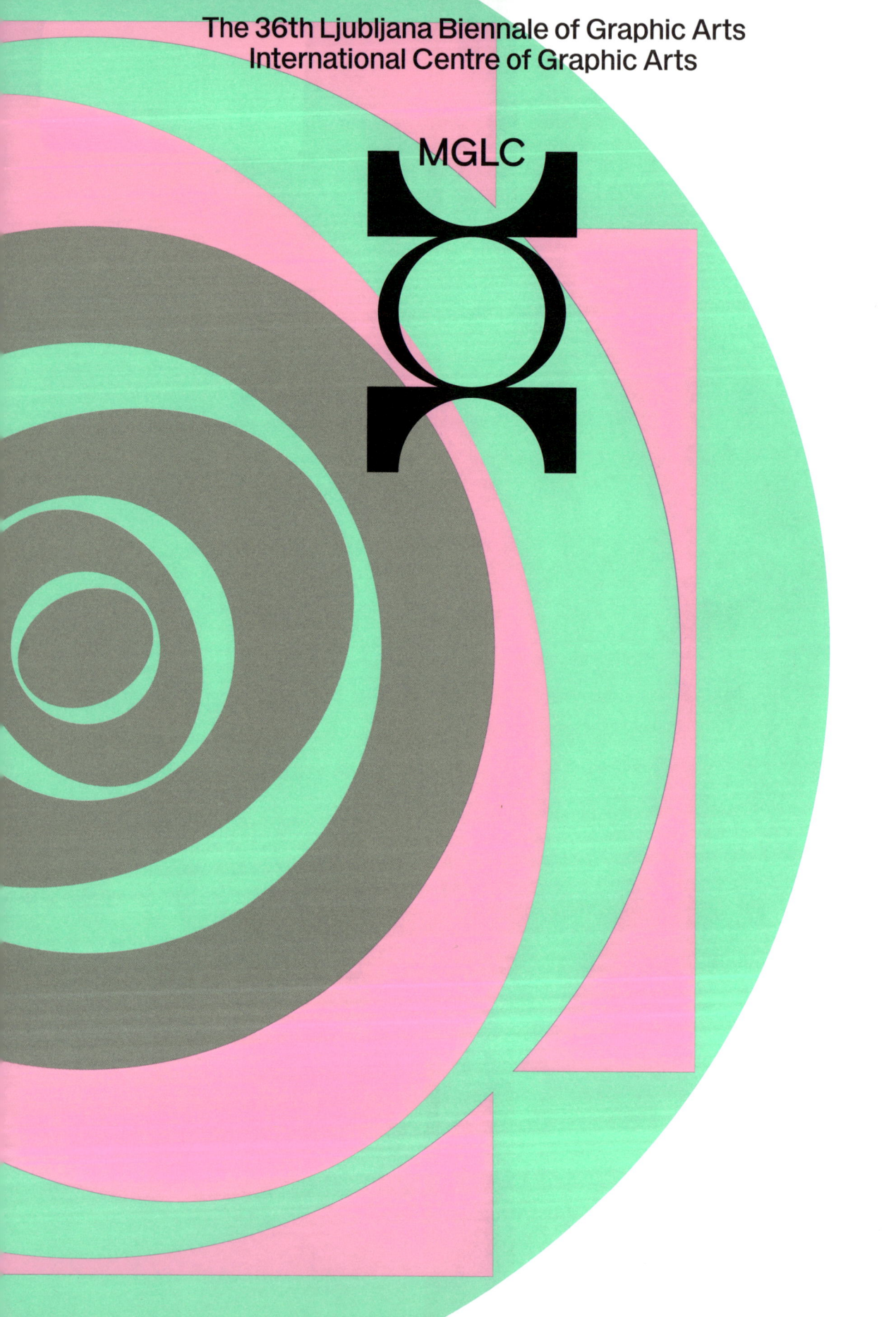

The Oracle:

ON FANTASY AND FREEDOM

Edited by Chus Martínez and Ajda Ana Kocutar

Sternberg Press

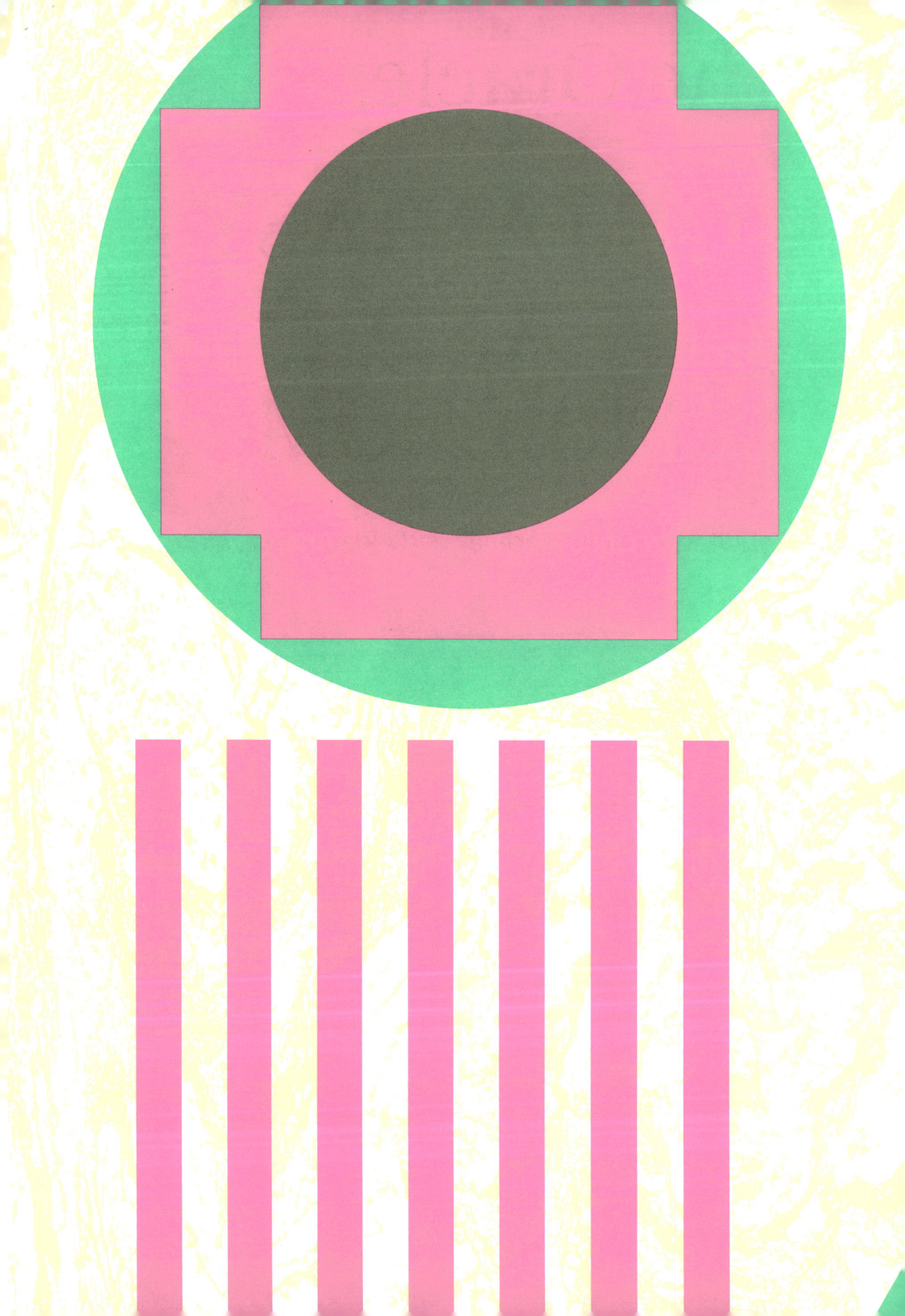

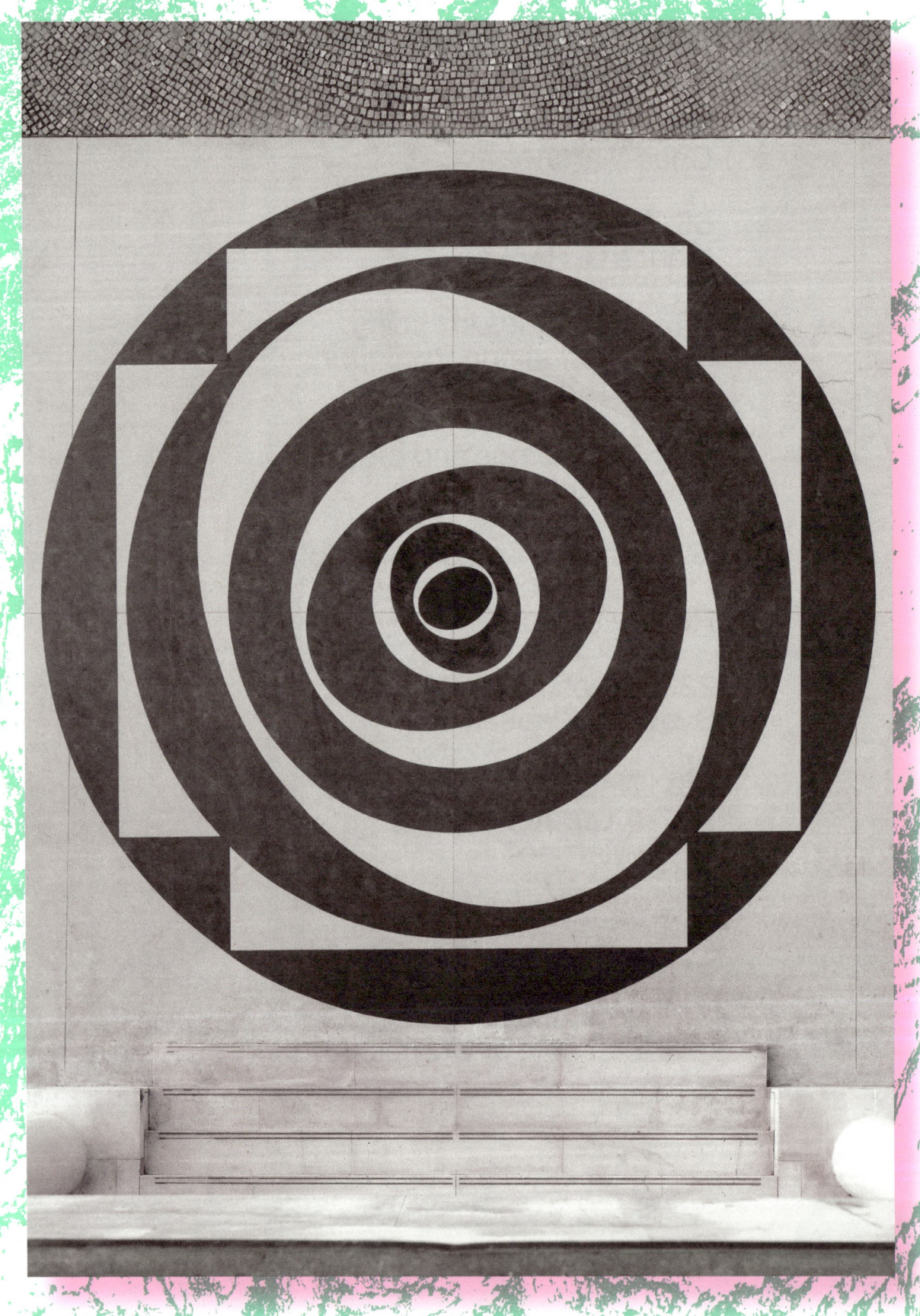

The Oracle:

ON THE FUTURE OF COEXISTENCE

Chus

Martínez

Chus Martínez

PART I:
THE ORACLE
AND THE PUPPETS

The reason I named an exhibition—the 36th Ljubljana Biennale of Graphic Arts—and this book *The Oracle* is because art embodies the existence of an extraordinary "place"—a fantastic site—from which to think in freedom. At this moment in history, I doubt whether people are capable of recognizing the value of art in helping them to realize a social project based on the values of equality and respect for life. That's why my first appeal in this place is to the puppets.

But first the Oracle ...

I have an interest in people's search for special—even privileged—places to ask important questions. It is possible to think that great questions arise in our minds in miserable places. But humans are a cautious species, aware of the existence of times of profound crisis and deep fear of what may lie ahead, and for this reason they have built places where the transmission of their desires and hope for answers takes place in a privileged, almost superhuman manner. Amazing scenic points across the seas, such as the Delphi Temple situated on Mount Parnassus, overlooking the valley of Phocis; the temple of the oracle of Ammon situated in the Siwa Oasis in Egypt; or the unfinished temple of Apollo at Didyma, in Turkey. The massive temples in Central America and Peru are not oracles in the ancient Greek sense of the word, and yet they were made for human-to-deity communication. The Temple of the Sun in Machu Picchu is situated on a misty ridge at over two thousand meters of altitude between two mountains in the Andes, encircled by an exuberant jungle; the Temple of the Feathered Serpent in Mexico also stands at

On the Future of Coexistence

two thousand meters above sea level, emerging in an unending highland plateau (the Valley of Mexico) and surrounded by distant volcanoes; or the Tikal Temple in Guatemala, the tallest pre-Columbian structure known is located deep in the jungle, with temples peeking above the canopy almost like mountains. I could continue my list with temples in India or the massive shrines in Japan, etc. The effort made to locate a point where communication with deities could happen was so extraordinary because the deep concerns of humans are equally exceptional. Industrial capitalism and modernism shifted the search for locations in nature to the creation of museums and libraries that could equal the sacral function in a secular form. The Kimbell Art Museum by Louis Kahn, constructed in 1972, for example, uses the dialogue between concrete and the sun in such a way that it feels reminiscent of divine illumination. Even more secular buildings, such as the Philips Pavilion, built in 1958 for the Brussels World's Fair by Le Corbusier and Iannis Xenakis, were conceived as a polyhedral cathedral of sound and space for a *Poème électronique.* The international exhibition held in 1970 in Osaka flourished with these ambitions, immersive examples of futuristic architecture all oriented towards the creation of a unique experience in time through space. The bubble-like Marine City by Kiyonori Kikutake was a prototype intended to innovate the possibility of a system of floating oceanic architecture. The whole project echoed Buddhist concepts in futuristic form. The Space Frame Pavilion by Arata Isozaki, a crystal temple for a cybernetic emerging brain. The Tower of the Sun by artist Tarō Okamoto, a 70m-tall, three-faced totemic shrine to human evolution. The Fuji Group Pavilion, by Yutaka Murata, a giant white dome with projection shows inside. I wrote extensively in the past about a similar experimental pavilion created by Venezuelan artist Jacobo Borges Imagen de Caracas in 1967. It was commissioned to celebrate 400 years since the foundation of the city. The artist created

Chus Martínez

an immersive vanguardist multi-channel film projection space where images were displayed across various surfaces: walls, fabric, floors, and semi-transparent screens. Instead of celebrating the colonial power, he offered the authorities multiple violent re-creations of the colonial battles and massacres that led to the founding of Caracas and subsequently to its independence struggles.

We can also claim that Brasilia, whose construction began in 1956, conceived by the architects Oscar Niemeyer and Lúcio Costa, was also a project for a city that wanted not only to create housing but to renew its relationship with the oracular, envisioning a life in peace with possibilities.

What ancient places have in common with the secular surreal exercises of modern times is the search for and actual belief in the "place." The possibility of designing and constructing a place and being immersed in it, so that we are charged with the energy to face what is about to happen, the time ahead. The only important exception is the pavilion created by Jacobo Borges because he included the colonial past and the suffering of millions as a crucial element of the "temple." Celebrating 400 years of Caracas is the same as asking the deities for another 400 years, or at least to go on. His intelligent inclusion of the past disrupts this wish and renders it impossible for it to become a collective wish. The wish to continue living equals the will to perpetuate a history crafted through crimes and inequality. Learning how to take the past into account, or better said, to take the pain of the past into account, in the oracular exercises that we use to—and continue to—perform is something crucial.

"The Oracle" is the place. "The Oracle" is not the questions we posed or the answers we may have received, but the place we choose to exercise this very special transmission between us and the forces that surpass us. This place, though, has dramatically changed over the centuries. Even if culture—as the Western world conceives it—places enormous importance on physically built places, on temples and monuments, on the possibility of a place to represent power (the power to address deities, the power to be above others in the social sphere)—this idea no longer holds. Representation is too odd, and even if we are impressed by it, we have turned our backs on it in many ways. Meditation, identity politics, and checking one's social media accounts in important and monumental buildings all speak of an abandonment of these architectural temples. What, then, can replace the places that hold a unique meaning and manage to create a sense of transmission that is so powerful and bonding that it makes us feel a sense of togetherness and belonging? And was this abandonment of temples something that happened later in history or something that has actually been occurring since ancient times—but is only now being comprehended?

My answer to the first question is clear: art is the place. Art as a practice, art as a substance, art as an imagination that—as the eco-anthropologist Tim Ingold[1] claims—is for real, as real as the world itself. In Western culture—as Ingold also explains—imagination (and I extend this to art) is under-stood as something that happens inside the head, something that is not present, as a simulation, or as a simple tool for creativity or escapism. Tim Ingold claims that imagination is not a departure from reality, but a way of fully engaging with it. To imagine is to participate in the ongoing becoming of the world. Art has been with humans since ancient times, and has also been learning to become this participatory force in the making of the world. It has been learning to represent less, to take its distance from taste, from form, from subject, even. Art has been learning how to become immaterial and also to live in the bodies of those performing it, performing art. Art has also been learning to be less autonomous—as defined by modernism and its philosophers—and paradoxically, since

1   Tim Ingold, *Imagining for Real: Essays on Creation, Attention and Correspondence* (Routledge, 2021).

Chus Martínez

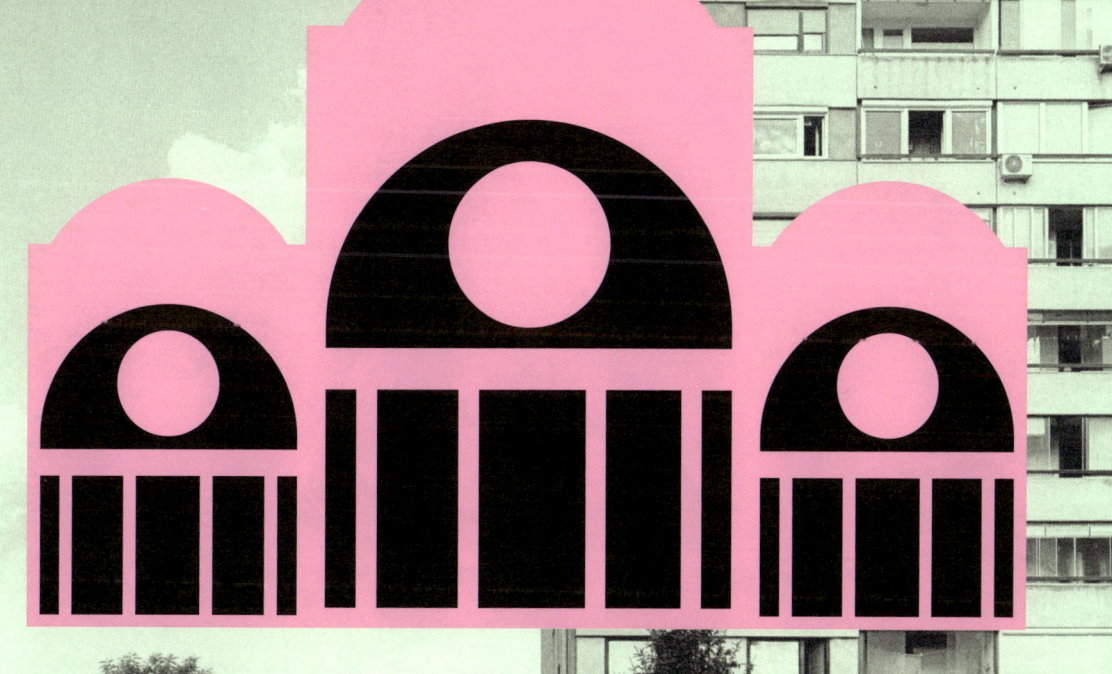
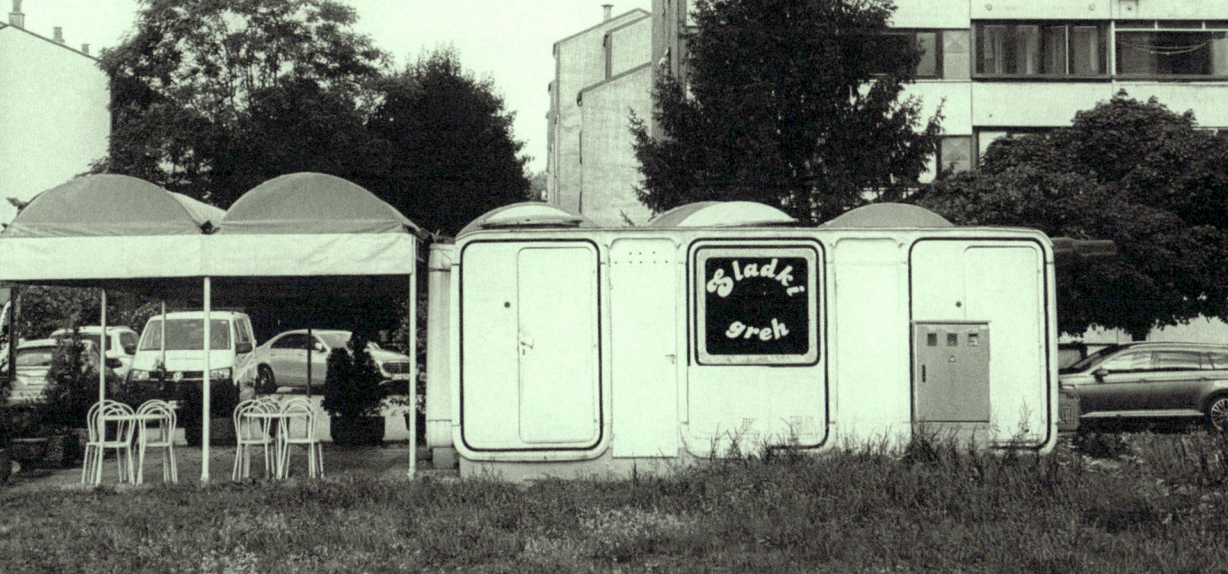

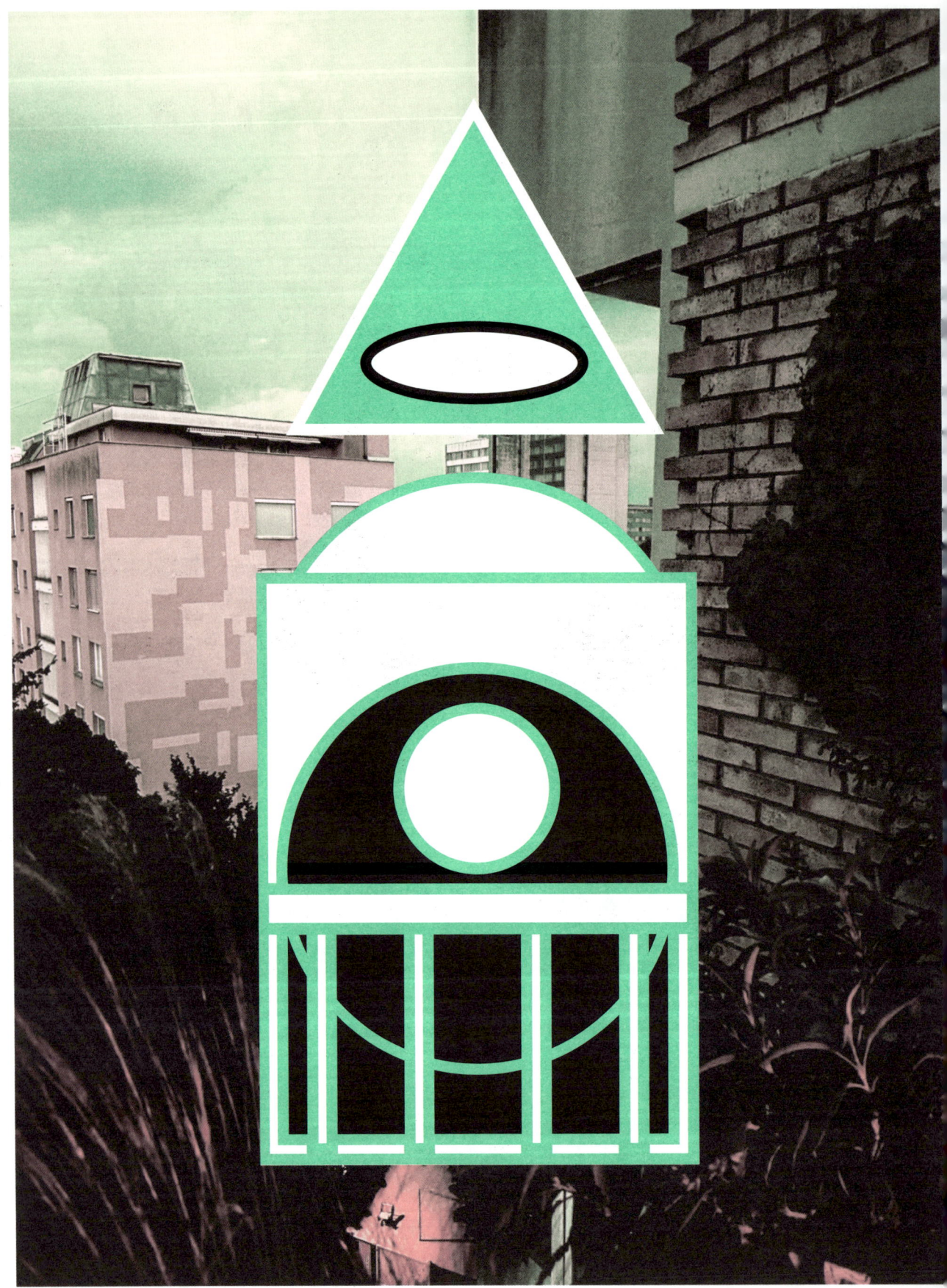

this constraint was lifted, art has felt more at ease engaging with other fields, ideas, and disciplines. Art has been learning to speak the tongue of the oceans, to reactivate the spirits of ancestors, to reflect on the polymorphic textures of identity and the social fabric. Why then? Why would a substance that for centuries was treated as a mere "discipline" of knowledge unleash itself so radically? To replace the temples. People are turning their backs on culture. It feels remote or foreign. Religions are also back. The questions have given rise to a world riddled with Dantesque answers, with an evil simplicity that is leading us to a place where we have already been: violence and submission as the ultimate solution.

How can one produce the wonder of making culture and art appear as an ally of another great world-transforming force, education, at a time when everyone, or mostly everyone, seems exhausted by the idea of adopting new collective habits? Who but we—citizens and inhabitants—could make a last effort to think differently and act differently so as not to be swept along by what seems to be an inevitable current towards the destruction of the common good?

This is when, in the context of the history of this exhibition, I now return to puppets. I must confess that never before—apart from in the work of some artists—had puppets managed to arouse any particular philosophical interest in me. It all started with a text accompanying a review of the history of puppetry in Slovenia and, in particular, in Ljubljana after the Second World War. The text quoted a letter from the sculptor and puppet designer Ajša Pengov about the possibility of designing puppets completely independent of the human hand. The translation from Slovenian into English indicated the artist's intention to create indigenous puppets. The term, so far from its usual usage, assaulted my mind, creating all sorts of speculative scenarios. Indigenous puppets could be something like a distinct species with a culture and knowledge of their own. If these puppets are not

On the Future of Coexistence

moved by hands but by very long, invisible strings, what is their purpose? With what mission have they come into the world? It is very difficult to imagine the level of despair and destruction in Europe after the Second World War. At a time when everyone seems to see glory in the rearmament of nations, it is important to remember the pain generations endured to rebuild and achieve the rule of law. It was clear that the will to create puppets on the part of a number of artists and intellectuals was directly related to two important and fundamental goals: to create creatures capable of living for us and to create an eloquent language capable of speaking to everyone, of reaching everyone without raising suspicions of belonging to an elite culture.

The particular story that caught my attention, Žogica Marogica, is about a little ball that is adopted by an elderly couple. The character was actually created in 1936 by Czech puppeteer Jan Malík. It was first staged in Ljubljana in 1951 at the City Puppet Theatre (today's Ljubljana Puppet Theatre). In the early twentieth century, the Czech puppeteering tradition experienced a great transformation, and particularly between the 1910s and 1950s Czech puppetry evolved into a highly respected art form, into a blend of politics, modernism, and avant-garde theater that was still able to remain a form of folk entertainment. This development also took off in Slovenia, somehow, around the post–World War II period, particularly from the 1950s through the 1980s, when puppetry transformed into an experimental form. Fundamental to this transformation was the establishment of the City Puppet Theatre in 1948—the first professional puppet theater in Slovenia, and the fact that puppet theater was a state-supported cultural art that enabled the formation of clusters of visual artists, composers, and directors to push the form beyond simple entertainment. By "simple entertainment," I mean that from the beginning all these artists and intellectuals saw the potential of a form that appeals mostly

Chus Martínez

to children but that they see with parents. Puppet theater was seen as an invaluable educational language that was relatively ideologically safe while suitable for promoting socialist values such as cooperation, collectivism, and equality.

It seems a little bit radical to turn to puppets in an age when digital animation does not even need a hand to draw the characters. However, that is one of the elements that interests me: can we merge the thousands of years of puppetry, from ancient Egypt and India, to Indonesia and Central Europe, with the new media cultures of storytelling? We are mostly seeing new media culture in the form that big corporations have given it. Social media belong mostly to private companies, and their logic is profit and not education or the common interest. I do not wish a return to puppetry culture, but to look at it for a moment and see if its ancient history and evolution could inspire a movement in forming clusters of artists and practitioners to access the many neighborhoods that exist both physically and online. I am advocating here for an avant-garde of social mediation that would be nourished by the same willingness to tell stories and myths of self-fulfillment and liberation. And yes, I imagine the funds that are used for military purposes being invested in all-encompassing research on how to implement several factors at once: education, arts and culture, scientific research, and technology. Indeed, there have been several public initiatives that have explored the potential of building digital and social media platforms independently from corporations. Mastodon in Germany, ActivityPub, initiated by the European Union following the same protocol as Mastodon, the Digital Democracies Institute in Canada, anchored at the Simon Fraser University, etc. If you ask researchers and experts about the reasons why public social media platforms lack appeal—even if many millions are dissatisfied with the existing corporate ones—the answer is unanimous: a lack of funding. The open-source public media digital research initiatives lack the funding needed to develop user interface designs that are appealing, real-time updates, machine learning moderation, and content discovery algorithms, for example. However, if we are experiencing as a danger the change of heart of millions regarding their preference for democracy, wouldn't it be more important and decisive for our future to invest in peace? But how to do so? Do we need public money to be invested in privately developed weapons, or do we still have the option of ensuring the safety of the citizenry without investing in defense? Indeed, public investment in weapons and the military significantly surpasses global spending on education and civilian technology. We do so because our governments supposedly perceive a danger. But could we fight the danger by other means? Are all these weapons making us safer?

At the core of our problem is the perception of the problem. Governments want to feel safe in the event of a foreign intervention, e.g., the corruption of the citizenry, tsunamis of distorted realities generated and spread through technological channels, commercial wars aimed at the procurement and extraction of rare minerals, etc. But wouldn't it be wiser to invest in forms of technological, educational, and artistic research that would create a real shield at the sites where the attacks actually occur?

I would argue that the design and development of vast programs to mobilize the population towards the values that have shaped our imperfect but still operative democracies is a matter of national defense. I would argue that doing so is an urgent matter and that it needs to be done now. Global democracy is experiencing a decline. According to the Economist Intelligence Unit's Democracy Index, only 6.6% of the world's population lives under a full democracy, a decrease from 7.8% the previous year. Approximately 45.4% reside in some form of democracy, including both full and flawed democracies. In contrast, about 39.2% of the global

Chus Martínez

population lives under authoritarian regimes, a proportion that has been increasing in recent years[2]. One could argue that it is a good moment to start. If one were to continue this research on democracy by roughly determining the number of foundations dedicated to the arts, education, public health, and culture, one would arrive at an estimate of 400,000, concentrated mainly in the United States and Europe (there are few comprehensive listings about the rest of the world). If the climate emergency is added, the number rises to approximately 550,000 non-profit foundations worldwide.

What can we learn from these numbers? From the first, the Democracy Index, we simply need to push democracy as a system further. We need to grow if we want the guarantees of equality and freedom to grow. From the second number, we learn that from public governments to privately initiated foundations, we lack synchronicity. I would say that the climate emergency has been a leading force mobilizing many different disciplines and sectors towards working together in a successful way.

But still we may lack congresses and summits initiated by the people—and not by the leading powers, as was the case with many of the historical communist congresses worldwide—to coordinate action between all existing stake-holders to secure the future of democracy. We do not seem to have a lack of tools, and yet they are clearly not synchronized towards the interests of citizens in a world at peace, in health, and in securing basic needs, education, and access to culture.

What would be the motor of thought oriented towards the development of this type of action? Actions that would equally mobilize technology and the arts, science and the

2   Alicja Hagopian, "Only 25 countries in the world are fully functioning democracies—and the US isn't one of them, report claims," *Independent*, February 27, 2025, https://www.independent.co.uk/news/world/democracy-index-data-economist-governments-b2705687.html.

On the Future of Coexistence

arts, puppetry and democracy for education would need a common philosophy. We are lacking the capacity to build a thinking substance—a thinking mass—able to surpass the volume of anti-thinking. Scholars and thinkers capable of collaboration with artists and scientists have been disempowered and disenfranchised. Art and the many disciplines in the humanities, and also in the life sciences, capable of complex speculation and the development of networks are under suspicion for not being productive. They produce democracy, but over the past two decades, numerous philosophy and classics departments worldwide have faced closures or restructurings, often due to financial constraints, declining enrollments, and shifts in institutional priorities toward more market-driven disciplines.

But what am I proposing here? Social media platforms initiated by the public sector have failed not only because of funding, but also because we are too late to mimic and replace the existing platforms. People are unwilling to leave the communities they have built, even knowing that the powers that sustain them are unjust and ultimately pose a threat to democracy. We are too late—in other words—to evacuate millions of citizens from corporate platforms to public ones of a similar kind. It is also wrong to regulate people's behavior in the existing platforms via strong rules and censorship so that people would act according to the democratic game. The only way out is to invent something else. And that something else needs to happen, at least for a while, partially through private platforms. Now that everyone is addressing the negative impact of artificial intelligence and robotization in the labor market, there is a sector where humans are still needed: puppetry. My "puppets for democracy" is both a proposal that you can take literally and an image that may ignite many different genres of social interaction that may have nothing to do with puppetry in the end. But both the literal presence of puppet theater productions in schools, neighborhoods, care

Chus Martínez

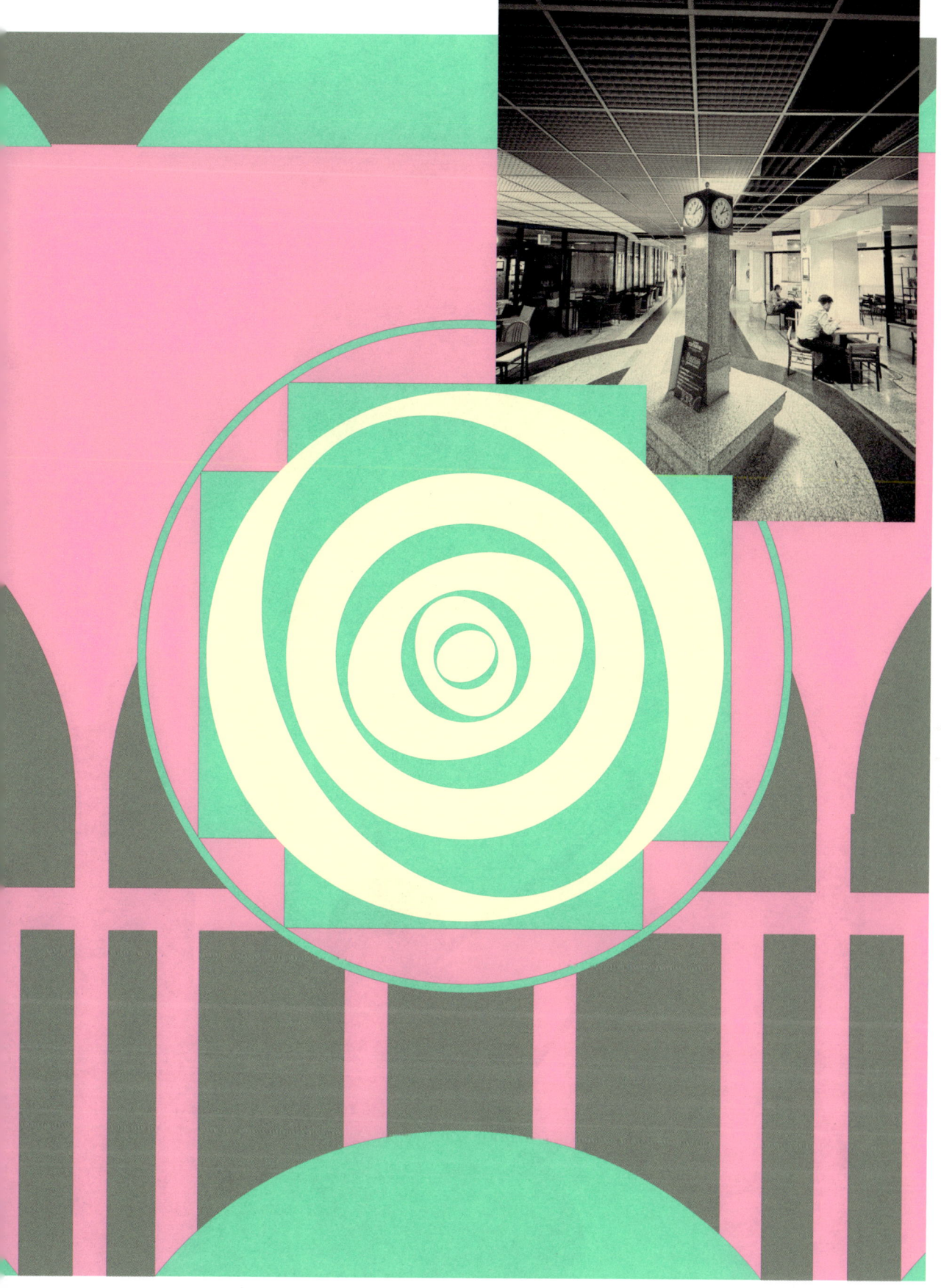

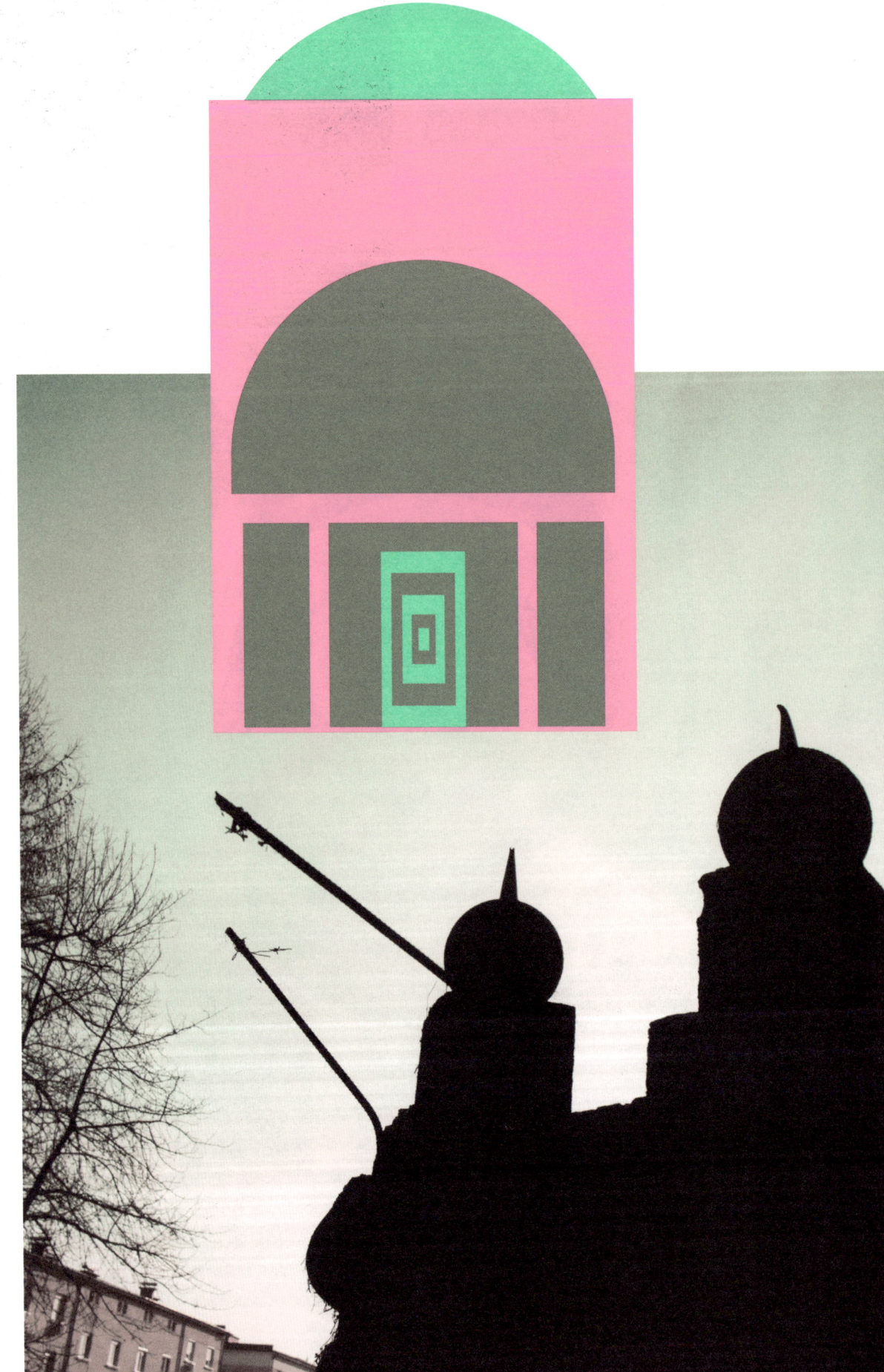

homes, hospitals, etc., and the more extravagant take thereon, combining different genres of entertainment and fantasy to reach out to people, have in common the necessity to be at street level for a while. This is a very budget-demanding enterprise that would need extensive collaboration among many sectors and experts to carefully develop forums where people and their problems are addressed. Eliminate your prejudices regarding the word entertainment and go back to its Latin roots: *intertenere*: inter = among, between, and tenere = *to hold*. Literally: "to hold among" or "to keep together." I believe that we could create a new avant-garde with anagogic interaction, revisiting the world's repertoire of narratives and tales while engaging amazing artists, scientists, and intellectuals in creating new ones. Imagine new crazy versions of the world using all types of technologies and gaming devices, ready to display reality and being played in public by many people. New versions of *Pulcinella*, rooted in the sixteenth-century Italian *commedia dell'arte*; *Wayang Kulit* shadow puppet theater from Indonesia; *Karagöz* and *Hacivat* from Turkey; and *Bunraku* from Japan. No one is interested in puppetry if you ask. Our interests are so clearly designed and determined by industries—work and corporate entertainment—that no one would respond "yes" if questioned about it. It possesses no cool, no edge, no trend. It may just become the most down-to-the-street project, as well as the most honestly surprising project for the population. This street puppetry for democracy allows itself to be combined with many other different methods that have proved effective, such as music education—like El Sistema, created in 1975 by economist, musician, and visionary José Antonio Abreu, a community-based, publicly supported music education program that uses orchestral and choral training as a way to promote social inclusion, personal development, and cultural enrichment.

On the Future of Coexistence

Let's fill the world and the streets with this fantasy. Let's believe that fantasy is real, that it is a constitutive element of the future of the social on the verge of a radical transformation that demands analogue artistic and other programs to hold people's minds and bodies together. This may be a transitional phase that we need to implement in order to balance the impact of certain technologies on our social and mental health. I do not believe in boycotting any existing platform. I only believe in forgetting them for a while, in making them just a tiny part of our lives because we have something else, more important, going on. Human excitement is magic, we cannot fight the global burnout with anything else than with the exhilaration of having a wonderful time, having hope.

Yes, I do believe in puppets as agents capable of taking all the blame, all the pain, and giving us in return all the joy. Yes, I do believe that puppets, digital, technological, or however you dare to imagine them can serve the mission of creating an eloquence for the many millions of people that are functionally illiterate—not completely illiterate, but suffering from a lack of sufficient reading, writing, and comprehension—or just plain illiterate. Puppets can tell and explain the world to those who cannot read, or have stopped reading, or lack trust in reading. "Puppet" here is just another name I am giving to a form of education and politics, deeply public and committed to the common good, which will just start engaging in using fantasy to talk in the social sphere.

But what then is the role of this exhibition, *The Oracle*?

Why an exhibition and not a street puppet theater right away? In 1917, Viktor Shklovsky wrote a text that I consider crucial today: *Art as Device* (*Iskusstvo kak priem*).[3] There, he introduced a concept that, subsequently, greatly influenced

3   Viktor Shklovsky, "Art as Device," in *Theory of Prose*, trans. Benjamin Sher (Dalkey Archive Press, 1990), 1–14.

Chus Martínez

the thinking and theater ideas of Bertold Brecht: *Ostranenie* (*Остранение*)—defamiliarization. He argued that when everyday life becomes automated, we stop noticing the world around us. Art, therefore, must *defamiliarize* the ordinary, make it strange, so we actually *see* it again. This idea resonates in the proposal of Ajša Pengov to create indigenous or radically autonomous puppets. Puppets that are not puppets anymore. It is important to understand that we cannot simply employ any genre—puppet theater or politics—in the state they are today. We need a threshold—and exhibitions like this are intended to be read this way—to be able to reinvent all the premises of the game, all the rules, to soak the very substance of all thinking and creative forms we are familiar with in a fantasy that may then emerge with a different language and force. In the words of Viktor Shklovsky, the purpose of art is to impart the sensation of things as they are perceived and not as they are known.[4]

We need epic forms—as Bertold Brecht wrote about theater—epic genres.[5] But the new avant-garde I have in mind should also reverse the premises of the former one. Brecht said theater must make you think, not just feel. I say—with Hayao Miyazaki,[6] one of the founders of Studio Ghibli—that we should prioritize real emotion over spectacle and modern ideas of thinking. Brecht said that theater should help us to analyze society, rather than just relate to characters. I would say with Miyazaki that we should suspend and avoid moral binaries and assist minds to move organically through the different scenarios that unfold in the social sphere, without judgment. Brecht said: recognize injustice and be moved to

4   Viktor Shklovsky, "Art as Technique," in *Russian Formalist Criticism: Four Essays*, trans. Lee T. Lemon and Marion J. Reis (University of Nebraska Press, 1965), 16.
5   Bertolt Brecht, *Brecht on Theatre: The Development of an Aesthetic*, ed. and trans. John Willett (Hill and Wang, 1964).
6   Hayao Miyazaki, *Starting Point: 1979–1996*, trans. Beth Cary and Frederik L. Schodt (VIZ Media, 2009).

On the Future of Coexistence

act, not just sympathize. I would say, let's avoid polarization at all costs and reject the traditional three-act structure that resolves injustice in justice and instead allow for the thousands of stories to unfold in an infinite flow with no clear antagonist, climax, or resolution. Art is not the Supreme Court. Art and exhibitions are spaces to exercise the possibilities of imagination and—I think—wild fantasy.

PART II:
SOCIAL SIMULACRA OR
SAYING THE SAME AGAIN
WITH OTHER WORDS

My ideas so far: art is the place; art is the place to generate a new folklore, new myths, new languages, strategies, and methods to positively affect the regeneration of our democratic forms of organization. Joseph Campbell, an American mythologist, wrote in *The Hero with a Thousand Faces* (1949) that many myths from various cultures share a fundamental structure, which he termed "the monomyth."[7] We can read the last decades of artistic production as a critique and as an expansion of Campbell's idea of the monomyth. Art has understood the importance of storytelling and the structure of folklore to address complex questions like non-human intelligence, but also that we must push beyond the Western-centric, masculine, and often individualistic structures to include more diverse narratives, cultures, identities, and ambitions towards the social. Art has understood that an important task has been to redefine the existing heroic narratives (patriarchal and colonial), challenging them with

7   Joseph Campbell, *The Hero with a Thousand Faces*,
     3rd ed. (New World Library, 2008), 23.

Chus Martínez

queer, Indigenous, and collective journeys that allow us to break free from the Western ideas of the return (of the hero), the conquest (of territories and peoples), and linear progress. Art has done this. And now the question is how to regenerate the exhausted tissue of the social. How to be regenerative and not only critical.

Art can be regenerative by giving a body to the inexpressible. An exhibition can do so by giving a dramaturgy to the forces, feelings, and questions that resonate with our current existence. Historically, no other substance than art has been so invested in creating conditions for us to foresee the many dimensions of the world through experience, through the possibility of gaining through experience a different thinking, and with it, potentially, implementing a different behavior.

Having been educated during the political transition of Spain from a dictatorship to a democracy, my generation was taught that art is a repository of recent historical memory and a guarantee of freedom and of the preservation of human and social rights. Back then, I was very aware that this extreme reading of artistic practice had so much to do with our own historical and social conditions. But, viewing the current global expansion of authoritarian rule, I am returning to a question inspired by this notion: How can we move art and non-art audiences to believe that art is a fundamental substance through which we all can gain a sense of fulfillment? How can an experience made in the context of an exhibition positively affect the choices we make? How can we move away from the new authoritarian essentialist models that populism, certain sectors of capitalism, and technology industries are spreading? How, also, can art and culture give a new impulse to the idea that *the people* is an open concept from which new, unprecedented forms of democratic organization may emerge.

Imagining scenarios together is the exercise of creating a language together through an experience we share. The bonding that happens in such a context has a positive impact on how we read the public space we inhabit. The experience of being part of a relevant development, an event of collective significance, challenges the fear that every form of truth and security can be appropriated or subjugated and jeopardized. It is the exercise of trying to return to a state of openness and possibility where we can disagree but guarantee civil rights and freedom.

How to do this?

I imagine an exhibition like the opera *The Magic Flute*, by W. A. Mozart, that is capable of creating through artistic practices an incredible space for the collective understanding of one's own language, and appealing to those unfamiliar with or disinterested in art. An exhibition able to put to work a dramaturgy of questions and responses, leaving a trace in the memory of the audiences that sparks joyful fulfillment.

Imagine the important questions unveiled before your eyes through the work of artists in such a form that you feel motivated to experience more, to see more. Can we create a sensorial language capable of embracing the relevant questions in a fantastic way? Dramaturgy needs to be applied to prevent defensiveness in dealing with the urgent issues: Is the social sphere going to rupture without us being able to act? Is the agency of nature going to affect the way we perceive, educate, and legislate in the future? Is bad mental health irreversible? Is labor ending? Is the emergence of automatic weapons going to facilitate permanent attacks and unending conflicts? Is conscious behavior towards the Earth going to impact the way we deal with mining, waste, and pollution? What is technology going to turn into? Are we witnessing the end of any consensus on the common good?

Chus Martínez

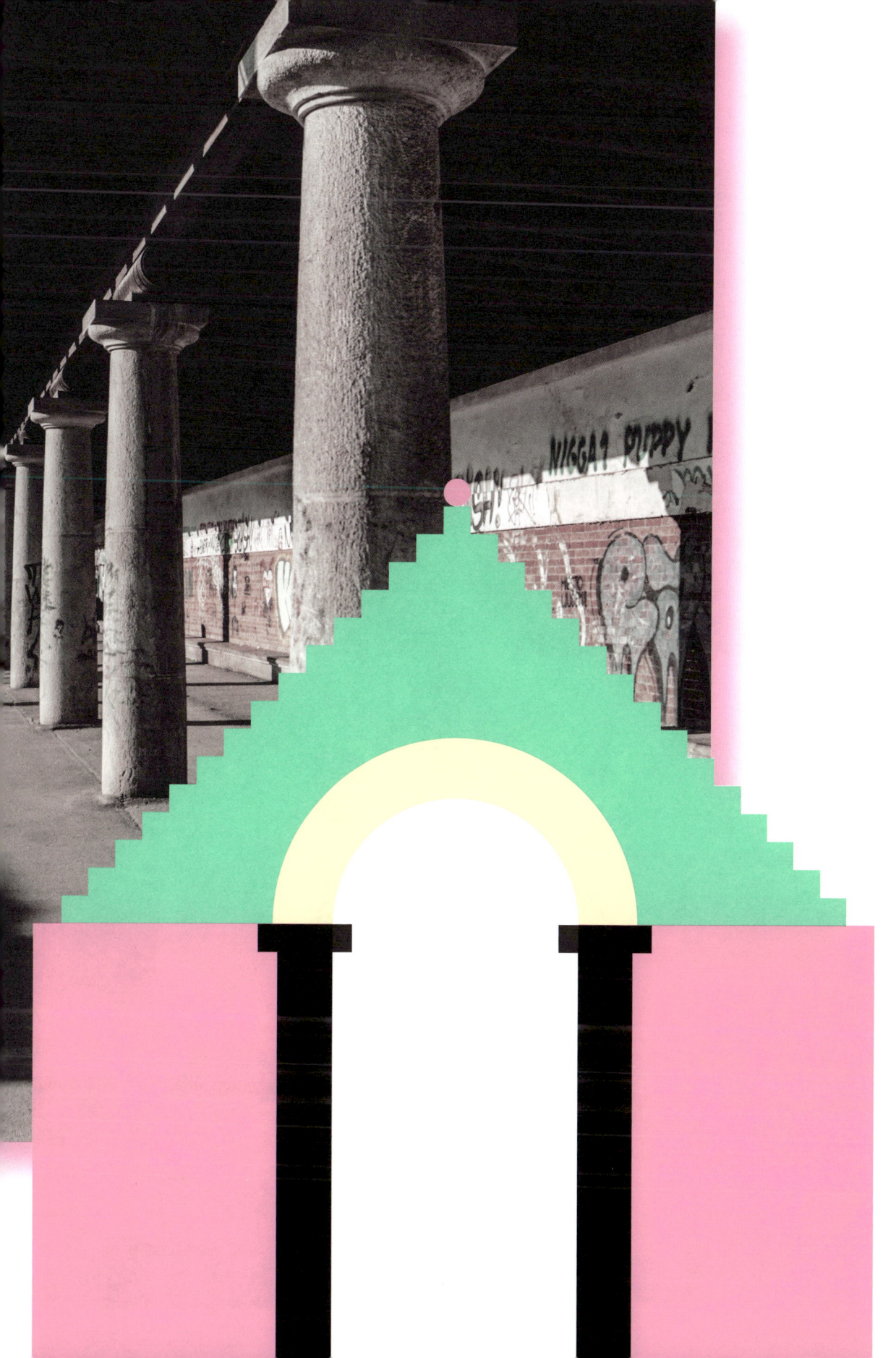

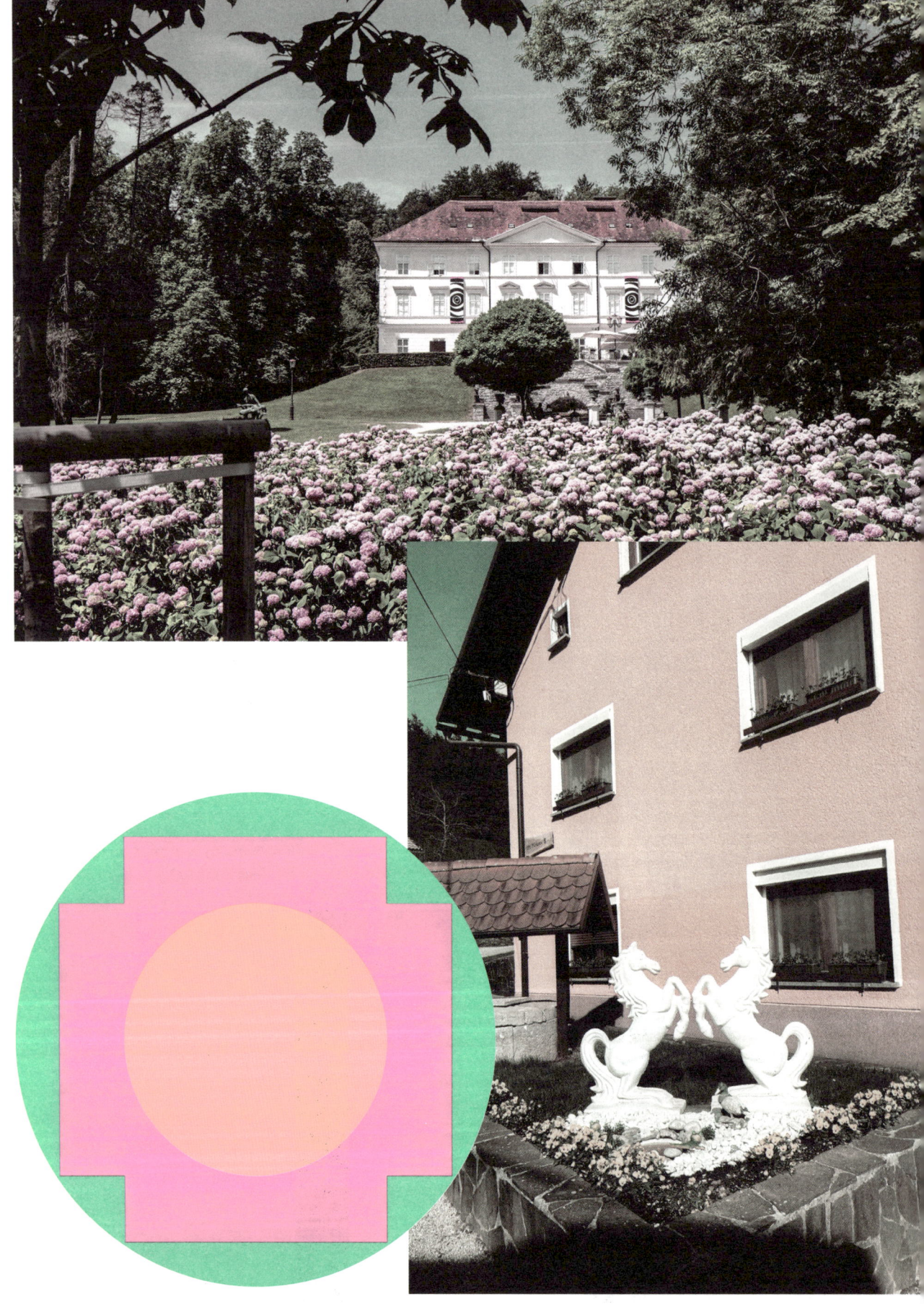

Questions are infinite, but one suggestion would be to re-invent the exhibition format as a *Singspiel* in the spirit of *The Magic Flute*, a hybrid lyrical language able to enact important moments of our current and near future concerns—created and produced in close collaboration between artists and practitioners coming from different fields such as neurolinguistics, biology, dream research, indigenous epistemologies, public interest thinking, choreography, ethnomusicology, gaming, technology, and nuclear waste management. The premise is to create a scenario of conditions where a hypothesis can be experienced, talked about, and reversed. A scenario where certain models are presented to facilitate a set of experiences and interactions, respecting the key criteria for inclusion.

An exhibition is one of the most incredible tools we have created to display forms of appearance: symbols, themes, emotions, cultures, values, aggression, destruction, etc. The exhibition emerges as a world that gives birth to worlds and enhances the conditions of participation.

To say that an exhibition is conceived under the premises of creating social simulacra—scenarios of the possible—is to focus on the importance of linking sensorial perception with our ability to produce versions of the real.

The Crisis of Reading and the Era of Conceptual Blending

Every transformation responds to a set of conditions. We can perceive this transformation as a big loss, or we can morph our social systems and languages to the new reality and produce possibilities out of it. The Western world has not properly acknowledged the consequences of our readership cataclysm and has not invested enough in researching new transmission and education methods. It is time to present exhibition-making as a great generative ground and transmission model in the post-reading paradigm. Exhibitions are indeed the best environment to explore the way we think. Exhibitions are perfect environments for exploring conceptual blending—a model that moves away from logical-argumentative reasoning to explain the way we think. Neuroscience[8] is trying to explain that thinking happens in between the blended space created by an unconscious coming together of images dynamically connected to the emotions and signals that assist us in creating interpretations of the situations we are in. Our mind needs the imaginary situations as much as the perception of facts, forms, and images in order for ideas to emerge. The important part of this theory is that all these blended spaces act in networks. We constantly connect them independently of their actual meaning, allowing us to activate unexpected types of thinking. Crucial to this model is that for complex thinking to emerge our minds need to be exposed to a vast number of inputs.

This model of conceptual integration networks provides us with a way of imagining exhibitions far beyond the three dominant models: the display model—centered around the presentation of artworks in a public space to human perception; the art-as-social-competence model, where the goal is to reverse certain narratives of domination, class, and access; and the awareness model, wherein facing urgent questions through the artistic language should create awareness and, causally, a change in behavior. By blending experience with orality, an exhibition can indeed become the very substance that allows every individual—independently of their educational or cultural background—to develop thinking

8   I am referring to the research by Gilles Fauconnier and Mark Turner and their book *The Way We Think: Conceptual Blending And The Mind's Hidden Complexities* (Basic Books, 2002).

Chus Martínez

in an open and complex way. An exhibition can become a cognitive test space wherein we regain trust in our capability to generate images and ideas that sustain the feeling of personal self-fulfillment and foster an inclination to be open and generous. The exhibition develops into a space where unruly emotions and experiences are allowed and serve the purpose of generating a view, a personal and collective vision that can be discussed, assumed, or rejected.

From the Literal, Through Fiction, Towards Fantasy

In recent decades, art and artists have guided us towards a multi-layered and diverse comprehension of the real and the texture of time. Art practices have assisted us in critically reflecting on the monolithic and colonial substance of time as history. The archival, the documentary phases of art, were immensely important in grasping the role we attribute to facts and memory. To leave some traumas behind implies not only remembering from the point of view of the state, the winners, or the victims, but also multiplying the points of view to such an extent that even forests and mines could possess a memory of the actions inflicted by humans. Art assists us in creating exactly that possibility. While still relying enormously on documents, discourses, ideology, and text, art practices have started to open up to the possibility of a multiple coexistence of times and narrative voices, implementing the emergence of fiction to address relevance.

Fiction has surely been a key element in discerning non-human intelligence, in conceiving nature as being us, in breaking the binary culture–nature. Fiction has made space for poetry and has turned speculation into a valid method for re-establishing a relationship between artistic practices and questions and concerns that affect the future of life. In fiction, we have not only seen the emergence of nature, but also the eloquence of indigenous and vernacular cultures and their values, vindications, and ideas on the future. The incredible importance of fiction, however, has also been misused by many who saw this increased openness as an opportunity to trespass the line between fiction and fakes, the line between storytelling and the fabrication of lies. A normal impulse in order to balance these floods of negative impulses coming from the media, capital interests, and authoritarian regimes is to believe that we can create even harder control systems. Like in modern times, our ideas regarding events and their development are highly influenced by notions of centralized power and an overruling that believes in filters, promotions, and dams that stop the anti-democratic social flows. It is not thinkable—from my point of view—to advocate for the regeneration of democracy and the rehabilitation of contemporary art and culture in the eyes of citizens with only the assistance of a damage prevention system. Rather, the contrary is true.

Fantasy strongly emerged in the nineteenth century as the force that re-invented folklore and also the national state myths attached thereto. It was invented to revive oral history and reintroduce tradition. And, therefore, it has retained a suspicious status that has excluded fantasy from being further developed in art and philosophy, as fiction has been. This specific gap between fiction and high culture, on one hand, and fantasy and popular culture, on the other, has been maintained without much effort to revise or rescue fantasy for the sake of freedom and the common good.

Like some of the technologies that are being developed—AI, to name the most obvious—fantasy has not been very present in the artistic discourse because we feel we lack control over it. Only now can we perceive a growing interest

Chus Martínez

from many artists worldwide in returning to fantasy as an ally in order to gain eloquence in the public sphere, a sense of charisma to address fundamental subjects.

As Ursula K. Le Guin demanded in a text back in 1975,[9] it is urgently necessary to create a different, less patriarchal kind of fantasy. But it is also important to transgress its current, predominantly commercial forms of consumption (reading, watching, computer gaming). Fantasy deserves to expand to its full emancipatory potential through a non-hierarchical encounter in real space, the exhibition.

While fiction is more linguistically oriented, fantasy's logic is loose. It resembles the way neuroscience envisions the networks created by conceptually blended spaces in the brain. Fantasy has always been there, but I believe that a large group of younger artists is turning toward it to surpass the polarizing language of responsibility and awareness. When I say fantasy here, it is not to imagine a genre-like exhibition, but an exhibition that pursues an intense sense that expression and self-expression are fundamental to understanding our lives. Fantasy equals here a very accessible transmission language, orality, spaces where people can be open about who they are, what they feel, and how they wish things to be.

Fantasy has, historically, not played a major role in the definition of the social, so there is more of a reason to research this path, so embraced, for example, in Afrofuturisms. Also, in addressing the exhibition as a test space for regaining a sense of individual and collective interconnectivity, it has the capacity to motivate people through the emergence of rich spaces of perception. An exhibition conceived by trusting in fantasy means that the exhibition should possess a highly inclusive philosophy, being able to create exceptional identification with those participating

9   Ursula K. Le Guin, "American SF and the Other," *Science Fiction Studies*, no. 7, vol. 2, part 3 (1975): 208–10.

and visiting it. Bringing together cognitive blending and fantasy is a way of contesting the capitalist ambition to design the social as a set of immersive spaces, collapsing thinking instead of addressing how thinking and judgment happen.

Which Social Simulacra? Which World's Fantasies?

Mental health or the comprehension of mental states, poverty, the future of waste, intelligences, the automation of weapons, war, the future of transmission and education, aging, the aspiration for a non-violent life …. Again, the project: puppets for democracy.

SINZO AANZA   NOOR ABED
GABRIEL ABRANTES   SAELIA APARICIO
MARIA ARNAL   CANAN   GABI DAO
MANCA G. RENKO   GRUPA Ee
MILES HOWARD-WILKS
JOAN JONAS   JANE JIN KAISEN
EMA KUGLER
NICOLE L'HUILLIER
SVETLANA MAKAROVIČ
YAREMA MALASHCHUK & ROMAN KHIMEI
MANUELA MORALES DÉLANO
EDUARDO NAVARRO
INGO NIERMANN & MAYTE GÓMEZ MOLINA
SILVAN OMERZU   AJŠA PENGOV
NOHEMÍ PÉREZ
JUAN PÉREZ AGIRREGOIKOA
VESNA PETREŠIN WITH
PROF. DR. EUGEN PETREŠIN
MAJA PETROVIĆ-ŠTEGER
SADIE PLANT   TARTA RELENA
RENATA SALECL   KATHRIN SIEGRIST
SVETLANA SLAPŠAK
MLADEN STROPNIK
OLGA SUBIRÓS   DEREK TUMALA
AILI VINT   TAKESHI YASURA

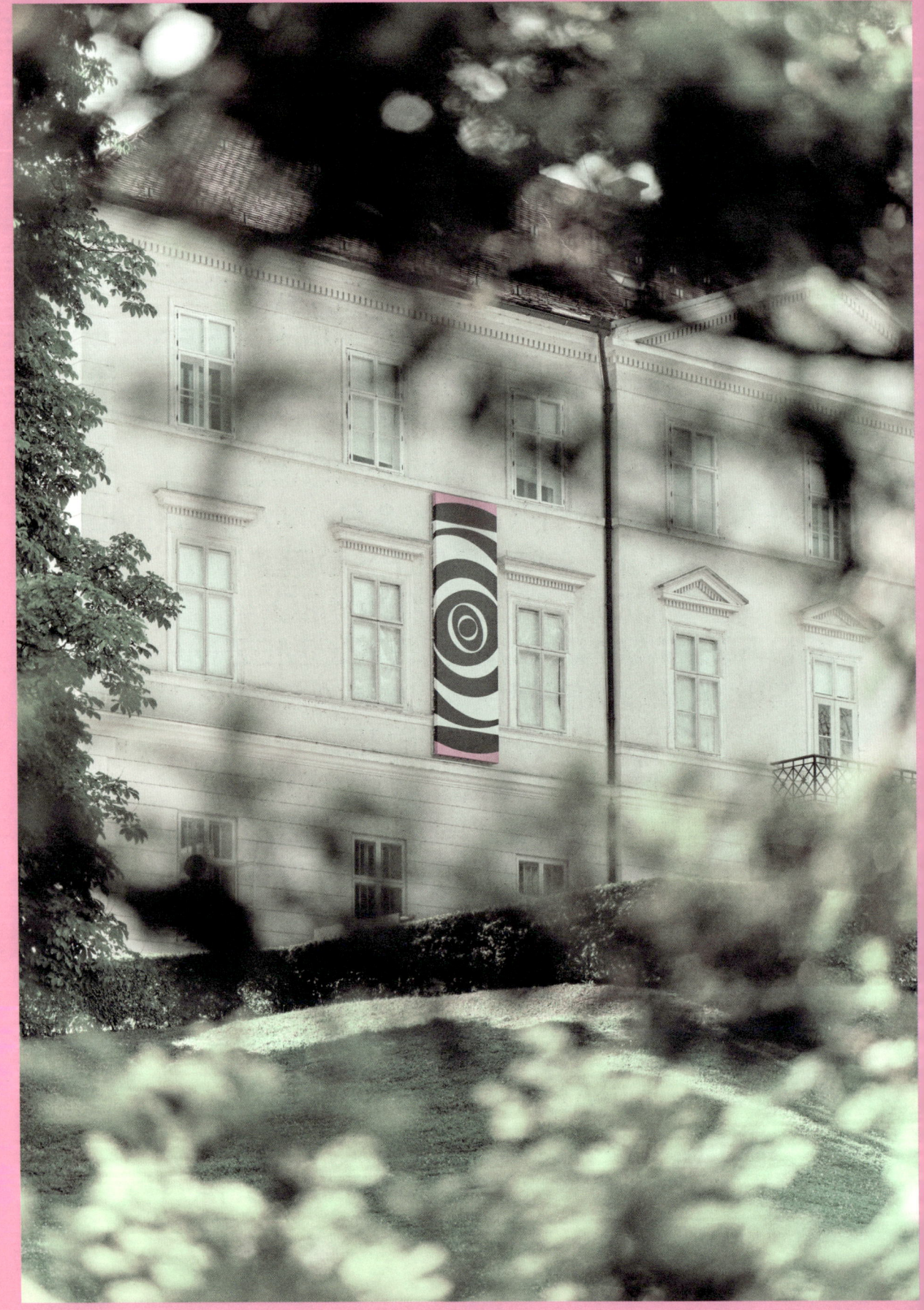

Walk-through of the Exhibition
Chus Martínez

You will encounter three artists at each of the four venues that constitute this Biennale: Silvan Omerzu, whose work is deeply connected to the Slovenian puppetry tradition, and Svetlana Makarovič, one of the most prominent Slovenian literary figures. On the opening weekend, you will hear the voice of Maria Arnal, an artist and singer, who is interested in the voice in its various forms of existence. For the Biennale, she has created a series of songs that she will sing live to signal the beginning of the Biennale and the passage to another world. Departing from existing songs and their historical meaning and function, she has decomposed them to create new pieces. Synchronizing us with ourselves, and ourselves with our past and future, is the aim of this invitation to not only listen, but to sing together at the entrance of each venue.

MGLC Grad Tivoli:
Meshwork, Magic and Emotions

One should enter an exhibition with the mindset of entering a new world. A world where senses are in a state of alertness and oriented towards a new configuration of the real. MGLC, the seat of the Ljubljana Biennale of Graphic Arts, is situated in Grad Tivoli, the oldest building in the area of today's Tivoli Park. Its story goes back to the thirteenth century, having witnessed the constant changes of power, sentiment, and history. It is for this reason that the non-human, from mosquitoes to ghosts, is a central motif of this venue. Here you will encounter the work of five artists: Gabi Dao, their installation located by the entrance, on ground level; Silvan Omerzu, the first work when you come up the stairs; CANAN, when you turn to your right; Manuela Morales Délano in the middle of the first floor; and Gabriel Abrantes, the cinematic installation in the last four rooms. The common denominator of the works presented in this venue is the power of artists to form new narratives, new folklore, even out of the world's disasters.

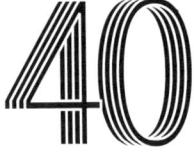

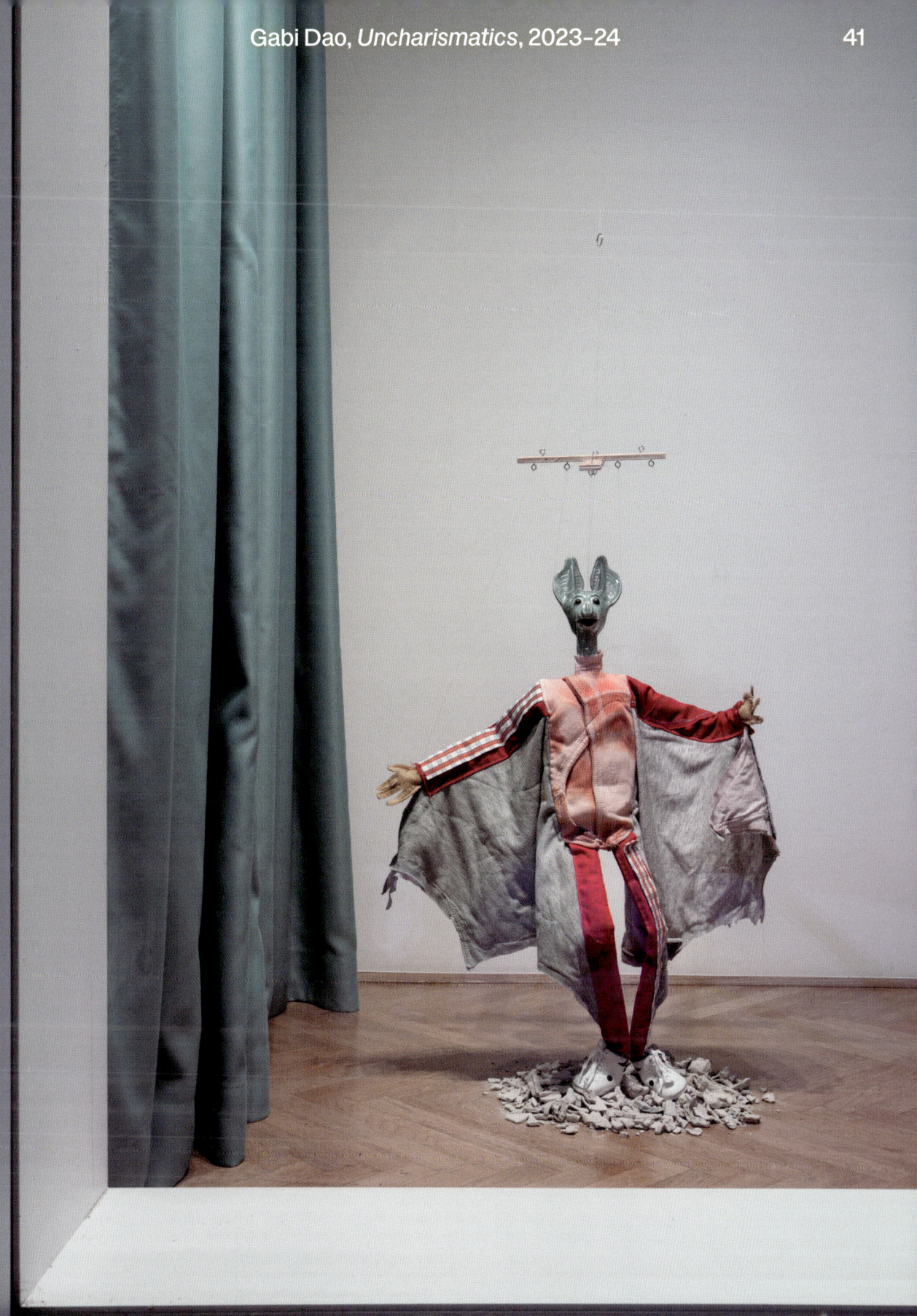

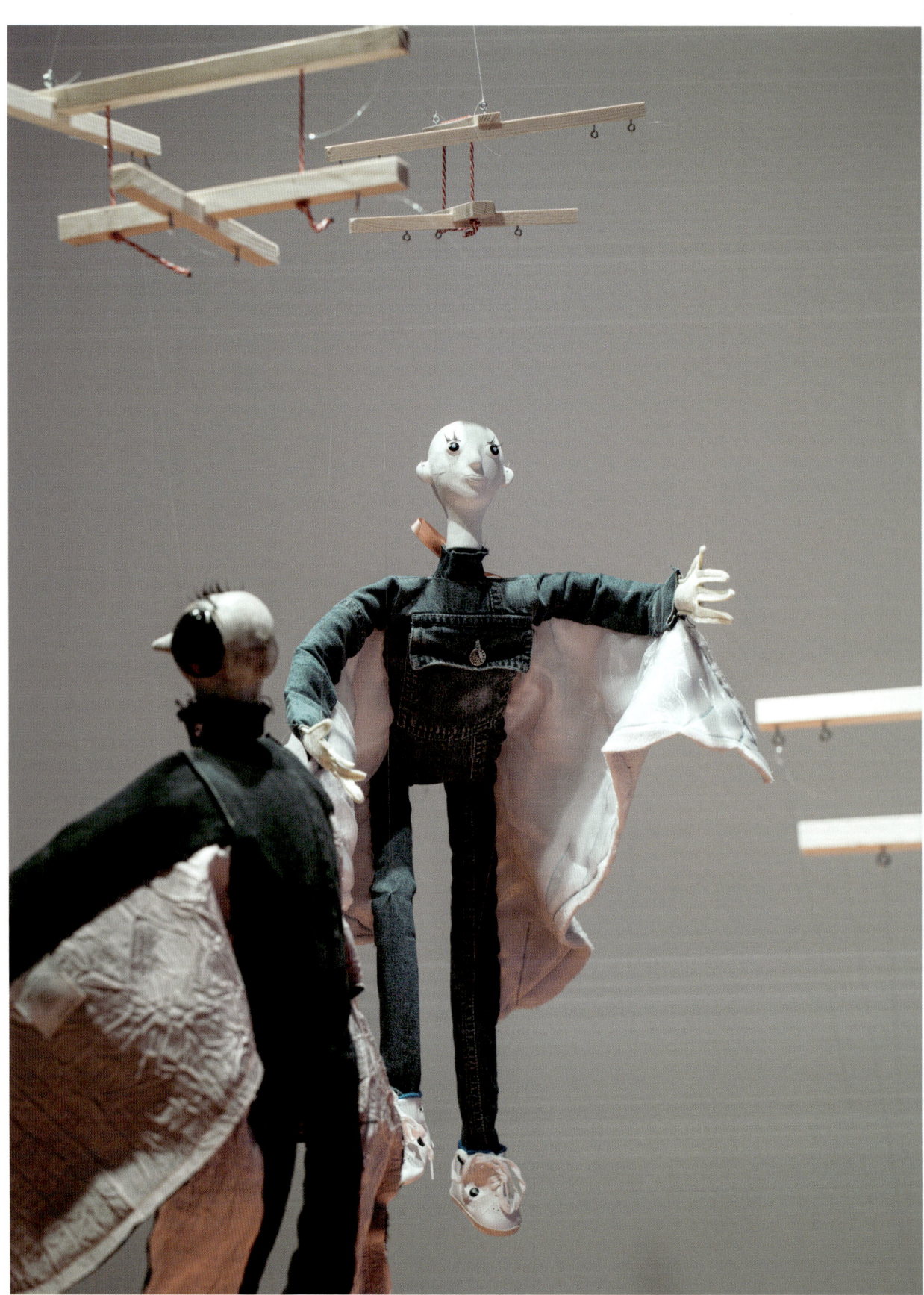

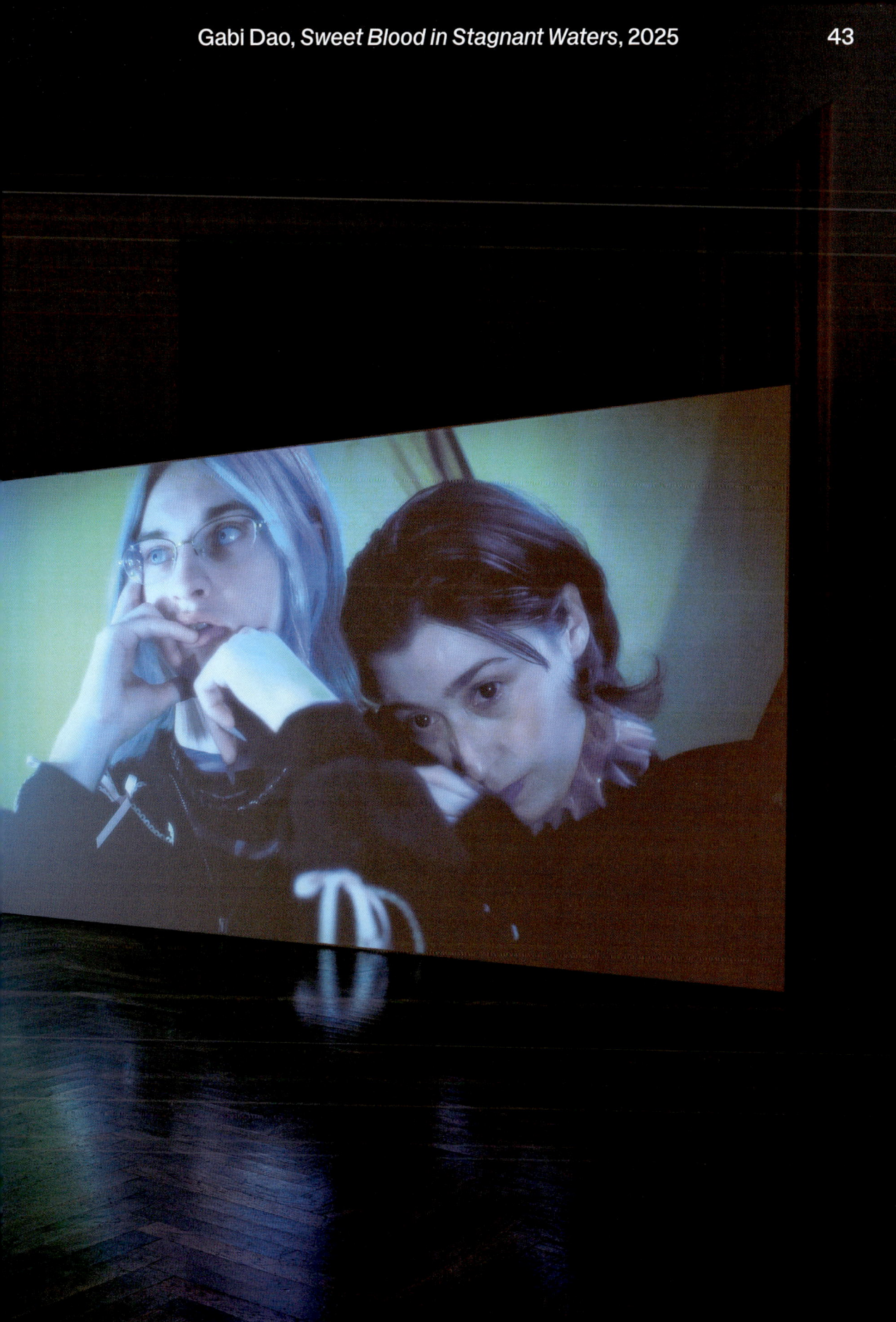

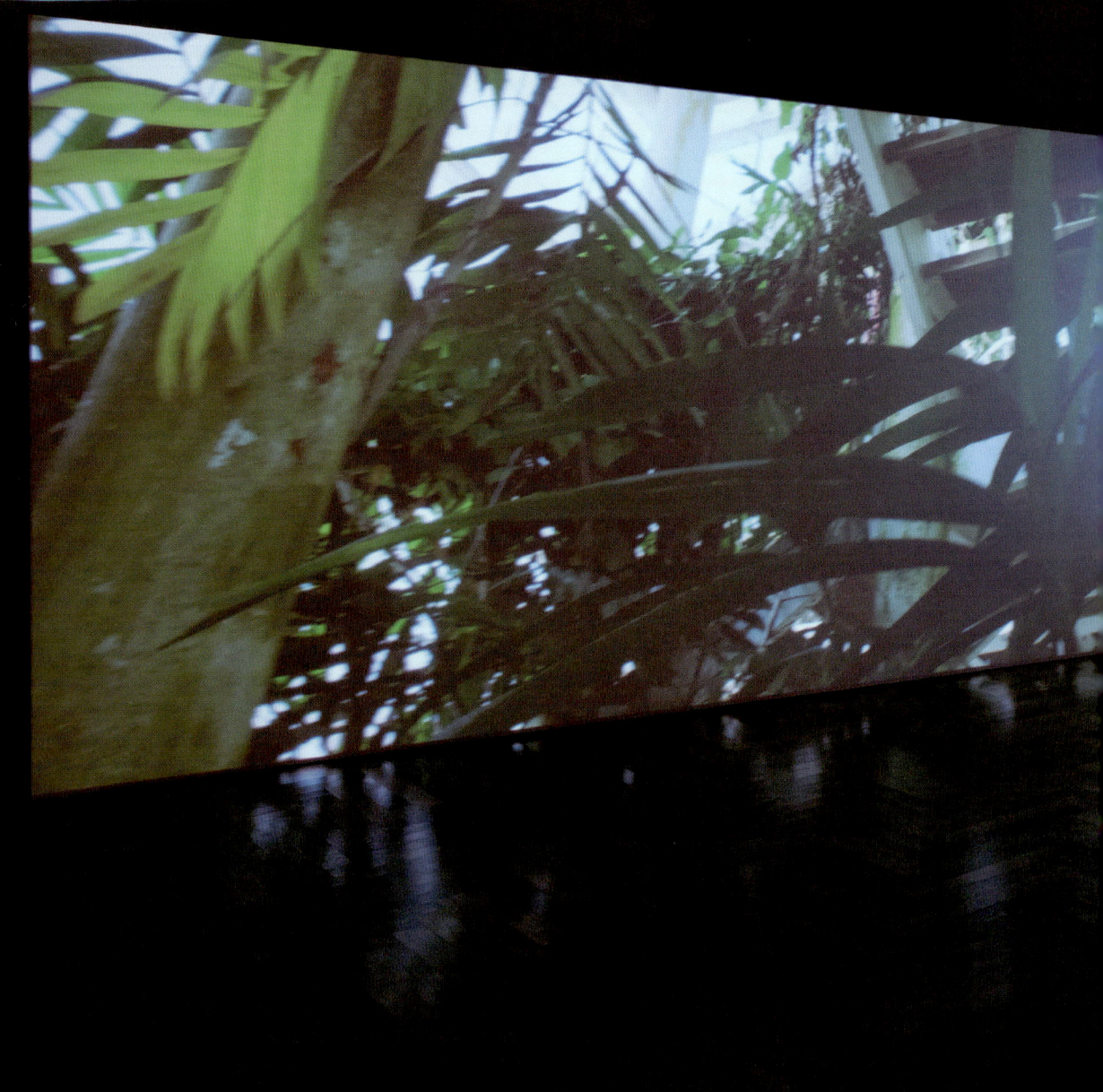

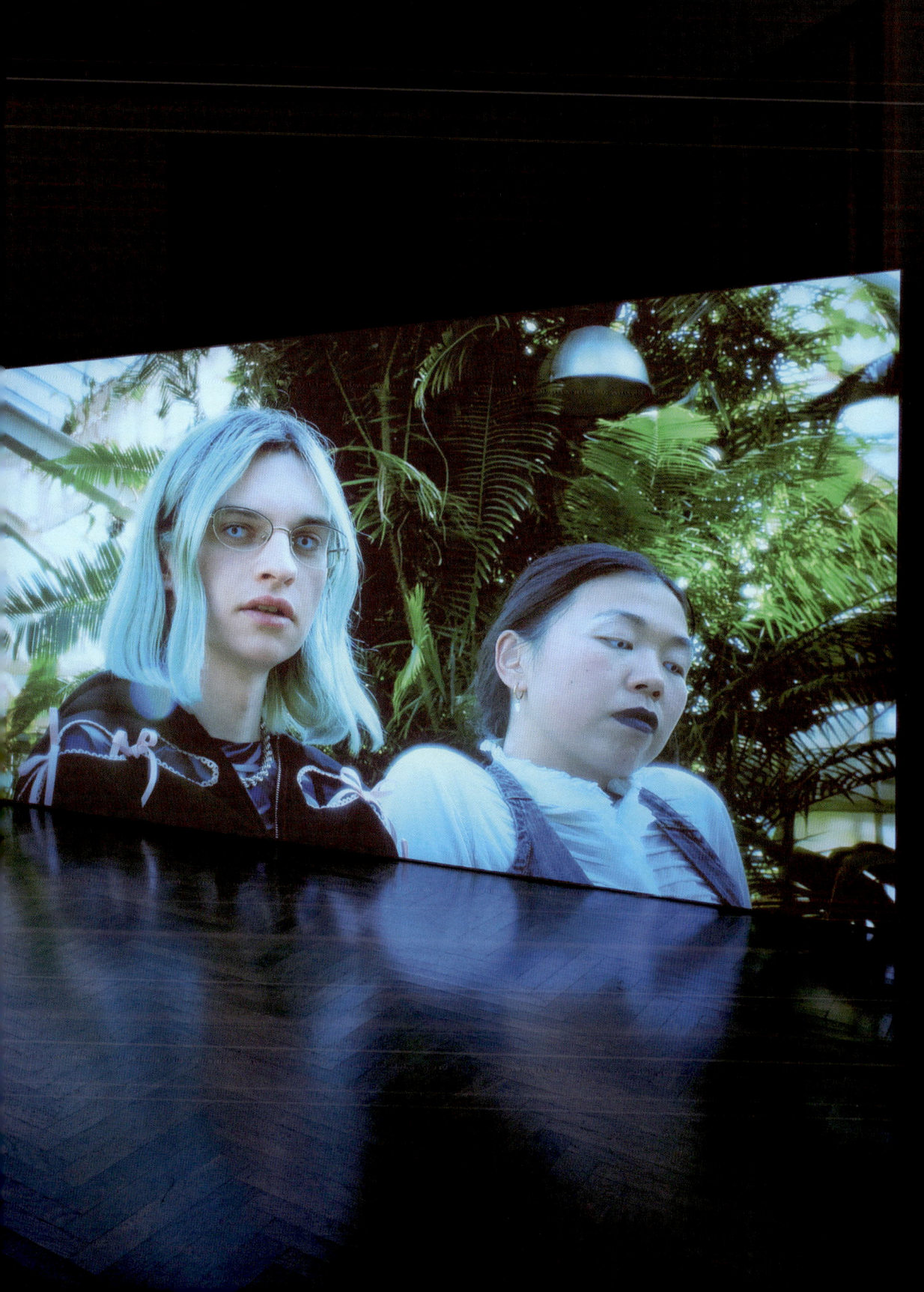

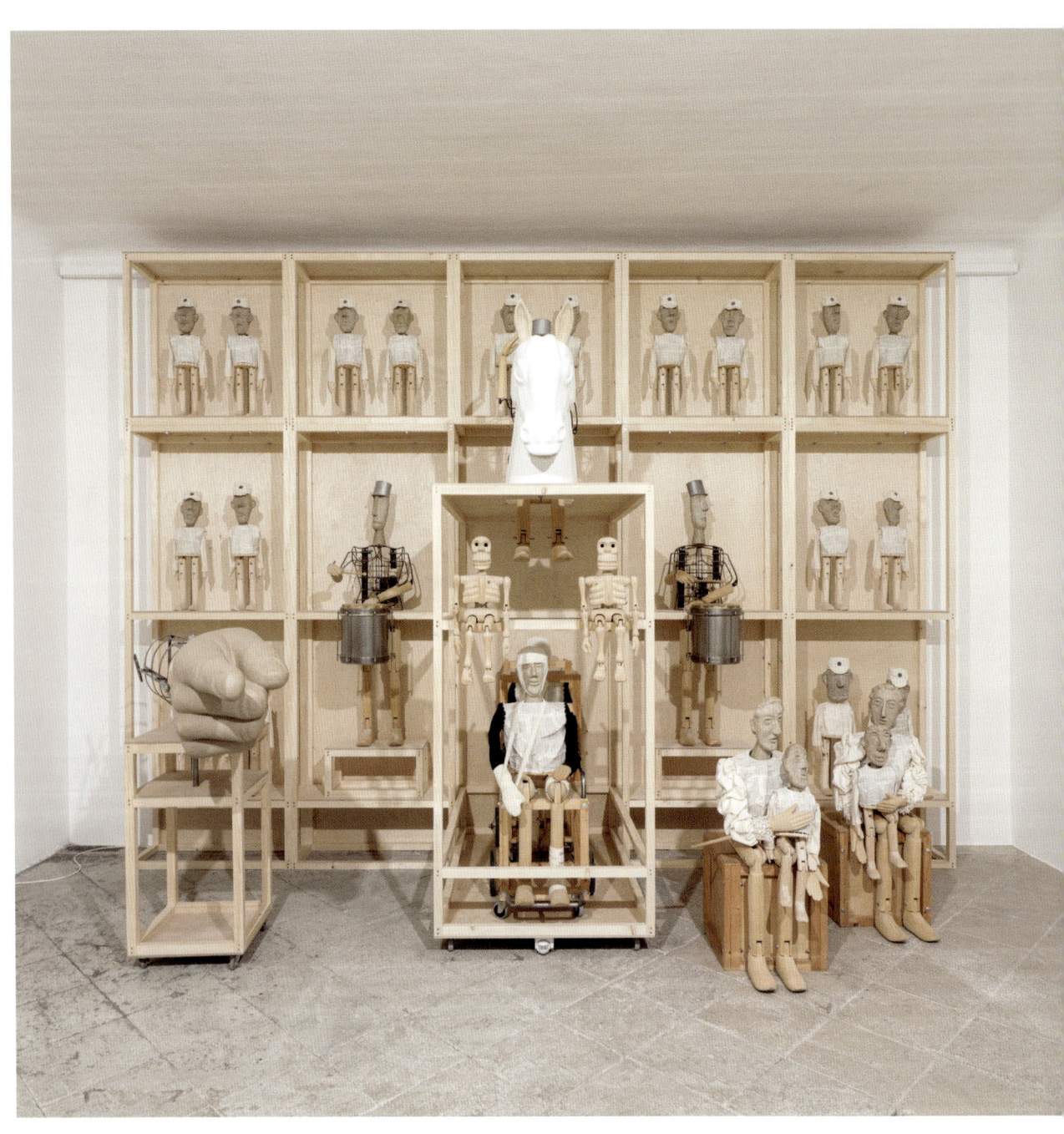

Gabi Dao's *Sweet Blood in Stagnant Waters* is a film and a mosquito puppet installation. Dramatizing epidemic imaginaries, colonial geographies, science fiction, militarism, and queer ecology through the study of mosquitoes, the artist creates an experimental sci-fi film. A hybrid documentary, experimental, multi-channel video installation to give voice and agency to a whole series of characters that become the storytellers of a new order. The goal? Re-enchanting meaning-making from the ruins of culture.

Silvan Omerzu's piece possesses a strong anti-war message, highlighting the inhumanity and devastating consequences of war. A work that refers to the history of the very Mansion where the exhibition takes place. Grad Tivoli served as a military barracks and a hospital for a while. The Provincial Estates later sold the property to Emperor Franz Joseph I, who gifted it to the Habsburg Field Marshal Joseph Radetzky. He renovated it and opened this part of the park to the public. His statue stands in the courtyard. Through mechanized puppets and automata, it creates a sense of the military system's callousness and the suffering of the innocent.

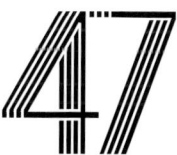

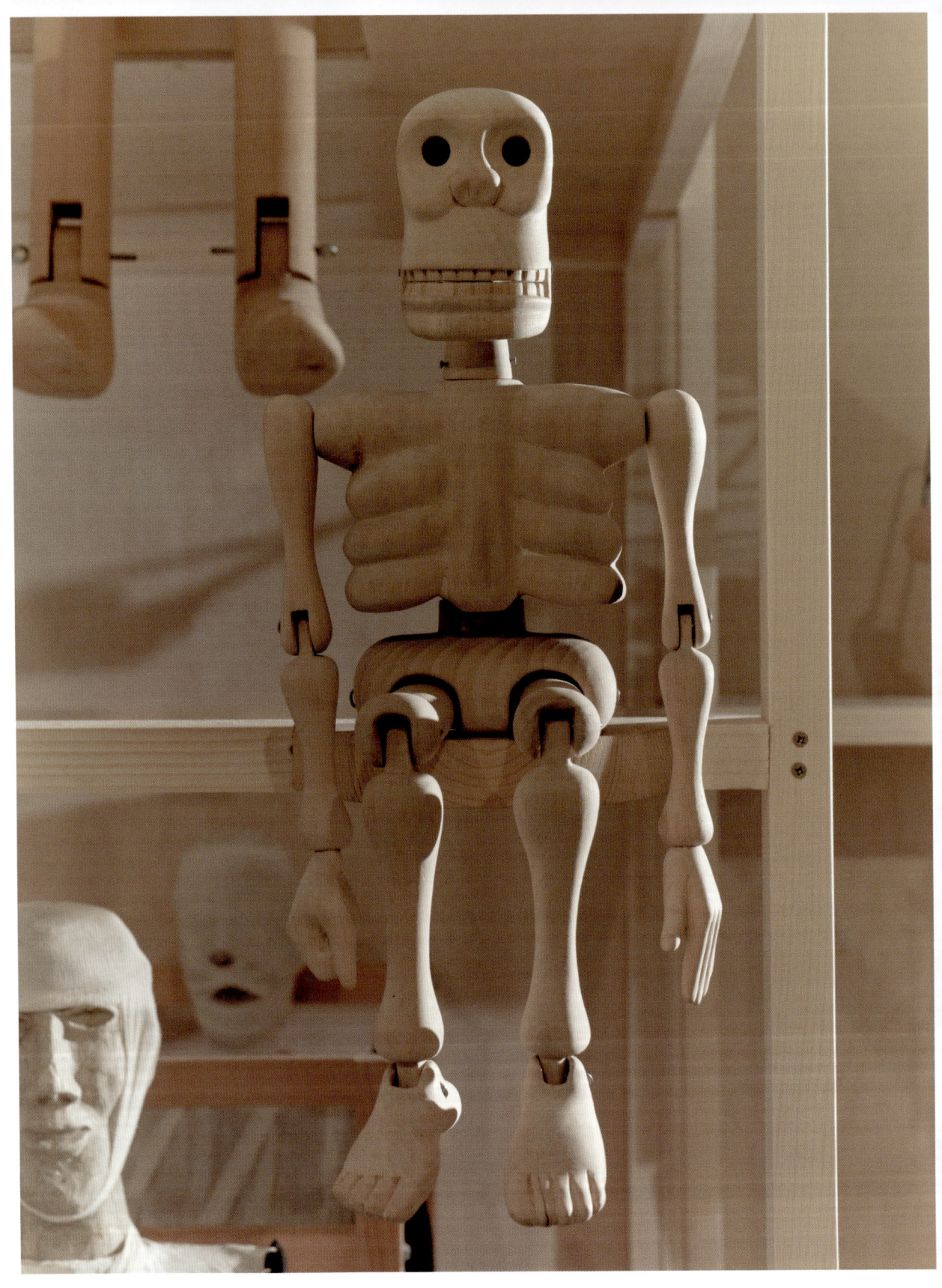

Silvan Omerzu, *Mr. Captain*, 2025

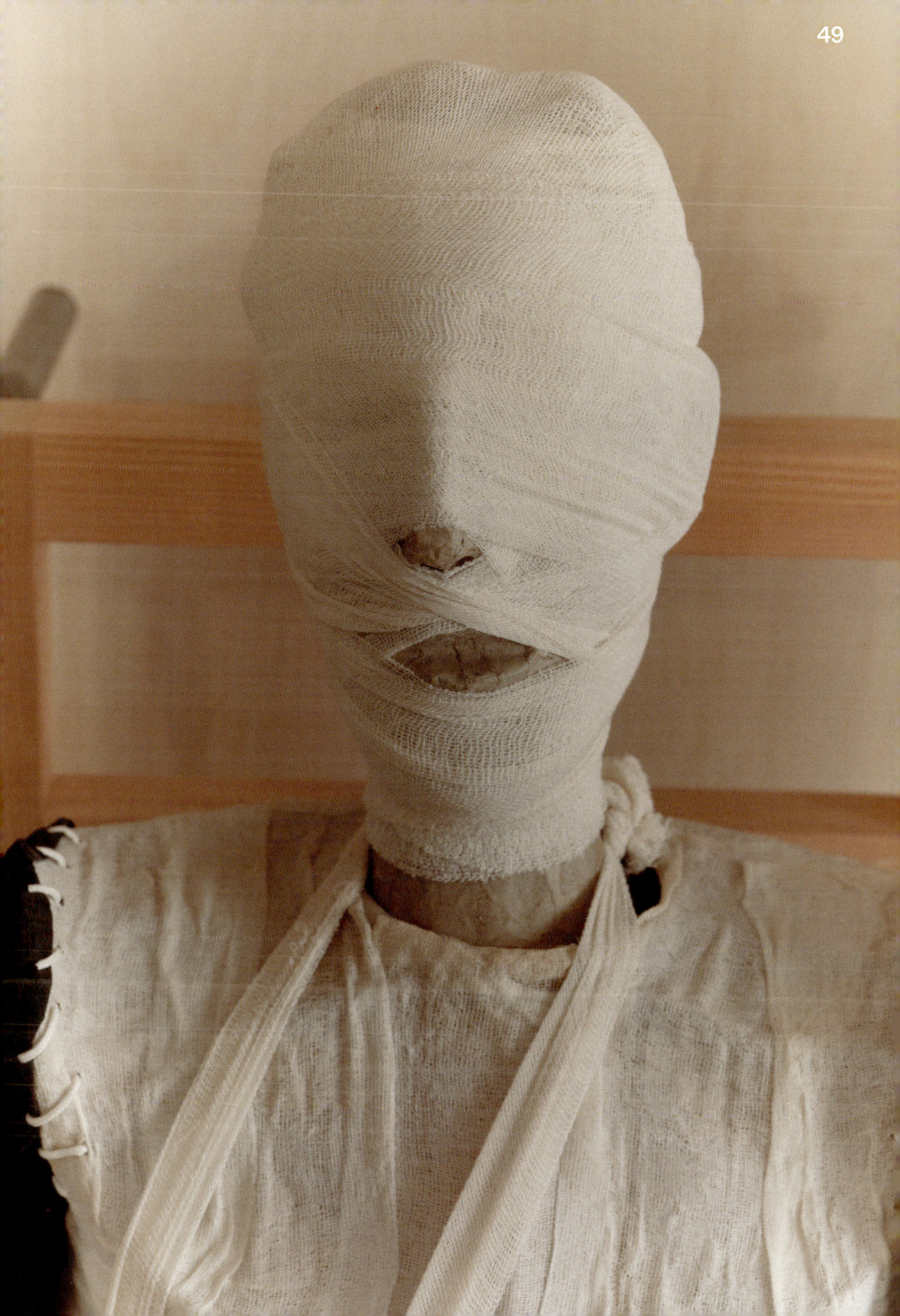

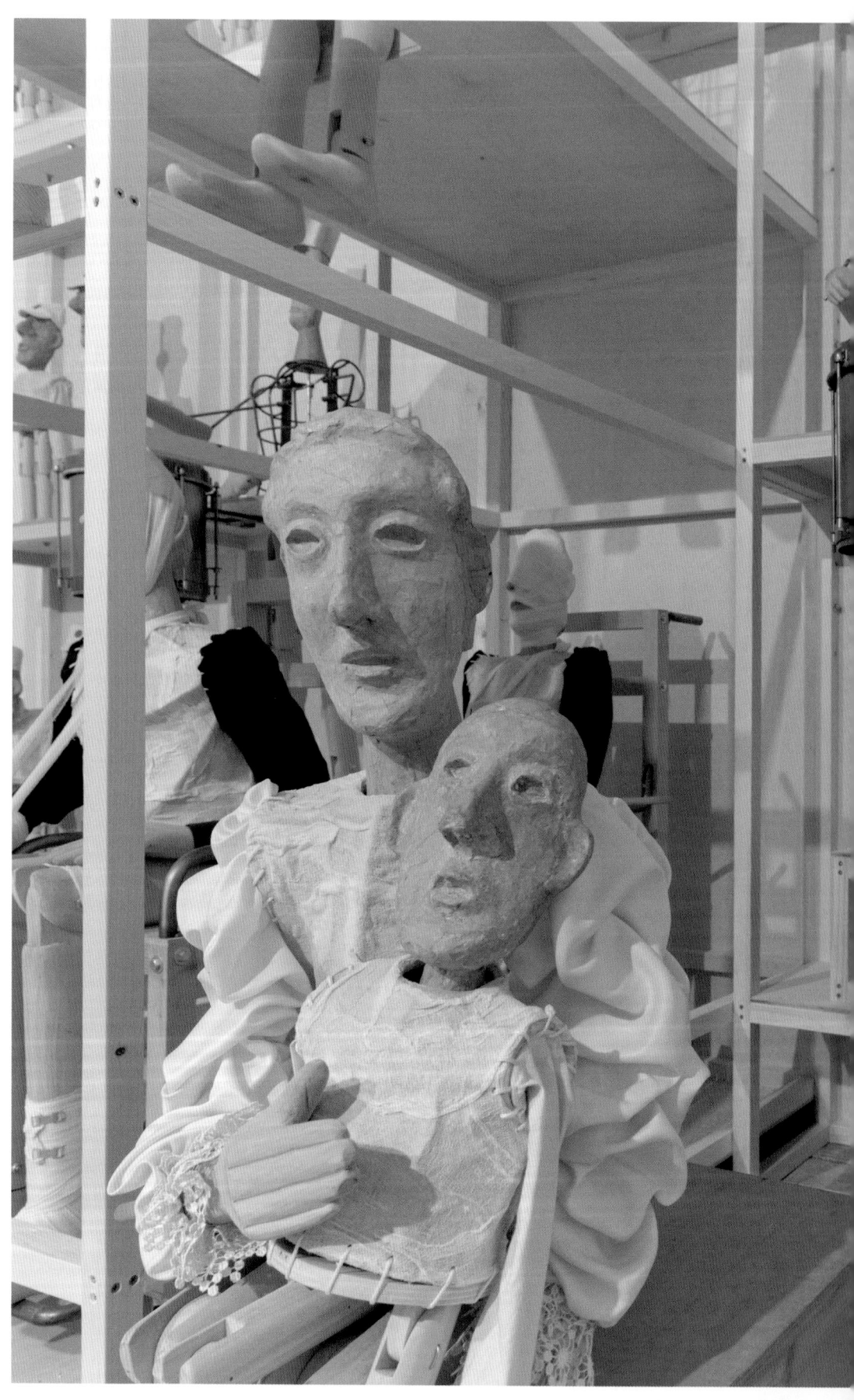

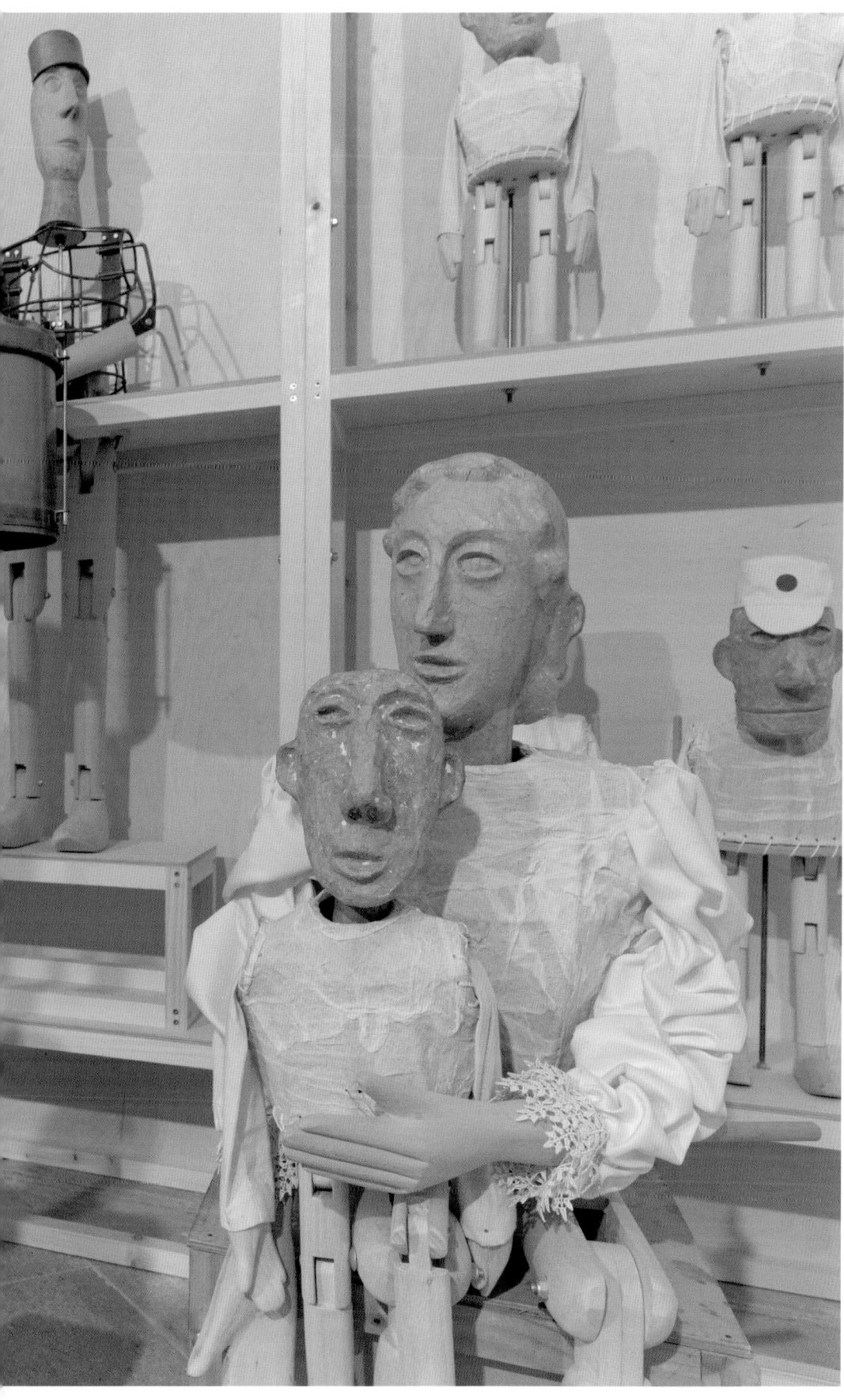

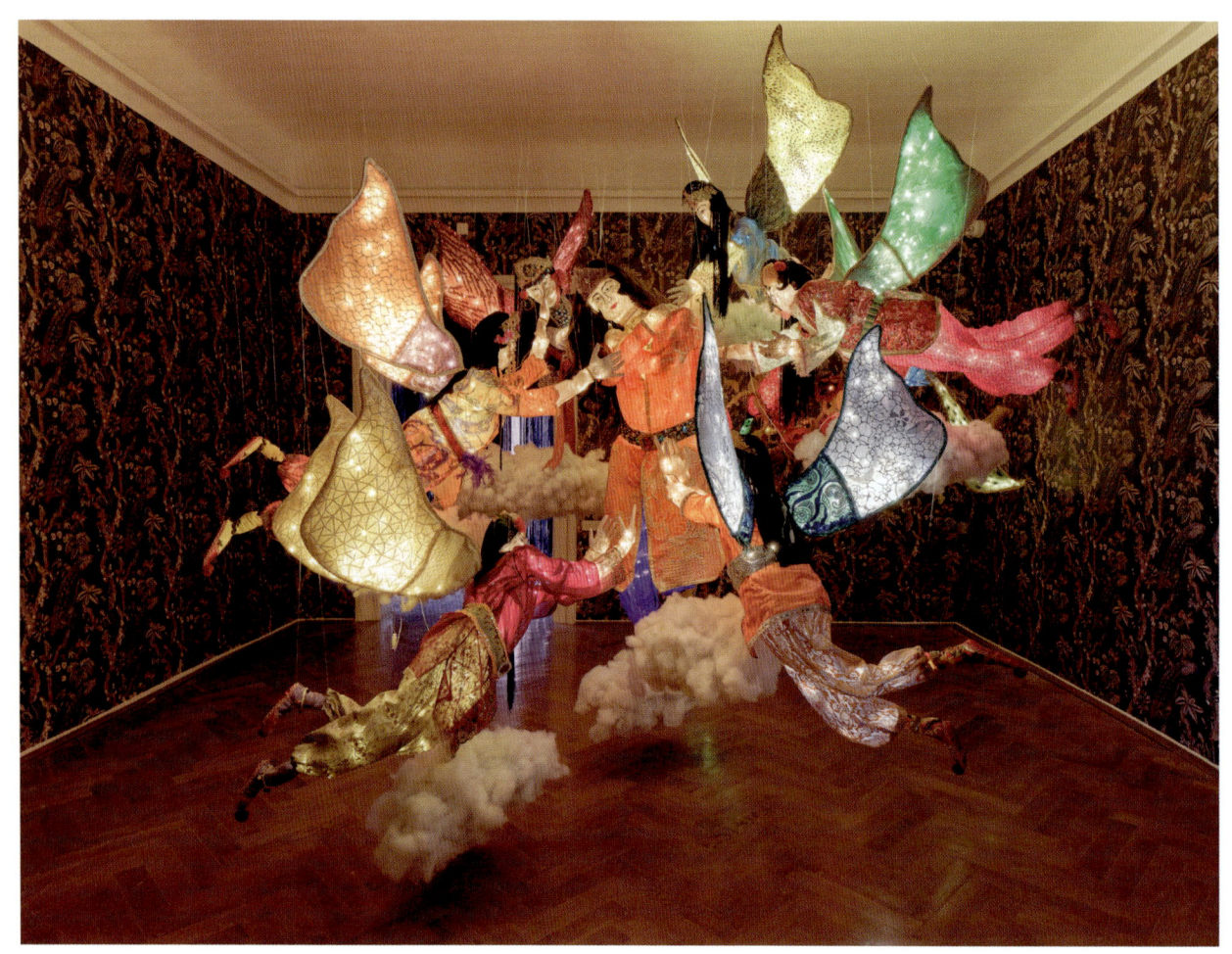

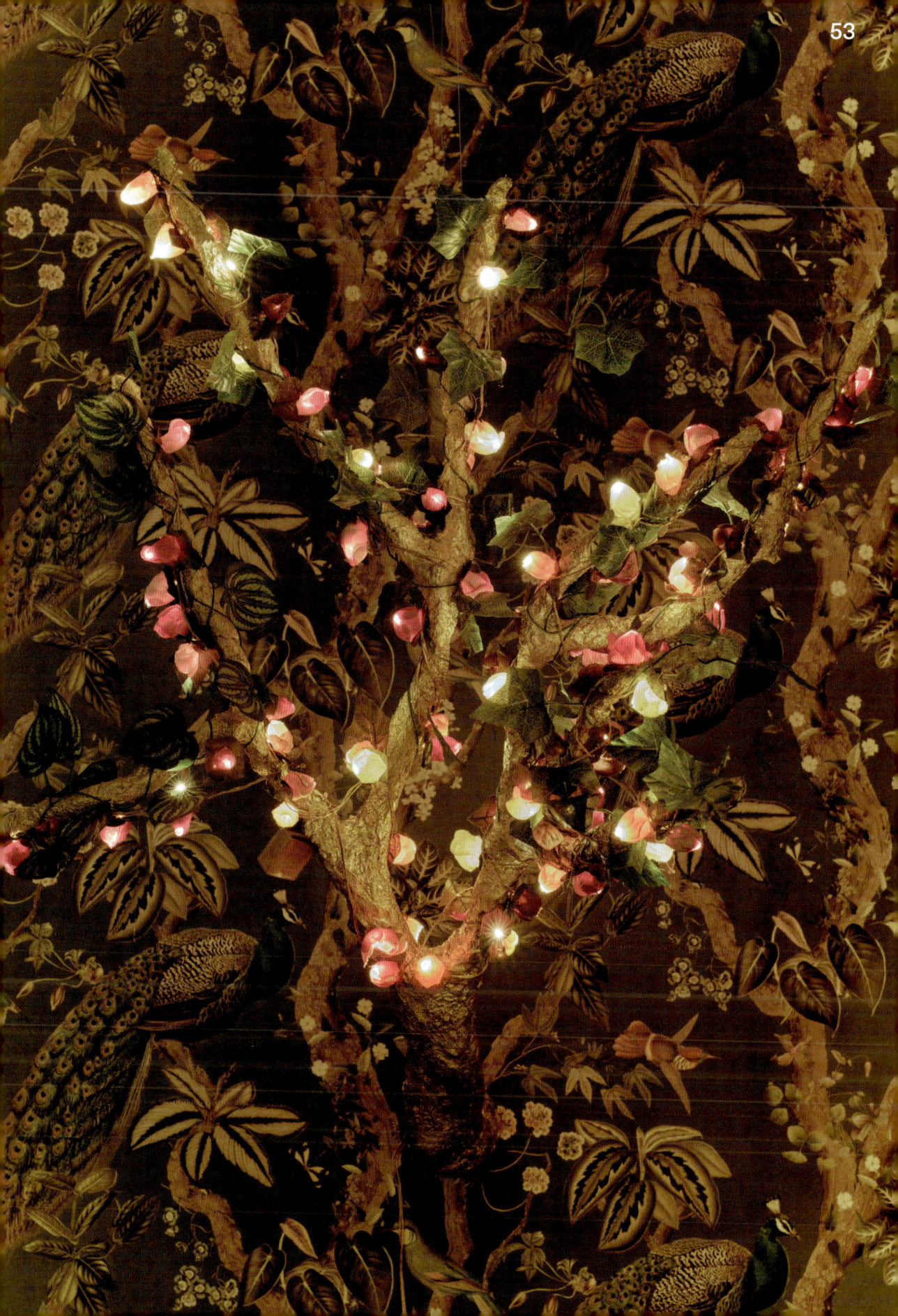

CANAN's installation takes over from this idea, immersing the viewer in a four-step voyage to self-valuation as the original title, *Kıymeti Zatiyye* (*Intrinsic Value*), implies. The first room asks you to distance yourself from the outside world, to create a sense of privacy. The second room calls for compassion—a sentiment so important. There, a female figure inspired by miniatures is surrounded by angels, forming a lighted sculpture group. The faces of the angels are identical to the face of the female figure. The body structure, made of iron and aluminium wires, is covered with fabric and sequined materials and is illuminated from the inside. The third room is called *The Mercy Room.* Mercy with oneself and others. The room is a sort of fabric-fresco featuring human, mythical, and animal figures that evoke mercy. Viewers here are invited to lie on the floor and look up at the ceiling, then listen to a story written and narrated by the artist. The last room—*The Value Room*—is a cylindrical installation made of golden bridal veils and golden copper wires holding golden inscriptions—"I am valuable," "I value myself," "I show compassion and mercy to myself," "I am at peace with myself" in various languages. Hanging inside the cylinder are red roses, symbolizing worth.

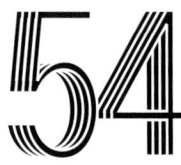

Walk-through of the Exhibition

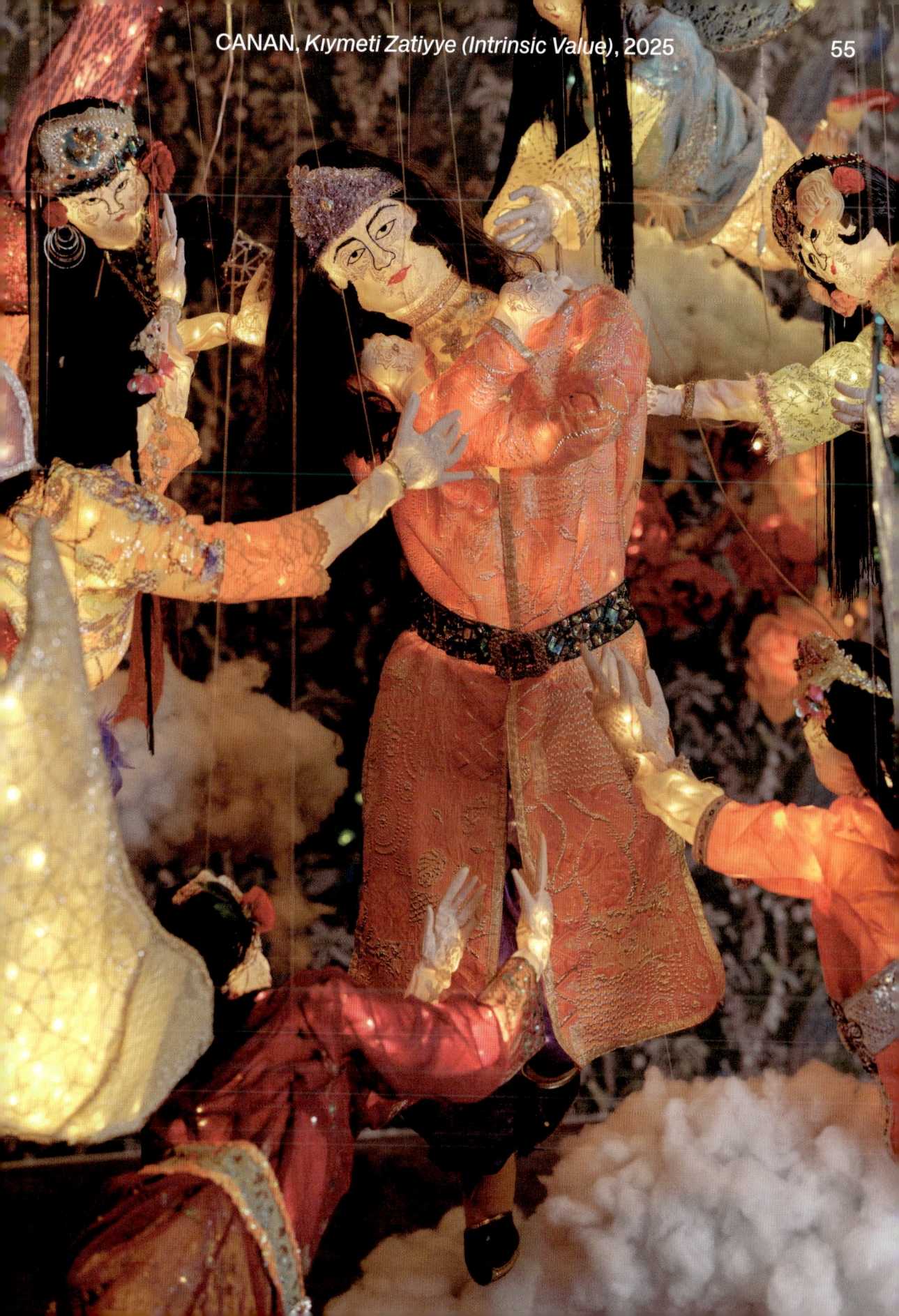

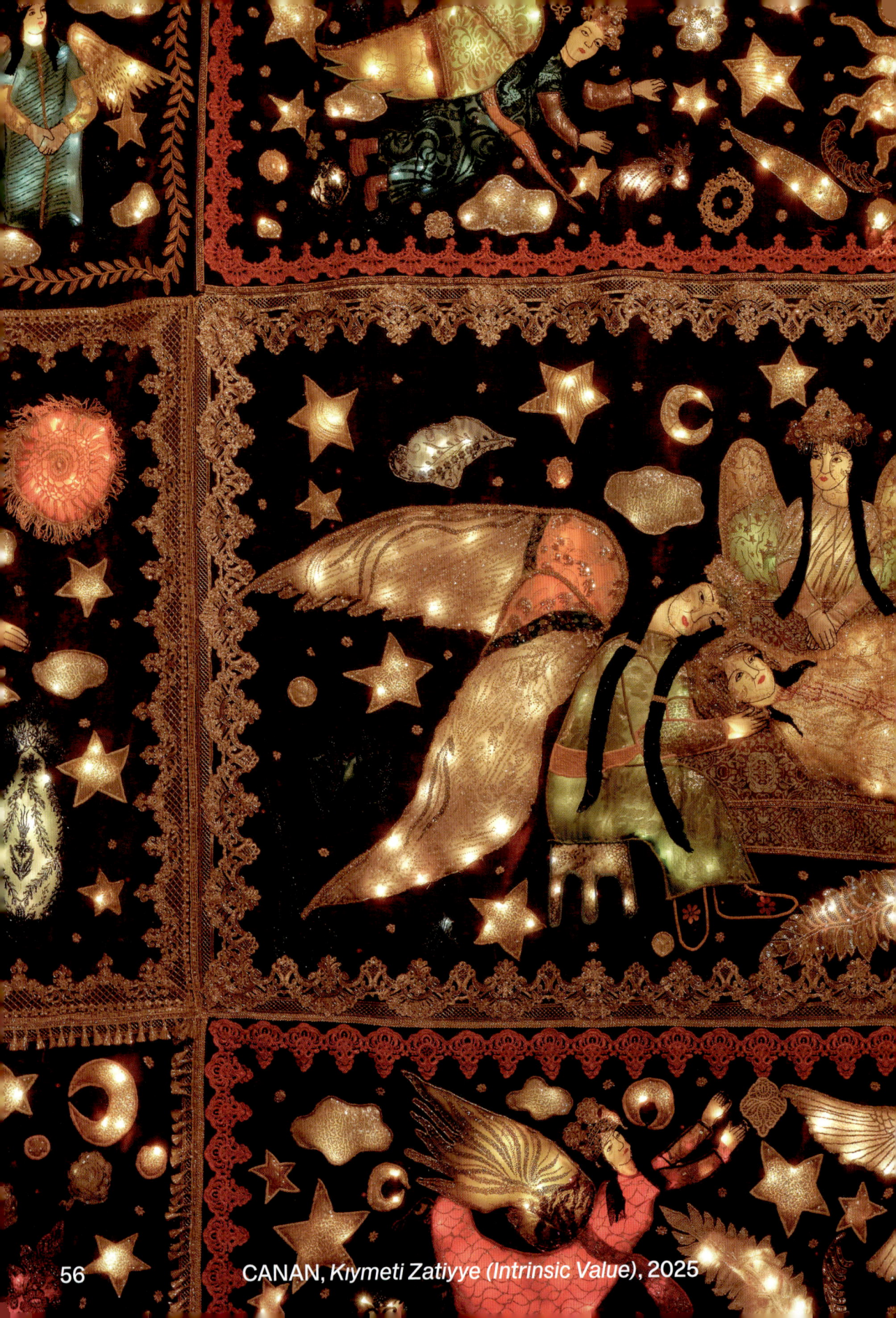

CANAN, *Kıymeti Zatiyye (Intrinsic Value)*, 2025

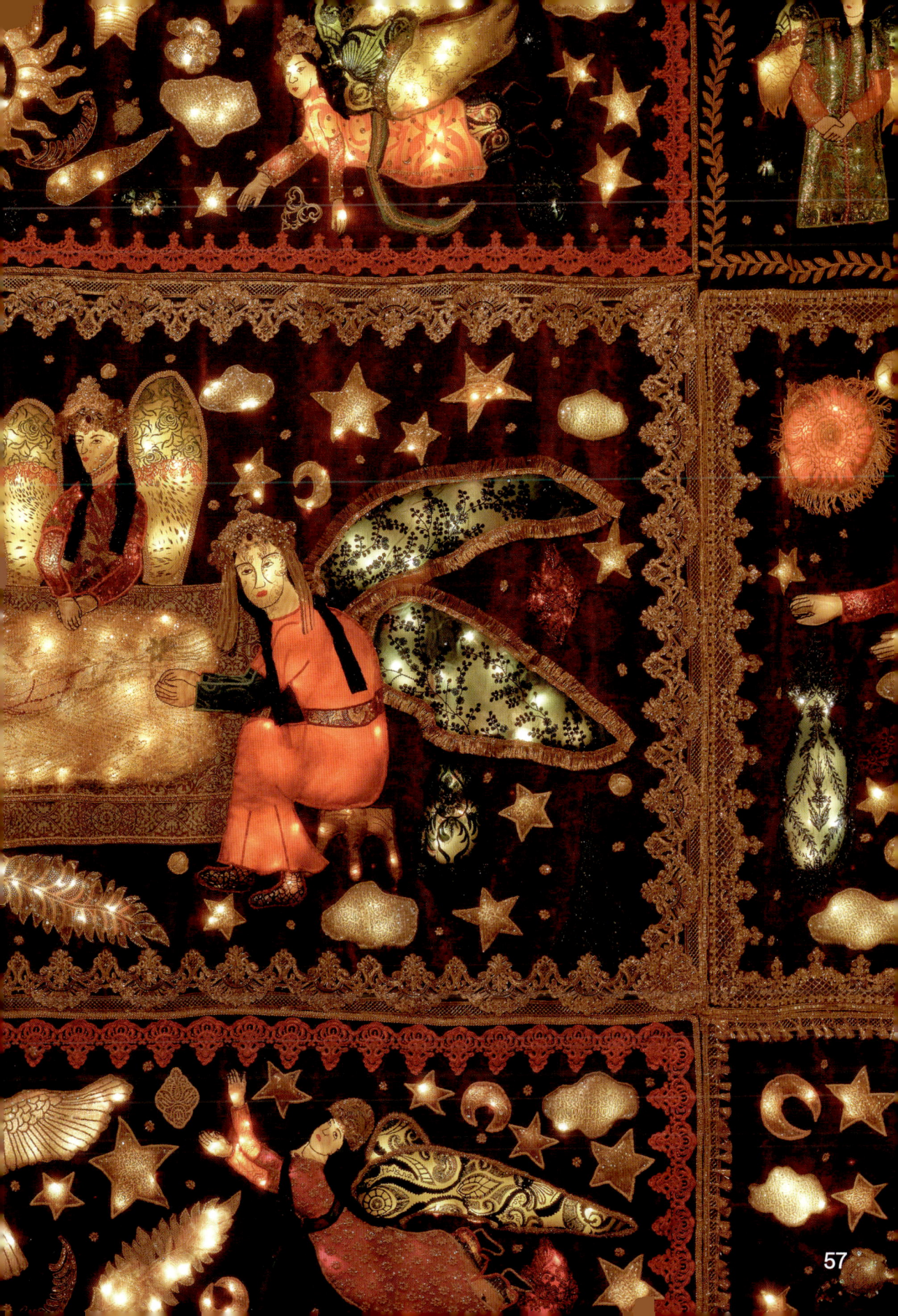

Manuela Morales Délano, *Espantapájaro con ojo (Scarecrow with Eye)*, 2025

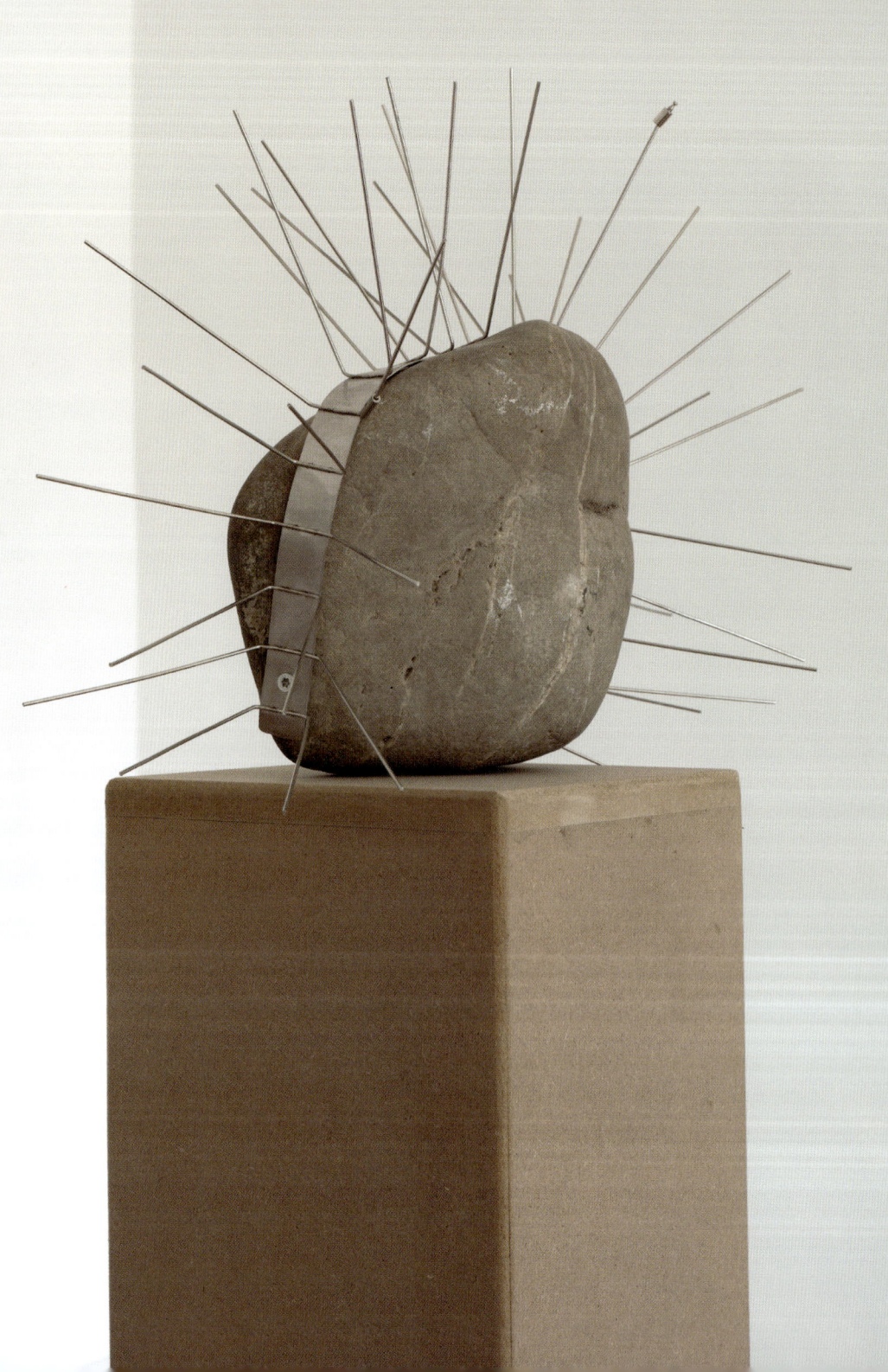

In the small room right after this dense installation, you will find two stones by Manuela Morales Délano. The stones—like the puppets by Silvan Omerzu at the entrance—are heads, insensible heads that wear a strange war attire. What these stones are wearing reminds us a little of the Roman war hackle, a short spray of colored feathers that was attached to a military headdress. The metal pieces here are anti-pigeon skewers that the artist found on the street. Another war, a war against nature. Another piece by Manuela Morales Délano—a drawing installation—is situated downstairs at the Museum of Modern Art.

From here, you will enter the dimension of the bardo, *The Bardo Loop*, a video-musical installation by Gabriel Abrantes. The bardo is the name of a transitional state between death and rebirth in some schools of Buddhism. Four rooms with a singing ghost: *the sad singer*, *I want to have a baby*, *victim,* and *break up*. The beautiful singing ghost performs a pop-classical ballad on a grand piano within the decrepit setting of an abandoned Lisbon palace that might once have been a political party's headquarters. The song mourns "being too late" — but too late for what? This space-opera layers improbable readings, twisting traditional narratives while flirting with absurdity, folklore, humor, and politics. It builds on the appropriation of Hollywood genres, such as melodramas, romantic comedies, war films, adventure movies, etc., and stirs it with a familliar archive of symbolic references, popular culture, and contemporary anxieties.

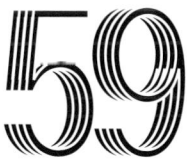

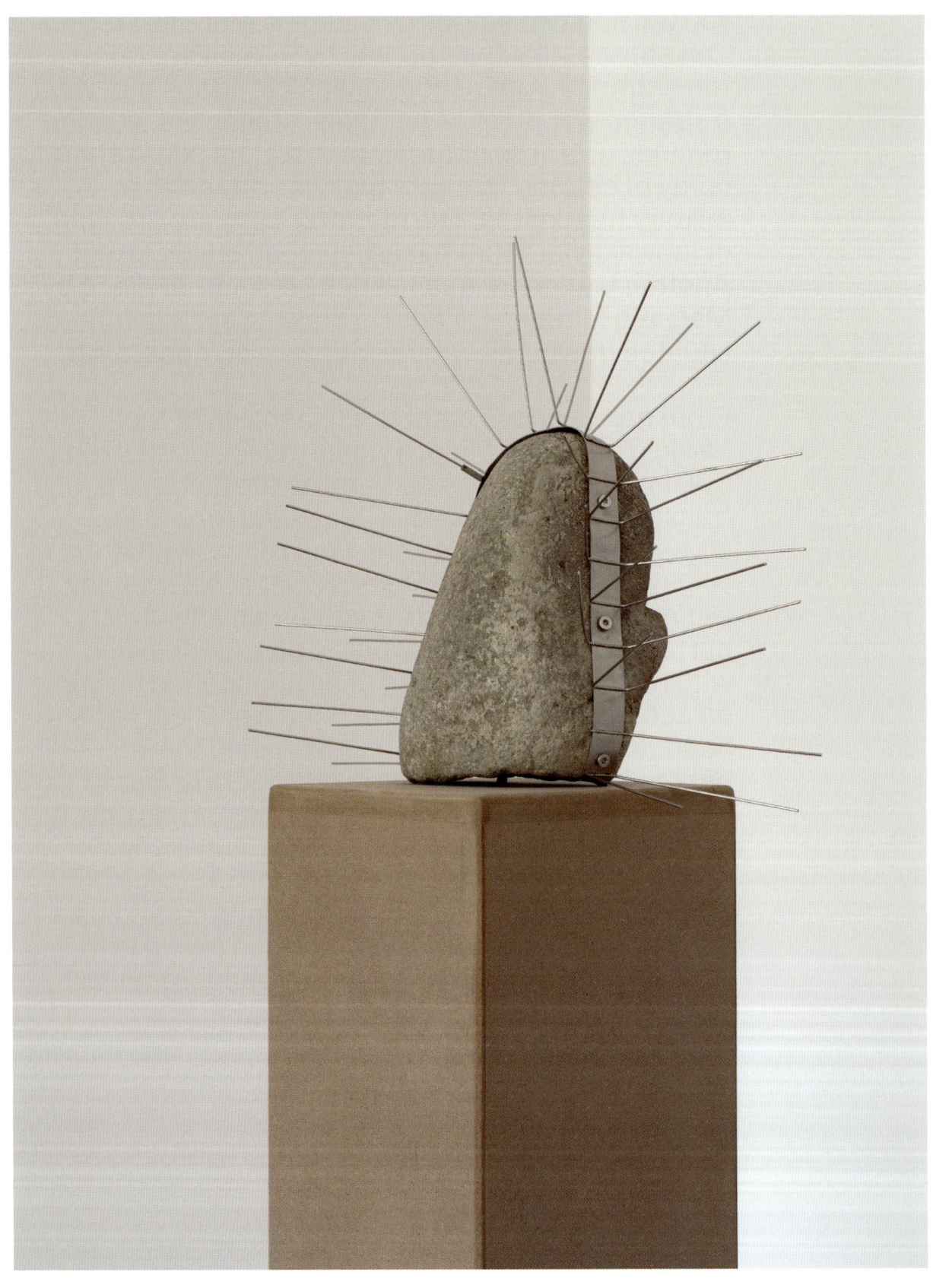

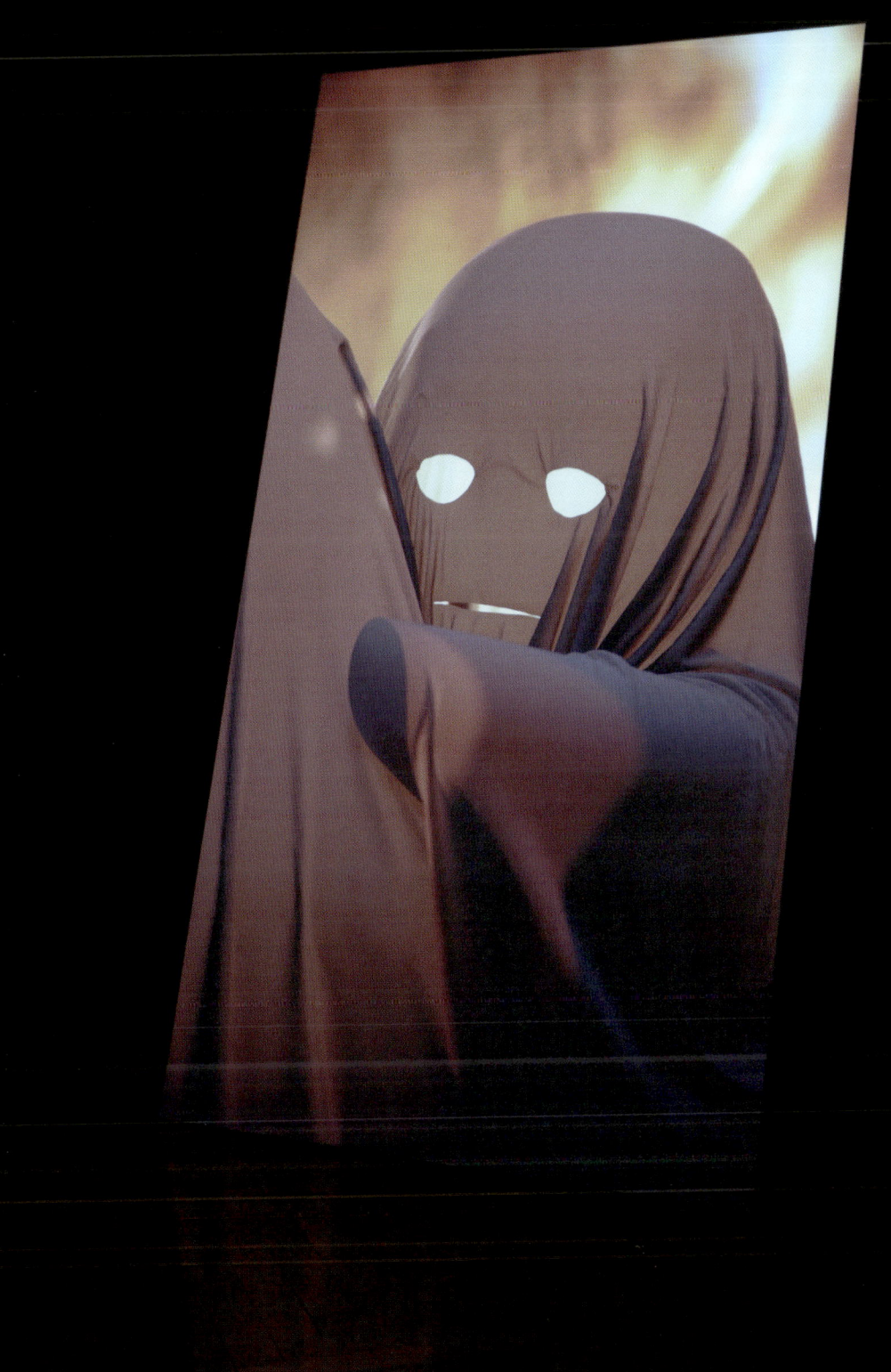

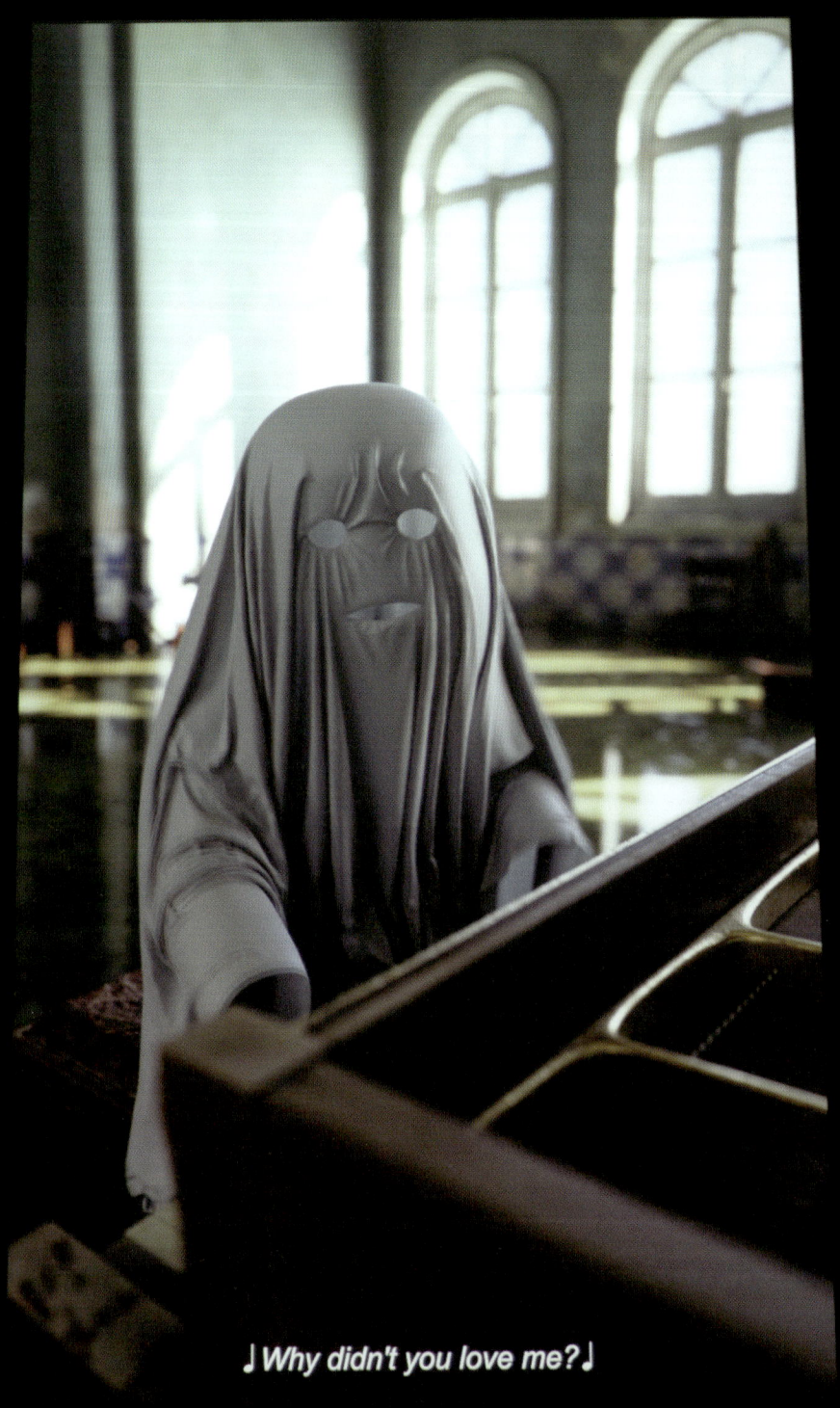

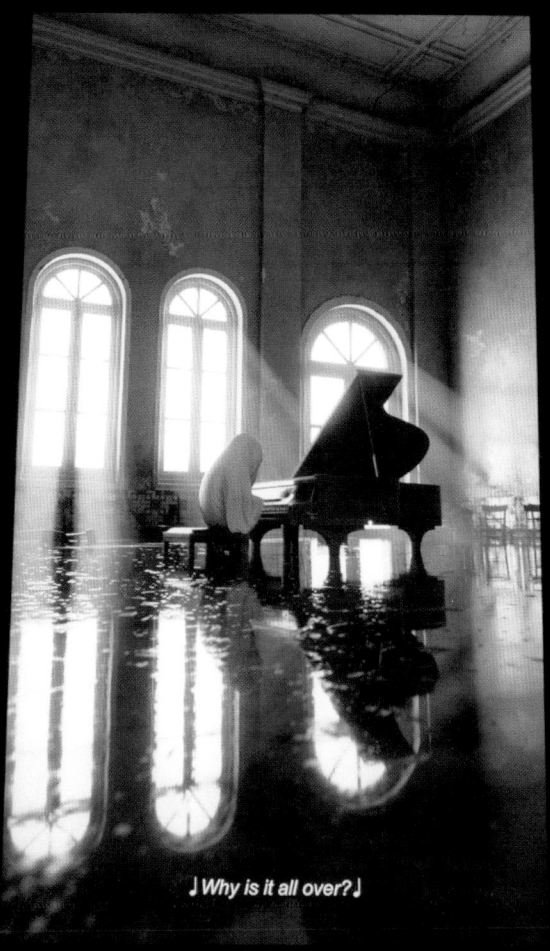

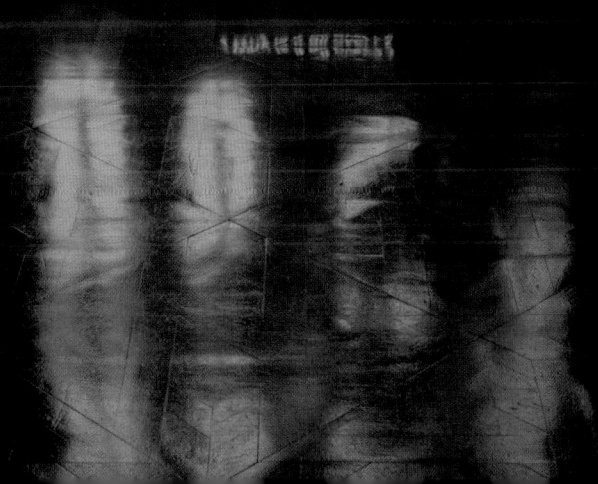

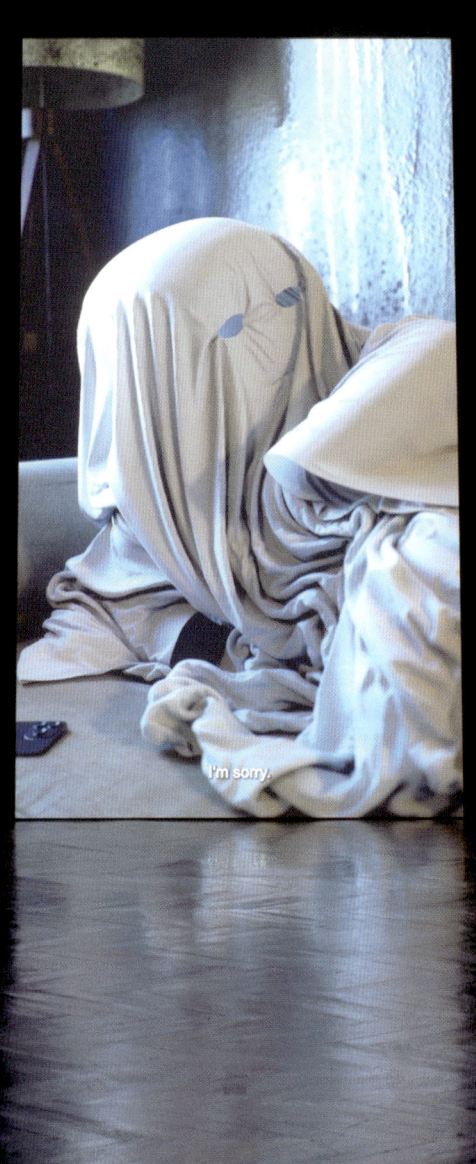

Gabriel Abrantes, *Bardo Loops*, 2024

LIFE
ON MARS?

Manca

G. Renko

Manca G. Renko

Stefan and I were born in different republics of the same country, and we both studied history and spent part of our student years in Germany. Since our niche interests coincide in some respects, we have lately been meeting at scientific conferences. We also share a similar taste in memes, which we like on each other's Instagram profiles. They are mostly Trotskyist jokes with a contemporary twist, and I suspect that Stefan is actually fonder of Trotsky than I am. But that doesn't really matter. At the end of February, on a day that couldn't have been more spring-like, as we were walking in Rome from the Fondazione Gramsci, where the archives of the Italian communist movement are kept, to Sapienza University, where we were both presenting papers on the same panel, he told me that he would like to invite me to give a guest lecture in St. Petersburg, where he has been living and working for the past few years, and present my work to his students. I was very happy as well as honored.

A few hours later, I read in the news that Slovenia, as a member of the EU, had imposed new sanctions against Russia. I wondered whether I would even be allowed to go on a work trip to Russia; could any of my temporary employers in Austria or Slovenia have a problem with that? Am I immoral for wanting to go to Russia again? Then I remembered how my PhD supervisor had told me more than a decade ago that he thought the most important thing I could take away from my doctorate was to learn at least the basics of using Russian archives and libraries. He was afraid that soon there would be no one left in Slovenia who knew how to use them and that the knowledge which had been passed down from generation to generation since the nineteenth century, linked by a thin thread of enthusiasm, curiosity, personal relationships, and Russian imperial ambitions, would be lost forever. I remembered my trips to Moscow, where everything was more or less left to chance, where I had difficulty communicating, and where strict

Life on Mars?

archivists were willing to only let me look at a few files, which ended up being not particularly useful to me. I photographed the documents secretly, in constant fear that I would be discovered and banned from entering the archive forever. Despite all this, it seemed to me at the time that I was doing something important and that the world was opening up, and that Moscow would gradually feel closer. It was only a matter of time, I was convinced, before I would be able to announce my visit to the archive online rather than via the ominous telephone in the entrance hall. In short, had I had to predict the future a good decade ago, I would never have said that I would one day wonder whether I would be allowed to visit Russia for work. Nor could I have imagined that a Ukrainian colleague, just a few years younger than me, would—while showing me her apartment in Vienna—almost advise me not to rent it, saying she had never felt more depressed than she did there after learning that her partner had been killed by the Russian occupiers. I also wouldn't have predicted that nearly the only people of my generation with stable employment in my field—those not adrift in the harsh seas of the international academic precariat—would be working in Russia, China, and Alaska.

I was in no way prepared for this world and how it would shrink: summer Interrail, Erasmus exchanges, and direct easyJet flights from Ljubljana to Berlin in my early twenties represented the promise of an open world, a liberal Europe that would continue to expand. Today, in my late thirties, I travel from Ljubljana to Vienna by FlixBus instead of by high-speed train, because the bus is more reliable than the Slovenian and Austrian railways, even though it is sometimes stopped by the police and everyone who is not fair-skinned is thoroughly searched. I remember all too well the talk of a "two-speed Europe" and the "Franco-German train." At the time, I could have predicted that we would never be on the same train, but I didn't think that the train would soon cease

Manca G. Renko

to exist altogether, and that we would be divided into those on FlixBuses and those in Teslas.

When, by a series of coincidences, we find ourselves halfway between the Fondazione Gramsci and Sapienza University, and when we mention this in an essay, some may think that we have, as they say, made it. The names of ancient European institutions sound prestigious, but we are mostly just humble pilgrims who meet at agreed-upon times and places in these sanctuaries, which open their doors to us for a day or two, throw a feast for us, and give us a sense of community, and then turn into fortresses. And so, we find ourselves back on a FlixBus, on our way to the next institution, hoping that it will accept us. When we talk to friends, we always say Sapienza or Humboldt or Charles University, but never FlixBus, even though it is one of the few constants in an uncertain world. On the FlixBus, we meet various *gastarbeiters*, workers who, like us, work in precarious conditions. The precariat has always existed for the working class, but it was only when academics and journalists found themselves in it that it became a topic we discuss when talking about so-called late capitalism. I am not inclined towards utopias, but if I were, I might write that FlixBus could become a revolutionary cell of a future classless society.

At first glance, these institutions with their illustrious names appear to form the backbone of Europe. On closer inspection, however, it becomes clear that they, like Europe itself, do not know what to do with their heritage, let alone what their role in the future will be. In this sense, they are no different from other venerable European institutions, such as galleries, museums, or theaters, nor from liberal democracy as a postwar consensus, which has been kept alive by economic interests established over decades. Liberal democracy as a unified system of the Western world is in its final throes, as it is conditioned by American hegemony, which is disintegrating among other, stronger empires that

Life on Mars?

will subjugate national states (which will resist fiercely, so we can prepare ourselves for several decades of intense, but ultimately unsuccessful nationalism). If, with the fall of the Berlin Wall, a significant part of Europe placed its hopes in the new system of liberal democracy, more than three decades later, it seems that we are witnessing a hopeless disappointment: liberal democracy works best as a promise, not as a practice. Nothing has improved liberal democracy more than the desire to establish a better counterweight to socialist countries, where the foundation of anti-fascism played a key role. The moment socialism ceased to exist as a rival political system and the anti-fascist foundation wore thin, liberal democracy began to lose its focus, as can be clearly observed today. However, as a woman who came of age when her country joined the European Union, I have also experienced firsthand the progress that has been made in the area of gender equality and the LGBTQ+ community, just as I fear I will experience firsthand the erosion of these rights. No achievement of liberal democracy in recent years has provoked a stronger reaction than gender equality and LGBTQ+ rights. The same was evident in 2024 in the US election campaign, which was based primarily on the idea that men should be able to feel like men again, whatever that means. This photogenic retraditionalization played a partic-ularly strong role on social media, where beautiful, young, urban people talked about wanting a return to traditional gender roles and the normalization of hate speech, the only two things that liberal democracy seemed to have partially succeeded in abolishing or at least limiting.

Still, I don't have to go to America to see how the liberal order I've internalized is falling apart. In the United Kingdom, the Supreme Court ruled that a woman is defined solely by the sex organs she was born with, which means further marginalization of transgender people and the revocation of the rights they had. I see trans women as my community.

Manca G. Renko

It is from British authors such as Shon Faye and Paris Lees that I have learned a great deal about myself as a woman: transitioning provides insights into the body and society that I would not have been able to gain on my own, as I have only ever known life with the gender I have identified with since birth, the blind spots included. But we don't even have to look as far as the United Kingdom; I can just look across the border to neighboring Hungary, where parliament has amended the constitution to recognize only two genders, and prior to that had banned the Pride Parade. At around the same time, European citizens received a letter of deportation from Berlin because they opposed the genocide in Gaza. This is a precedent; until now, it seemed impossible that EU citizens who had not been criminally charged and found guilty could be expelled from another European country. And not just from any country, but from Germany, from Berlin, the metropolis of my generation, a transnational utopia, an illusion of a different world, a fantasy of community. And all because of something as fundamental and self-evident as opposing genocide. This is not the world I was born into, nor the world I grew up in. This is something completely new.

I had to write all this in order to start talking about the future, which depends primarily on the point from which we observe it. It is no different with the past, which is also at the mercy of our position (ideological, class, gender, geographical), although some historians would confidently disagree with me. I would even go so far as to say that writing about the future is much more difficult than writing about the past. When dealing with history, we rarely encounter our own mistakes, the dead remain dead, historical sources are always incomplete, and the utopia of the past that we imagine is a much safer haven than the future. If nothing else, at least we know that we will never have to live in the past.

It is difficult to imagine life in a political system we were not socialized into. Alhough I was born in a socialist republic,

I actually grew up in various forms of liberal democracy. As a child, I navigated the political transition from socialism to capitalism, which, by the time I was old enough to be aware of the world around me, I had already internalized as the only possible economic system. Liberal democracy was also the only political system I really knew and it seemed important to me to participate in it. I couldn't wait to turn eighteen and vote for the first time. I was willing to despise any young woman who did not participate in elections or was not interested in politics (*Do you even know the risks women in the past had to face so that you can vote today?!*), I fanatically followed political events and mapped out a network of political shifts in my head in order to understand as accurately as possible what had been happening since 1991, when Slovenia became "independent." I simply couldn't avoid transferring the taken-for-granted nature of liberal democracy and contemporary feminism into my research of the past, until years ago, when I came across the relativization of voting rights in one of the key feminist and communist texts of wartime Yugoslavia, entitled *Žena v današnji družbi* (*The Woman in Contemporary Society*) by Angela Vode (1934). Vode, the most prominent feminist and communist woman of her time, believed that women's suffrage could not be the key political goal since the democracy she knew was a poor political system. She did not believe in the bourgeois-royalist alliance of wartime Yugoslavia, so she felt it was more important to overthrow this system than to participate in it. She considered women's economic independence to be much more important than women's suffrage, as she believed that this was the only means by which women could truly become equal to men. If a woman believes that she is worth as much as a man, she wrote, this is a much richer legacy than a law written on a piece of paper that can be changed at any time. She was not alone in her conviction; many other Yugoslav and European leftists wrote similarly, arguing that defending democracy

Manca G. Renko

meant defending capitalism, which was directly linked to fascism. Let's not forget: German women had both passive and active voting rights, and Hitler still came to power. Women's suffrage can't save democracy. The greatest power of history is perhaps that it shatters our assumptions, and for me, who considered women's right to vote to be one of the most important achievements of civilization, reading literature that shattered my assumptions meant confronting the extent to which I transfer the dominant political order of my time into the past as a matter of course. Women whose writings I've read had just recently encountered attempts at democracy, which they understandably saw as something new and therefore flawed. For me, this system was no longer new; I belong to the third generation of women who have been able to vote . But the reflections of women who lived through the Second World War enabled me to gain the crucial insight that I, too, can question liberal democracy as the only possible system. Just as it hasn't always existed, it means that it will not last forever either. In other words, what good is the right to vote if parliaments and courts deliberately harm marginalized minorities? What good is the European Union to me if it increasingly restricts freedom of movement? What good is the concept of human rights if every morning I wake up with the genocide live-streamed right on my phone?

Perhaps that is why I was so angered by the film *There's Still Tomorrow* (*C'è ancora domani*, dir. Paola Cortellesi, 2023), one of the most successful contemporary Italian films. At first, it reminded me of literature very dear to me, of Alba de Céspedes, Natalia Ginzburg, and Elena Ferrante, who tell stories of women in post-war Italy caught between the patriarchal expectations of society and the desire for self-fulfillment. The director builds suspense when she sends her protagonist, a victim of domestic violence, economic deprivation, and a patriarchal environment, a mysterious letter, which she carefully hides from her husband. One morning, she rises earlier than usual, gets dressed, and sneaks out of the house. Will she leave her husband? Run away with another man? Sail to America and start over? None of the above. The protagonist simply goes to the polling station with hundreds of other women. And that's how the film ends. Her husband will continue to beat her, she will still only be able to do the lowest-paid jobs and hand over the money to her husband, and she will be nothing more to her daughter but a weak and submissive woman. Since nothing interprets contemporary times better than popular culture, this is the ideal film for Giorgia Meloni, Italy's prime minister, who is the political successor to the fascist party, a woman who has transcended the role traditionally assigned to her, yet defends traditional ("Catholic") values. Symbolic victories such as the right to vote—or the first female prime minister—do not in themselves guarantee systemic change unless economic or social realities change as well. I would like to say that feminism can stand up to fascism, but no one in their right mind can actually believe that.

When I think about the future of liberal democracy, I cannot help but think about fascism, too. I am not referring to hysterical cries of *fascism!*, a combination of moralism and an unreflected desire for privilege and/or social power, but rather to fascism as a vibe. With Donald Trump's re-election, the phrase "vibe shift" immediately began to appear in the media and on social networks. Some described it as a more relaxed and less politically correct atmosphere, others as a return to tradition, some linked it to politics as spectacle, and again, others speculated about the shift in geopolitical forces. But in many ways, even historically speaking, fascism was nothing but an atmosphere. Unlike Nazism, which had clearly defined programmatic and ideological precepts, Italian fascism could change its form on a daily basis, depending on the whims of the moment, and was based on ruling by decree and on the general mood of the society. In fascism, violence could

Manca G. Renko

be combined with Dionysianism, progress with art, ideology with lifestyle, and rules with exceptions. I have a feeling that Donald Trump's and Elon Musk's America could also move along this spectrum, as long as their alliance lasts, of course. Perhaps this is the clearest thing I dare to predict in this essay: it will not last, but the breakup will not be fatal either. Perhaps it will implode before this essay is even in print.[1] How can one predict the future at a time when change is the only constant?

When I was invited to write this essay, one of the suggestions was to write about how art, fantasy, and science can help preserve democracy in the broadest sense. How important they are. Instead, this essay has strayed and come to the conclusion that democracy as we know it may not be something worth defending at all costs, but rather something we should learn to think critically about. Even at the cost of being prepared to live with the consequences of its collapse. Art, fantasy, and science cannot do anything instead of us. In Europe, liberal democracy will run its final lap, and we will watch it run out of steam during our lifetimes, but we will not witness its final breath. At the same time, we will see art that will outlive us and that will be able to exist in the full sense of the word even in a different social order.

There have been moments in history when art was not only a reflection of social reality, but also its catalyst. However, women who wanted to change the world knew that art alone was not enough. This was also understood by the Yugoslav intellectual, politician, and revolutionary Mitra Mitrović, who wrote in her memoirs that literature played a key role in her joining the communist and anti-fascist movement.

1   After clashing with top White House officials, Elon Musk left Trump's administration at the end of May 2025—just in time for the final corrections to this essay. I've deliberately left the original prediction in place to highlight how we live in a time when only fleeting online interactions can keep up with the pace of events. Writing an essay, by contrast, is already a gesture of the past—too slow to ever truly catch up.

She did not write this in a sentimental, sugary way. She did not write about literature as a lifestyle choice, but as a necessity. In the 1920s, a twenty-year-old woman in Belgrade believed that only new literature could offer new answers to the key questions of her contemporaneity.

However, reading books was not enough for her. She had to take to the streets and be imprisoned. Just like the Italian photographer and revolutionary Tina Modotti had to leave her camera in Moscow in the mid-1930s and organize an anti-fascist movement in Spain and France. (Photography is work, not art, she said.) Like Claude Cahun, who protested with art and humor in Nazi-occupied Jersey. (To laugh until the end, even when you are condemned to death.) Like Alexandra Kollontai, who believed in love in a new society even before that society existed. (The question is whether it ever will.) Like Nawal El Saadawi, who knew that with every word she wrote, she was in danger, but never stopped writing. (To be free to do whatever you want, but also to be free to do nothing.) And finally, like Angela Vode, who believed that women's emancipation was more than just the right to vote, and then, a little over a decade later, lost all her civil rights as a dissident. It was at that time that she translated Stefan Zweig's *The World of Yesterday* into Slovenian, which, among other issues, discusses how even the most perceptive intellectuals and the most sensitive artists only notice that the world is falling apart when the roof of their own house collapses.

Good art first accurately recognizes the world as it is, and then, if it is transcendent, offers images of the world as it could be. Such images can be completely abstract or emotionally direct and scientifically accurate, but they always address something that has not yet been addressed. They look at the world as if they were seeing it for the first time, but at the same time, they know it through and through.

In his speech at Donald Trump's inauguration, Elon Musk talked about how magnificent it would be to plant

Manca G. Renko

the American flag on Mars. Although the following day most people were primarily appalled by his right arm raised in a Nazi salute, I found the crude desire to colonize space much more frightening. In it, I recognized a vulgar inability to visualize complex images of the world. Space can be a place for imagining a new political and social order, as Liu Cixin has shown in his literature. It can be a place for projecting dreams and desires, as David Bowie captured in his songs. But what we got a few months after Musk's speech was an all-female expedition into space aboard the Blue Origin spacecraft, owned by Jeff Bezos, a billionaire and one of Donald Trump's men. While the flight to the edge of space lasted eleven minutes, the singer Katy Perry caught the most attention among the aspiring astronauts, singing *What a Wonderful World* to her fellow passengers during the flight and then kissing the ground after landing. The project, which used the illusion of female empowerment as an advertising campaign for the private corporation Blue Origin, turned out to be just another vulgar form of touristification.

Only time will tell whether Katy Perry in her space outfit is the new icon of the Cold (or perhaps not so cold anymore?) War. In the flood of bizarre, tacky, and terrifying images that bombard us through our devices' algorithms, it is impossible to know which ones will be swallowed by time and which ones will linger on the surface of the internet. However, it is clear what emotions these three types of images evoke in us: dismay, emotionality, and anger. These emotions paralyze art as well as intellectual work more than they deepen it. In other words, art and science are not interested in merely travelling to the edge of space, but rather in how to be alone with ourselves under the vast sky without fleeting impulses, rooted enough in our own time and space to be able to overcome the point of discomfort—and how to reach from that point for what is available to us so that we can think what transcends us (spiritually, intellectually, emotionally,

Life on Mars?

or scientifically). Art, fantasy, and science will not save democracy—nor is that their task—but they can help us think about what kind of order to strive for while billionaires play space tourism on Mars. Perhaps they can give us enough courage to let things fall apart. After all, art, science, and fantasy teach us that if we want to move forward, we often have to discard the very things we have devoted most of our time to and loved the most. This is frightening—but it is also the only true freedom.

Manca G. Renko

MGLC Švicarija:
The Secret Solution for World Peace

In this venue as well, you will encounter an installation by Silvan Omerzu welcoming you right after passing through the door. Here, his work refers to the history of the building you are in. After the earthquake that devastated Ljubljana in 1895, a large reconstruction and modernization of the city were underway. Soon, the wooden guesthouse of Švicarija no longer met the modern needs of the city, and a hotel was to be built in its place. It opened in 1909 and quickly became the social and cultural center of the park and a meeting spot for artists and intellectuals. Among them was Ivan Cankar, one of Slovenia's most important writers, poets, and playwrights, who called Švicarija "the refuge of sinners." After its closure in the 1930s, Švicarija became home to many people in need. Ghostly figures stand at the entrance and further along the corridor, symbolizing the darker sides of human nature and history. At the end of the corridor are dolls of sick girls in wheelchairs, flanked by two angels, and an image of Mary, Help of Christians, as a metaphor for hope and salvation.

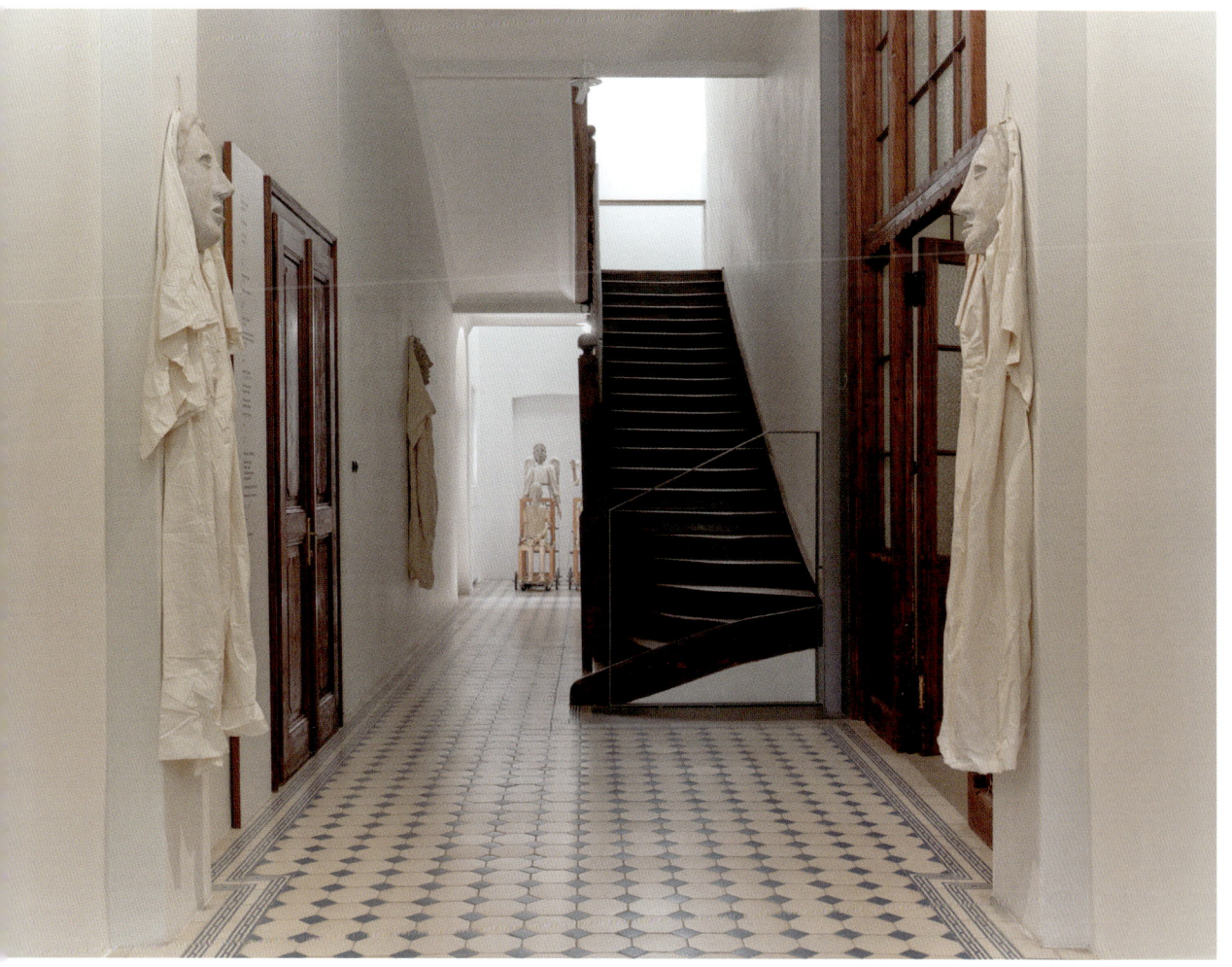

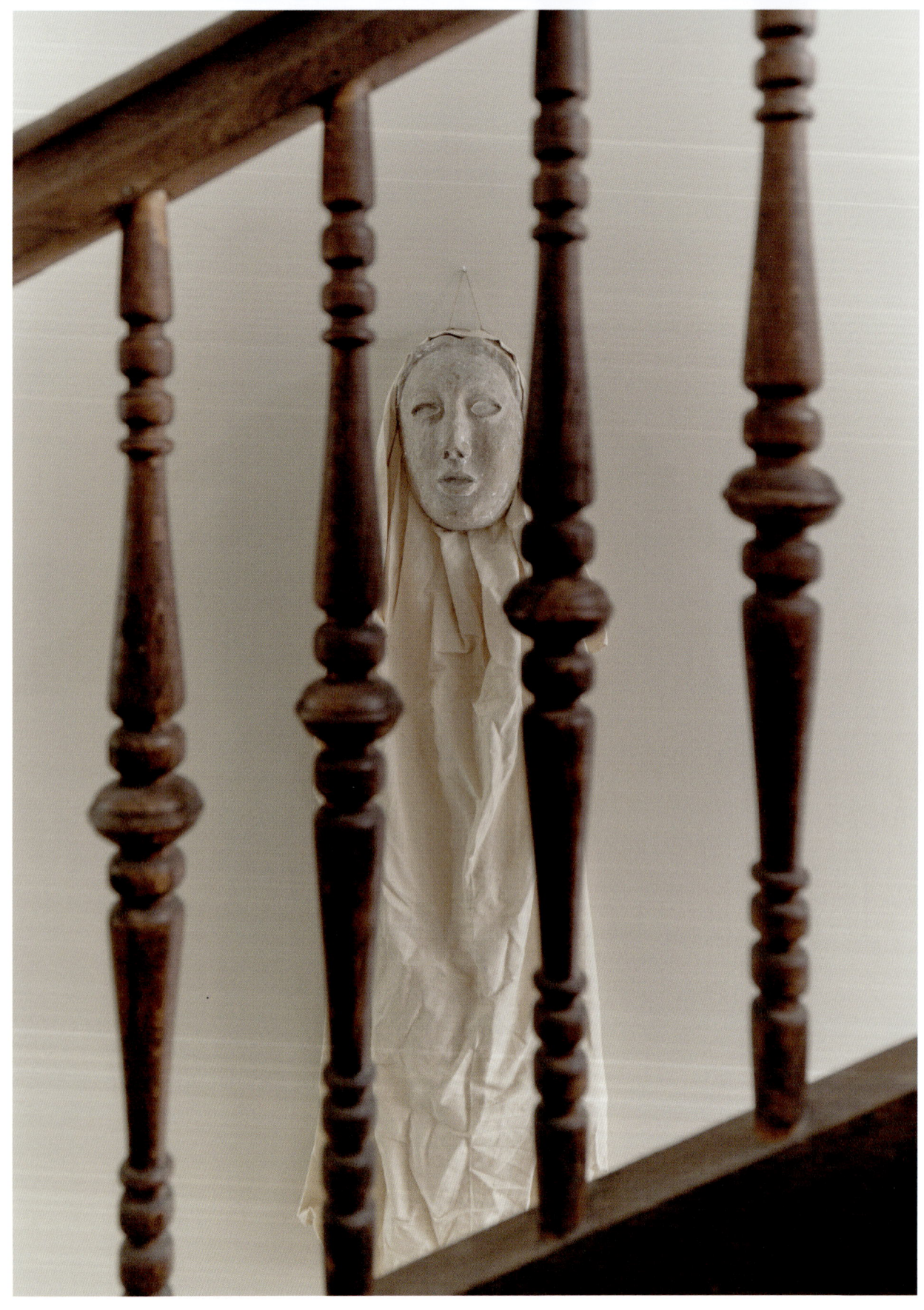

Silvan Omerzu, *The House of Our Lady, Help of Christians*, 2025

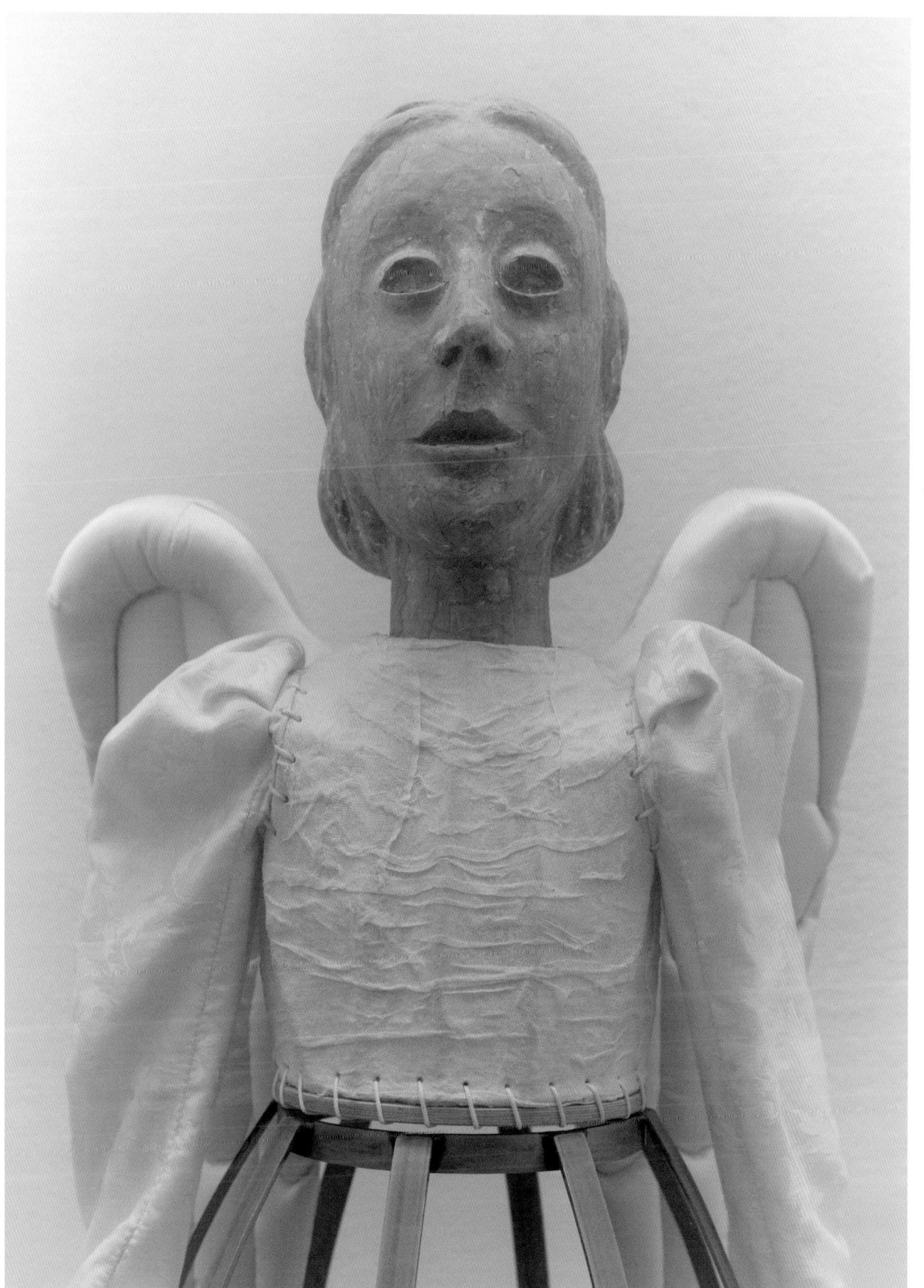

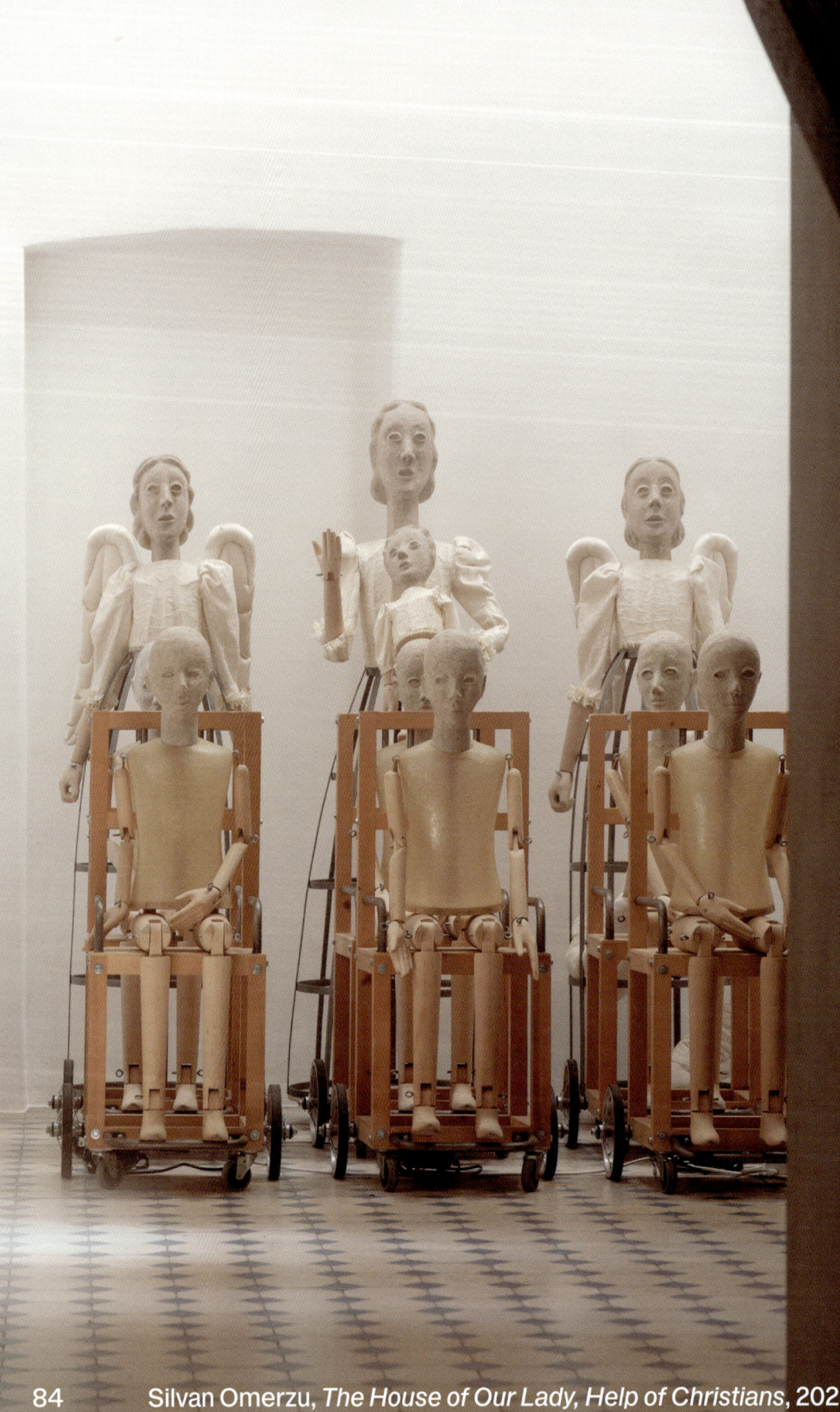

Silvan Omerzu, *The House of Our Lady, Help of Christians*, 2025

Vesna Petrešin in collaboration with Prof. Dr. Eugen Petrešin, *Autonomous Energy Machine*, 2025

85

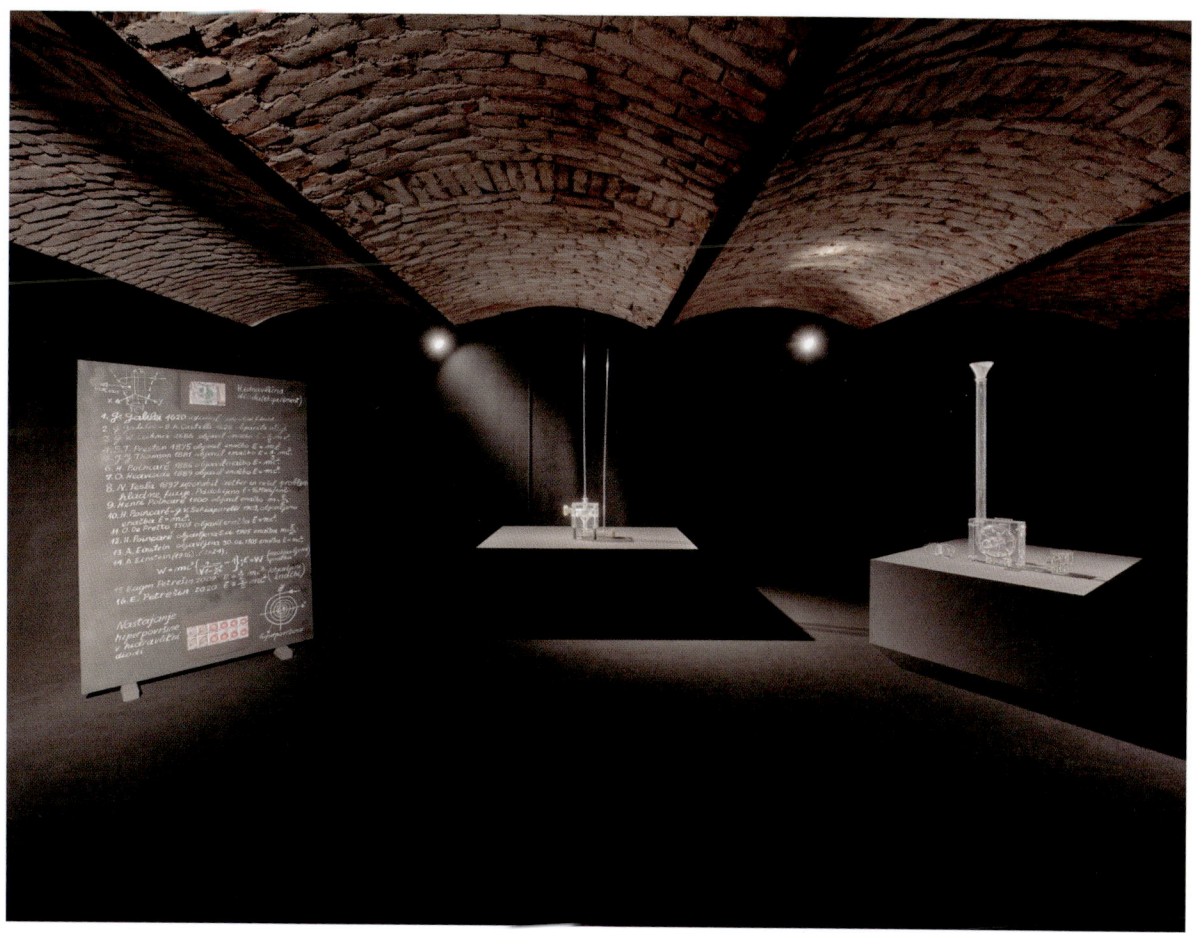

The Švicarija venue is, indeed, dedicated to salvation. One of the secrets of salvation would be to find the key that guarantees all beings a peaceful coexistence. Peace is also dependent on resources—energy—to continue living. One of the most precious secrets in this respect is kept in the basement of this house: the possibility of fulfilling the dream of generating enough energy for just about everything by simply using water. If you go to the basement, you will encounter a room created by Vesna and Eugen Petrešin. Vesna Petrešin was an artist who, for years, has worked together with her father, Eugen, a distinguished Slovenian civil engineer specializing in hydraulics and water management. His marvellous research: the possibility of generating sufficient energy and doing so only using water. Hydropower has a long history, and yet—until now—we cannot subsist without carbon fuels or nuclear power plants.

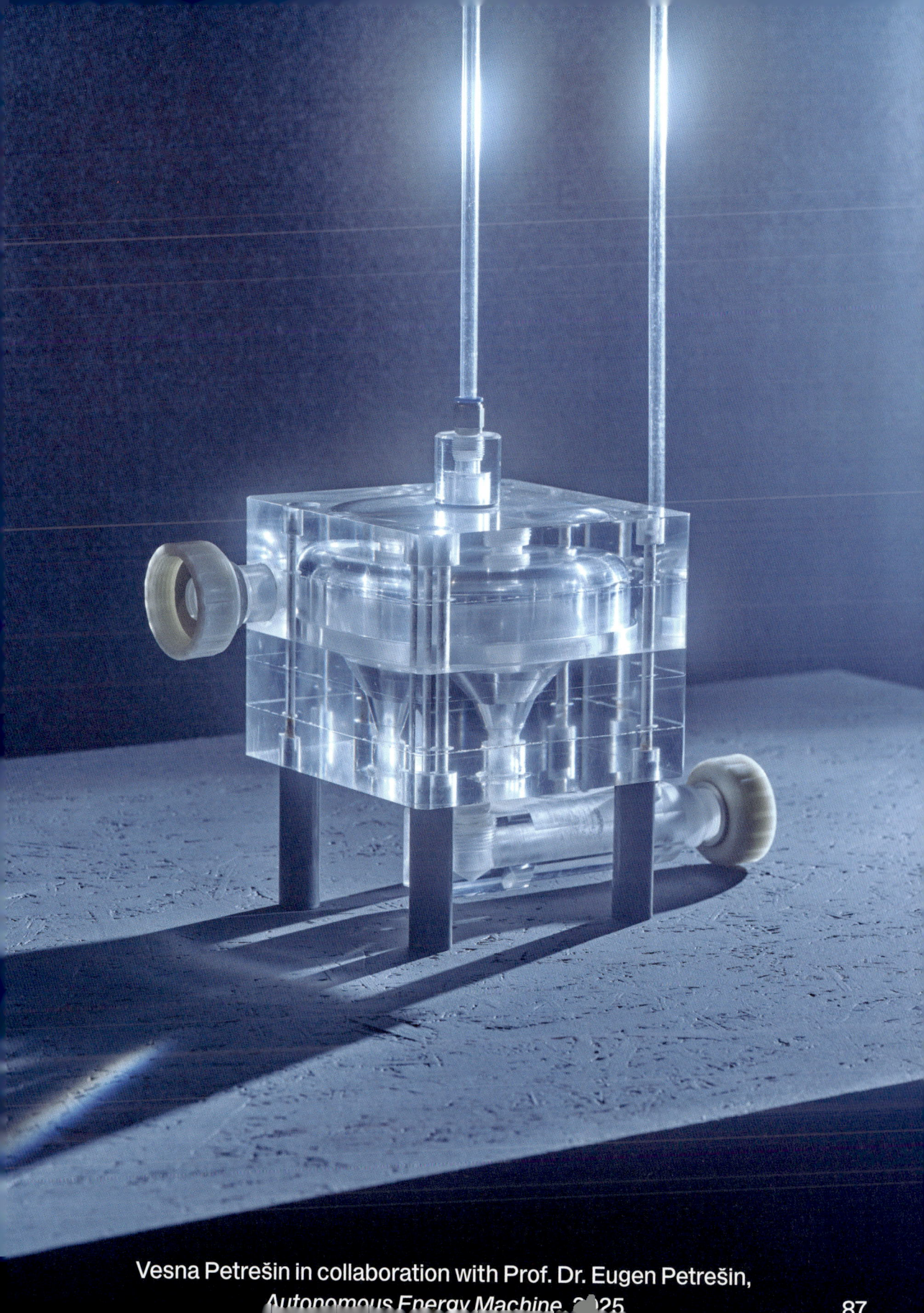

Vesna Petrešin in collaboration with Prof. Dr. Eugen Petrešin,
Autonomous Energy Machine, 2025

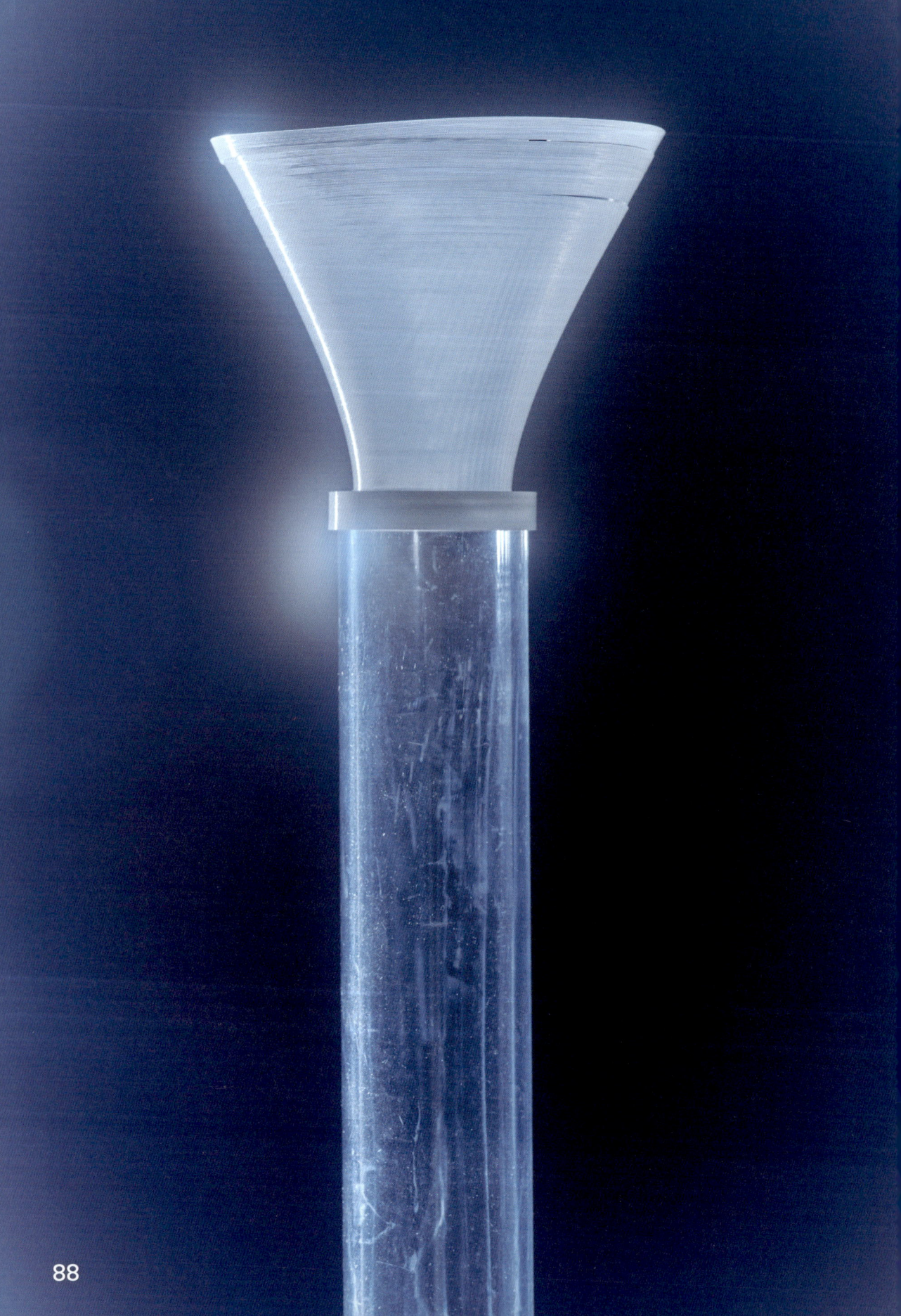

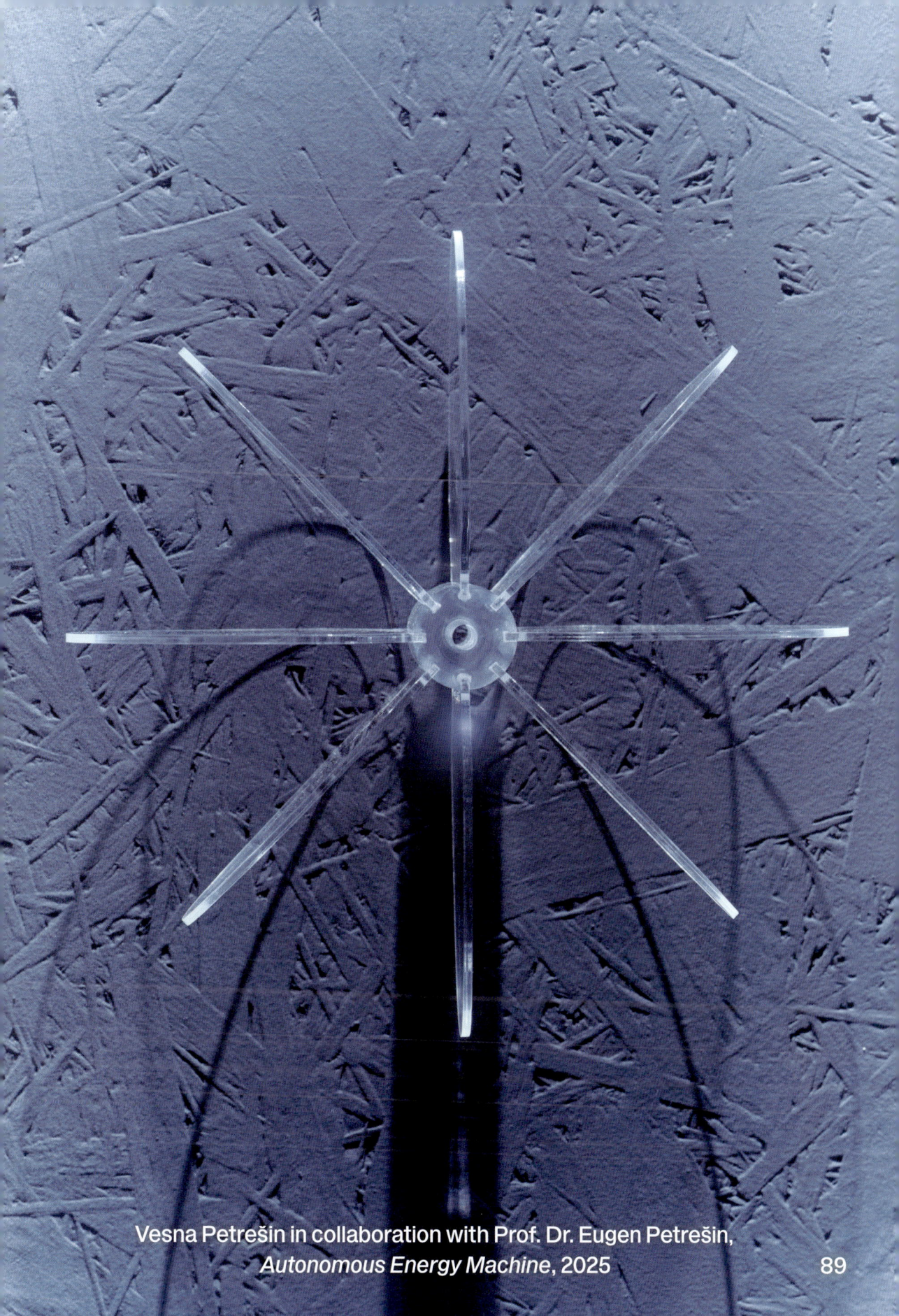

Vesna Petrešin in collaboration with Prof. Dr. Eugen Petrešin,
Autonomous Energy Machine, 2025

Vesna Petrešin in collaboration with Prof. Dr. Eugen Petrešin,
Autonomous Energy Machine, 2025

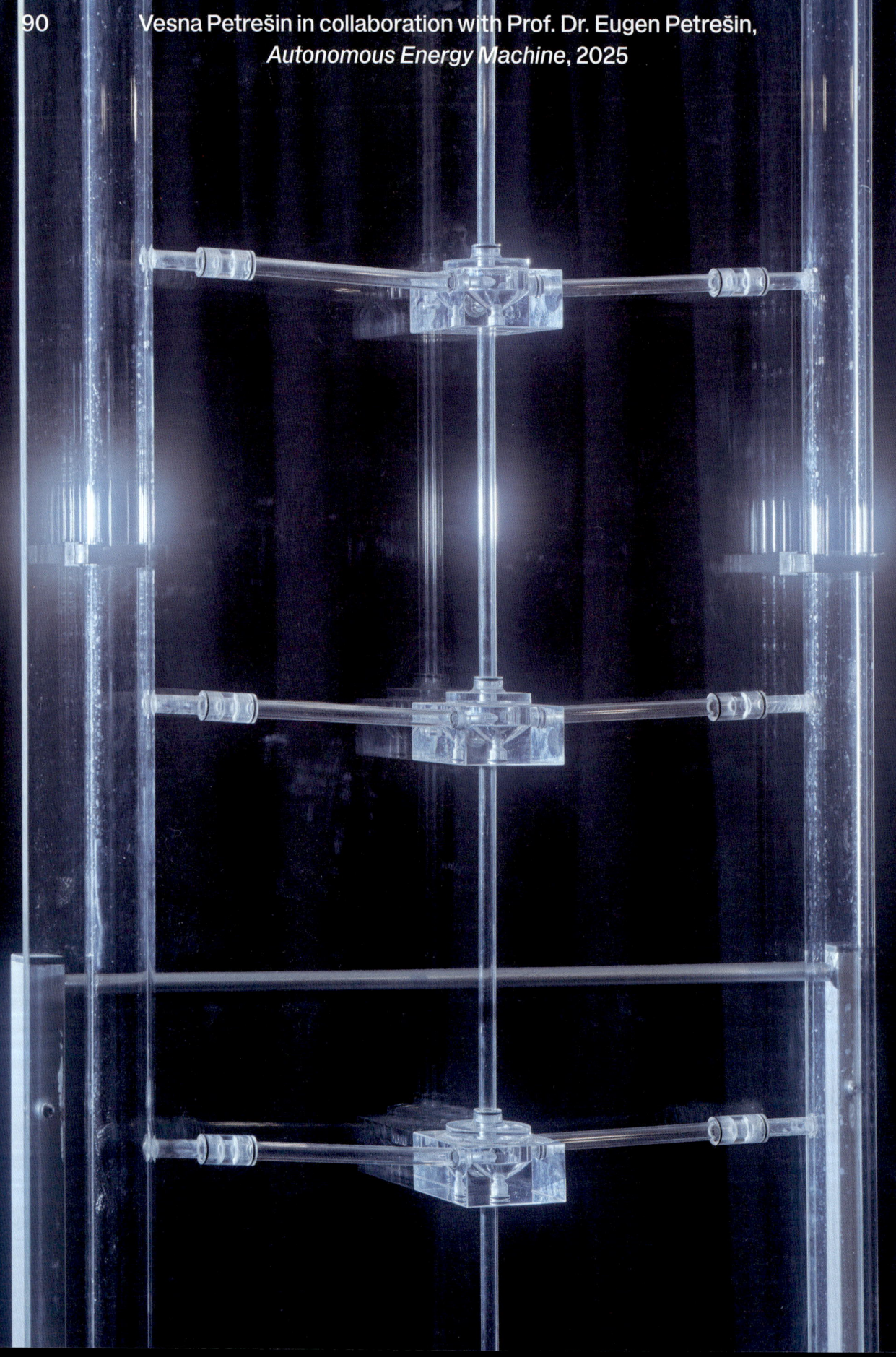

Hydropower is also dependent on certain geo-characteristics, such as mountains and rivers. Europe's first concrete dam was built in 1872 at Pérolles to the south of Freiburg, Europe's first arch dam (Montsalvens) in 1921, and, at 111 meters, the world's highest water barrier in 1924 in Wägital. But could you imagine the possibility of generating energy only with water, only generating movement, and a movement dynamic enough to create electricity easily? Eugen Petrešin, a scientist and inventor, has dedicated his life to developing a device capable of absorbing water's force. This innovation involves a system designed to gradually absorb force impulses and turn this water force into energy. Research in the field of energy generation technologies using water is proving that there is a chance of obtaining enough energy to run our world without polluting it or needing to fight or colonize to obtain energy resources. Together with his daughter, Vesna, they have created a chamber of secrets, an immersive installation using mathematics, sound, light, and drawings. The quest for clean and sustainable energy independence is the quest for a world of peace.

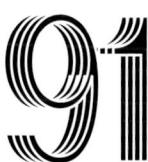

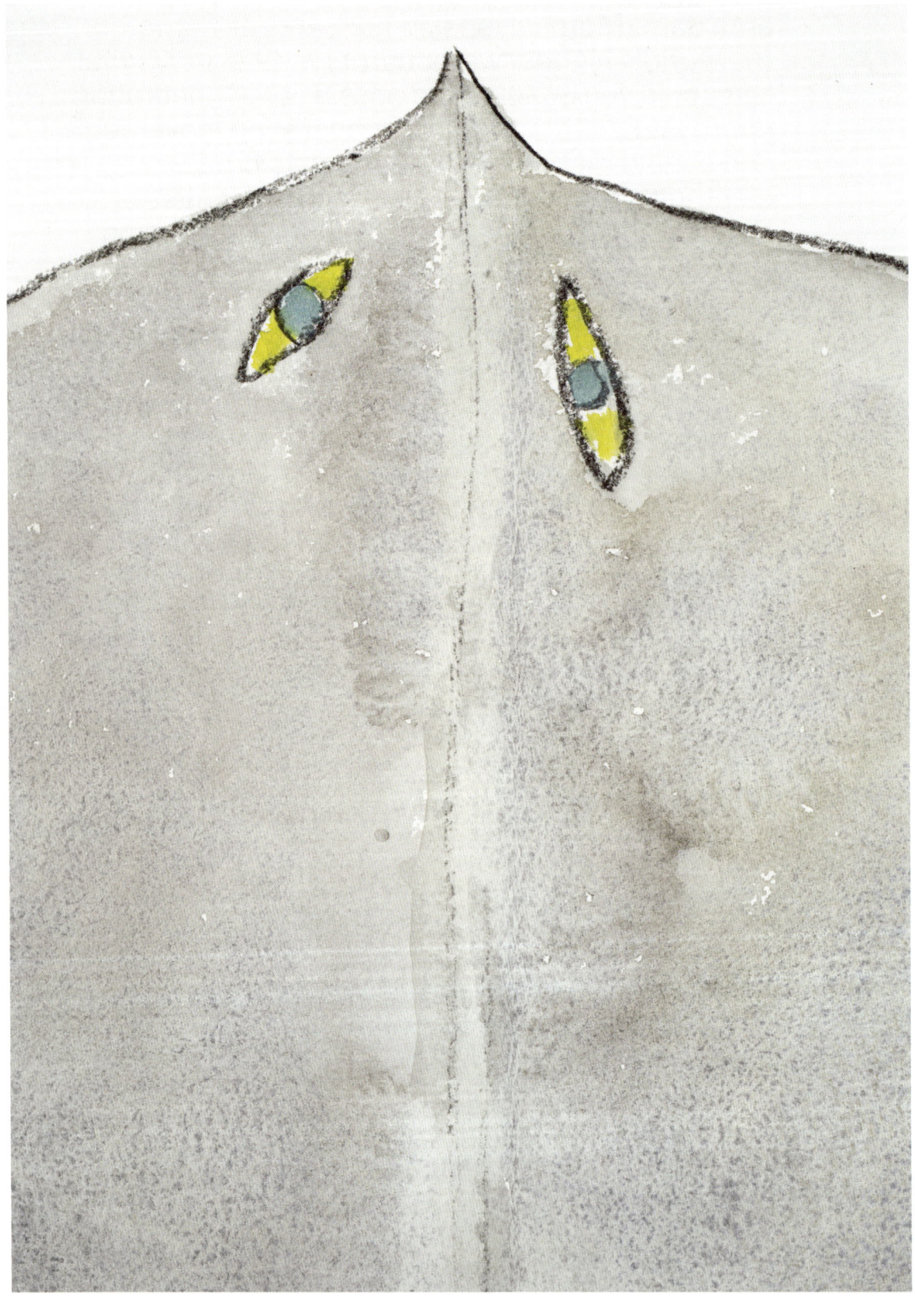

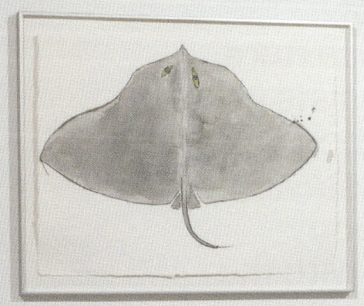

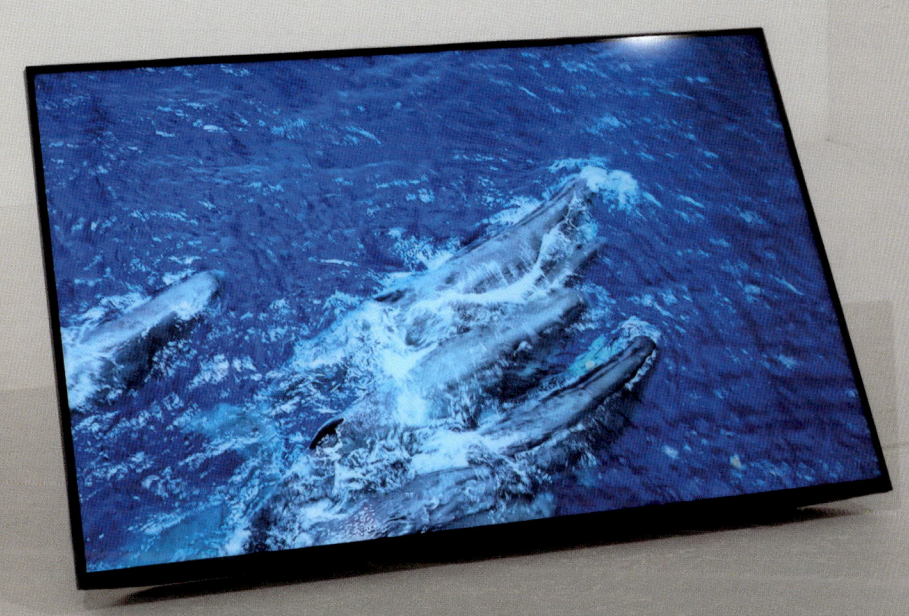

Joan Jonas, *Ray*, 2018, and *To Touch Sound*, 2024

When returning to the ground floor, you will encounter a gallery with two artists. Joan Jonas and Miles Howard-Wilks. Joan Jonas is indeed an inspiration for the whole biennial. Her work embodies the capability to recover and regenerate from the disastrous. Exercising the force of imagination upon the real, the real regains texture, color, and brightness. A brightness that assists us in perceiving the immense intelligence all beings possess, an intelligence oriented towards staying alive and joyfully so. The discovery of the body performing small gestures, synchronizing with the wind and the elements of nature, shows us other ways of communicating with life and also another way of using technological tools. Joan Jonas is present in the exhibition with a drawing. A drawing that is a well, a source, a place in the mind. It seems little, but it is just enough to inspire all of us. On the same floor, there is also the work of Miles Howard-Wilks, an artist whose painting works aspire to establish an immediate connection with all the animals in the world. For years, his interest has focused on Australian animals as if he would like to expand democratic rights and give them a voice. Surreal at times and very dynamic in the use of line and color, his work on birds and animals of the seas is a way to share his view of the world as someone with a neurodiverse condition.

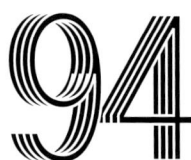

94

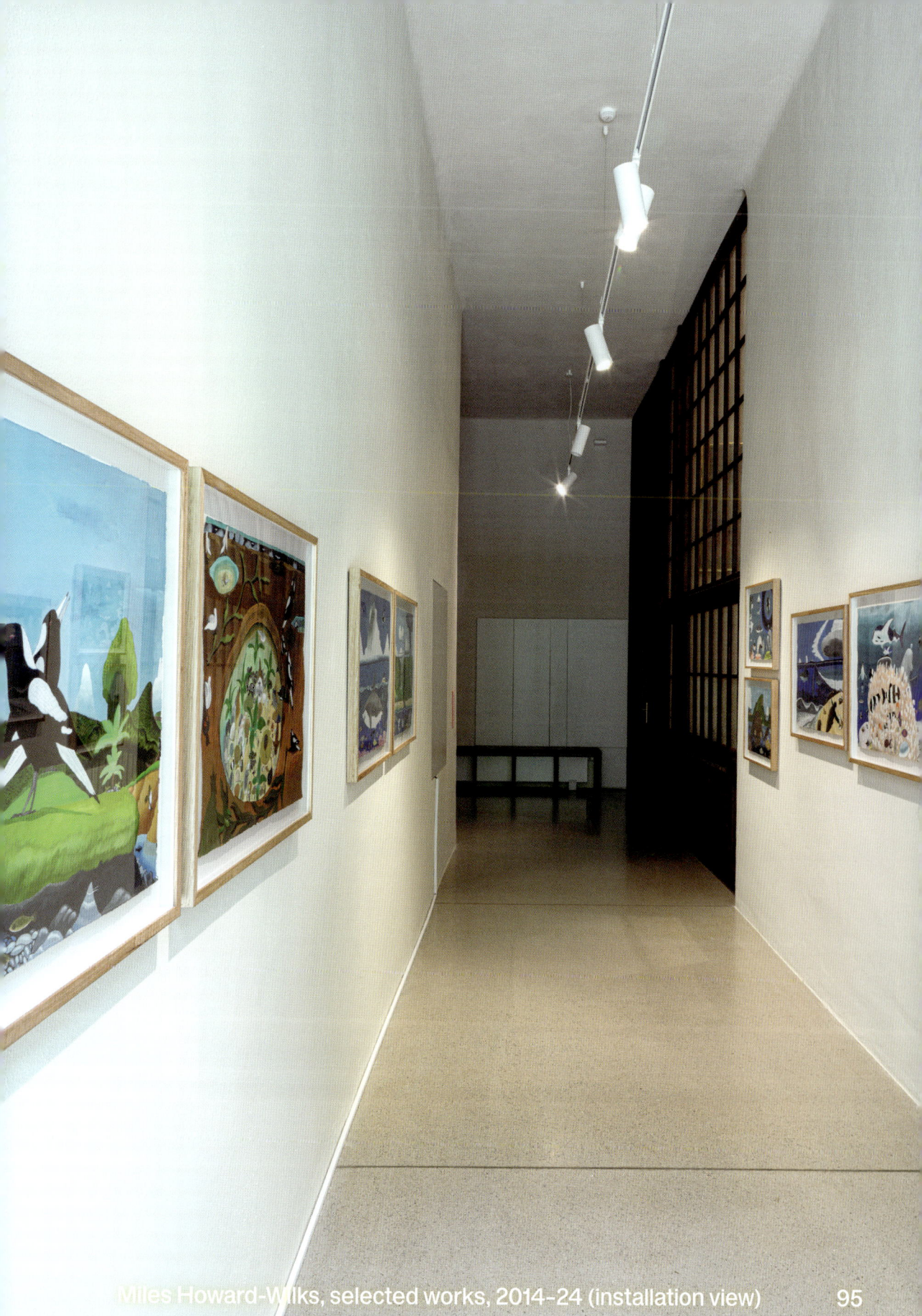

Miles Howard-Wilks, selected works, 2014–24 (installation view)   95

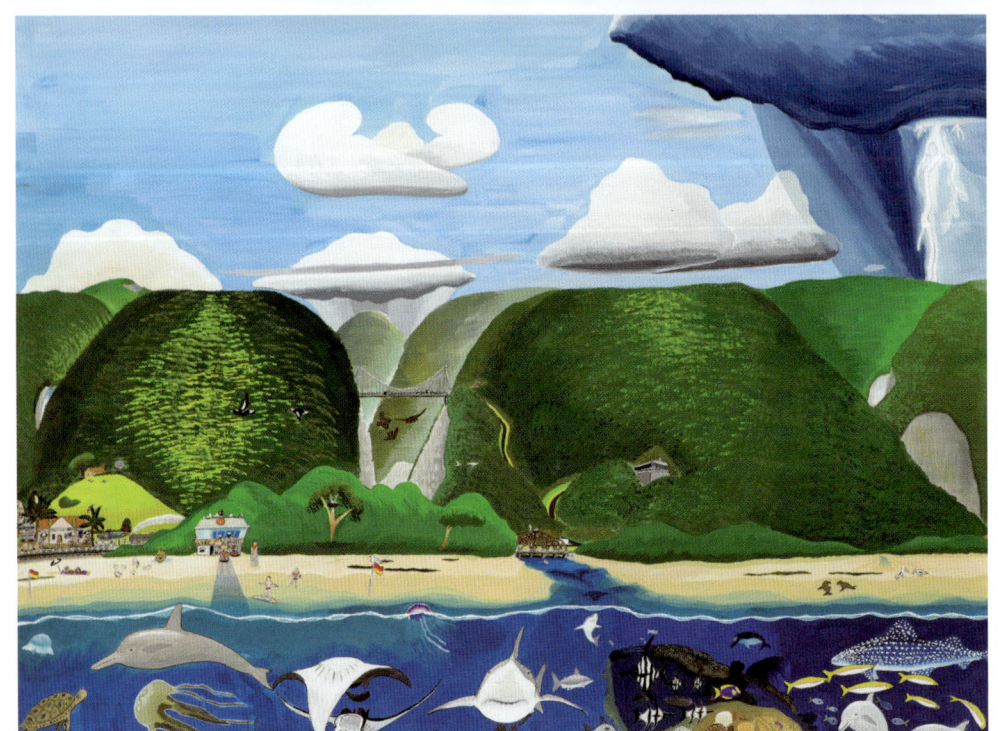

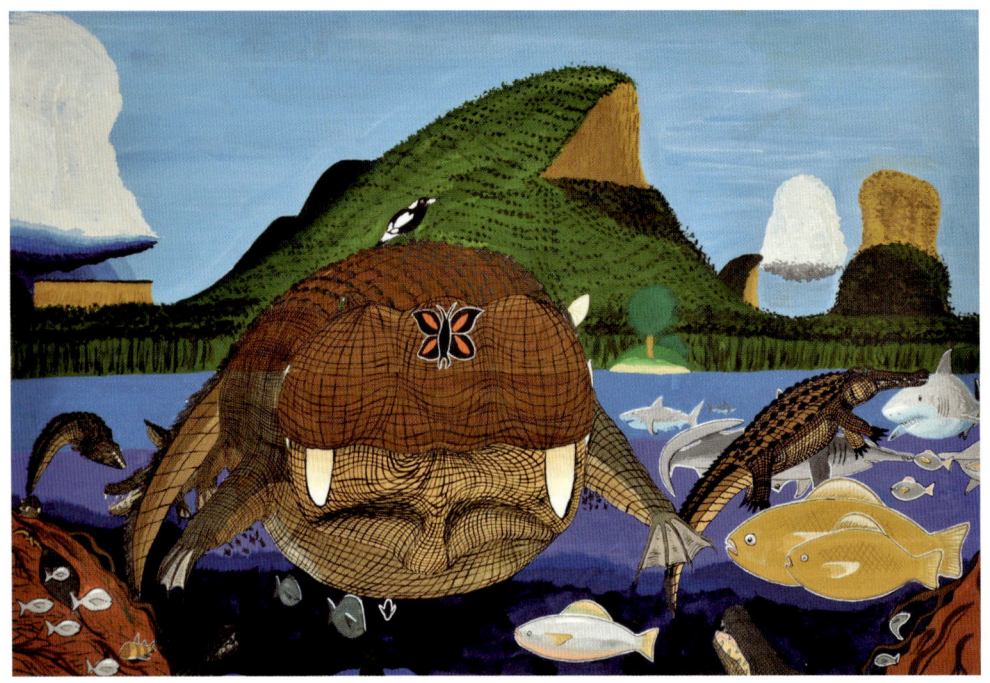

Miles Howard-Wilks, *Untitled*, 2022, and *Untitled*, 2014

Visionaries in Hiding:

FIGURING AND PREFIGURING

Maja

Petrović-Šteger

Maja Petrović-Šteger

Imaginative projection, including prefiguration and vaticination, has always designated an important set of ways to relate to the world, to make it. Historians, poets and warriors have described many contexts in which our predecessors and contemporaries have sought ways to anticipate and (perhaps relatedly) to bring about change.

In ancient Greece, Egypt, and the Middle East, in the Americas, in India, Tibet, Mongolia, Japan, Korea, and throughout Africa, knowing the world and bringing about change therein was often linked to mantic practices. Guidance was sought either through consulting mediums—channels of psychic information sent by ancestors or more-than-human agents—or by using other methods of divination—from reading patterns of cracks in oracular bones to patterns in dust, from examining the stars or the entrails of sacrificed animals to scrying, shamanic dreaming, fasting-induced trances, dancing, ingesting hallucinogens, and fixating on mirrors, *thangkas*, amulets, labyrinths, yarrow stems, and mandalas.[1] Divinatory enquiries looked into the future, but also raked over past catastrophes whose causes could not be explained; they sounded unknown things, hidden from view, or far away; appropriate behavior in critical situations, including the healing of illness, the determination of appropriate times and modes of religious worship, and decisions about particular tasks.[2]

1   See also Barbara Tedlock, "Divination as a Way of Knowing: Embodiment, Visualization, Narrative, and Interpretation," *Folklore* 112 (2001): 189–97.
2   See Barbara Tedlock, "Toward a Theory of Divinatory Practice," *Anthropology of Consciousness* 17, no. 2 (2006): 65. See also Michael Winkelman and Philip M. Peek, *Divination and Healing: Potent Vision* (University of Arizona Press, 2004).

While divination continues to be practiced worldwide,[3] today other ways of being, seeing, understanding, and imagining the world are made available for philosophical speculation and everyday use through science, economics, art, technology, AI, religion, and politics. Since 1789, prefiguration has been singularly tied to practical politics. Protest and revolutions have come to be understood as particularly effective in engendering transformations of social relations.[4] To prefigure, then, is, in everyday parlance, often to reimagine society on a political level and allied with the strategies and practices of activists seeking to build alternative systems. The social and protest movements that have flourished since the 1960s, based on principles such as participatory democracy, strict horizontality, inclusivity, and direct action,

3   See Niels Bubandt, "Interview with an Ancestor: Spirits as Informants and the Politics of Possession in North Maluku," *Ethnography* 10, no. 3 (2009): 291–316; Patrick Curry, "Embodiment, Alterity, and Agency: Negotiating Antinomies in Divination," in *Divination: Perspectives for a New Millennium*, ed. Patrick Curry (Ashgate, 2010), 85–118; Martin Holbraad, *Truth in Motion: The Recursive Anthropology of Cuban Divination* (University of Chicago Press, 2012); Diana Espírito Santo, "Fluid Divination: Movement, Chaos and the Generation of 'Noise' in Afro-Cuban Spiritist Oracular Production," *Anthropology of Consciousness* 24, no. 1 (2013): 32–56.

4   See Charles Tilly and Lesley J. Wood, "Contentious Connections in Great Britain, 1828–34," in *Social Movements and Networks: Relational Approaches to Collective Action*, ed. Mario Diani and Doug McAdam (Oxford University Press, 2003), 147–72; Suzanne Staggenborg, *Social Movements* (Oxford University Press, 2016); Vincent Bevins, *If We Burn: The Mass Protest Decade and the Missing Revolution* (Wildfire, 2025).

are widely recognized as organized means of trying (and failing) to proactively project and change the future.[5]

Readers should not be misled into thinking that I am outlining two apparently opposed modes of prefiguration, indeed of metaphysical enquiry, as proxies for notions of the irrational and the rational. It does not seem entirely satisfactory to equate modern ways of imagining and shaping the world with rationality, and ancient and indigenous ways with unreasonable methods of prediction. Nor do I think that the assumption of a continuity between these two ways of acting in the world—one based on a notion of prophets and sensitives making sense of the inchoate, the other on organized community intervention—is unassailable. Rather, I want to draw readers' attention to ideas of imagination and conceivability, and to processes of divining immanent in the conditions and acts of prefiguration—in both the sybillic and political spheres. This contribution is an invitation to reflect on and move beyond received thinking as to how change comes into the world.

BIDDING FOR TRANSPARENCY

As an anthropologist, I have long been interested in the contexts in which people express a need for change, and the conditions, both societal and personal, under which they come to see the world differently. I began my main, long-term research in Serbia in early 2000. Ever since the country started to emerge from the Yugoslav wars of the 1990s,

5   See Guilherme Fians, "Prefigurative Politics," in *The Open Encyclopedia of Anthropology,* ed. Felix Stein (2023), http://doi.org/10.29164/22prefigpolitics; Mathis Ebbinghaus, "Decoupling Social Movements from Modernity: A Critical Reappraisal of Charles Tilly's Theory on the Origins of Social Movements," *Theory and Society* 53 (2024): 1152, https://doi.org/10.1007/s11186-024-09569-0.

Serbia has been predominantly, even stereotypically, portrayed in the media, academia, and popular culture as broken and in need of social and political restitution. I have also been documenting stories of people who feel stuck, out of place, alienated, in denial, and financially and emotionally troubled for too long (for them and possibly for me). My interlocutors often complain that in comparison to the immediate postwar period, the last twenty years have been even more precarious and unpredictable. Many feel they are running on empty, drained by the stagnant and treacherous political, economic, and psychological ecology of their nation. They insist that they live in a structurally compromised country run by exploitative leaders, where party patronage and political clientelism are naturalized and expected. All too aware of the politics of the past, many portray their prospects—political, economic, and moral—as boxed in, as a general rule. They are exhausted because their future has been preemptively preconceived by the expectations of both local and international policymakers.[6]

6　　See Maja Petrović-Šteger, "Parasecurity and Paratime in Serbia: Neocortical Defence and National Consciousness," in *Times of Security: Ethnographies of Fear, Protest and the Future*, ed. Morten Axel Pedersen and Martin Holbraad (Routledge, 2013), 141–62; Maja Petrović-Šteger, "Understanding Self-Care: Passing and Healing in Contemporary Serbia," in *Materialities of Passing: Explorations in Transformation, Transition and Transience*, ed. Peter Bjerregaard et al. (Routledge, 2016), 113–29; Maja Petrović-Šteger, "O 'Odprtem pogledu'. Miselne pokrajine in doživljanje časa družbenih podjetnikov in vizionarjev v današnji Srbiji," *Glasnik slovenskega etnološkega društva* 58, no. 3–4 (2018): 7–23; Maja Petrović-Šteger, "Calling the Future into Being: Timescripting in Contemporary Serbia," in *Biography—A Play? Poetological Experiments in a Genre Without Poetics*, ed. Günter Blamberger, Rüdiger Görner, and Adrian Robanus (Wilhelm Fink, 2020), 163–79; Maja Petrović-Šteger, "On the Side of Predictable: Visioning the Future in Serbia," *Etnološka tribina: Godišnjak Hrvatskog etnološkog društva* 50, no. 43 (2020): 3–67.

Maja Petrović-Šteger

Some of the people I work with seem politically apathetic and genuinely disengaged from everyday politics. Others, even those once feisty and articulate, have toned down their political views and retreated into private life. They often feel despondent because they see no way to alleviate the systemic exclusion and discrimination they face, the forms of which are constantly mutating. Many others, however, can be described as part of the hundreds of thousands of Serbs who have taken to the streets at one time or another since 2016 in a series of massive anti-government demonstrations against Aleksandar Vučić and his ideological set, to whose leadership they attribute Serbia's malaise. These demonstrators have demanded accountability from Serbia's leaders over a wide range of issues: e.g., the Belgrade waterfront construction project; alleged fraud in parliamentary elections; the government's greenlighting of plans for a controversial lithium mine; and gun violence connected to a school shooting. Most recently, the collapse of a concrete canopy over a railway station in Novi Sad, which killed fifteen people in November 2024, led to widespread protests calling for an end to corruption and genuine monitoring of spending and maintaining public infrastructure. Over the past four-and-a-half months, hundreds of thousands of people have marched across Serbia demanding the release of all documents related to the renovation of the station, the dismissal of charges against the demonstrators, and an increase in the budget for higher education. The protesters see their demands not as a call for revolution but for reform—as a fundamental plea for transparency, for respect for the rule of law and the constitution, and for holding public officials responsible and accountable for eliminating structural negligence. Despite the government's various strategies to quell the demonstrations, the protests are gaining momentum. Universities have been occupied and organized strikes, road blockades, and peaceful guerrilla actions have taken place across the country. A number of large and small businesses, cultural institutions, theatres, libraries, museums, shops, and even nightclubs and bars have closed in support. The protesters organize themselves through student plenums and other assemblies, where everyone has the right to speak and all decisions are voted on. The movement survives on food donations and operates independently of university adminis-trations and opposition parties. The energy that accompanies the protests—usually of highly articulate, calm, caring, young people, eager to show solidarity and mutual recognition, who clear the streets of rubbish and other traces when they're finished with a protest—is inspiring to many. One can also note, of course, a mounting impatience and aggression. As tensions rise between those who support the demands of the protesters and their opponents, there is a growing practice of filming the demonstrations. Social media offers hundreds of clips from multiple perspectives purporting to show the authorities' intimidation, but they are also used to publicly shame pro-government activists. The protests' hypervisibility is taken as a bid for transparency—an ideal invoked by both the government and the dissidents.

"GROWING IS INVISIBLE."

Ana is a sixty-eight-year-old woman with a light grey bob that frames her dark, inquisitive eyes. She moves with noticeable grace in her loose, warm-colored clothes. She lives alone in a small flat in an apartment tower in the Novi Beograd (New Belgrade) district, near the Sava River. Over the past five years, I have spent considerable time with Ana in her cramped kitchen, decorated with plants and her amateur paintings. After retiring, Ana developed a naïve style, usually reserved for depicting folk and rural life, but applied it to urban, almost technical settings. Her paintings of concrete

Maja Petrović-Šteger

halls, factory workshops, and laboratories are bathed in soft light, often suffused with burnt orange. Impressed by her reinterpretation of the industrial landscape as soft and luminous, I asked Ana several times what made her paint these scenes with such counterintuitive colors and technique. I knew she had worked for forty years as a chemical engineer, specializing in the protection of metals from corrosion, in a large company making paints and varnishes. Her work, though, clearly had other inspirations and sources. She never answered. Instead, she would turn around or look through the balcony doors, which were almost always ajar, and draw my attention to the birds, or children screaming with joy, or people passing by, or arguing over a parking space. Often, we would just continue to sit in pleasant silence. And sometimes she would pick up where we left off, talking about life, the family that raised her, her deteriorating health, her financial situation, her ideas about eternity, or the death of her son twenty-nine years ago. Ana is open, warm, direct, and responsive in the way she looks at you and moves her hands and body. But sometimes she chooses not to answer questions.

Tetka Ana, auntie Ana, as everyone affectionately calls her, is seen as the person to go to if someone needs advice, if an issue needs to be raised at the tenants' council, or if someone wants to learn about the neighborhood gardens. In all these exchanges I've seen, Ana's way of relating to people, whether peers, teens, or children, palpably makes a mark. People love to talk to her, to be recognized and greeted by her. I've seen people join us just to walk beside her in silence. Her rapport is always engaged, and the stability and vitality she exudes is much appreciated.

Marko, a friend who introduced me to Ana, said that everyone knows her as "the hood's spirit-keeper," as somebody who renewed and is deemed to sustain thc unusually good atmosphere in the neighborhood. Twenty-six years ago, she started planting roses, herbs, bushes, and trees in front of her block of flats, and later in the surrounding green spaces. At first, she was seen as an oddball, coming home from work in heels and work dresses, yet picking up litter or straightening rubbish bins on her way. It was known that she was a respected engineer. Some thought her to be haughty, over-proud of her superior cleanliness. Others were puzzled by such herb gardens in public places, or her stubborn protection of crab apple trees and particular plants such as mugwort, nettles, plantain, and fennel, which are barely distinguishable from weeds. But she never reprimanded anyone for stepping on her plants, littering, spraying graffiti, or trashing park equipment. Even when it would have been possible for her to finger culprits from the balcony windows of her kitchen, she just kept tidying up, planting, labelling herbs and trees, tending their foliage, and picking their leaves. There is an anecdote that for a while Ana regularly interrupted the late-night drug sales of a local small-time dealer. She would come and hang out by the same bush or in the same little corner where he had set up his makeshift "stall." Unfazed by him and his clients, Ana would appear, ask him something, offer him a cigarette, or just clean up the area while he tried to do his business. A few years later, another neighbor, a math teacher, arranged for the students in his class to join Ana and help her prepare and fertilize the soil around the fruit trees. Ana shared many stories about roots and stems, air, and light. The community's legends about her tend to be simple and short. They all more or less repeat that "planting is silent" and "growing invisible." That "what you see, and what is hidden from the view of others, make your ultimate resources," that "plants' spirits are always here and are timeless, but need to be related to and given a home in real turf to be felt." She neither preaches nor organizes. When members of the Green (Ecological) Party approached her a few years ago about joining them and standing as a local councilor, she

Maja Petrović-Šteger

flatly turned them down. Whenever I tried to find out more about what motivates her devotion to plants, she ignored my questions. They were superfluous. Instead of answering, she would simply continue to smell the bark of the trees. Or offer me a tea from her herbal treasure trove. Or move her hands in a ceremonial way, which she often does, as if searching for something in the undergrowth and gathering something in the lower parts of the hedges. The environment Ana has created is not decorative, just exceptionally alive. Green islands that surround concrete blocks have become a refuge for birds and passersby who just go there to sit and rest, contemplate, tidy things up, plant something, serenade each other, or hide. As regards its atmosphere, this neighborhood truly differs from its surroundings.

PREFIGURING RENEWAL

The political as a mode of analysis enjoys a certain representational hegemony over Serbian life, both for Serbian citizens and observers thereof. It tends to trump all other possible analyses or ways of understanding their sociality and society's unfoldings. Obviously, the daily national and international politics have an enormous impact on the economic and mental well-being of Serbians. After years of the country's machinery refusing to acknowledge any war crimes, and then years of smaller and larger protests, as well as engineered apathy (motivated by a fear of retribution), the current student-led protests arguably mark a breakthrough in galvanizing massive numbers of people into action.

For some of the people I spend time with in Serbia, however, political action as a medium for genuine change seems hollow. Their sense of their past and future would imply that these interlocutors see formal politics—i.e., the government, formal institutions of power, the media coverage of party politics, the state of emergency and its normalization, aspirations for change led by new political organizations—as not only trite, uncaring, and ineffective, but also empty. Their conception of the political is that of a machine that grinds down whatever is fed into it, then spits it out. By extension, they refuse to associate themselves or judge their own lives through a political or politicized lens. Fully aware that Serbian politics (even with its conflicts) has the effect of cynically invalidating any appeal to anything beyond politics to the extent that its interpreters could be wary of that call and find the concept of the "non-political" rather vacuous, they still refuse it. It is not that they claim to be "apolitical." They lean towards one side or another, seek independence from orthodoxies, and, just by dint of their profession or activism, form part of various institutions and networks. Their social, intellectual, and (if they are lucky!) financial capital means they have to acknowledge the force of ideological and political endowments in their lives. However, all of them feel that systemic politics aims to impoverish them. It holds them too tightly and constrains their vision and actions. They avoid framing any criticism or aspiration in an untrustworthy political syntax, instead looking for other, more adequate, designations for a range of experiences and hopes vital to their lives and connection to larger interpersonal, social, and natural systems.[7]

Observing people's frustration with standing restrictions on how they are officially invited to make sense of their times, my research over the last six years has moved away, ethnographically, from its earlier predominant themes of political and economic hope and hopelessness. I have begun to focus on individuals and collectives who refuse to be perceived or fully subsumed within left- or right-wing political

[7]   See Maja Petrović-Šteger, "On the Side of Predictable: Visioning the Future in Serbia," *Etnološka tribina: Godišnjak Hrvatskog etnološkog društva* 50, no. 43 (2020): 3–67.

Maja Petrović-Šteger

identities, and who are concerned with renewing their personal and social resources in alternative ways. I've begun to pay attention to practices, narratives, signs, and "visions" of social change that inform the collective consciousness in non-obviously political ways. Besides taking stock of what builds out of observable facts, I have sought to attune myself to what is hibernating (while seeking expression) in mindsets and social conditions.

I started to follow the work of a public health planner, an educator, a carpenter, a biological archaeologist, and a few inventors. Other interlocutors include traditional musicians, a gynecologist, athletes, herbalists, and painters. These individuals, of different ages and life experiences, transcend their vocational identities in thinking about how change in society might emerge and be conceptualized. The specific fieldwork cases that I work on include a project founding and financing orphanages across Serbia, set up to attract the best social and natural scientists and educators; a public education project offering tours of Belgrade's catacombs and underground public infrastructure as a way of rethinking what city resources are; a project devoted to creating unusual libraries of herbal medicine and thus the rethinking of environmental taxonomies; and a project using Orthodox sacred music in medicine. The research follows people who believe that prefigurative actions, as they bear on matters of societal reconditioning, should count for more than being political in the right way, and should extend into the realms of coherence, order, morality, aesthetics, the sacred, and inspiration. My visionaries seek society's psychological and structural transformation through individual investment, intentional community projects, and scientific and spiritual activism, oriented to a supposed renewal of Serbia's spiritual fabric and well-being.

Some of these visionaries, inspirers, and makers are highly accomplished in socially recognized ways, with leading positions in their fields. Others are known for their imaginative and unexpected configurations of ideas about how social and state processes might align in new, unentrenched ways. Still others are recognized for their personal vitality or ability to carefully nurture the fragile relational threads in their communities. This is how I met Ana. Marko recommended that I meet and spend time with her, as she is regarded in some circles as a person whose actions, imagination, and force of mind have had a real impact on what people around her understand as possible and conceivable. Her imaginal practices, her vision of knitting the neighborhood together by single-handedly providing spaces where they can appreciate their surroundings, seem to be about finding sustenance and integrity. The fact that she does not compete for visibility, resources, or power, and does not seek to validate her vision and practices in political terms, is precisely why she is so respected.

THE REALM OF THE IMAGINAL

In social science and philosophy, imagination is usually conceived of as an individual's capacity to represent what is not there—the unreal, whether a hallucination or the projection of a scenario yet to come.[8] The concept of the social imaginary (a derivative term), on the other hand, is understood to be socially embedded and constrained. The term "the social imaginary" claims our ability to project what is not there as socially embedded, introducing a limitation: a society can only imagine what its members have been socialized to regard as possible, as noted by Castoriadis, Árnason,

8   See Chiara Bottici, "Imagination, Imaginary, Imaginal: Towards a New Social Ontology?," *Social Epistemology* 33, no. 5 (2019): 433.

La Caze, and Bottici.[9] As Bottici notes, if the imagination is a faculty we possess as persons, the social imaginary, by contrast, possesses us.

Anthropologists, philosophers, and other social scientists[10] have recently started to revisit the concept called the "imaginal." In contrast to both "imagination" and "the imaginary," the "imaginal," designating what is made of images, may be the product of both an individual faculty and a social context, and of their mutual interactions. As a term or a concept, the imaginal ought to help overcome tensions between the social and the individual.[11] Furthermore, in contrast to the imaginary, which is often associated with the unreal and fictitious (something that is and remains outside of being and existence—in brief, something *utopian*), the imaginal makes no ontological assumptions as to the reality of the images that compose it, or the presence or absence of what its images represent.

As a concept, the imaginal was first coined by Henry Corbin, who in his writings critiqued the circumstance that the kind of consciousness that has increasingly dominated Western culture since about the twelfth century is characterized by a critical disconnection between thought and being. Corbin defined *l'imaginal* or *mundus imaginalis* in the context

9   Cornelius Castoriadis, *The Imaginary Institution of Society,* trans. Kathleen Blamey (MIT Press, 1987); Jóhann Páll Árnason, "Reason, Imagination, Interpretation," in *Rethinking Imagination: Culture and Creativity,* ed. G. Robinson and J. Rundell (Routledge, 1994), 155–70; Marguerite La Caze, *The Analytic Imaginary* (Cornell University Press, 1996); Chiara Bottici, *Imaginal Politics: Images Beyond Imagination and the Imaginary* (Columbia University Press, 2014).

10   See Cynthia Fleury, ed., *Imagination, Imaginaire, Imaginal* (Presses Universitaires de France, 2006); Stefania Pandolfo, *Knot of the Soul: Madness, Psychoanalysis, Islam* (University of Chicago Press, 2018); Jean Hunleth, "Zambian Children's Imaginal Caring: On Fantasy, Play and Anticipation in an Epidemic," *Cultural Anthropology* 34, no. 2 (2019): 155–86.

11   See Bottici, "Imagination, Imaginary, Imaginal," 433–41.

of Islamic Sufi traditions as a concept designating fantasies, meta-psychological representations, as self-sustaining and real. The *mundus imaginalis*, in his theory, is a world of "metaphysical images, having the same consistency and reality as the world of Platonic ideas." It is "a world that is ontologically as real as the world of the senses and that of the intellect. This world requires its own faculty of perception, namely, imaginative power, a faculty with a cognitive function, a noetic value which is as real as that of sense perception or intellectual intuition."[12] Imagination, as an organ of perception, is required to enact a mode of being and of consciousness. Corbin was not merely theorizing nor philosophizing: he was describing something that for him was real.

My work seeks to identify individual and societal visions and imaginal practices in a social context crying out for radical overhaul, transformation, and community healing. In portraying and analyzing alternative social scenarios in Serbia vouched for by "visions" bigger than political, my aim is not to put forward a study of otherworldly fantasies, but to show that they are real, or can have real effects. My ethnography is concerned with worldly, mundane strategies tied to historically specific ideas, actions, and people. Yet, visions are hard to pin down or follow, for they are usually recognized only after their social impact has been measured, after a certain "facticity" has been added to the images and imaginaries that compose them. I met Ana twenty-two years after she had started planting her herbs and trees, that is, years after her vision (of which she never really speaks) started to change her neighborhood, and only after she had been recognized as the originator of that change.

Indeed, there is a question of when visioning becomes visible enough to become analyzable. It is easy to be drawn to

12   Henry Corbin, *Spiritual Body and Celestial Earth: From Mazdean Iran to Shi'ite Iran,* trans. Nancy Pearson, Bollingen Series XCI: 2 (Princeton University Press, 1977).

Maja Petrović-Šteger

objects and processes after they have appeared, and to movements or expressions of opinion after they have manifested
themselves. But in what forms were they inchoate? And
might we have seen and sensed them earlier? How do certain
imaginal relationships with the future emerge and gain social
recognition in the first place? Who is a "visionary"?

STEPPING OUT OF
SHARED IMAGINARIES

Anthropological work strives to recognize, and then com-
municate, how the conditions under which something has
been experienced become essential for understanding that
experience. We do not seek new and novel findings as such.
Rather, we aim to understand a phenomenon, an event, a
relationship, people's practices and ways of narrating the
world in a given society. We do that by attending to the ways
in which phenomena find their register and voice, and articulate themselves as, or in response to, the questions they find
vital. By providing a context, we attempt to ensure that the
phenomena we depict find their proper expression. We strive
to find analytical methods that draw phenomena of different
orders—discursive, material, or conceptual—into a coherent
field of understanding.

I understand the visionary to require subjects to step
out of the routines of group thinking, predictable responses,
and the regimes of shared imaginaries. The visionaries
I describe work not only with what is known—objects,
people, things, beliefs—but also with what is partially known,
unknown, and only incipiently realized. It is therefore all
the more important to resist the premature "coding" of their
ideas and actions politically (which typically means in terms
of moral partisanship), as my interlocutors themselves do not
perceive their actions and philosophies this way. Jumping to

conclusions about the sustainability of their visions will not make them more intelligible. Every time we reach an intellectual or emotional impasse, we would do better to just observe and listen. To wait. And to not ascribe political significance to an excess that, at that moment, cannot be contained in cognitive, social, perceptual, or emotional registers.

In the context of Serbia, what I have just proposed— consciously resisting the political as the focal resource for self-identification and making sense of the world—could be considered almost offensive. My analytical proposal, as well as the actions of some of the people I describe, could be seen as delusional and unpalatable. They could be understood even as morally wrong in a world continually remade by populist authoritarians, in which the credo of the left is to push back against their interventions.

Such moralizing calls have consequences. A few years ago, it was easier for me to start a conversation with people about those they admired as visionaries. Now the question of who has interesting ideas about societal revision often elicits cynical answers. My interlocutors now see these people as exceptionalists or obscurantists. Moreover, even some of the interviewees whose work I have been following for some time, and who seem (to me at least) to have the most interesting ideas, are themselves falling increasingly hushed. One interviewee, now a good friend, who was on the verge of implementing profound change in the Serbian preschool education system and then failed, has almost gone into hiding. Not because of the "failure," but because she cannot explain to her friends, colleagues, and family the conditions under which her project failed. She feels incredibly isolated. More and more people I work with choose not to share their plans with others for fear of ridicule, or for fear of them being thought too grandiose and pie-in-the-sky. Their ideas are dismissed as unrealistic. As a result, some drift into quietism.

Maja Petrović-Šteger

As Edwin Ardener wrote, a prophet is understood as incomprehensible or banal before the prophetic fulfilment (should any occur), and as intuitive and commonplace afterwards.[13] The prophet speaks not of the future, but from it, so until that time arrives, he remains opaque, and when it does, he becomes *passé*. Similarly, Chapman comments that "in a situation of theoretical and conceptual innovation, statements from within a novel structure of understanding are always likely to be perceived, at worst, as laughably meaningless, and, at best, as oracular—an oracle spiced, perhaps, with the exciting hint of fulfilment."[14]

In attending to how people in contemporary Serbia conceive their intimate and collective conditions, and how they foresee changing them while dealing constructively with their past, present, and future, I realized that one of the biggest changes they aspire to concerns proximity. Many speak of the need for proximity—to oneself and one's society, as the most important component that their work of social criticism seeks to illuminate.

When documenting a society's travails, and evolutions in the direction of change, one should not, I suggest, be too hasty to characterize the mediators of socio-historical transition. We should stay or tarry with the imaginal and not appropriate it too quickly to the language of the political. As Corbin wrote, the imaginal guides, anticipates, and molds sensory perception; it transmutes sensory data into symbols in ways that are vastly transformative. This applies to Serbia, but it could apply to other places too.

13   Edwin Ardener, *The Voice of Prophecy and Other Essays* (Berghahn Books, 2006).
14   Malcolm Chapman, "Introduction," in *The Voice of Prophecy and Other Essays*, by Edwin Ardener (Berghahn Books, 2006), xxvii.

P.S. I spoke to Ana on the phone the other day and asked her if she was demonstrating. She said that she was not attending the protests, but had sent five batches of *orasnice* (soft walnut cookies) to two daughters of a neighbor, who are very active organizers. Later, at the end of our conversation, Ana added: "No, I did not go to the protest. I am very impressed by how articulate and spirited some of the youth are today …. But you can't be in the streets all the time. At some point they will want to go home. They will need a place to recharge their batteries. And they will appreciate finding a new bench beneath the crab apple tree in full bloom."[15]

15 Acknowledgments: I am grateful to Chus Martínez for inviting me to join her in thinking within the framework of this book. My interlocutors in Serbia could not have been more generous and stimulating, and I thank them sincerely for their trust. Financial support from the Slovenian Research Agency (ARIS J6-3127) enabled me to carry out this research.

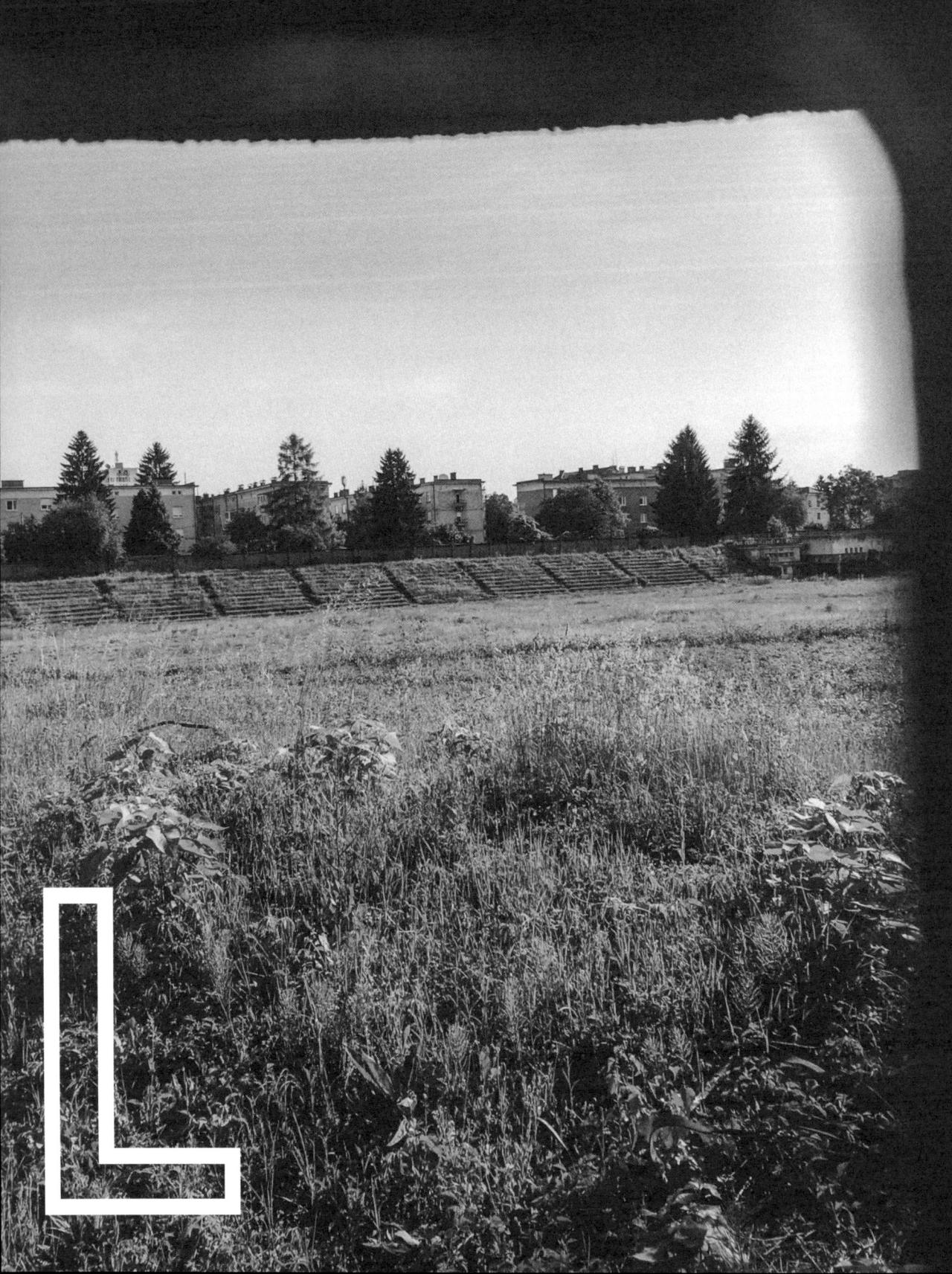

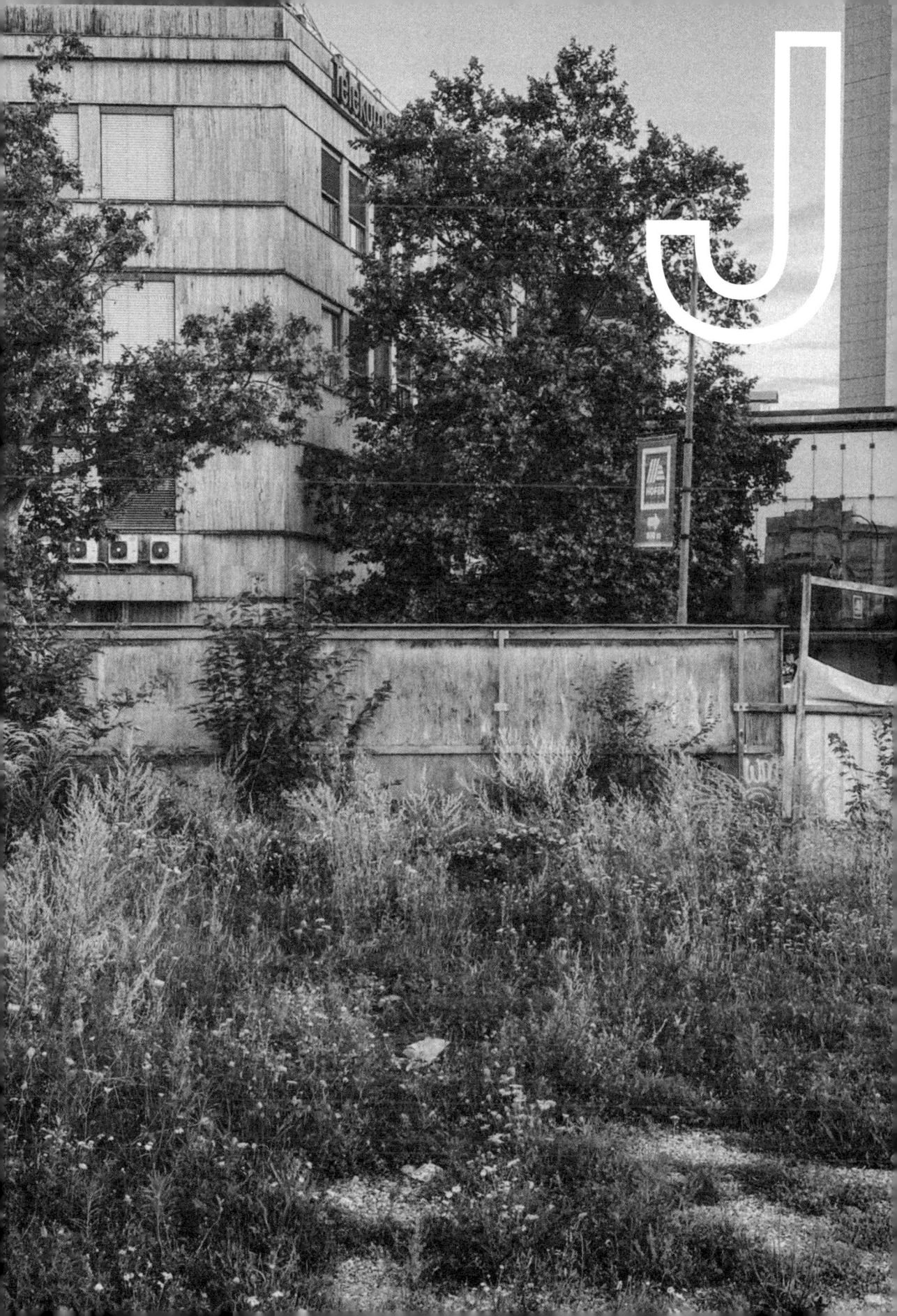

Tivoli Park:
A Flower I Will Become

The Park is one of the most glorious venues a biennial could dream of. The place, in its openness to the city, can be considered a work in itself. The Jakopič Promenade that connects the Museum of Modern Art with MGLC is an outdoor exhibition space that regularly hosts large-format exhibitions, providing cultural and informational displays about history and environmental issues in Slovenia. At first, I was sceptical, as only certain communities dealing with contemporary art can be. And yet, going up and down the park daily in my research visits to Ljubljana, I became familiar with the presence of these panels, as if they were guardians of the way. I also loved how people stopped by them and had conversations about their content. In winter, my parents visited, and both loved the promenade, too. They made me reflect on the times—right after the dictatorship in Spain during the early steps towards democracy—when people took refuge in the parks for picnics, but also amusement parks were populated with information panels about the new order. Indeed, when going out meant bringing your own food or a book to a park and reuniting with friends, the cities of Spain also thought that parks were a good venue to talk about politics. Panels on hygiene, birth control or divorce were not rare at that time.

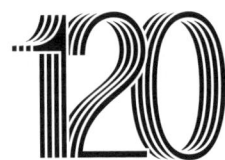

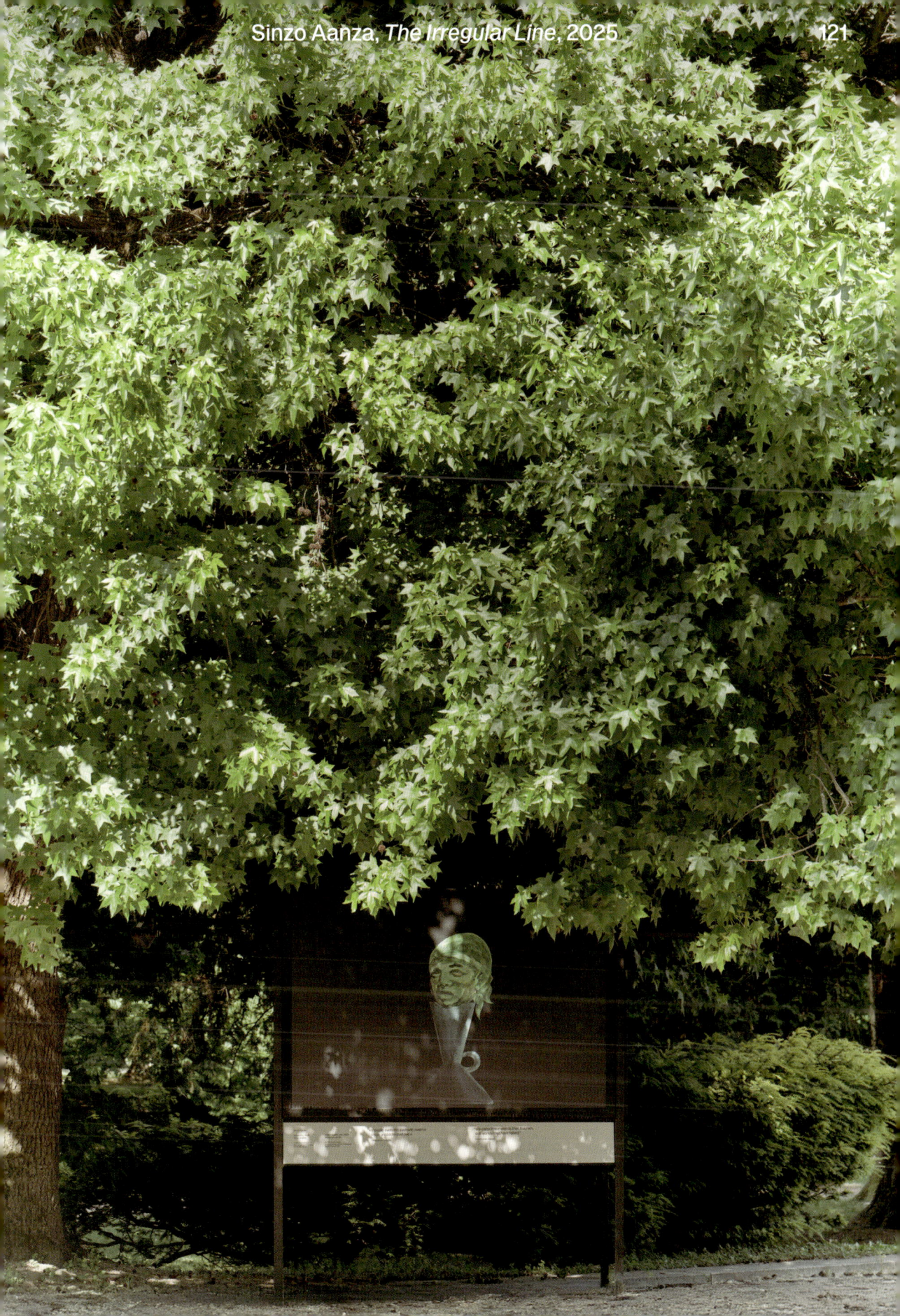

Indeed, I thought, the activation of the visit to the biennial has its backbone in this promenade. Or even better, this walkway—designed by the architect Jože Plečnik in the 1930s—acts like an umbilical cord connecting and nourishing the relationship between the public sphere and its child, the interiority of all the museums and collections that exist around the park, around this green agora of Ljubljana. Like a cat, Ljubljana has nine lives. One of them has to do with the Non-Aligned Movement. During the Cold War (1947–89), Ljubljana, as the capital of Slovenia, was part of Yugoslavia, one of the founding members of the NAM, along with India (Nehru), Egypt (Nasser), Ghana (Nkrumah), and Indonesia (Sukarno). The Ljubljana Biennale of Graphic Arts, established in 1955, played an important role in the cultural diplomacy of Yugoslavia's Non-Aligned Movement (NAM), becoming an important global artistic platform fostering artistic exchange between the East, West, and the Global South. For this reason, and given the fact that this year is the seventieth birthday of the Biennale, it is particularly interesting that the park exhibition is conceived by the artist and writer Sinzo Aanza, who for years has been researching the literal and symbolic meaning of this alliance of countries and political views. The Democratic Republic of the Congo (DRC)—where Sinzo Aanza is from—has had a complex relationship with the Non-Aligned Movement (NAM) since the early 1960s. As a former Belgian colony, Congo became a key area of Cold War tensions but also an important participant in NAM, seeking to balance its international relations while maintaining independence from both the Western and Eastern blocs.

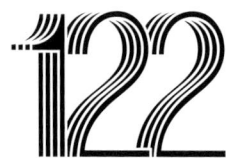

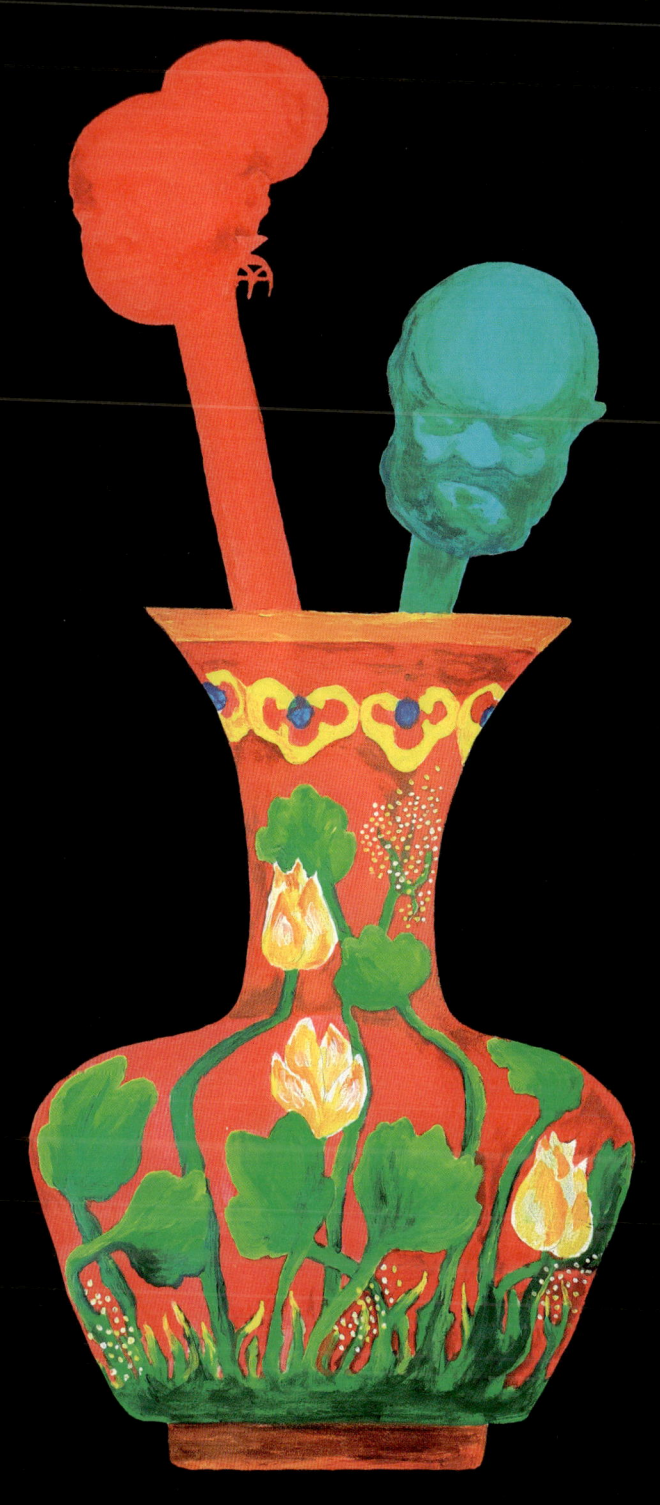

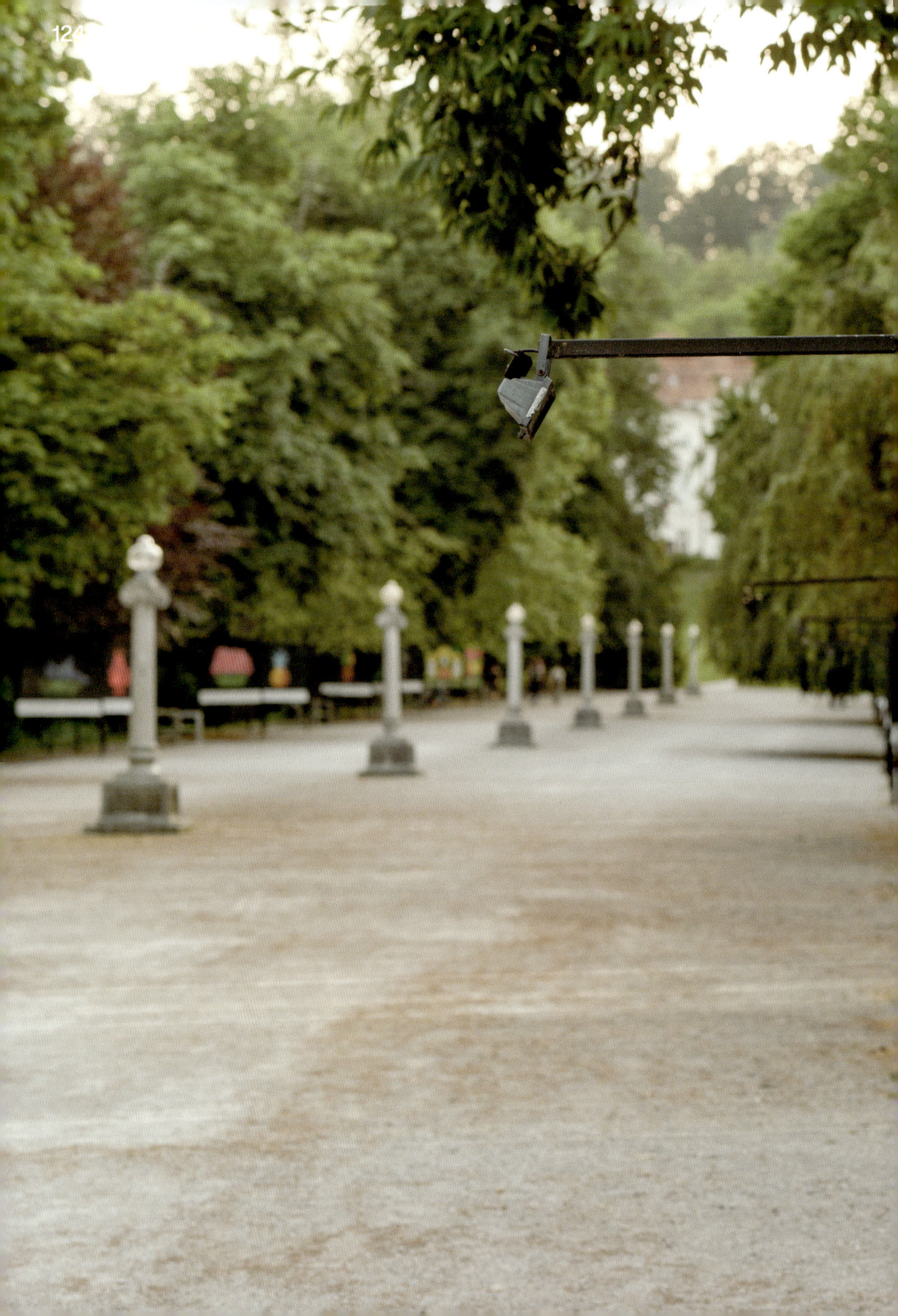

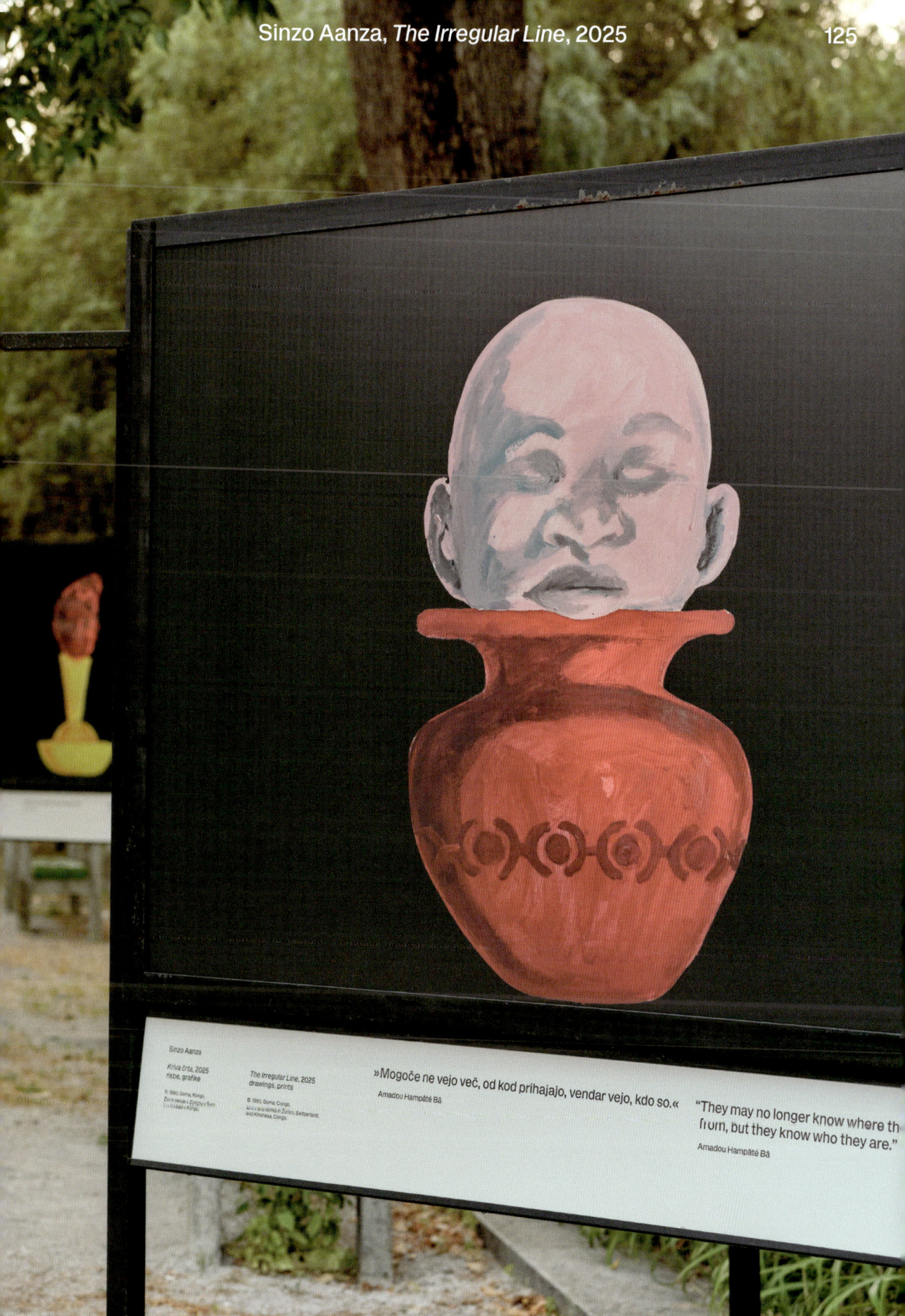

Sinzo Aanza

Kriva črta, 2025
risbe, grafike

R. 1960, Goma, Kongo.
Živi in ustvarja v Zürichu v švici
in v Kinšasi v Kongu.

The Irregular Line, 2025
drawings, prints

B. 1960, Goma, Congo.
Lives and works in Zürich, Switzerland,
and Kinshasa, Congo.

»Mogoče ne vejo več, od kod prihajajo, vendar vejo, kdo so.«

Amadou Hampâté Bâ

"They may no longer know where th
from, but they know who they are."

Amadou Hampâté Bâ

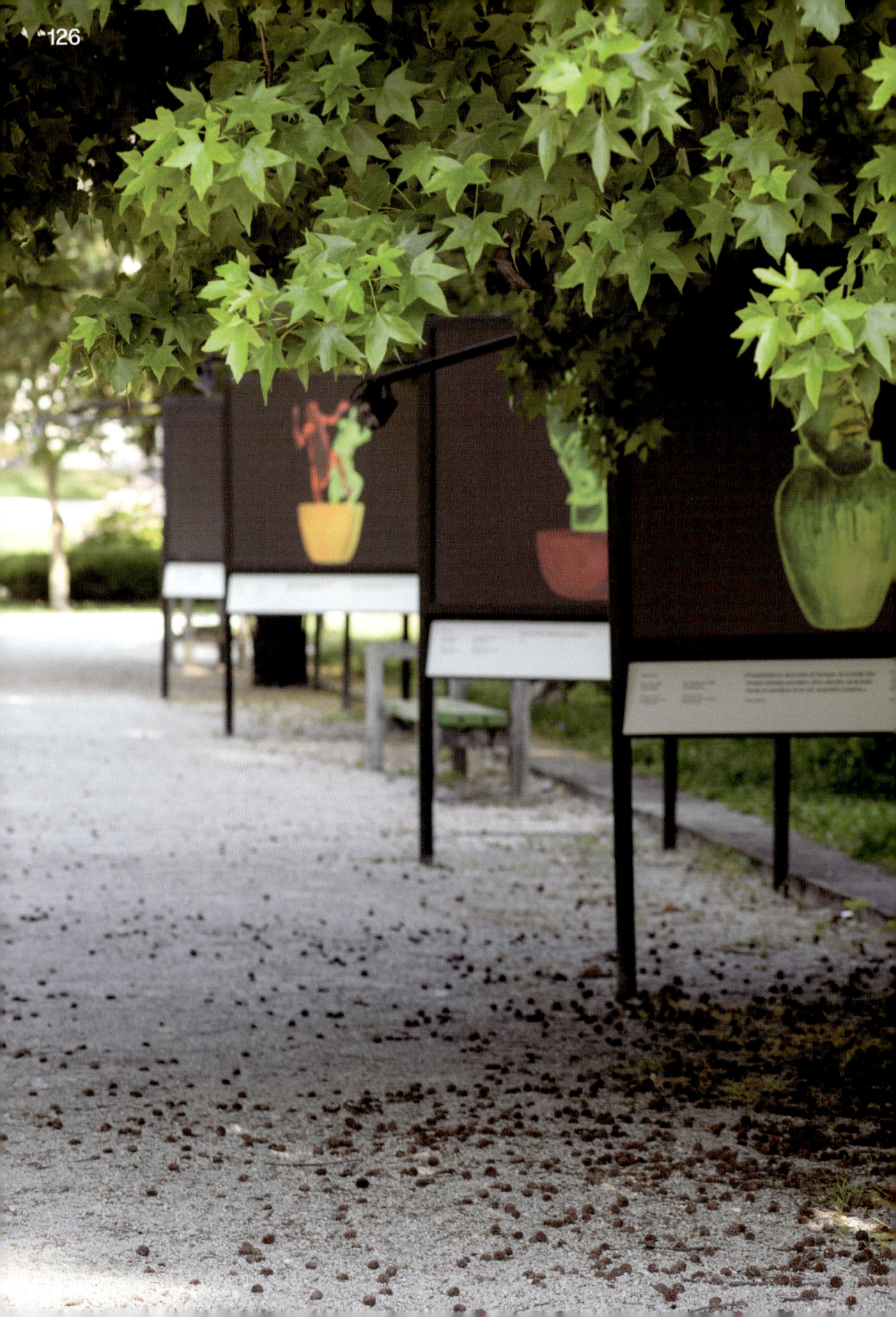

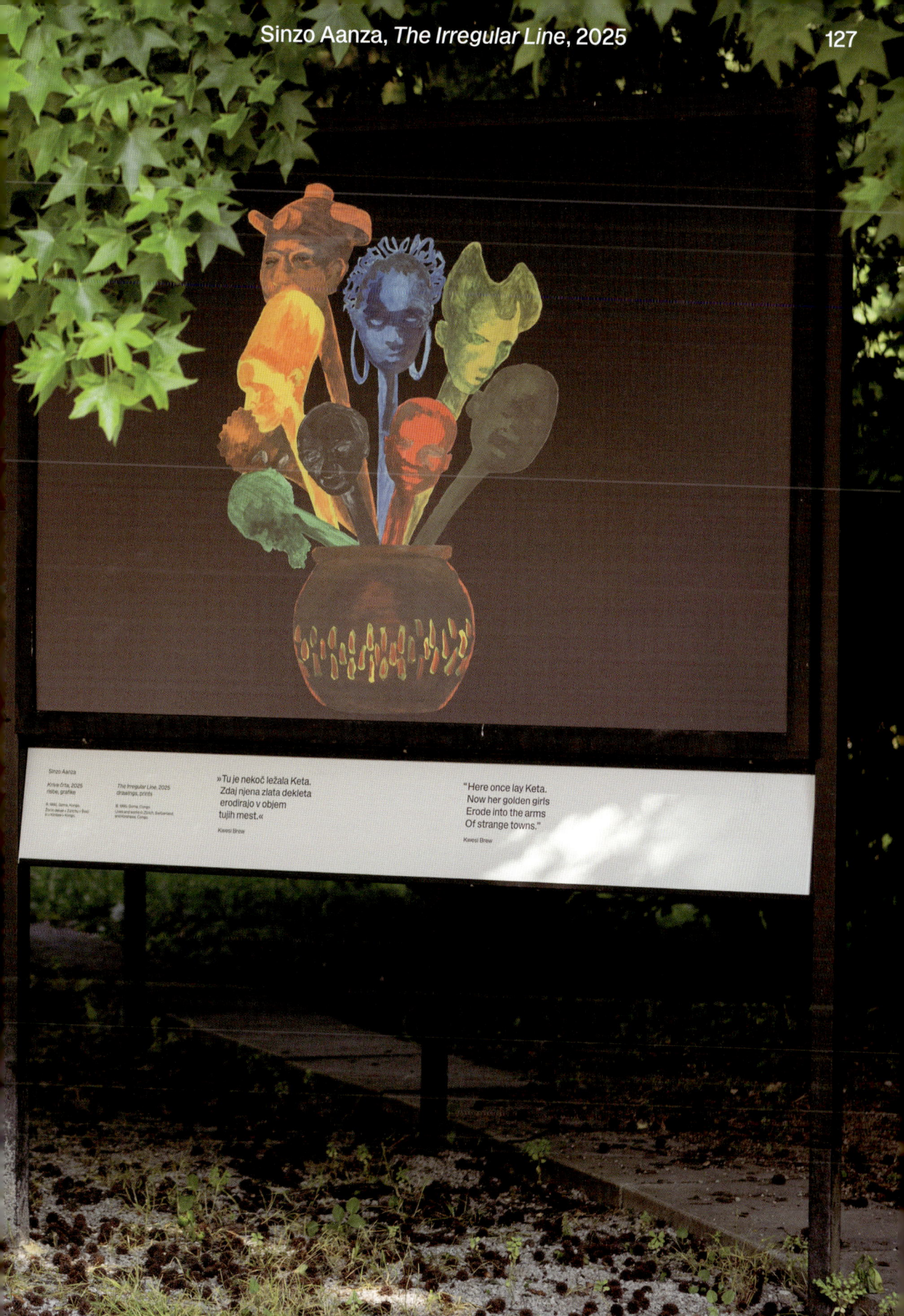

Sinzo Aanza

Kriva črta, 2025
risbe, grafike

Ž. 1991, Goma, Kongo.
Živi in dela v Zürichu v Švici
in v Kinšasi v Kongu.

The Irregular Line, 2025
drawings, prints

B. 1991, Goma, Congo.
Lives and works in Zürich, Switzerland,
and Kinshasa, Congo.

»Tu je nekoč ležala Keta.
Zdaj njena zlata dekleta
erodirajo v objem
tujih mest.«

Kwesi Brew

"Here once lay Keta.
Now her golden girls
Erode into the arms
Of strange towns."

Kwesi Brew

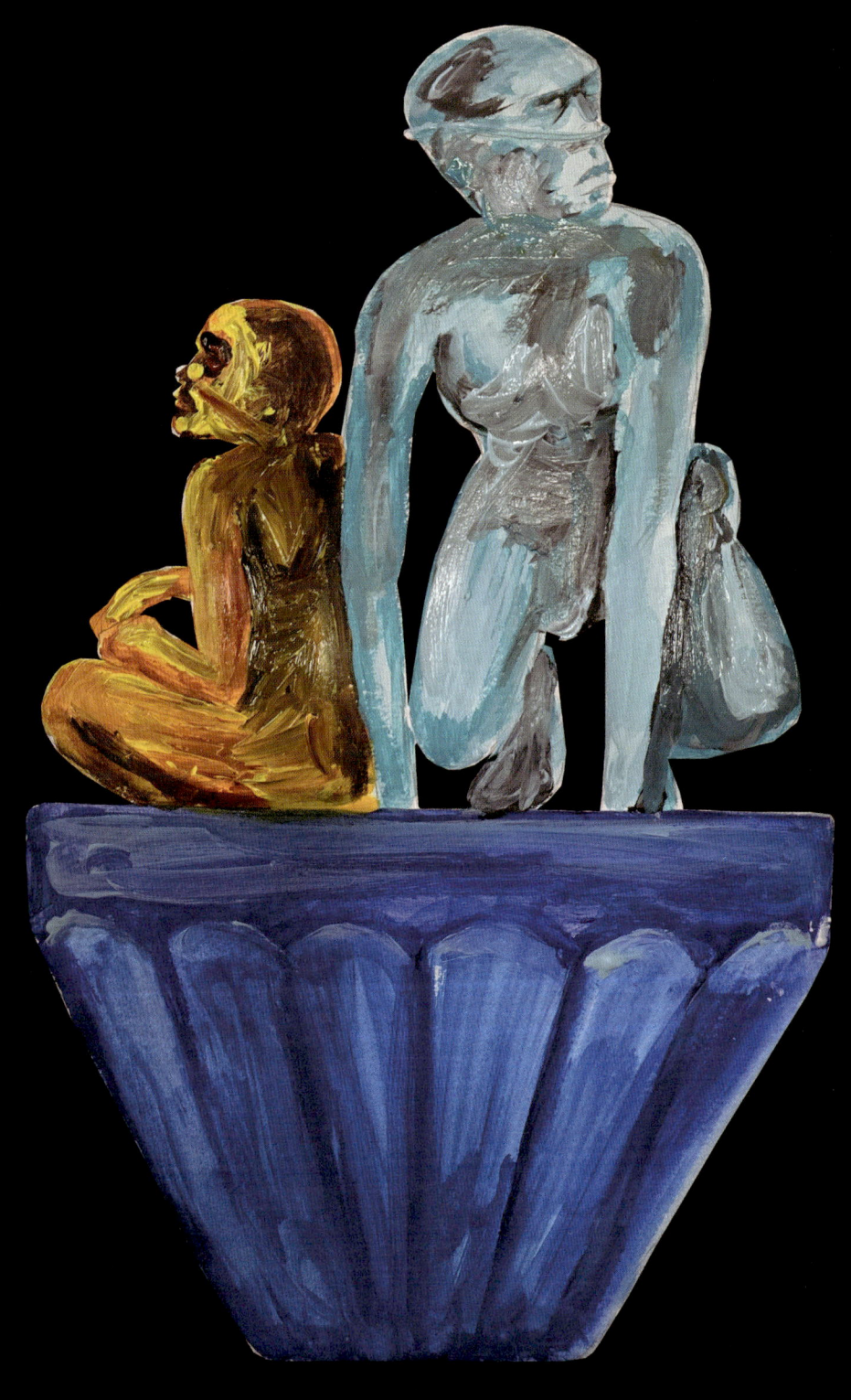

Sinzo Aanza has long pondered the relationship between the historical legacy of the movement, its core values—anti-imperialism, economic sovereignty, and cultural decolonization—and its artistic legacy. The very use of the metaphor of the "line" to represent the boundary that separates the two worlds, the East (Soviet bloc) from the West (NATO); the line is also a pathway that one follows or does not follow (the non-aligned), a different way .... Working on those questions, Sinzo Aanza has created a new pathway, a new promenade at exactly the moment when many are wondering about the forces and powers being created these days. The line is a metaphor that has a great appeal to human perception. A straight line, a ratio line, a right line, a line of order versus the curved lines, the lines of pain and expression. The metaphors used in geopolitics determine the way we read the spatial relationships between countries, the way we interpret the world and human engagement with the environment. The expressive lines that expand and grow are the lines of freedom and independence, the lines of self-recognition and solidarity, like the lines on our own hands. Those hands that we need to extend to others to hold, to hold together and resist the onslaught of emerging totalitarianisms.

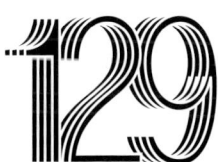

Walk-through of the Exhibition

Walking towards the MGLC from the promenade on your left, you will soon encounter a site-specific work by Kathrin Siegrist. The work is situated in the vicinity of the Plečnik Auditorium, originally designed in 1933. Inspired by Greek amphitheatres, it served as a summer theater and later as an open-air cinema until it fell into disrepair after World War II. In 2022, the auditorium underwent a thoughtful renovation led by the architect Rok Žnidaršič to reinterpret Plečnik's original design, maintaining its historical integrity while revitalizing the space for contemporary use.

The work by Kathrin Siegrist is loosely inspired by some of the forms and motifs developed in the architecture of Jože Plečnik. He often used pyramidal and triangular forms in his buildings. There are many reasons for this, including an interest in spirituality and an admiration for classical geometry and symbolism, but also structural stability. Plečnik admired ancient architecture, particularly the works of the Egyptians, Greeks, and Romans. His use of stepped and pointed pyramidal forms reflects this.

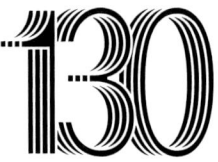

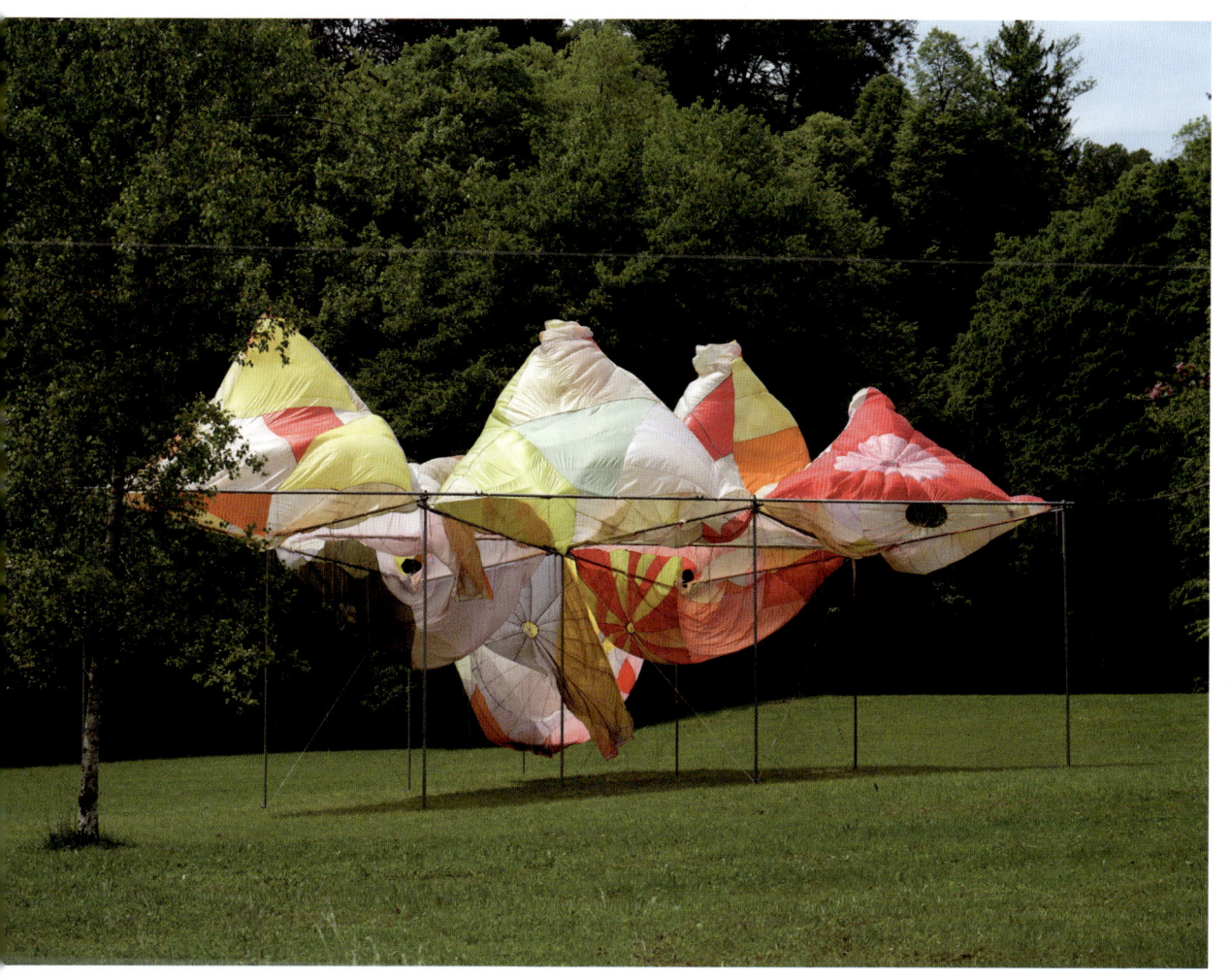

Using scaffolding and fabrics designed for parachute and paraglider manufacture, Kathrin Siegrist creates a group of inverted pyramids. Colorful, light pyramids, suspended in space, susceptible to being moved by the hands of the visitors, by the wind .... Her work does not reflect particular admiration for ancient Western civilizations. Rather, her work admires the work of many female artists who have seen in textiles a way of escaping the rigidity of forms, the rigidity of materials, the rigidity of architecture, and rigidity in general. One work resonates especially in this public labyrinth in the park: *Divisor*, a work made in 1968 by the Brazilian artist Lygia Pape. The piece consisted of a large white cloth (approximately 30 × 30 m) with evenly spaced holes cut into it. Participants placed their heads through the holes while their bodies remained underneath, creating a collective moving sculpture. An iconic participatory work of the Neo-Concrete Movement in Brazil. In the same manner, Kathrin Siegrist's work tries to activate the idea of a shelter, protecting people in a public space. The work constitutes a labyrinth as well, the possibility of our public space being the place where we perform a collective—emotional, spiritual, political—journey towards the common good. And again, the work symbolizes through these light pyramids the stability and strength that we need to show as a society to protect the values of equality and freedom.

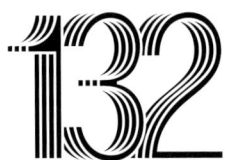

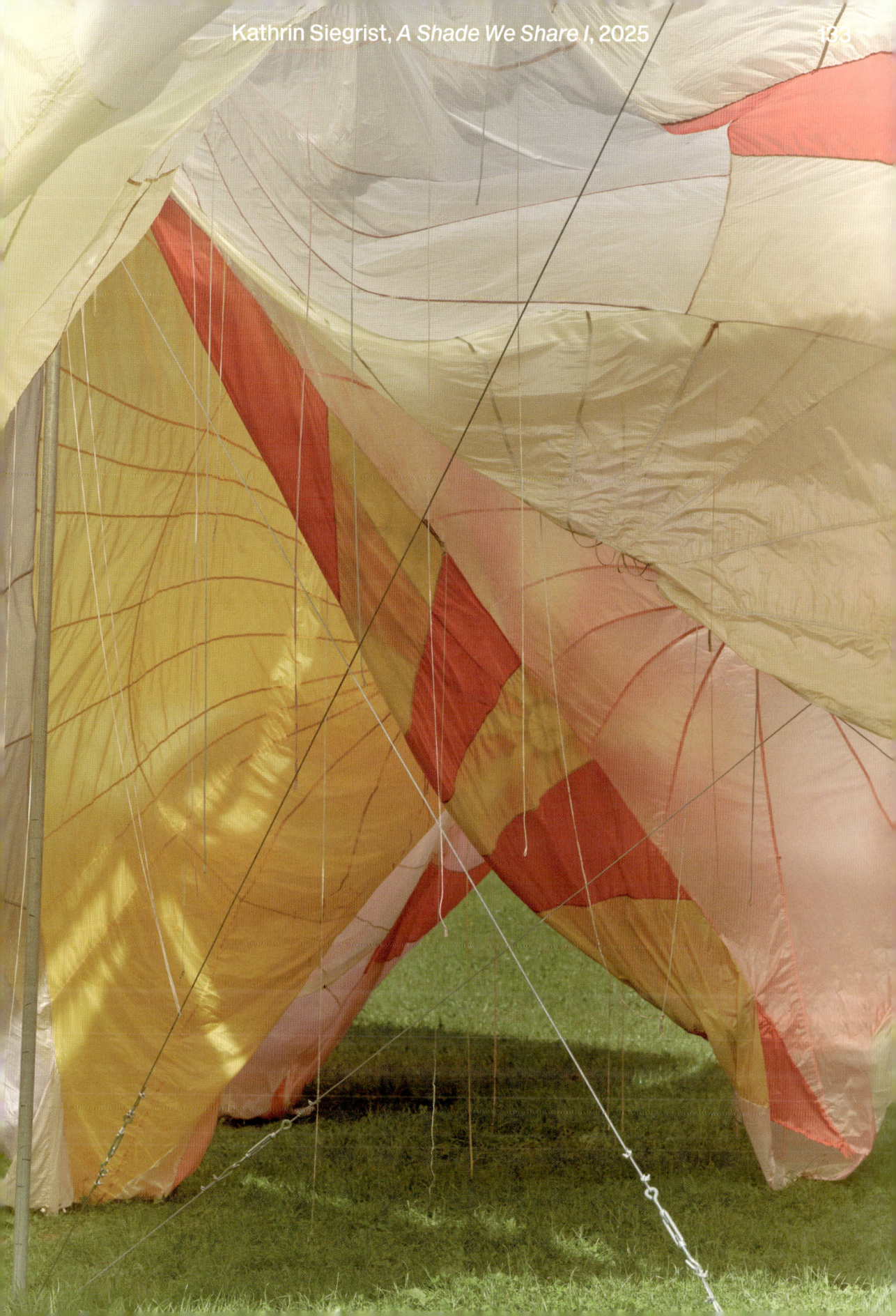

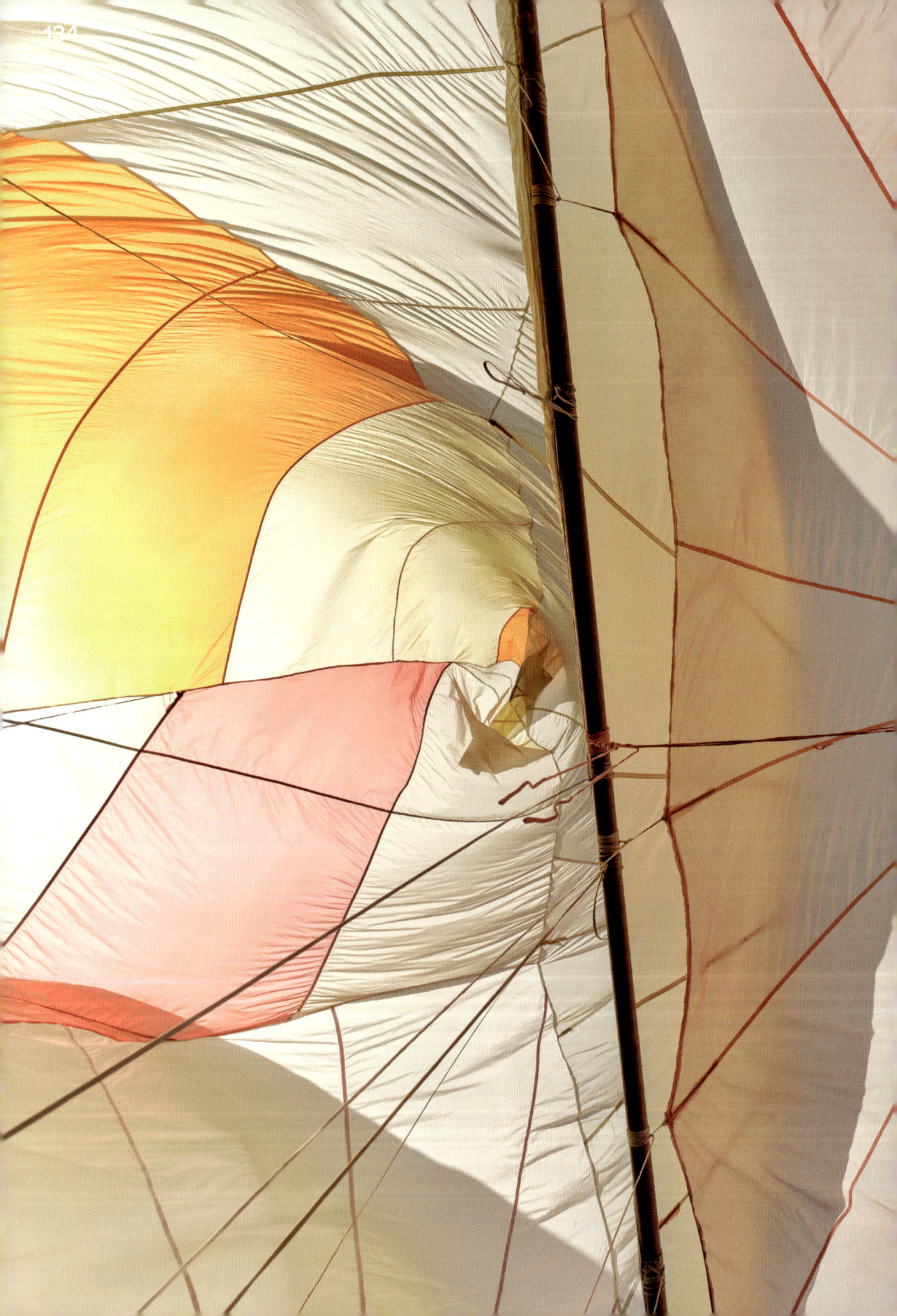

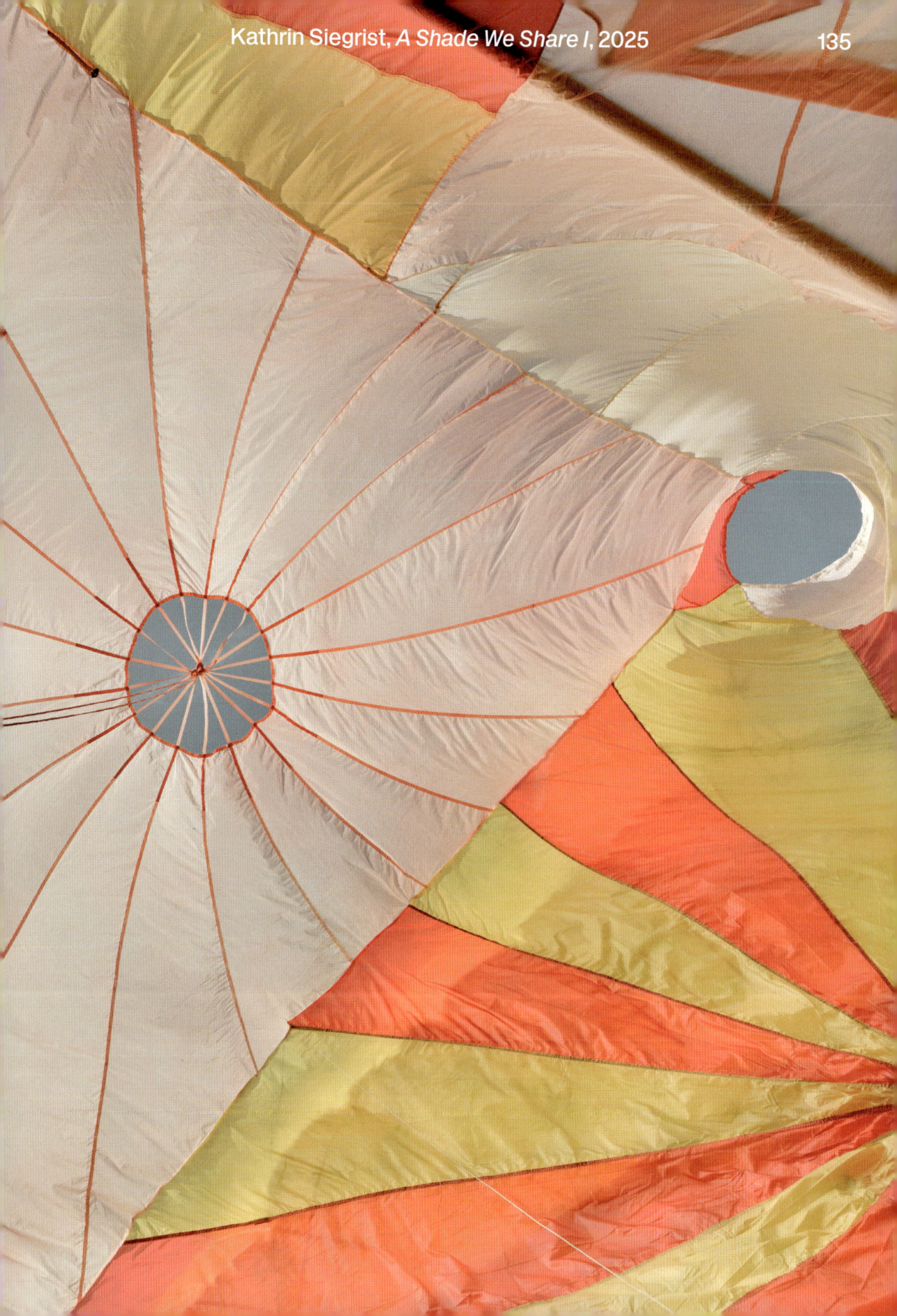

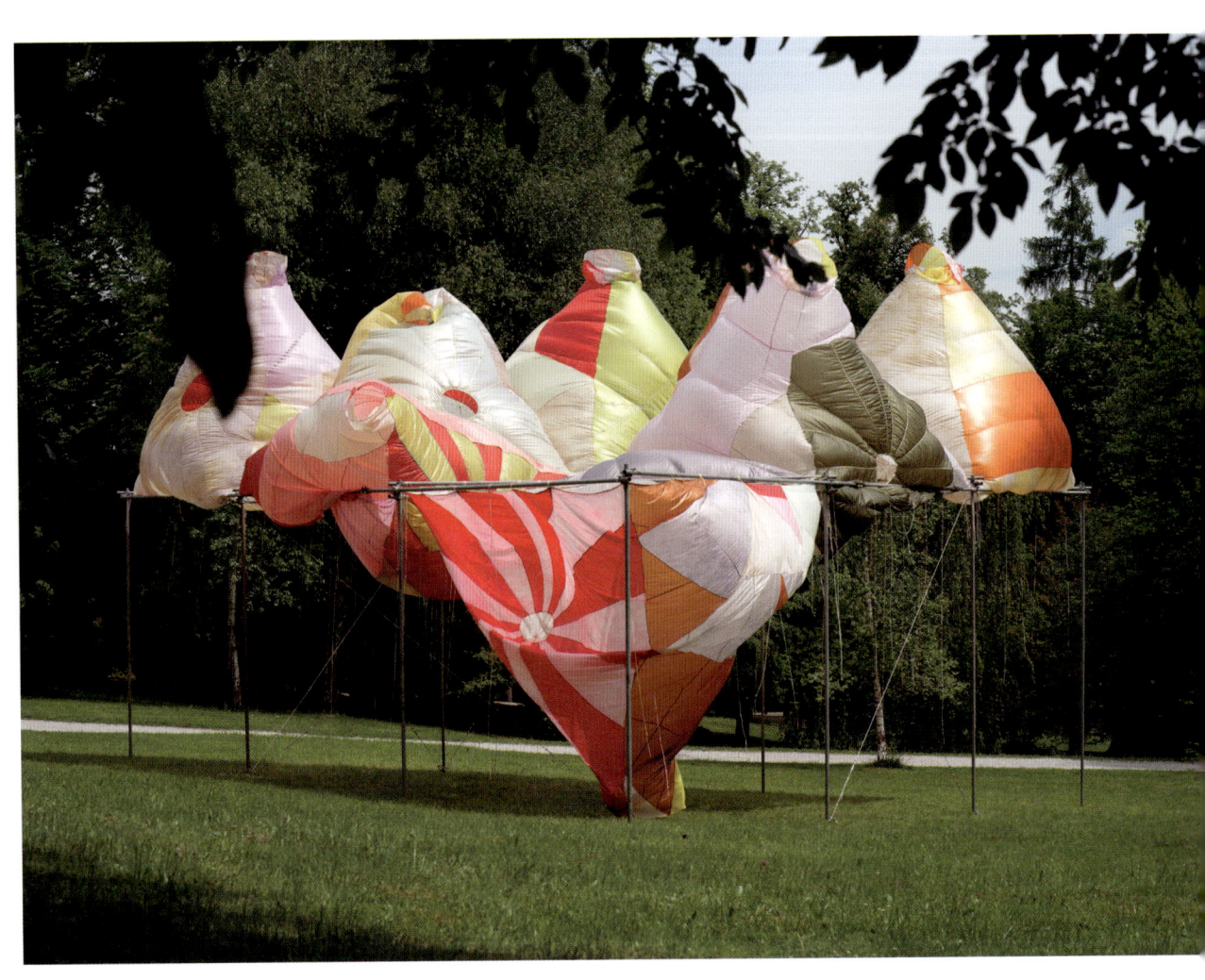

Kathrin Siegrist, *A Shade We Share I*, 2025

THE DEMOS AND THE DEMOS

Sadie

Plant

Sadie Plant

"Dissent is never counted; it is weighed."
Jim Crace, *Harvest*

Yes, yes, I know: they look the same, but there is nothing more to link the demos of democracy and the demos on the street.

In practice, however, they have a lot to say: to each other, and to all the ways in which demonstrations can feel as democratic as the exercise of democracy can be. They have certainly grown up together. It was O'Donnell's monster meetings across Ireland in the 1830s that won the vote for Catholics, and the Chartist demonstrations in Britain that extended voting rights beyond the three percent of the population that had such rights at the time, and the suffragette's call for "deeds not words" that won the vote for women too. Only by their physical presence on the street have those excluded from political participation won the right to have a say.

In the actually existing democracies within which many of us live today, the demos still operates this way. Free and fair elections are considered to define and guarantee a democratic society, but not everyone has the vote, and even those who do are often left with the feeling that it counts for little in the face of all the vested interests and the many other demonstrations of wealth and privilege that hold sway in actually existing democracies. When they feel this strongly, they demonstrate. They, too, want to give their views such weight.

In the older scientific meaning of the term, a demonstration is a way of proving a hypothesis, giving substance to something that would otherwise be nothing but a theory or a fiction, even a fantasy. On the street, in politics, a demonstration offers no such evidence. Its size is only ever approximate and always open to dispute: what it says about broader opinion, whether or how it has an influence, what, if anything, it can achieve, what counts as success; none of this can be measured or assessed with any certainty. What it

The Demos and the Demos

shows is not nothing, but it is inexact. A demonstration is an unknown quantity.

It is easy to underestimate how powerful this unknown element can be. There is always something disruptive, perhaps carnivalesque, about the simple act of using a street for something other than its normal business—putting the wrong bodies in the wrong places, as Jacques Rancière would say.[1] The tamest demonstration can remind people that they can have an impact, if only on a small part of a city on a Saturday. And even when it's calm, even perfunctory, there's always the possibility that something will happen, something unforeseeable and unpredictable. This not quite knowing what will happen, how big or effective it will be, is one of its defining qualities. More than expected is always a possibility.

There were certainly more people than expected at the poll tax demonstration held in London thirty-five years ago, exactly, as it happens, to the day on which I am writing this. The police had planned for twenty thousand people, but ten times more turned out. The poll tax was Thatcher's flagship policy, and we were determined to sink it, which we did.

Not, of course, because of this one day alone. The demonstration was just a small part of a long campaign against the tax, as well as the culmination of a long decade of mounting discontent with the government.

Officially known as the community charge, the poll tax was designed to replace the existing system of local taxation, based on the value of property, with a new charge on people, specifically those who were registered. In the government's view, this was only fair. "Why," asked one of its ministers, "should a duke pay more than a dustman?" Doesn't each have a vote, and with it an equal share in society?

The demonstration was an open call to anyone and everyone who thought about this differently. They wanted to

1   See, for example, Jacques Rancière, *Disagreement: Politics and Philosophy*, trans. Julie Rose (University of Minnesota Press, 1999).

be counted, but not like this, as supposedly equal individuals in a society otherwise bereft of equality. They wanted to give substance to their views, lend weight to their opinions, show their anger, and put their feelings on display. They formed a mass that was more than a large number of people, but people determined to matter, to make their presence, as bodies, felt.

There were plenty of factions vying for control and figures keen to lead, but the demonstrators had no unified identity, no leading party or coherent ideology. All they said was no to a policy that seemed to epitomize Thatcher's insistence that there were only individuals, and no such thing as society.

We made placards from some hefty bits of wood and hardboard found in my dad's garage. Be careful, he said as he waved us off: you could do some damage with those things.

Even on the journey, the atmosphere was cheerful, optimistic. We passed other coachloads of protesters, and the park in which we had arranged to meet was full to overflowing by the time we arrived. Music, dancing, picnics, sunshine, banners, flags, noise, all sorts of people, in ones and twos, friends and families, kids and dogs, campaign groups and ad hoc unions pouring in from everywhere. We smiled at each other as it dawned on us that something was happening, and we were it.

We set off, a sea, a stream, a flow, crossing the river, past the Parliament, heading to Trafalgar Square on a route that took us past Downing Street, home of the prime minister. Here we slowed, then stopped and hung around, and after a while, we sat down. Quite how it happened is impossible to say: thousands of people had passed this point without stopping to protest. Some said it was the work of provocateurs. The press blamed a handful of anarchists. In his account of the events, Danny Burns wrote: "at 3.00 p.m., twenty people staged a peaceful sit down opposite Downing Street." They were followed by several hundred more, "and then the police brought in the horses. Mounted riot police baton-charged the crowd. The crowd, angered by this violent provocation, retaliated by throwing sticks, banner poles, bottles—anything they could find. Young people, armed only with placards, fought hand to hand with police."[2] I heard my dad's words as I watched my own placard effort fly towards their ranks.

Later, when we all met up again—how we did so without mobile phones is also a mystery to me—some friends said the trouble had been planned; others were convinced we had been goaded by *agents provocateurs*. One couple confided, rather sheepishly, that the movement to sit down had started when they'd smoked a joint and could no longer stand. I still don't know what to make of that.

But we had been part of a movement, that was sure. No more or less than anyone.

"People sat down," a BBC reporter later said, "I think because we couldn't go forward, we couldn't go back [...] there were some thousands and thousands and thousands of people, and the route just couldn't cope with it."[3] In the records they later released, the police referred to this moment as a "SITREP," a situation to report.[4] "Nice bit of greenery to sit down and see if anything happens," one of the demonstra- tors said. "At this point it starts getting interesting [...] we're on this bit of grass opposite Downing Street [...] and then, god, all hell breaks loose!! Mayhem everywhere. A push, a shove the odd boot in here and there and then a running battle on the grass, everyone running this way and that, chaos, and in

2   Danny Burns, *Poll Tax Rebellion* (AK Press and Attack
     International, 1992), 89.
3   "We've Got the Power—The Poll Tax Revolt," 25 min., 52 sec.,
     https://www.youtube.com/watch?v=sh3baaSFH64.
4   Solomon Hughes, "This Confidential Police Log Shows
     How Cops Lost the Streets of London to Anarchists During
     the Poll Tax Riots," *Vice*, April 1, 2015, https://www.vice.com
     /en/article/poll-taxriot-anniversary-solomon-hughes-382/.

no time at all, horses appear." In the words of another eyewitness, "I don't know whether the cops deliberately provoked trouble on the march for reasons of their own, or whether they were just too heavy-handed to deal effectively with the small sit-down outside Downing Street (they baton-charged it, sparking a day of rioting), but either way, once it had begun, they rapidly lost control and had no clear plan of what to do."[5]

There were hundreds of thousands of people on the street that day. Not everybody took good stories home: many left with injuries, a few with looted goods, and hundreds were detained. But everybody felt they'd had a role to play, and all of them were right, even though it is impossible to say who exactly did what, and what effect it had, every gesture at the demonstration, and even the demonstration too: something, we were sure, had been achieved, but what it was, and how it had occurred, was impossible to judge. Had the demonstration been effective because of the violence of the police? What would have happened if so many people with such strong feelings had been left to demonstrate peacefully?

Either way, it did amount to something that was too much for the authorities: too many voices, too visible, too loud, too noisy and lively, too much to be contained. "These people are totally against democracy," was Thatcher's statement the next day. For these same people, however, it had felt like the most democratic exercise, a unique chance to participate, the best of demos and the demos at its best. "Extra-parliamentary action proved itself and in the process exposed the hollowness of our claims to democracy," wrote the *Observer* a year later, when the poll tax was finally abandoned. Their elected representatives had let them down, and "a rag-tag army of ordinary people" had done the work of democracy instead.

5   "Accounts of the Poll Tax Riots, 1990," libcom.org, submitted on March 9, 2009, https://libcom.org/article/accounts-poll-tax-riot-1990.

Perhaps this demonstration was a special case: an issue at the heart of democracy, a long campaign, its atmosphere of defiance and festivity, its sense of solidarity. Even the weather was on our side. It doesn't always come together like this. But it often has, and it will again as actually existing democracies tip further into autocracy. People can be so annoying when they keep interrupting things like this, making so much noise, making such a scene, so many situations to report: so irritating, such an inconvenience. Power can't stand the sight or sound of this. How smooth would be its exercise without this human error, these spanners in the works, these rough and ready bodies getting in the way, blocking traffic, sitting in the streets. How disruptive the demos and the demos can be.

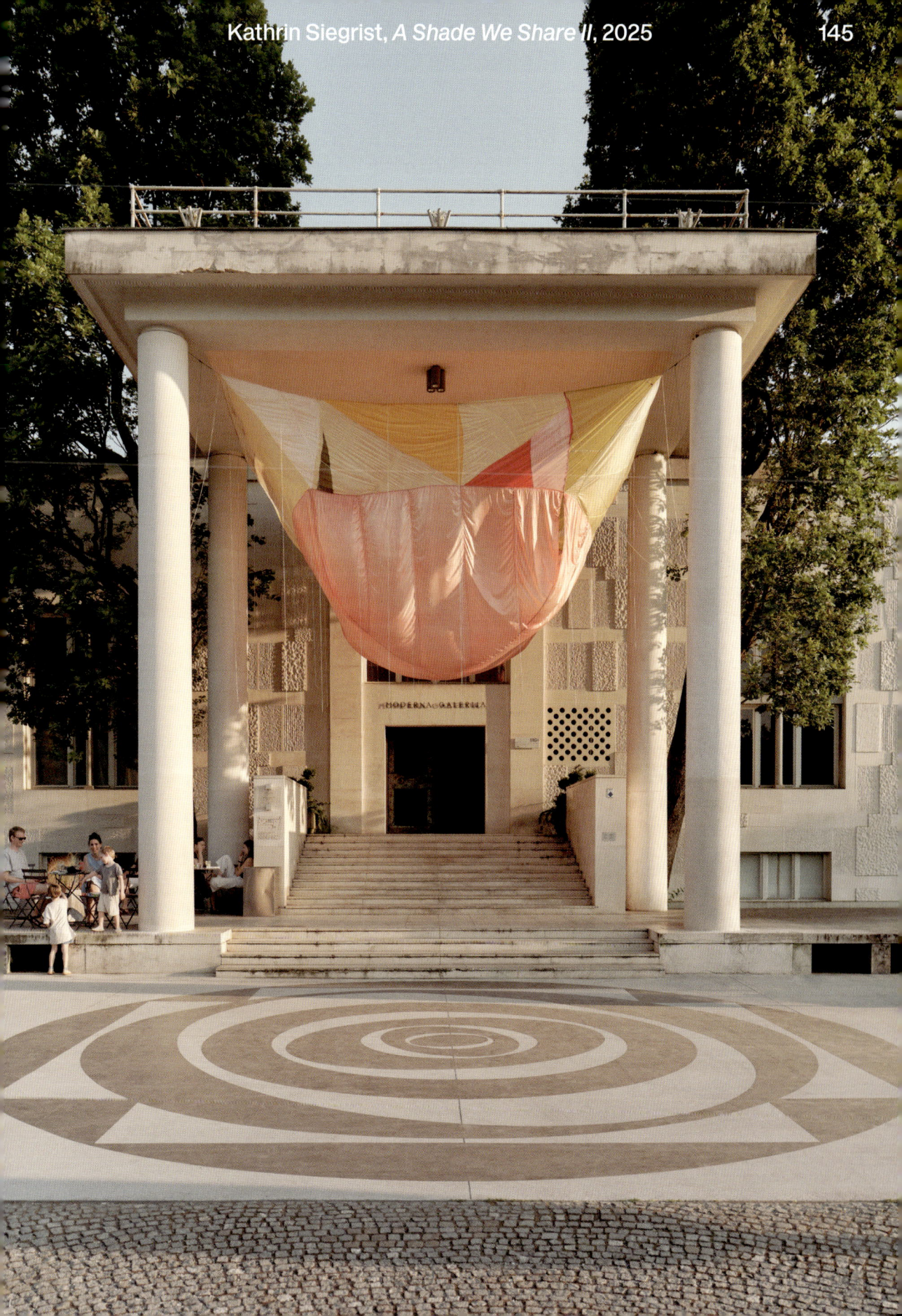

Museum of Modern Art:
Intellectual Courage

Outside the Museum of Modern Art, the first piece you will encounter is by Kathrin Siegrist. Her works are always made of fabric that is often used in sports, military parachuting, and paragliding. She frees this material from its original use to create dynamic interactive sculptures and installations. She processes the original material by re-dyeing it with natural pigments. Her work can be seen in two spots, up in Tivoli Park next to Plečnik's Auditorium and here. Plečnik's work plays a role in her pieces. She has departed from his love for certain universal forms, pyramids, and spheres, to nourish the idea that emotions, and even events, can manifest as visible entities. Her light textiles may appear vulnerable, but they are literally indestructible, creating a planetary problem. Emotions are indestructible as well and also produce global disasters when negative. Knowing the power of feelings and sentiments in our decision-making impulses, Kathrin Siegrist addresses the possibility of creating interactive public pieces to exercise the reprogramming of minor negative emotions such as irritation, paranoia, or anxiety through a pleasant experience.

You may have noted that poetry is a constant throughout the visit to the exhibition. I have immersed myself in Slovenian poetry with the guidance of Alojzija Zupan Sosič, a professor of Slovene literature at the

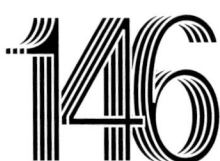

Walk-through of the Exhibition

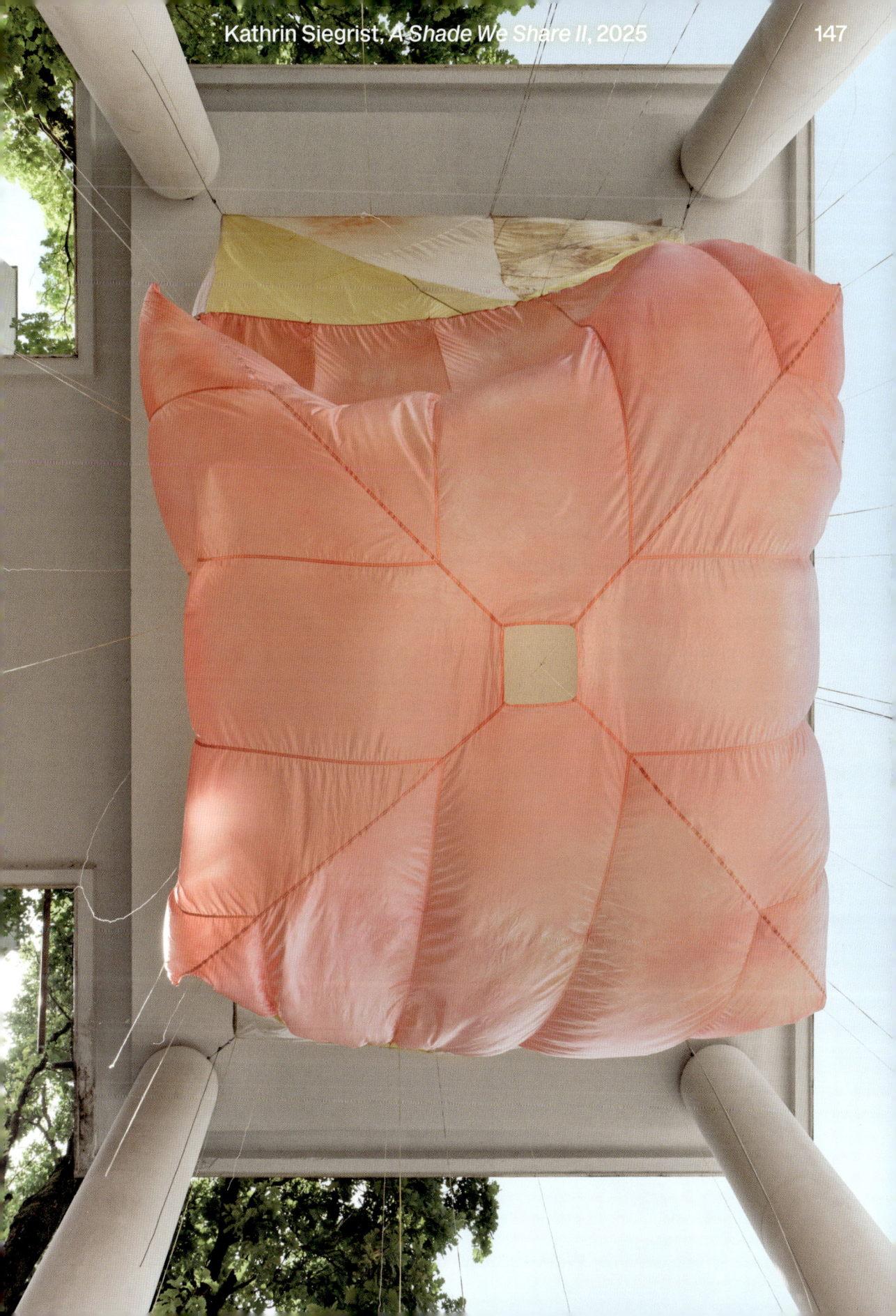

Department of Slovene Studies at the Faculty of Arts in Ljubljana. Poetry should be presented together with contemporary art as an incredible effort to hold the openness of the mind. The history of freedom is to be seen as intertwined with the findings of literature since even our brain is a literary machine. Our brain uses parables to understand space and time. Story, projection, and parable precede grammar. Therefore, language follows from these mental capacities. It is for these reasons that art and literature are fundamental, not because of taste, not because of form, not because of subject matter only, but because their mere existence guarantees that we will find a way to move forward, to rebalance, and restore the values of life and freedom.

In the first room, you will encounter the work of Ajša Pengov and another installation of Silvan Omerzu. Ajša Pengov was an artist and puppet designer active in the period following the Second World War. She created many figures, among them the puppets that are present in this room, a few from the performances *Zlata ribica* (*The Golden Fish*) and *Žogica Marogica* (*Speckles the Ball*). It will be difficult to find an adult in Ljubljana who does not know about the history of Žogica. The play, after a story written by the Czech author Jan Malík (1904–80), premiered in 1951 in what was then the City Puppet Theatre of Ljubljana. It tells the story of a childless elderly couple who adopt a ball that one day appears through the window. One day, bad kites appear through the window and try to take

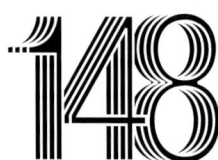

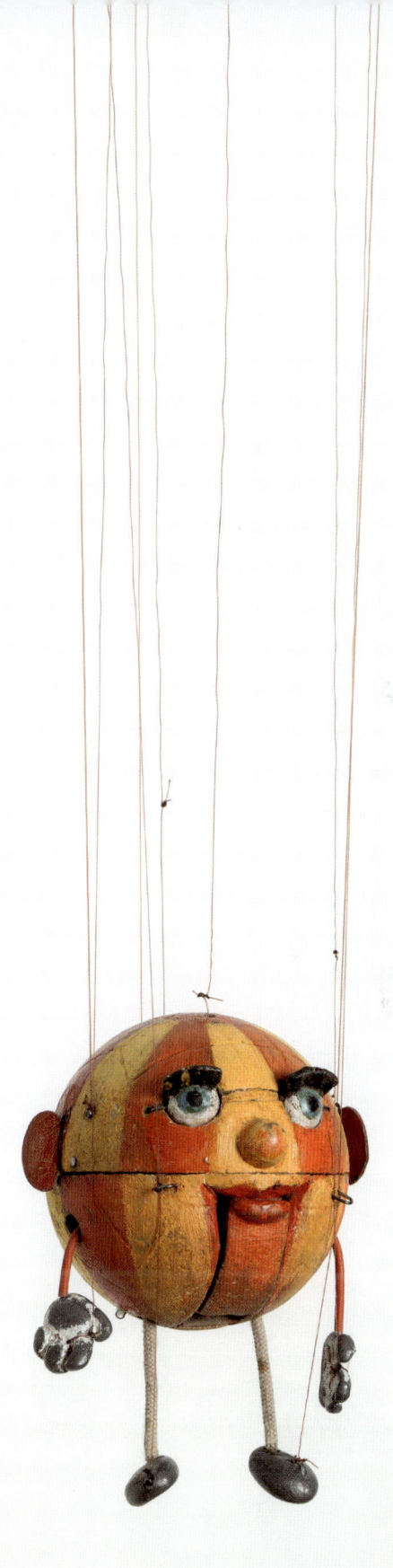

Ajša Pengov, *Žogica Marogica (Speckles the Ball)*, 1951

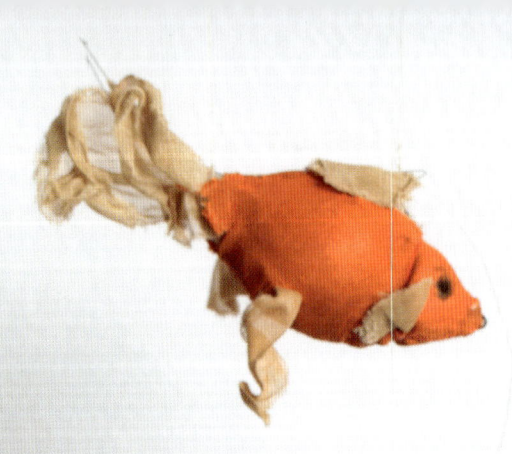

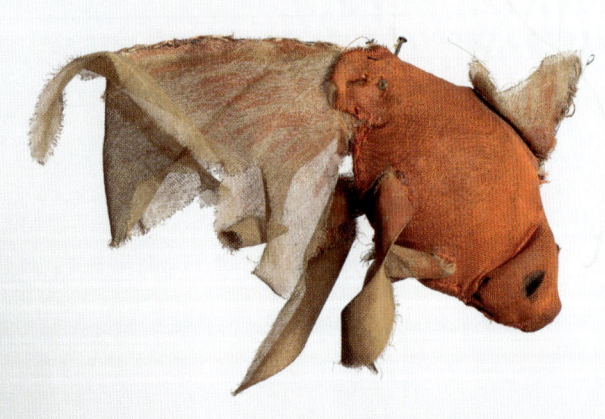

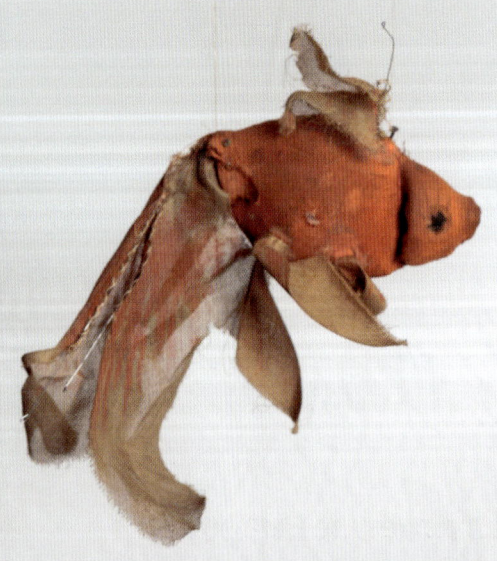

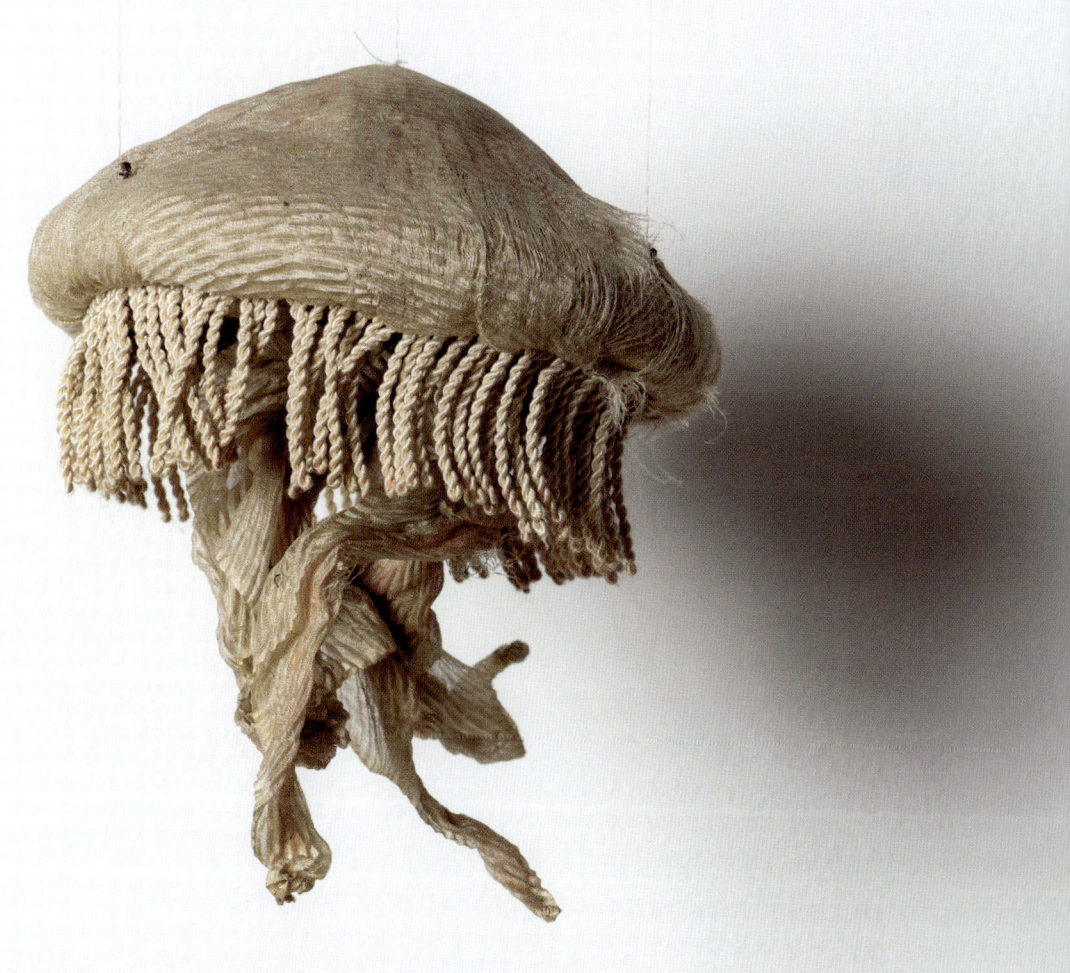

Ajša Pengov, Puppets from *Zlata ribica* (*The Golden Fish*), 1953   151

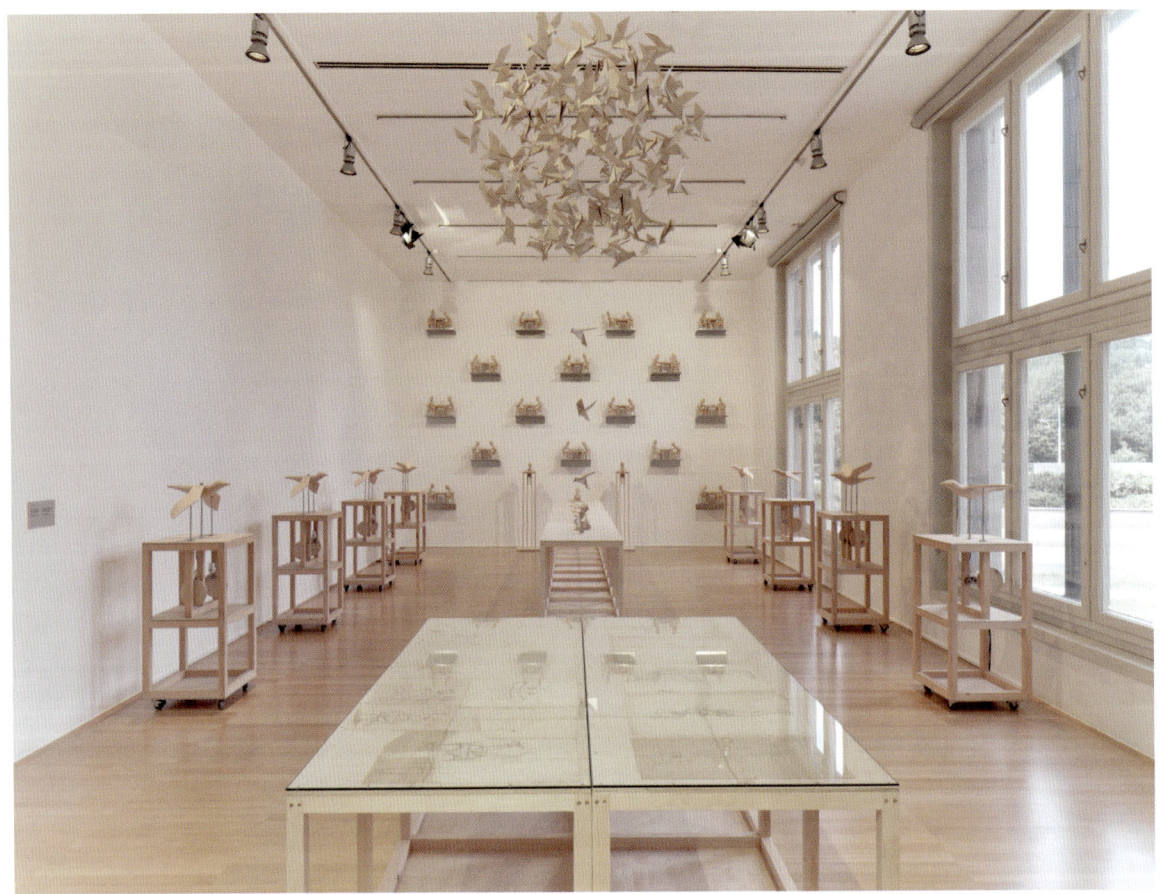

Žogica away. It is with the help of the children of the city that the couple reunites with Žogica, and it all comes to a happy end. In this room, it is important to not only observe the intricacy of the puppets but also the robot-like mechanization of their bodies. Are those who design, construct, and control them their owners? Is there a way to understand autonomy and the common good in the tools that humans create? The intellectual debate around the social, political, and pedagogical function of puppetry is inspiring today. It may serve us to develop a reflection about the need to address the needs of those who do not feel or cannot feel close to culture and education. The questions posed at the time by Ajša Pengov on the indigenous character of those puppets, about their autonomy from humans, are stimulating in light of the challenges we have ahead, the creation of a communicative language able to be understood in every neighbourhood. Like the puppets, we need to move to those places that do not welcome us. Or not yet.

The last wall of the room hosts the work by Silvan Omerzu. At a long table, a small figure of a poet sits on a tall, slender chair, writing. The sheet of paper gradually transforms—words written on it turn into an origami bird, which eventually takes flight and joins a multitude of paper birds hanging from the ceiling. This transformation symbolizes how poetry transcends the written word and spreads into the world. Behind the poet, small figures also seated at tables, writing,

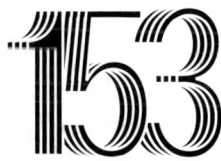

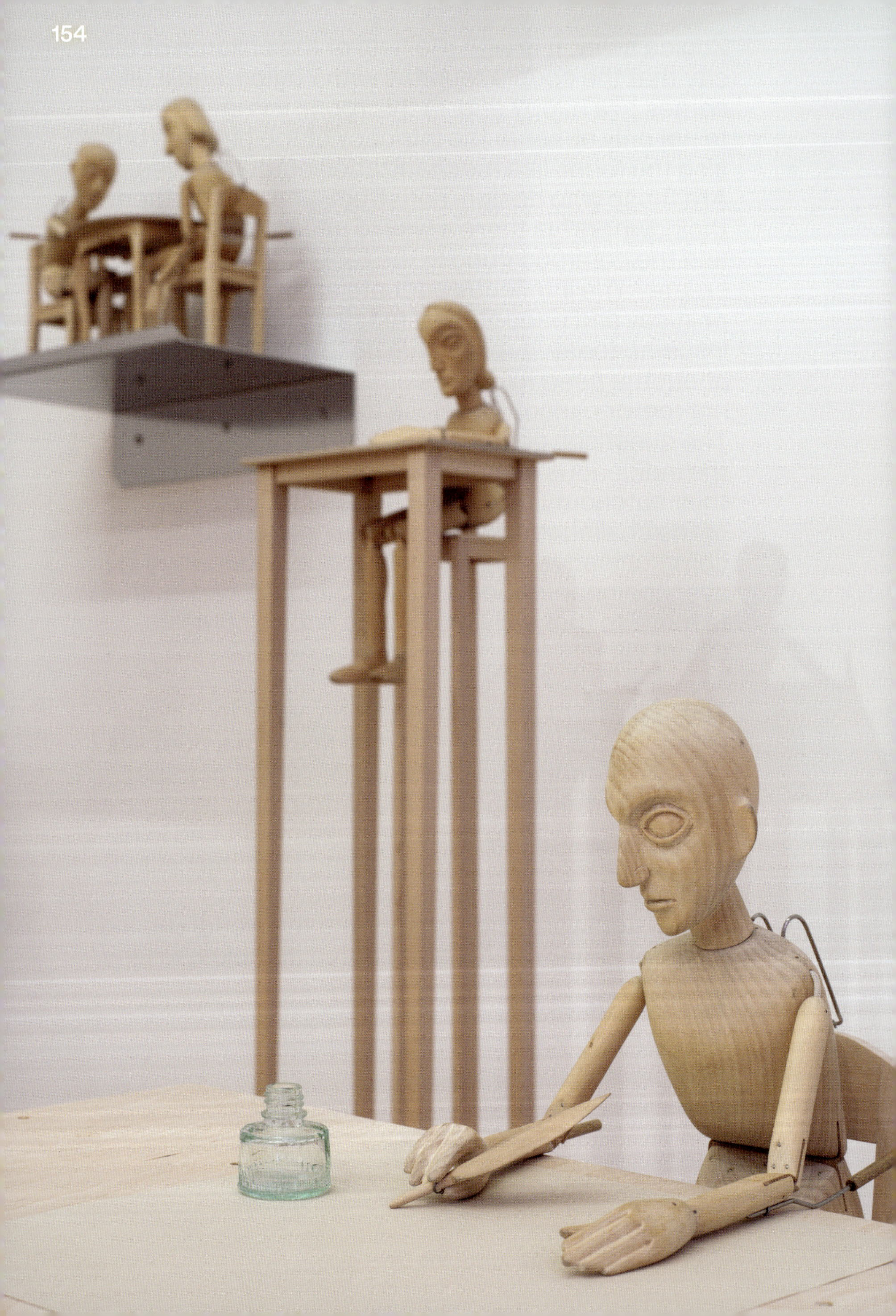

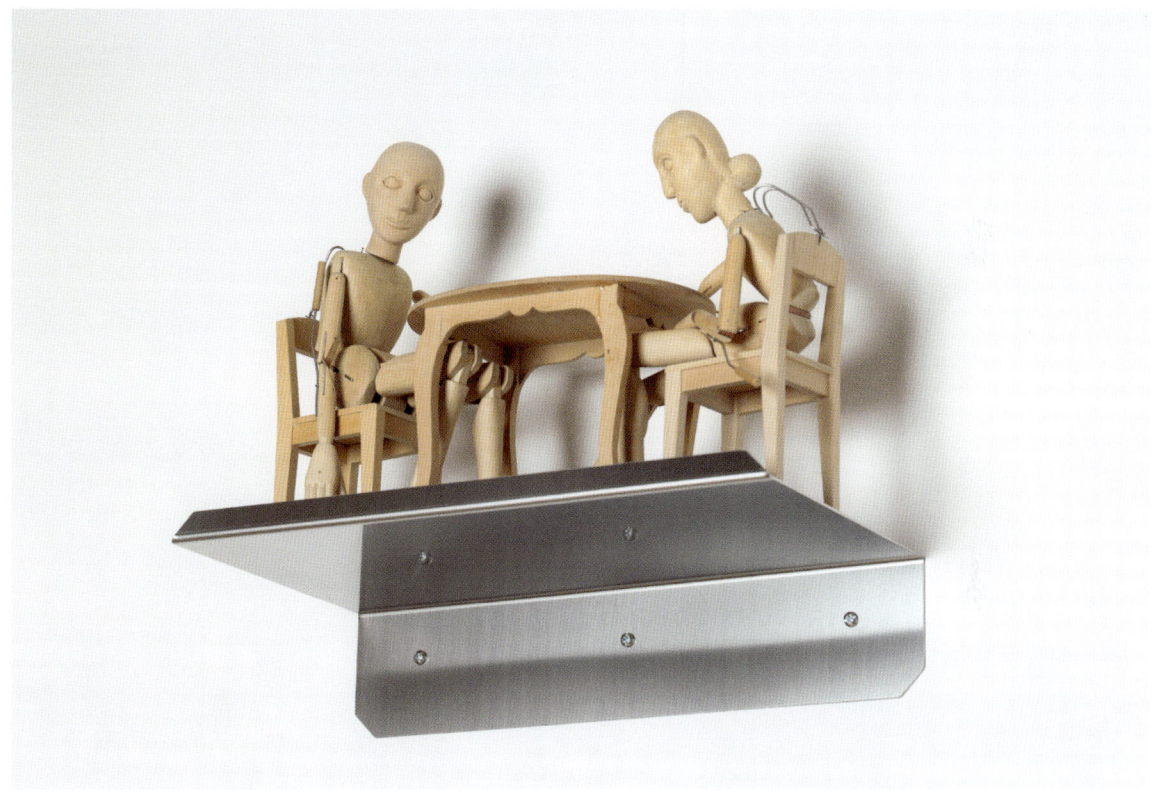

Silvan Omerzu, *Table for a Poet*, 2025

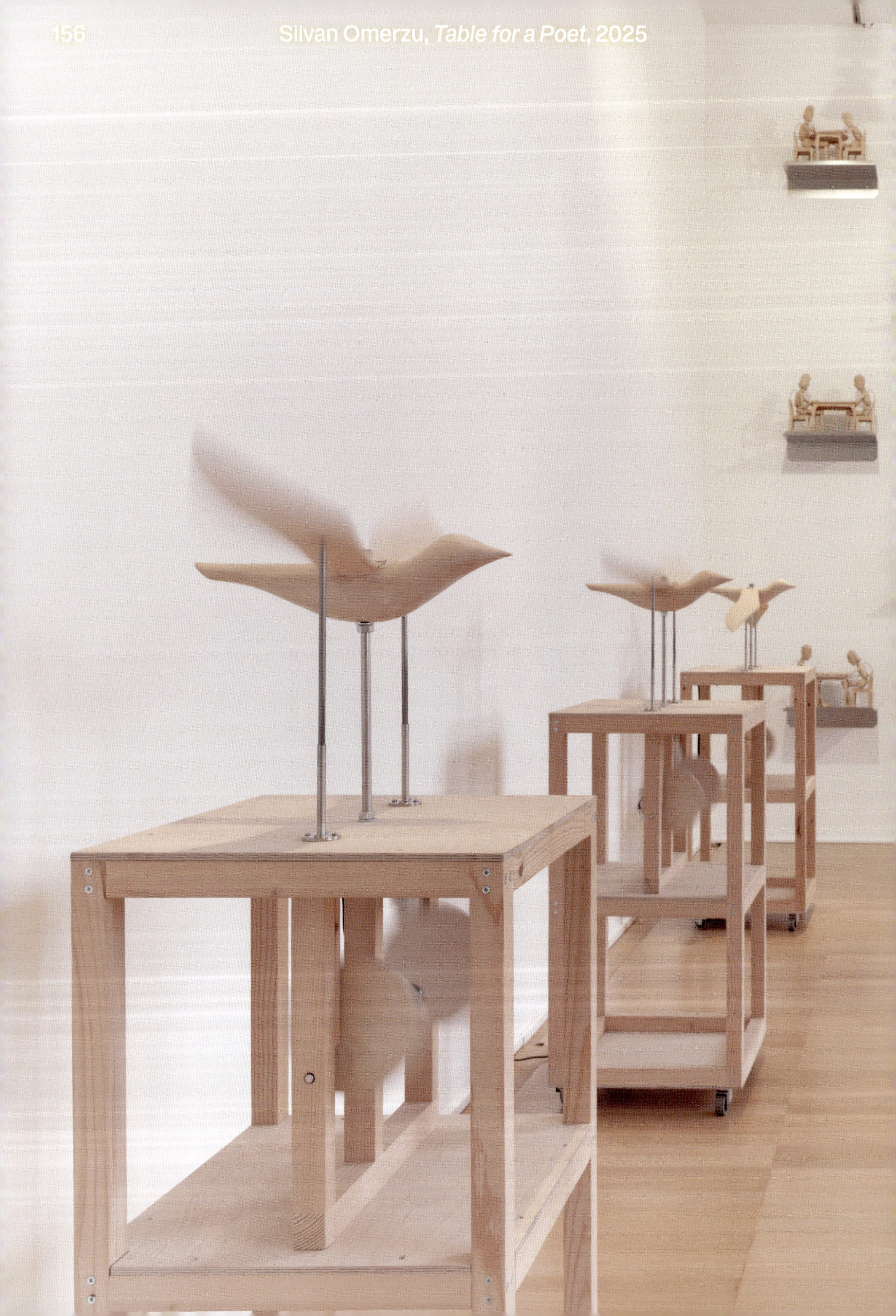

creating a recurring motif of poetic creation.
The installation of wooden puppets with metal guides
explores the relationship between creative freedom
and external constraints.

To continue viewing the exhibition, you need to exit this
room and go to the one on the other side of the wall
behind Omerzu's installation. There is the work of Noor
Abed. For this room, the artist created an installation
that refers to how drawing, photography and
performance interact in her practice. On one wall are
images of a female dancer (a fighter) with a stick, and
on the other side, detailed drawings of the stick and its
movements, accompanied by choreographic notations.
The stick, a simple element found in nature, is one of
the oldest material artifacts or tools used by humans.
Sticks have played a vital role in the technological,
social, political, aesthetic, and religious development of
humanity and some animal species. Here, it becomes
a medium of dance, and dancing with a stick becomes
a way to propose an eloquent way of addressing war
and the absence of war. The work of Noor Abed talks
about ways of igniting a collective dream and the public
imagination oriented towards protecting the vulnerable
and the marginalized. This dance is magic, a social
dance, a political dance, a war dance, and a dance for
freedom.

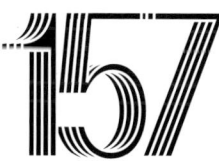

Walk-through of the Exhibition

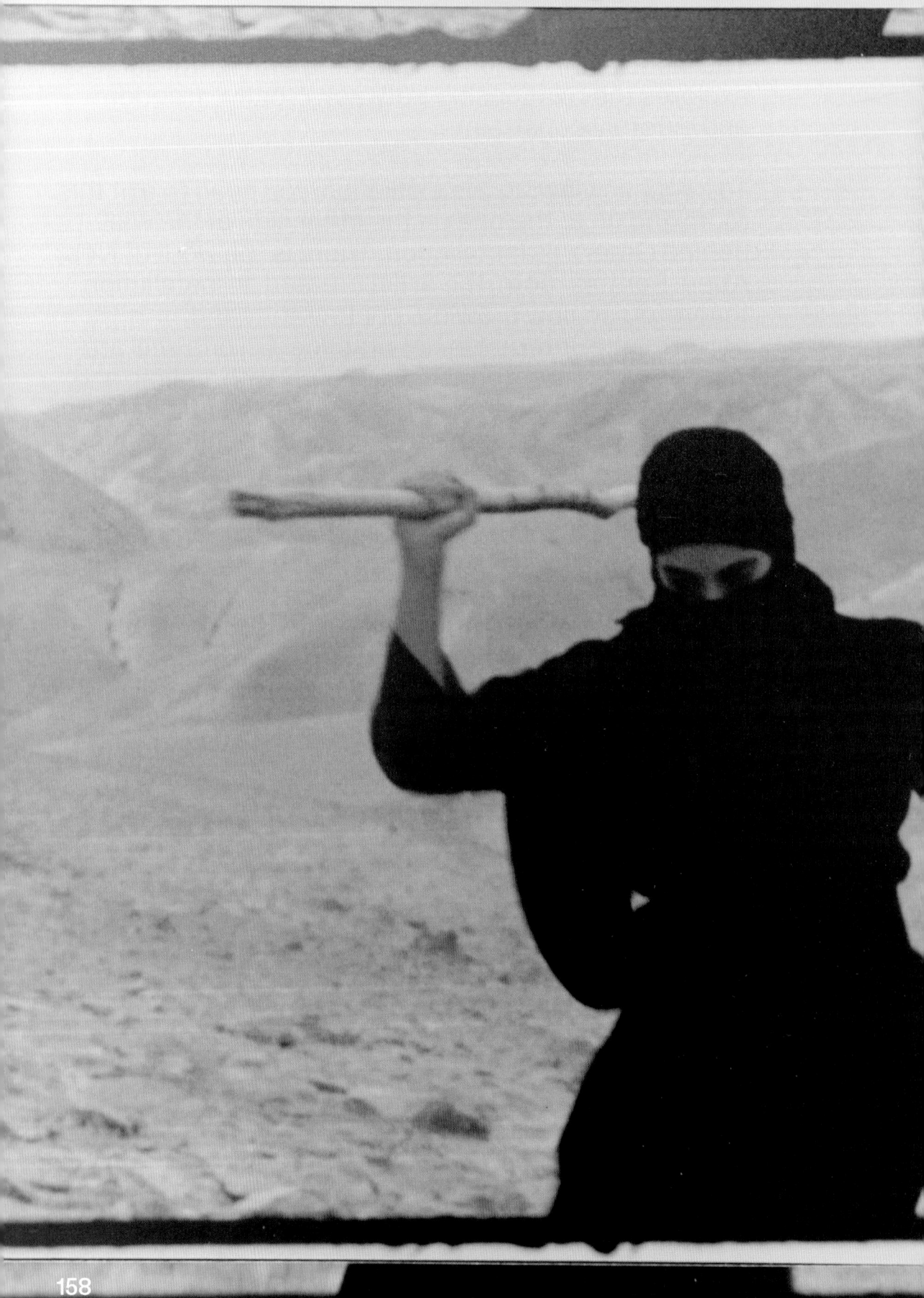

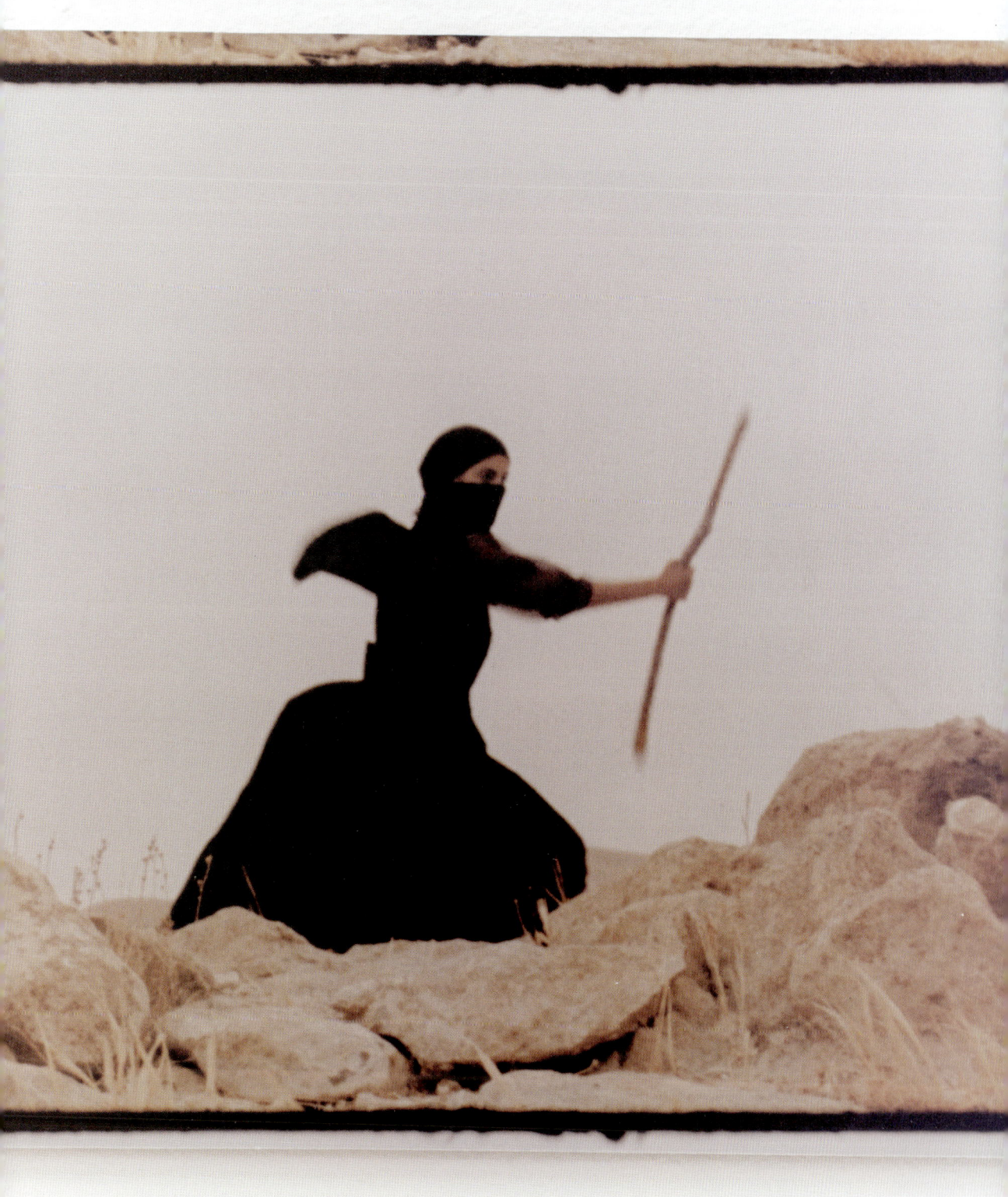

Noor Abed, *a study of a stick:*
movement notations and notes on defiance, 2025

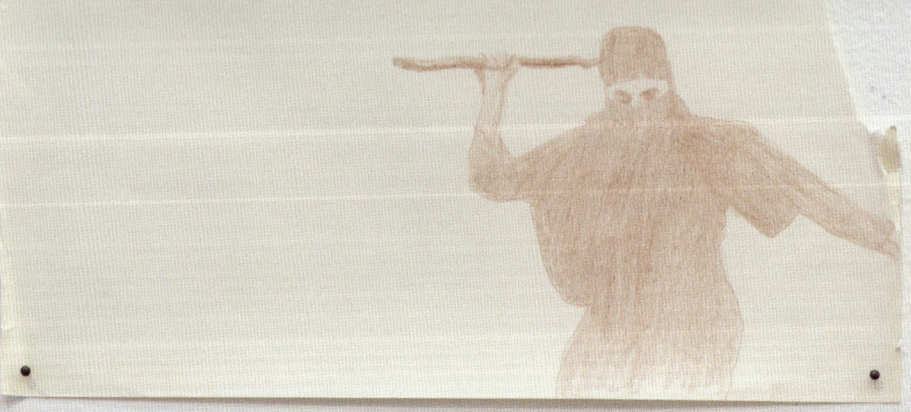

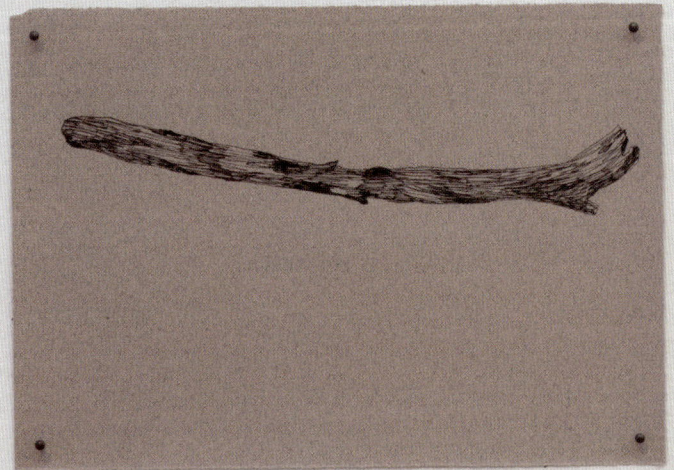

TEXT NOTATION

Key : R-arm : Right arm
L-arm : Left arm
Sh-Flex : Shoulder flexion angle (degrees)
El-Flex : Elbow flexion angle (degrees)
Motion : Movement description

1) "initial hold"
• R-arm : resting, wounded
• L-arm : partially resting
• El-Flex : ~ 45°
• Sh-Flex : ~ 20° (slightly raised)
• Stick — held loosely, angled downward
• Motion : preparing to move, minimal

2) "raising the stick"
• L-arm : moving slowly
• El-Flex : increases to ~ 90°
• Sh-Flex : raises to ~ 60°
• Stick — lifted upward, about 30–45° (horizontal)
• Motion : slow, insistence

3) "the throw"
• L-arm : extends,
• El-Flex : from 90° to about 150°
• Sh-Flex : steady, slightly forward (~60–70°)
• Stick — moving forward, upward, almost 45° (vertical)
• Motion : throwing motion

4) "stick release"
• L-arm : full extension
• El-Flex : ~ 150°
• Sh-Flex : stable
• Stick — released, upward
• Motion : stick moves away from hand

5) "after release"
• L-arm : drops down
• El-Flex : ~ 30°
• Sh-Flex : decreases, ~ 20°
• Stick — no longer in hand

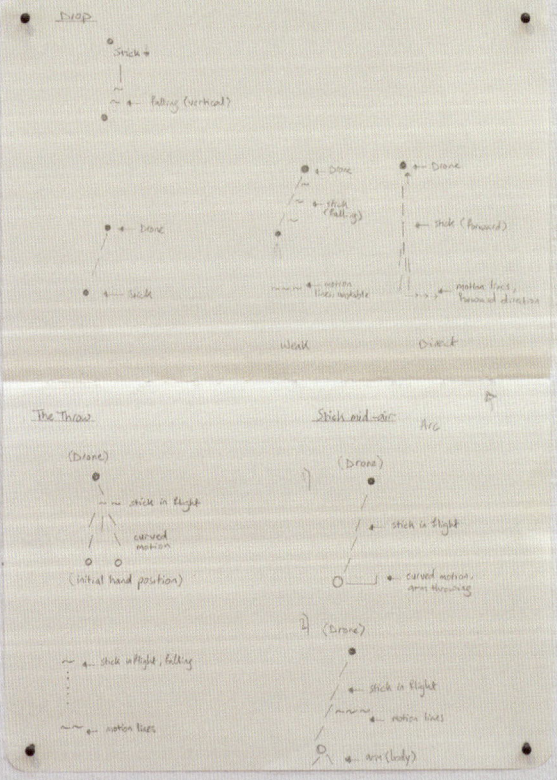

Drop

Stick ↑

~ ← falling (vertical)

The Throw

Stick mid-air   Arc

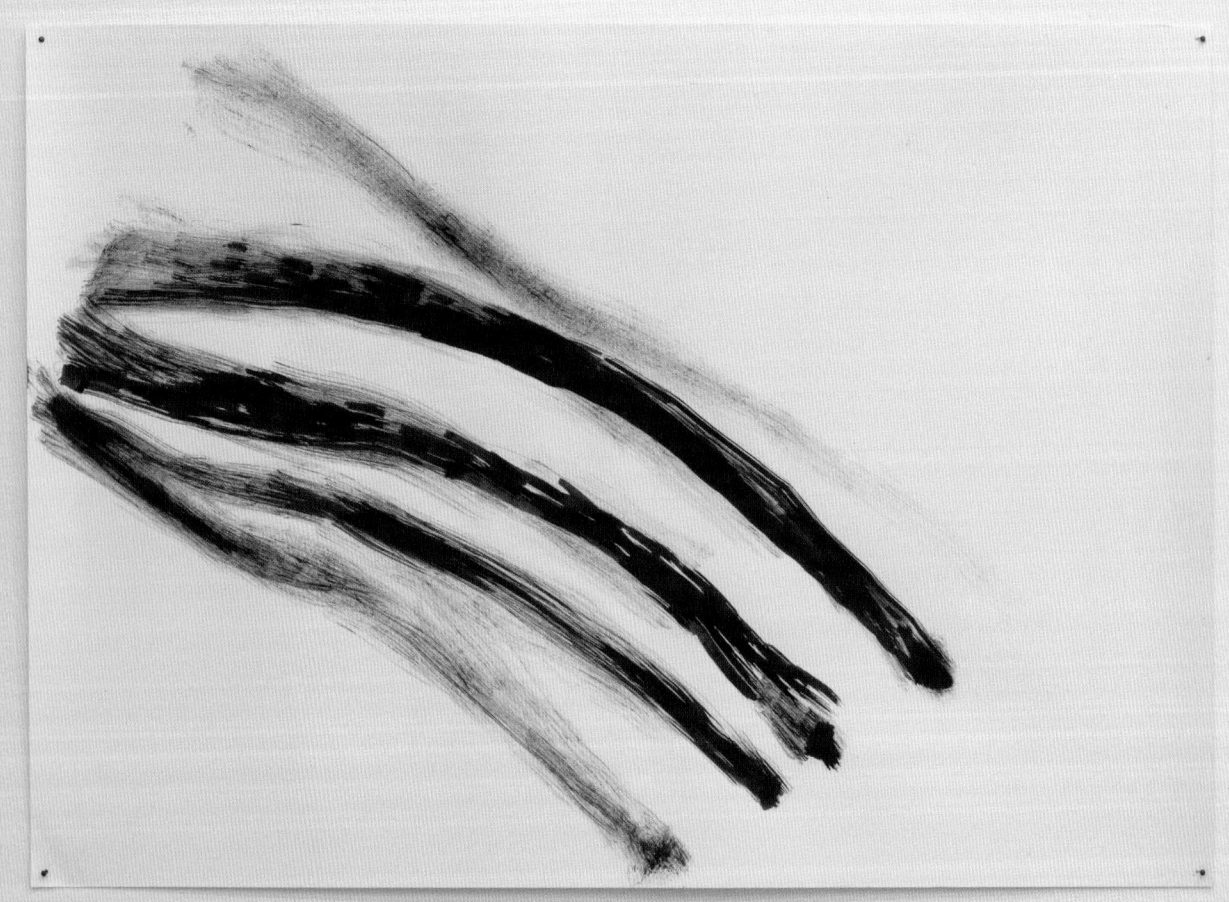

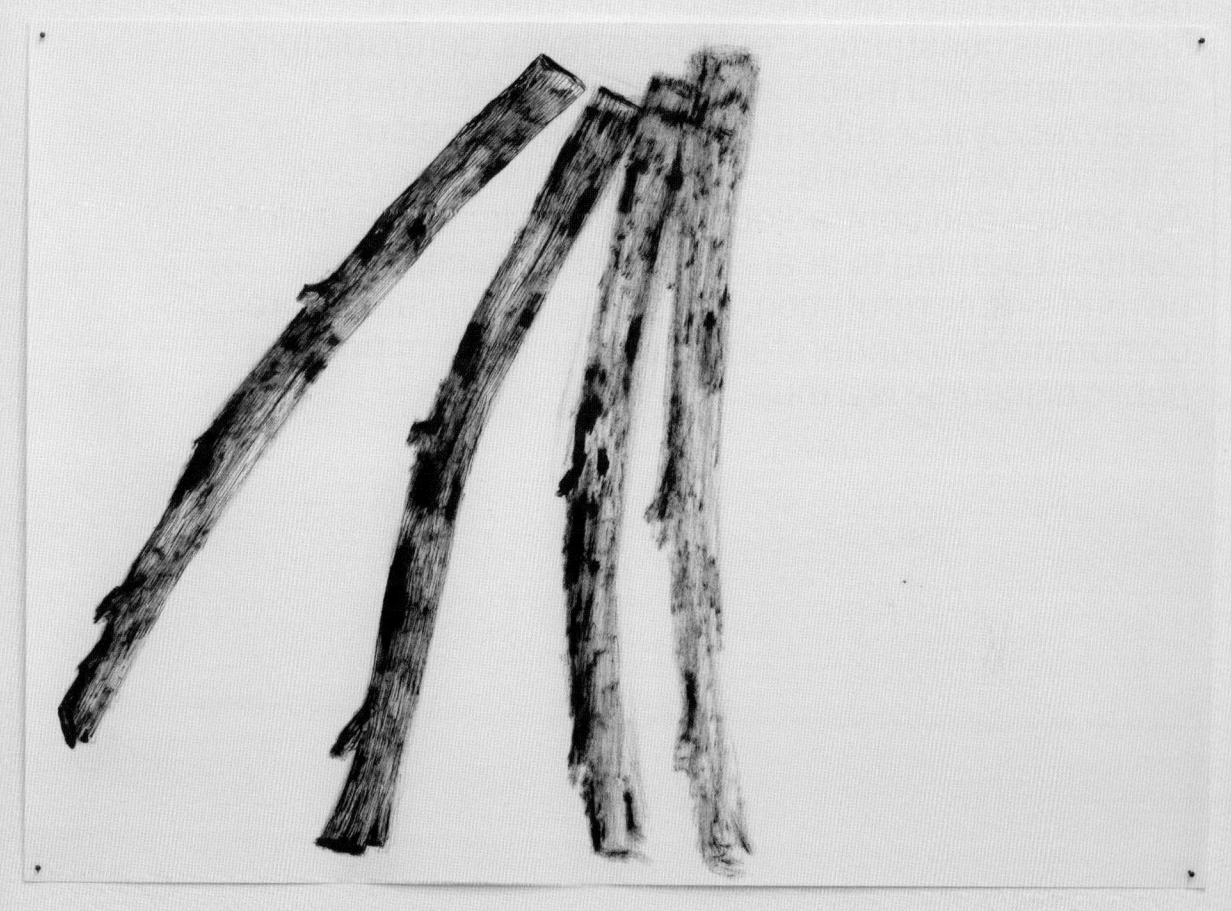

Noor Abed, *a study of a stick:*
movement notations and notes on defiance, 2025

When you leave this room, if you look to your right, you will find a monumental wall drawing by Juan Pérez Agirregoikoa. The piece with the ironic title *Who keeps the zoo?* is comprised of several diagrams inspired by the method of Venn diagrams, a visual tool that highlights the overlap between two or more seemingly contradictory statements that was popularized by the mathematician John Venn (1834–1923) in the 1880s. In his practice, Juan Pérez Agirregoikoa has always been fascinated by how politics and ideologies constantly create paradoxes, contradictory statements, and practices. And yet, far from being paralyzed by it or entering a permanent mood of cynicism, we need to accept this as a creative force. Paradoxes and contradictions are artistic forces inside politics. Learning to deal with this dynamics, going beyond simple refutation, and giving ourselves a more comprehensive understanding of the force of political public discourse is a must.

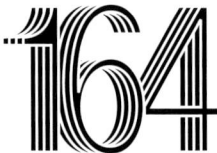

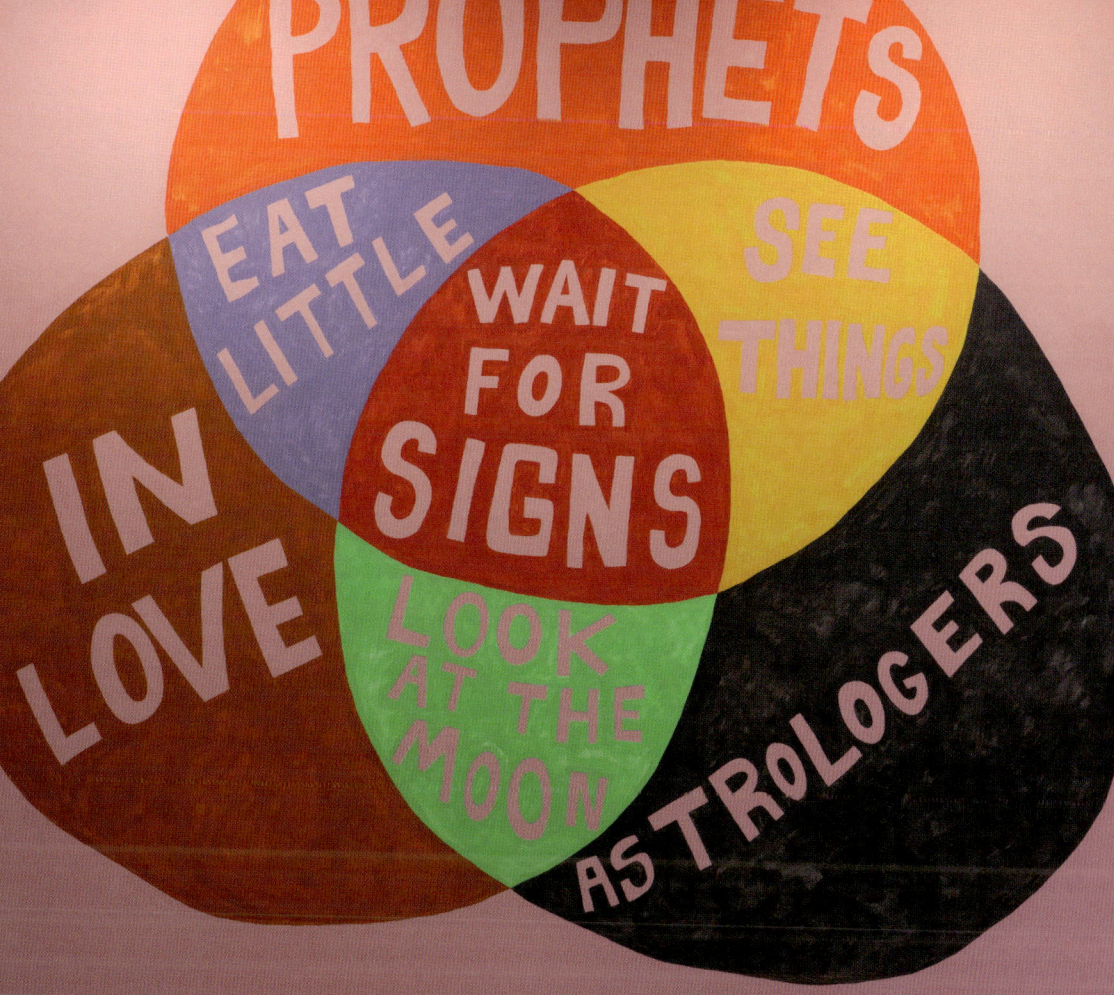

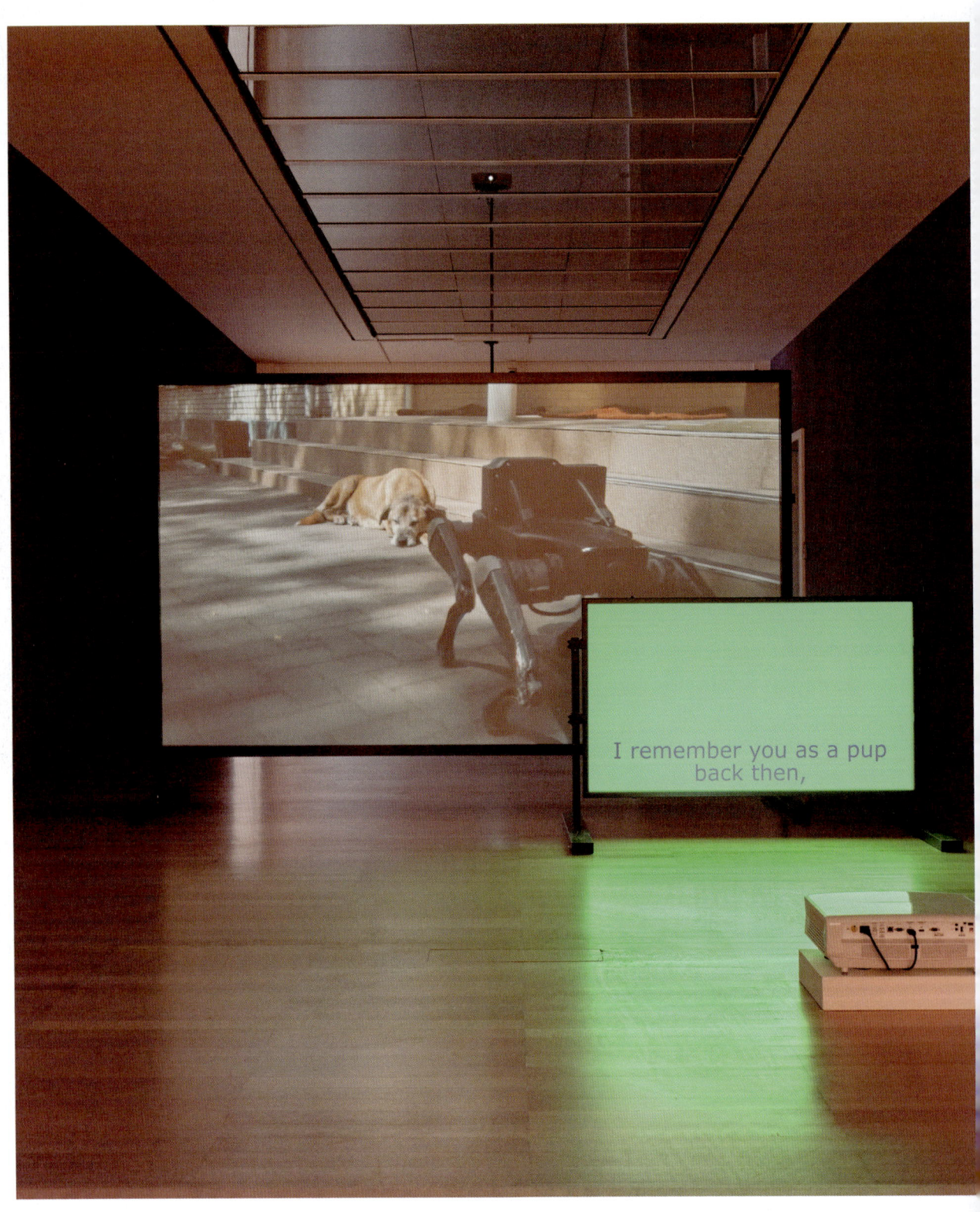

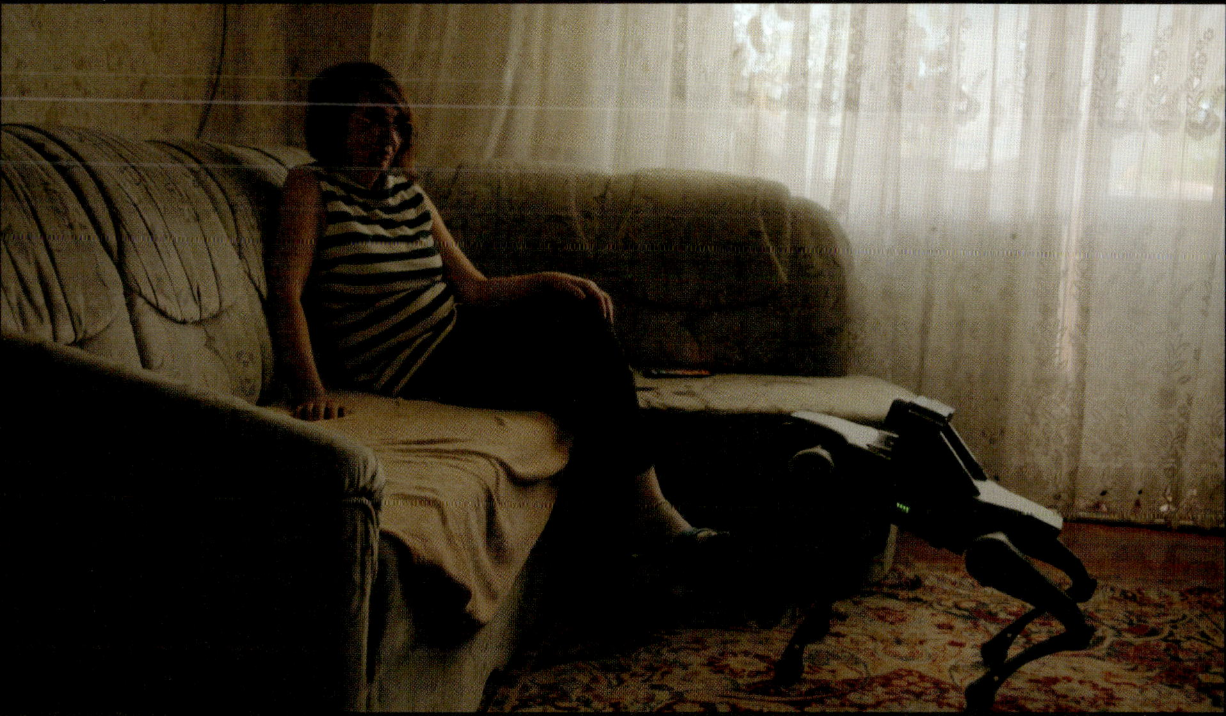

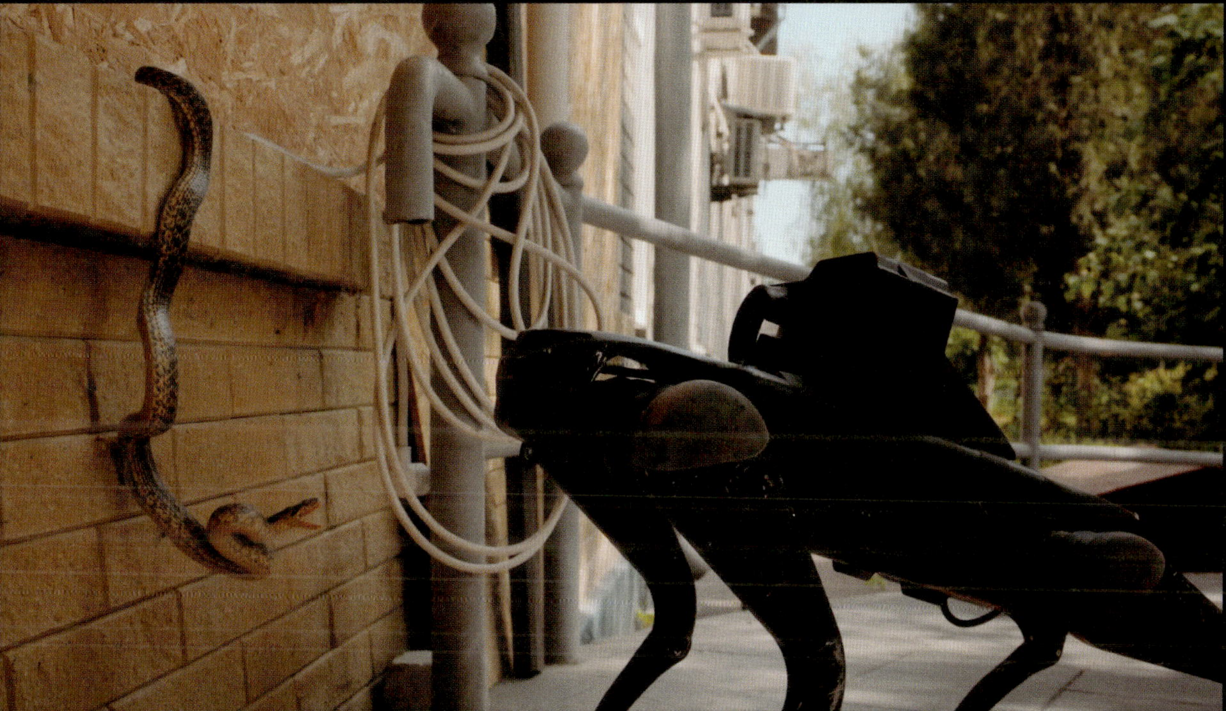

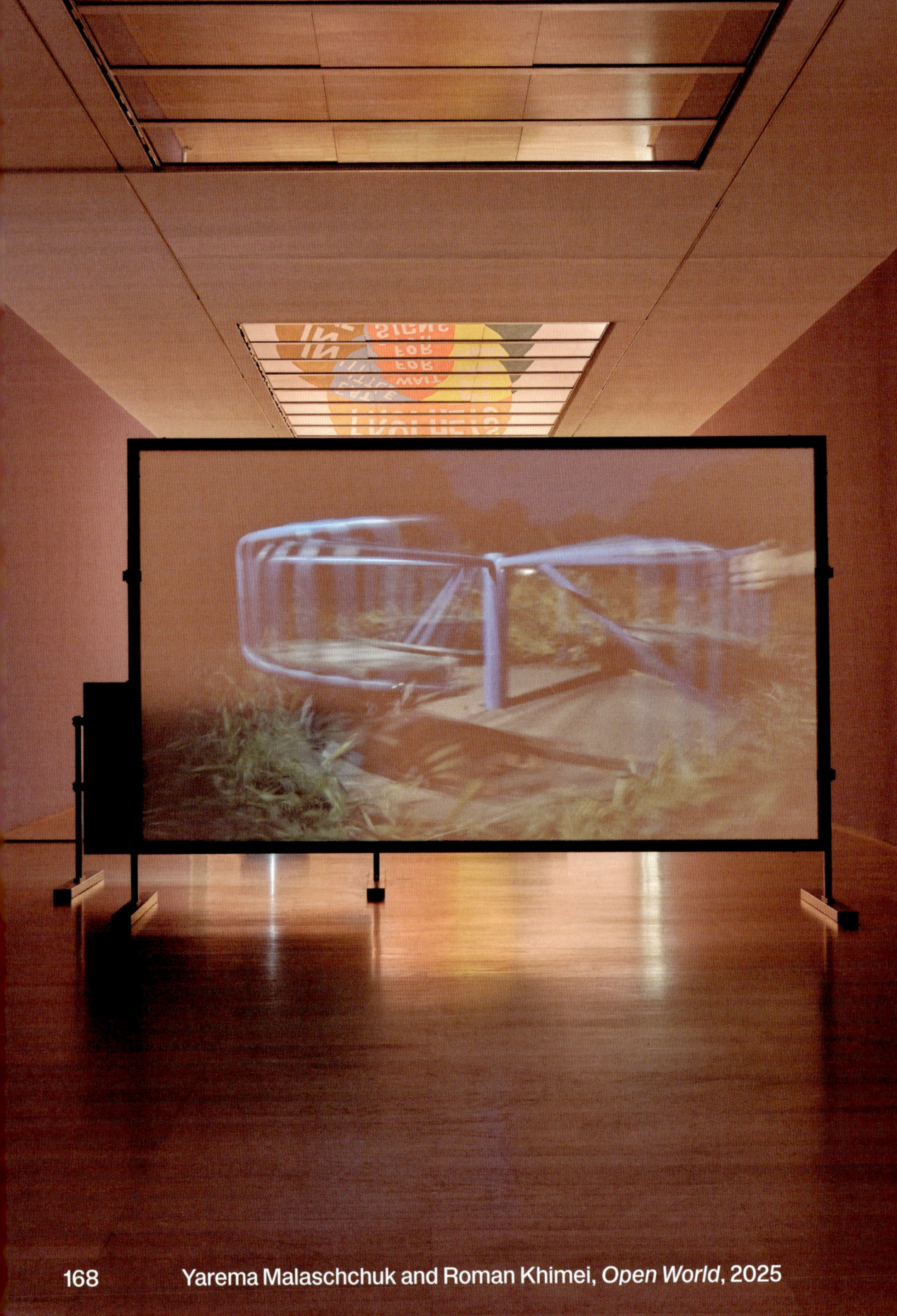

Yarema Malaschchuk and Roman Khimei, *Open World*, 2025

In the second gallery of the exhibition—its third room—there is the work of the duo Yarema Malashchuk and Roman Khimei. It is a two-screen projection work, a film telling the story of a young boy who was forced to leave his city due to relentless shelling by Russian military forces during the occupation of Ukraine. Living abroad, the boy discovers a unique way to reconnect with his homeland through the Robot Dog—an advanced robotic device recently acquired by the Ukrainian military for reconnaissance and defence. In a scenario reminiscent of a video game, the boy uses the Robot Dog to virtually navigate the streets of his former neighborhood, rekindling connections with neighbors and friends whose families remained behind. By highlighting the dual purpose of this technology—both as a tool for military operations and as a bridge for reconnection—the work delves into the complex dynamics of displacement, community, and the resilience of separated Ukrainians.

November, a double screen projection by Jane Jin Kaisen, occupies the next gallery together with the painting installation by Nohemí Pérez. The two works are deeply connected. The darkness of the night obliging our senses to adapt to be able to see and perceive has a stern parallel with the darkness of the crimes we are committing as a species. The darkness of our times takes a light gothic twist in Kaisen's work. In the dark, the world's logic is not the same as in the daytime. After continuous years of crisis—war,

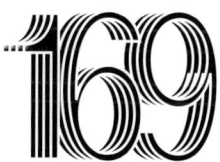

169

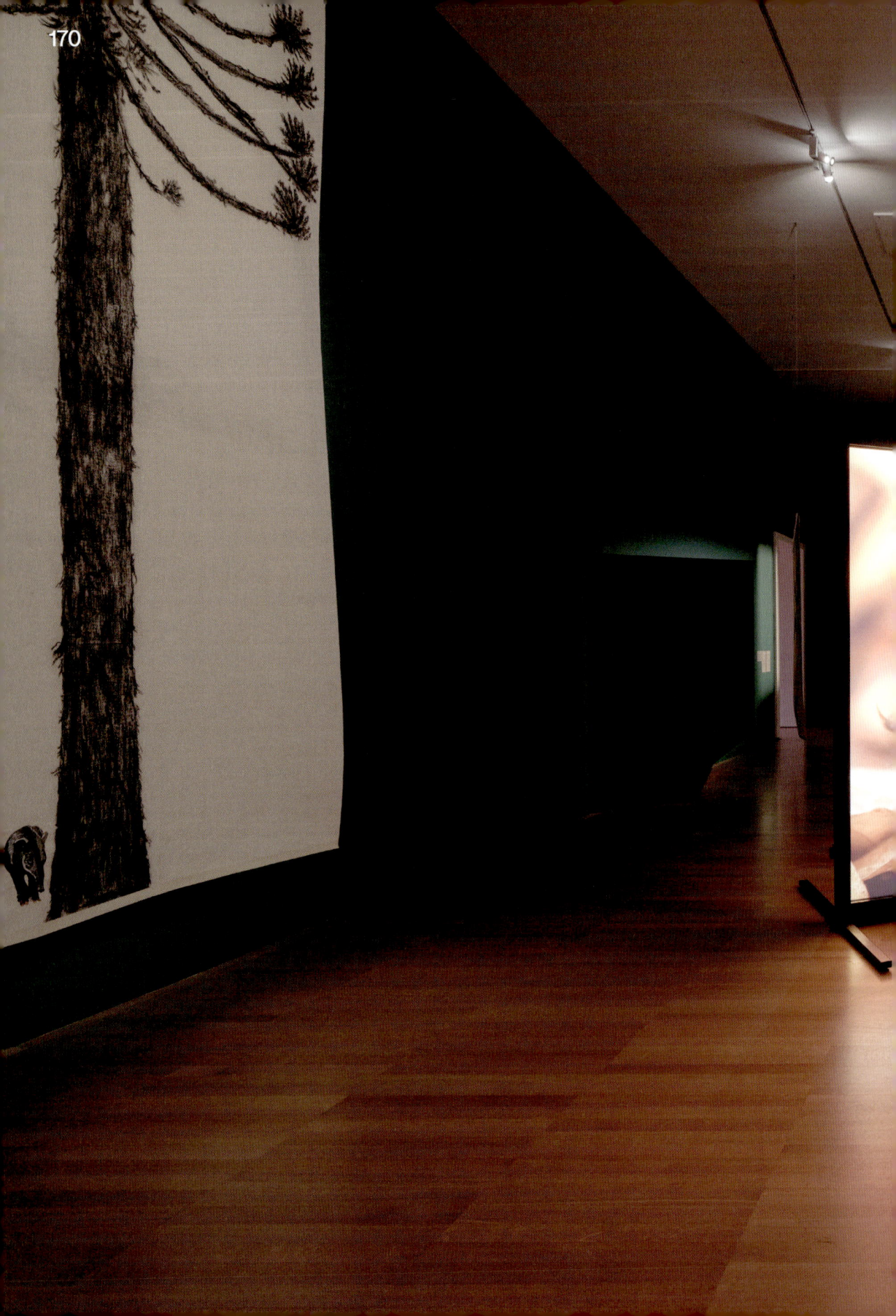

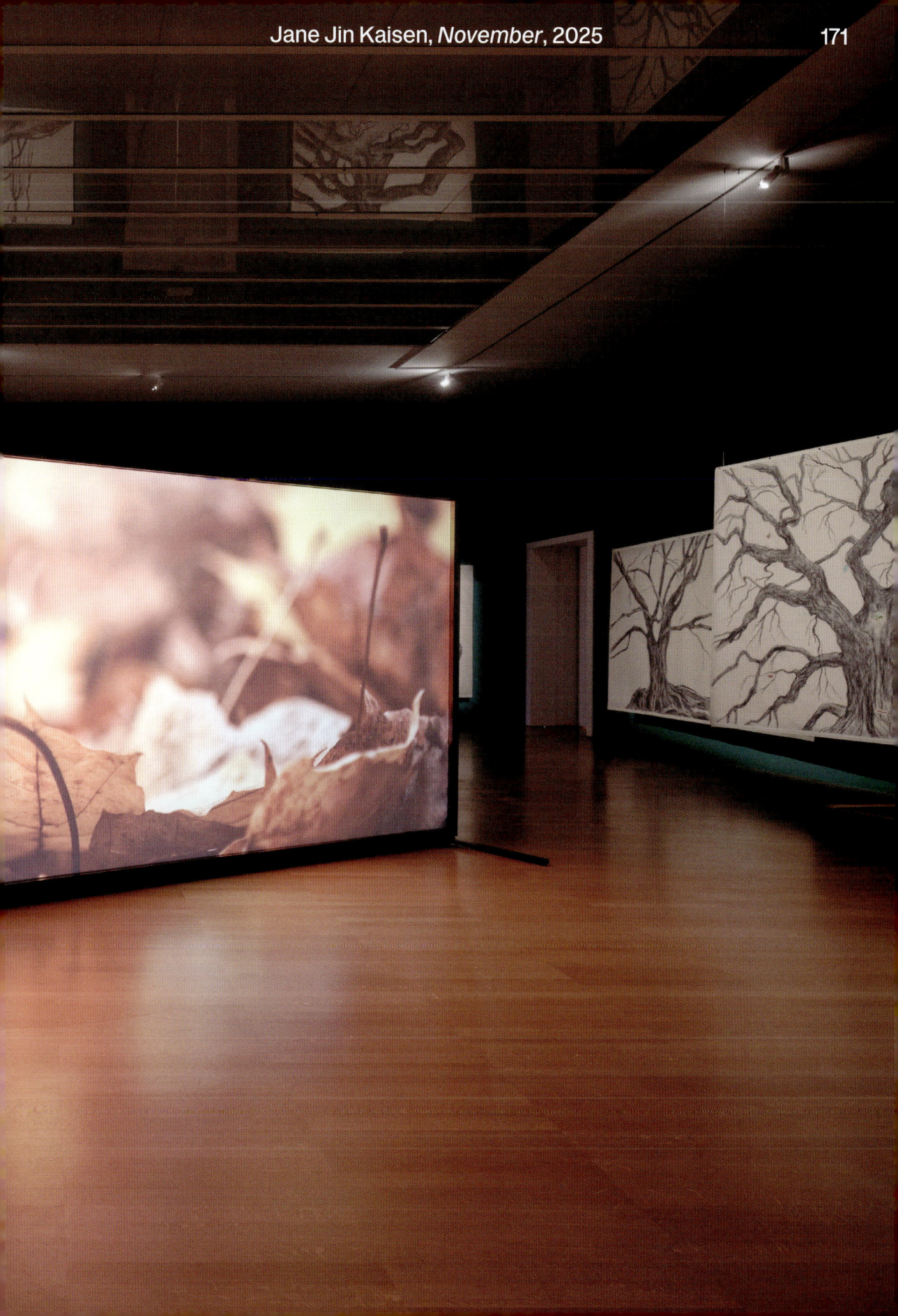

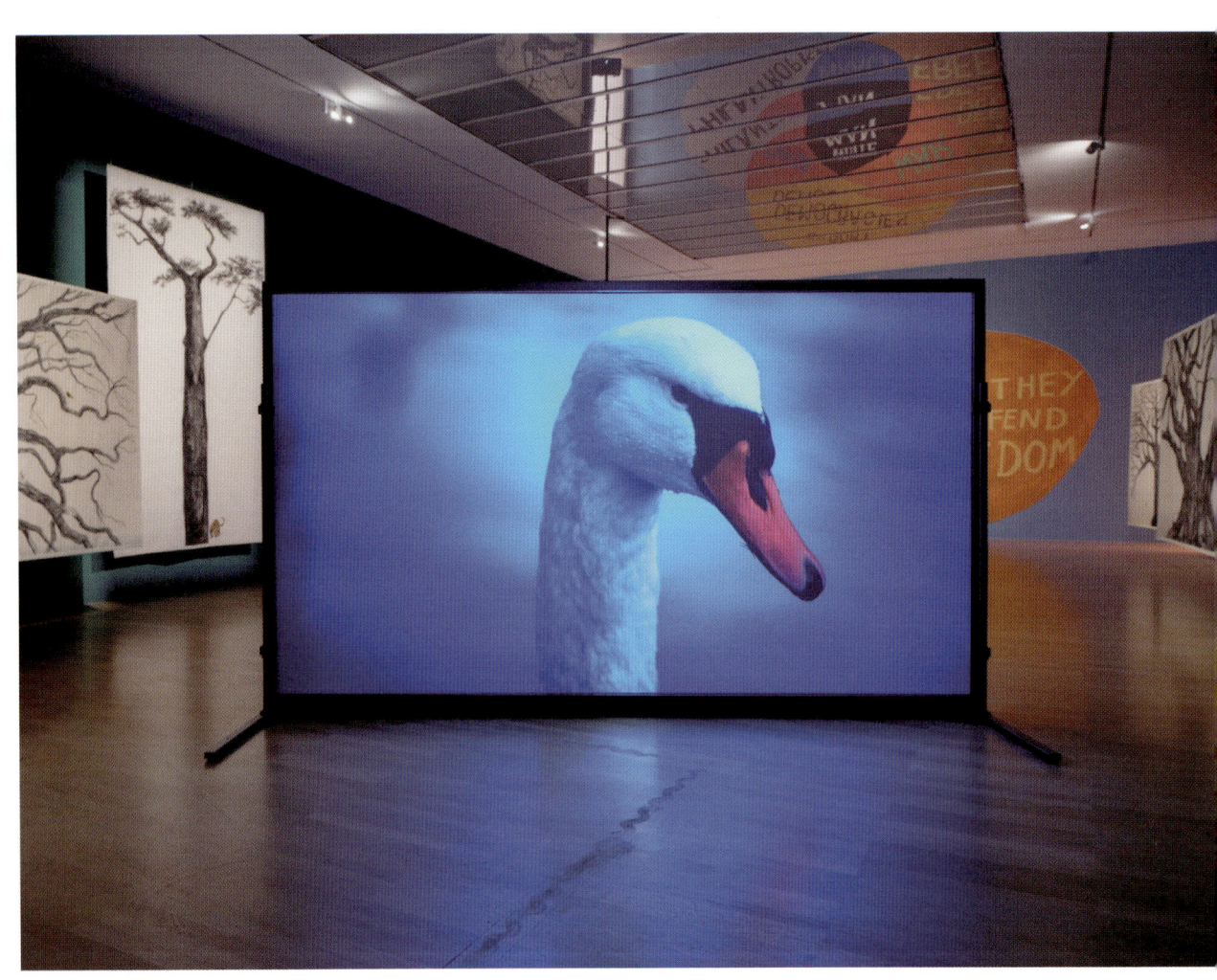

Jane Jin Kaisen, *November*, 2025

economic pandemonium, the rise of nationalism, advanced technologies deployed for profit and destruction, socialist advance followed by crushing defeat, and a devastating pandemic—learning to see and act in darkness seems a must. Including a poetic response to Kaisen's video by the Swedish poet Mara Lee, the work is both a *paideia* and a visual essay on the current moods. Paideia in the ancient Greek sense, given that the work refers to the development of moral character, intellectual ability, and civic responsibility through art-making and exposure to art. Nohemí Pérez's newly produced work, a forest of guardians, is also a story of darkness, about all the enemies of nature: humans, fires, extractivist disasters .... It is an installation made of tree witnesses in charge of the ecosystems and conservation of forests, valleys, and the wilderness of Earth. Among these gigantic trees, all painted black, color emerges through the presence of small embroidered animals. Embroidery here is more than just decorative needlework—it holds deep cultural, social, and symbolic significance. Its delicacy and its colors symbolize wealth and prosperity, one that is present in life but humans tend to disrespect. We can associate both the trees and the insects with the need to find immortality and wisdom. Pérez's work is pure ecology, visually presenting us with an incredible image of how species interact with each other and their surroundings, including climate, human, and cultural influences on nature.

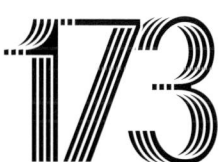

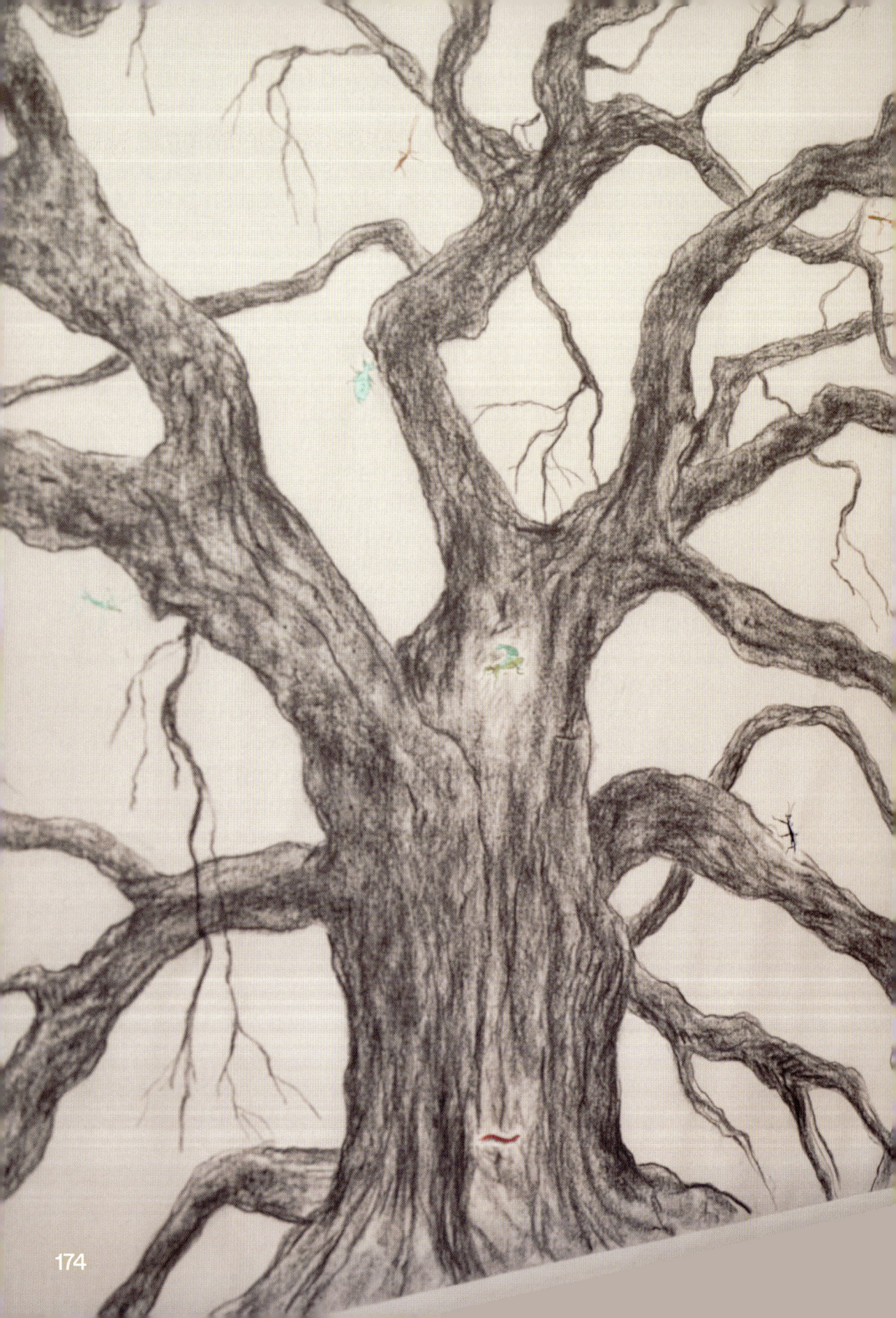

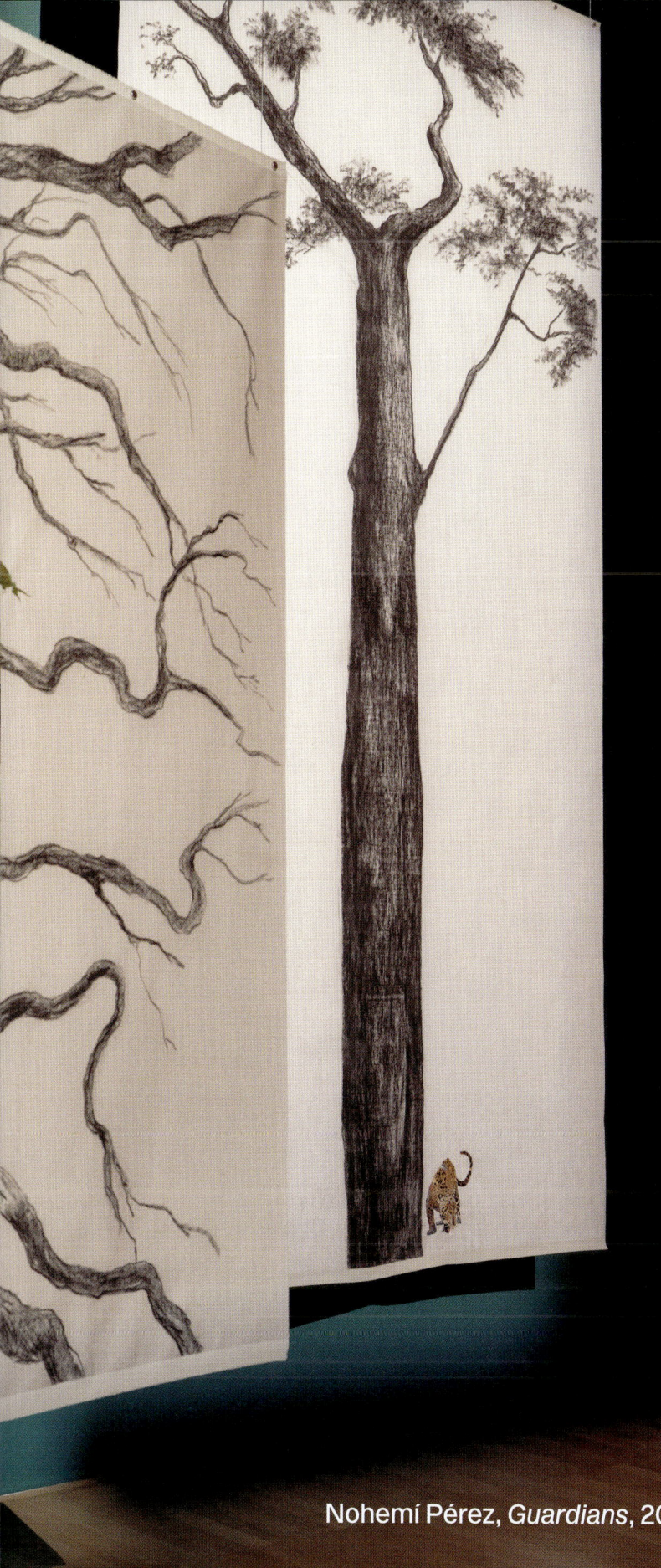

Nohemí Pérez, *Guardians*, 2025

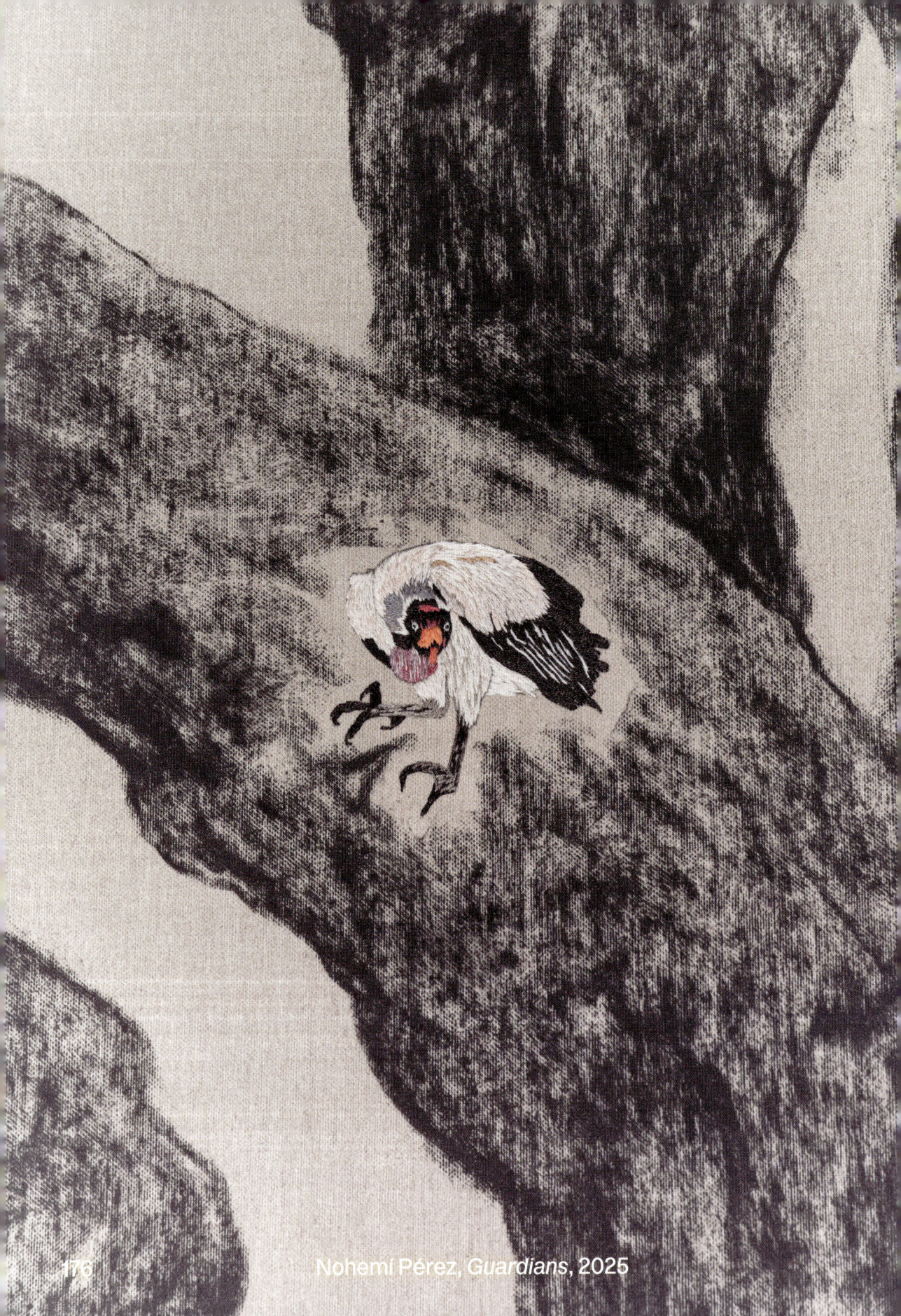

Nohemí Pérez, *Guardians*, 2025

Oracles and Sublimation:

FANTASIES OF THE END OF THE WORLD

Renata

Salecl

Renata Salecl

In the past, oracles have often predicted calamities such as plagues, earthquakes, and wars, or apocalyptic events, which would bring about the collapse of life on Earth. Oracles were sometimes living persons, but their wisdom was often linked to mythical figures found in religious texts, Greek mythology, or science fiction novels and films.

At a time when we are facing wars, climate change, and, in many countries, a turn towards authoritarianism, we may feel that the end of the world as we have known it is coming.[1] Unsurprisingly, oracles are making a powerful comeback today, drawing on their rich historical, mythical, and religious legacies while reinvigorating their role as modern-day prophets, analysts, and sophisticated algorithms. When predicting what is still to come, we see two distinct archetypes of oracle figures. On the one hand, we have authoritative voices, such as scientists and climate experts, who alert us to environmental crises, pandemics, and geopolitical upheavals. These oracles rely on research and data, and their forecasts warn about the potential trajectories our world may take if we ignore scientific discoveries. On the other hand, we have a new breed of leaders, from social media influencers and self-help gurus to charismatic religious figures, who deliver mystical and often apocalyptic predictions. These prophecies rapidly circulate through the mass media, social media platforms,

1 According to a Pew Research Center survey conducted in 2022, 39% of US adults believe that humanity is "living in the end times." This finding was part of a broader study examining the intersection of religious beliefs and environmental views. The survey revealed that this belief is more prevalent among certain religious groups, with 76% of historically Black Protestants and 63% of Evangelical Protestants affirming this view. In contrast, only 27% of Catholics and 23% of religiously unaffiliated individuals shared this belief. Jeff Diamant, "About Four-in-Ten U.S. Adults Believe Humanity Is 'Living in the End Times'," *Pew Research Center*, December 8, 2022, https://www.pewresearch.org/short-reads/2022/12/08/about-four-in-ten-u-s-adults-believe-humanity-is-living-in-the-end-times/.

and internet forums, and frequently contribute to increased anxiety in society, while some also provide false hope.

Prophecies raise essential questions about determinism and free will. Can the future truly be predicted? If so, does that knowledge fix our fate into an unchangeable reality? The question is also whether predictions become self-fulfilling prophecies. Take, for instance, climate change: alarming forecasts have the power to galvanize individuals and communities into action, sparking innovative solutions and collective initiatives. However, overly pessimistic predictions can also instill resignation, leading many to adopt a passive stance in the face of looming threats. In this case, despair easily fuels inaction and ultimately ushers in a bleak reality.

Canadian psychologist Steven J. Heine pointed out that regarding predictions that people try to get out of genetic tests, we need to consider that the oracle's crystal ball is made of mud.[2] Psychoanalysts would be interested in deciphering what this mud consists of and why people imagine mud to be a crystal ball. In this context, they do not look to oracles to tell them the truth but rather to hear something that resonates with their desires. People might also look at oracles to gain certainty about an uncertain future. Sometimes, oracles thus provide comfort and guidance, while other times they are punishing figures who increase a person's feelings of anxiety and guilt. No matter what people seek to get out of oracles, they reflect people's deepest fears and unconscious drives.[3]

2   Steven J. Heine, *DNA Is Not Destiny: The Remarkable, Completely Misunderstood Relationship between You and Your Genes* (W. W. Norton & Company, 2017).

3   For Carl Jung, oracles allowed people to converse with themselves. In performing this function of internal dialogue, oracles never spoke falsely, for they were a tool for the expression of people's unconscious, or as Jung said, they were the personification of the unconscious. See: Carl G. Jung, *Psychological Types*, ed. R. F. C. Hull, trans. H. G. Baynes (Princeton University Press, 2014).

Renata Salecl

Regarding predictions about the world's end, the anxieties and unconscious drives at work, and the fascination with the apocalypse today are becoming increasingly complicated to understand. For example, nowadays, a particular group of people is fascinated with the idea of the end of the world, which comes from the circles of those passionate about spreading fake news and conspiracy theories on social media. The paradox is that many of these people do not believe in what they spread online, but find a thrill in their messages being liked by their followers and in the angry comments of those who disagree with them. When US-Danish researchers led by Michael Bang Petersen[4] analyzed this phenomenon by interviewing more than 6,000 very active tweeters, they were struck by the fact that a third of those interviewed expressed a desire to see the world as we know it go to hell. For many, the aim was to cause chaos by spreading fake news and conspiracy theories or, like the famous Joker movie, to dream of the world as we know it burning down. These people often fantasize that in the rubble of this world, a small group of survivors could begin to create a new, better world.

Can the concept of sublimation help people deal with the conflicting feelings they might have concerning the destruction of the world, where they are both anxious about it and enjoy fantasizing about it? In popular discourse, sublimation is often apprehended positively as something that can lead to the production of art, literature, and other cultural artefacts. Sigmund Freud perceived sublimation as the redirection of instinctual drives, especially libidinal and aggressive energies, into socially acceptable or culturally

4   Michael Bang Petersen, Mathias Osmundsen, and Kevin Arceneaux, "The 'Need for Chaos' and Motivations to Share Hostile Political Rumors," *American Political Science Review* 117, no. 4 (November 2023): 1486–1505, https://doi.org/10.1017/S000305542200147. More in R. Salecl, *A Passion for Ignorance* (Princeton University Press, 2021).

productive activities. In this context, we can also understand oracles' predictions as a form of sublimation. Oracular texts and practices can be taken as symbolic expressions of psychic transformation. The question, however, is whether sublimation is still a relevant term today and whether it has changed from the time Freud and Lacan conceptualized it.

Italian psychoanalyst Rosella Valdrè[5] questioned whether sublimation is talked about less today because the possibilities of sublimation in contemporary humankind have drastically—and dramatically—diminished, both in patients undergoing analysis and in society. Valdrè sees one reason for that in the evolution of psychopathological cases. She thus points out that in contemporary clinical work, one observes fewer cases of classical neuroses and more pathologies on the borderline or the narcissistic spectrum, whose capacity and possibility to create symbols and metaphors is compromised or even absent, which might affect sublimation. Valdrè sees the second reason for the diminished power of sublimation in contemporary subjectivity, which, unlike the individual of the twentieth century, is marked by a tendency towards immediate satisfaction and discharge. Valdrè concludes that to understand the cultural complexity of today and to try to untangle what role sublimation plays today, psychoanalysis must turn to other sources, such as philosophy, sociology, and economic doctrine, on top of literature and art.

When we look at today's fascination with the idea of the end of the world, sublimation can help us understand how people channel the anxieties they face into socially acceptable forms of expression. However, the power of sublimation today does not lie only in art practices but also in scientific discoveries and religion.

5   Rosella Valdrè, *On Sublimation: A Path to the Destiny of Desire, Theory, and Treatment* (Routledge, 2019).

PANDEMICS AND THE DEATH DRIVE

At moments of great social upheaval, one can observe various forms of aggressions and regressions in people's behavior and, unsurprisingly, also new forms of sublimation. Equally, in moments of crisis, people often rediscover oracles' predictions, as well as long-forgotten scientific warnings.

If we take the example of the last pandemic (2020–23), one can see how the work of Sylvia Browne, a self-proclaimed psychic, was rediscovered when the world started dealing with COVID-19. In her 2008 book *End of Days,* Browne predicted, "In around 2020, a severe pneumonia-like illness will spread throughout the globe, attacking the lungs and the bronchial tubes and resisting all known treatments." Browne wrote this after the SARS pandemic, so it was unsurprising that she spoke about an illness that attacks the lungs. However, her prognostications have not proven to hold true since she also predicted the following: "Almost more baffling than the illness itself will be the fact that it will suddenly vanish as quickly as it arrived, attack again ten years later, and then disappear completely."[6]

Although these forecasts about the end of COVID did not come true, for many, Browne was an oracle who foresaw the pandemic. Strangely, scientific forecasts published decades before COVID got much less attention than Browne's book. As early as 1994, the American journalist Laurie Garrett predicted the emergence of new major pandemics. In her book *The Coming Plague: Newly Emerging Diseases in a World Out of Balance*, she says that people often feel that history is happening to "others" or in the past and that they are

[6] Sylvia Browne and Lindsay Harrison, *End of Days: Predictions and Prophecies about the End of the World*, Reprint edition (Dutton, 2009), 312.

Fantasies of the End of the World

somehow outside history.[7] Indeed, many aspects of history are unpredictable or only predictable in retrospect, such as the fall of the Berlin Wall. Nevertheless, we can foresee what might emerge in the future when it comes to the emergence and spread of infectious diseases. That is why Laurie Garrett warned that new diseases will mark our era, with epidemics spreading around the world, and new diseases will be transmitted from insects or other animals to humans due to the destruction of the natural environment humans are causing.

When the COVID-19 crisis hit, Laurie Garrett was bombarded with questions about whether she could predict what would happen after this pandemic. Although she fought against being perceived as a kind of latter-day Cassandra, Garrett nonetheless warned that people would not stand still for long as social inequalities increased with the new pandemic. She imagined that societies would face large protests against those who would start economically profiting from the pandemic. These protests did not happen. Instead, we witnessed countless small aggressions between people.

While most people were actively trying to prevent themselves and others from getting infected, some resorted to aggressively spreading the virus. For example, in March 2020, a sales assistant, Belly Mujinga, was on duty with a female colleague in London's Victoria Rail Station ticket office. One of the customers, who claimed to have COVID-19, started spitting on the women and coughing in their faces. A few days later, both employees contracted the coronavirus, and a few weeks later, Belly Mujinga died.[8] A similar attack happened in London two months later when a passenger

7   Laurie Garrett, *The Coming Plague: Newly Emerging Diseases in a World Out of Balance* (Penguin, 1995).
8   Matthew Weaver and Vikram Dodd, "UK Rail Worker Dies of Coronavirus after Being Spat at While on Duty," *The Guardian*, May 12, 2020, https://www.theguardian.com/uk-news/2020/may/12/uk-rail-worker-dies-coronavirus-spat-belly-mujinga.

refused to pay the taxi driver, Trevor Bell. When Bell insisted on receiving the payment, the passenger revealed that he was infected with the coronavirus and started coughing and spitting in the driver's direction. As a result, Bell fell ill and died from COVID-19.[9]

Elsewhere in the world, similar attacks were made by allegedly infected people. In the US, some shoppers started coughing and spitting on products in stores. In Missouri, for example, police arrested a man who was spitting on the sales items at a Walmart store while shouting, "Who's afraid of the coronavirus?" In California, a shopper was jailed for licking groceries in the store. One woman who coughed on the exhibited goods in the mall later argued that she was kidding. A similar claim was made by a police officer coughing at fellow Baltimore citizens.[10]

When the new coronavirus was spreading in China, news emerged that some people were trying to spread the virus by spitting on other people. However, much of this news about spitting has turned out to be fake. Nevertheless, the sharing (and creation) of films related to spitting somehow played the role of sublimation.

Particularly popular film footage involved an incident that happened in 2018 when two businessmen from Liangshan County in Guangdong Province clashed in front of a police station and angrily started a spitting duel. Police detained both businessmen because public spitting is considered a criminal attack in China. During the period

9   Simon Murphy, "Tributes Paid to Cab Driver Who Died of Covid-19 after Being Spat At," *The Guardian*, May 22, 2020, https://www.theguardian.com/uk-news/2020/may/22/tributes-paid-to-cab-driver-who-died-of-covid-19-after-being-spat-at.

10 Craig Jackson, "Psychology of Why Some People Are Deliberately Spitting, Coughing and Licking Food in Supermarkets," *The Conversation*, April 29, 2020, http://theconversation.com/psychology-of-why-some-people-are-deliberately-spitting-coughing-and-licking-food-in-supermarkets-137111.

of COVID-19, this clip was enthusiastically shared in China, and viewers often thought that it represented an incident that happened during the pandemic.[11]

Sigmund Freud[12] associates spitting with a form of infantile adverse reaction to someone close to us. Melanie Klein[13] also links this behavior to early childhood, especially with the fantasy of expunging aggressive self-affections through spitting, biting, or excretion that can be observed among young children. When an adult starts spitting, this behavior can be a regression to such childhood affects, but it can also be an individual's way of coping with anxiety or the desire to harm others. It is possible that an individual who resorts to such an activity cannot verbally articulate particular unconscious dilemmas. If we take sub-limation as a process by which individuals redirect socially unacceptable impulses into socially acceptable actions, we can say that making fake YouTube films about spitting in some way played this role of redirection. These films were not necessarily of artistic quality, however, many people watching and sharing them found quite a lot of satisfaction. Similarly, people in crisis digging for old prophecies that might have already predicted calamities are getting satisfaction not necessarily from the artistic value of these texts but from the redirection of their anxiety and other uncomfortable feelings that the crisis provoked.

At the time of the pandemic, for some, consumption became a way to express their anxieties. In the spring of

11   Sophie Williams, "Two Furious Chinese Men Engage in a Minute-Long 'Spitting War,'" *Mail Online*, March 29, 2017, http://www.dailymail.co.uk/~/article-4360356/index.html.

12   Sigmund Freud, "Papers on Metapsychology," in *The Standard Edition of the Complete Psychological Works of Sigmund Freud*, ed. James Strachey, vol. 14 (Hogarth Press and the Institute of Psycho-Analysis, 1953).

13   Melanie Klein, *Envy and gratitude and other works 1946–1963* (Hogarth Press, 1975).

2020, American psychologists wondered how to explain the large-scale purchase of toilet paper that led to stores being emptied of this product. Gail Steketee and Randy O. Frost had done a good deal of research on hoarding certain products.[14] Their explanation was that people usually accumulate for three reasons: because of some emotional or sentimental connection to a particular object, its aesthetic appeal, or its usability. However, when Frost was asked why people started hoarding toilet paper during the pandemic, he observed a shortcoming in these theories. People did not buy toilet paper because they believed it to be so essential to their lives; it was instead that the act of hoarding helped them cope with the unpredictability of the pandemic. Behind the accumulation of toilet paper was the fear of the unknown and not just the fact that toilet paper is good.

Freudian psychoanalyst Andrea Greenman tried to find the source of the urge to accumulate toilet paper in a child's relationship to his excrement and the desire to control his excretion. When people were forced to yield control due to the pandemic, for some, that meant a regression to a previous childhood condition. And some might have harbored the illusion that with a massive supply of toilet paper, they would not lose control and become powerless.[15]

Freud looked at children's relationship with their excrement through the light of their relationship with their parents. When children go through the anal phase, they might take the stool as a gift to their parents. Excrement can, for some children, look like something that has an exchange value, which will give them more love and attention.

14   Gail Steketee and Randy Frost, *Stuff: Compulsive Hoarding and the Meaning of Things* (Mariner Books, 2011).
15   Henry Alford. "What Would Freud Make of the Toilet-Paper Panic?," *The New Yorker*, March 23, 2020, https://www.newyorker.com /magazine/2020/03/30/what-would-freud-make-of-the-toilet -paper-panic.

A coffee shop in Australia saw an exchange value in people's obsession with toilet paper and decided to accept toilet paper as a substitute for money. One coffee cost three rolls, and for a kilo of coffee beans, thirty-six rolls had to be paid. The walls of this coffee shop were, of course, quickly covered by rolls of toilet paper. One cannot say that this action resulted in a work of art, but one might take it as a particular type of sublimation of the anal drives that went into overdrive at the time of the pandemic.

SUBLIMATION, SCIENCE, AND RELIGION

With people searching for oracles in times of crisis, we might also find a regression to childhood. As children find fascination with fairy tales, adults find satisfaction with the predictions that oracles provide. In the case of the pandemic, however, sublimation also involved articulating negative feelings through scientific discoveries.

When the pandemic was coming towards an end, I happened to be in Turkey to promote the Turkish translation of my book *On Anxiety*.[16] A few students from the Faculty of Pharmacy came to my book launch and invited me to give a talk at their book club. When I asked the students what motivates them in their studies, many said it was their anxiety over a repetition of the pandemic. However, in the most positive ways, they mentioned the Turkish scientists Ugur Sahin and Ozlem Tureci, the founders of BioNTech. For several students, doing scientific research that might lead to the invention of a new vaccine was a way to sublimate the anxiety over the pandemic.

16   Renata Salecl, *On Anxiety* (Routledge, 2004).

A form of sublimation can also be seen in how researcher Katalin Karikó came up with the original idea that led to the discovery of the COVID-19 vaccine. When Karikó left Hungary in 1985, the Hungarian government only allowed citizens to take $100 out of the country. Karikó decided to hide her money in her daughter's teddy bear. Later, she experimented with another type of hiding place. To obtain an effective vaccine, she decided to wrap the mRNA in a lipid droplet to prevent its degradation in the body and help it penetrate cells. Just as the teddy bear helped Karikó transport money to the West in the past, the lipid bubble carried the mRNA into the cells it needed to penetrate.

RELIGION AND THE END OF THE WORLD

Another answer to the anxieties that people are increasingly feeling concerning their survival and the survival of the world as we know it is religion. Sigmund Freud argued that religion serves as a collective neurosis for humanity, a way to channel and mitigate the inherent tension between individual desires and the demands of society. By sublimating primal urges into religious activities, individuals not only find a socially acceptable outlet for these impulses, but also gain the psychological comfort of belonging and the illusion of an ultimate protector in the form of God.

While building on Freudian theories, Jacques Lacan offered a different perspective on sublimation, which can be extended to religion. From a Lacanian standpoint, religious beliefs and practices can be seen as attempts to fill the fundamental lack or void in human existence with something that transcends the symbolic order of language and society. In this sense, religion can provide a way for individuals to confront and engage with the Real, an unrepresentable realm beyond the Imaginary and the Symbolic.

However, in the link between sublimation and religion, we should not forget the power of the death drive. Importantly, Lacan has linked this *creatio ex nihilo* with the destructive nature of the death drive. The latter is "a creationist sublimation, and it is linked to that structural element which implies that, as soon as we have to deal with anything in the world appearing in the form of the signifying chain, there is somewhere—though certainly outside the natural world—which is the beyond of that chain, the *ex nihilo* on which it is founded and is articulated as such." The death drive is a drive of destruction that undermines the social symbolic space; however, linked to it is a will to make a new start, a start from the point of nothing. Lacan also points out that the death drive "is to be situated in the historical domain, it is articulated at a level that can only be defined as a function of the signifying chain."[17]

Sublimation offers a creative way for the subject to relate to the fundamental lack or void that characterizes human desire. It is a way of transforming the death drive's potentially destructive push towards jouissance into something that can be expressed within the symbolic realm, albeit in a way that challenges and transfigures it.

Researchers Dov Cohen, Emily Kim, and Nathan W. Hudson examined the link between sublimation and religion[18] and looked at the variations of sublimation among different religious groups. They concluded that Protestants (compared with Catholics and Jews) were more likely to

17 Jacques Lacan, *The Seminar of Jacques Lacan: The Ethics of Psychoanalysis*, ed. Jacques Alain-Miller, trans. Dennis Porter (W. W. Norton & Company, 1997).
18 Dov Cohen, Emily Kim, and Nathan W. Hudson, "Religion, the Forbidden, and Sublimation," *Current Directions in Psychological Science* 23, no. 3 (2014): 208-14, https://doi.org/10.1177/0963721414531436.

minimize troublesome affects and displace them into creative work. Creative work, however, does not necessarily only mean the arts; it can also involve socially mobilizing activities that might serve particular political purposes.

Among Protestant Christians, a specific type of creative work can be observed among the fundamentalist evangelicals who have been very active in propagating the end of the world. For example, in the USA, among these evangelicals, more than sixty percent believe that our world will come to an end quite soon.[19]

America's large evangelical churches, however, not only believe in the end of the world, but they are also actively praying for that end to come. One of the most famous evangelical ministers, who is said to have over ten million followers in his church, John Hagee, likes to create colossal gatherings where his sermons look like rock concert types of performances where the priest in a trance-like state preaches about the fact that we are living our last days on Earth. He also suggests the possibility of a second coming of Christ, allowing Christians to go to heaven.

Evangelicals believe that Jerusalem must be under Jewish control for the second coming of Christ to be a possibility.[20] This is a crucial prerequisite for Christians to

19   In their documentary *Praying for Armageddon* (2023), Norwegian filmmaker Tonje Hessen Schei and American filmmaker Michael Rowley analyze the influence of fundamentalist evangelicals on members of the US congress and point out that without the support of these churches, no Republican presidential candidate today can hope to win an election. According to some estimates, more than 100 US congressmen have declared themselves members of these churches.

20   Philip Bump, "Half of evangelicals support Israel because they believe it is important for fulfilling end-times prophecy," *The Washington Post*, May 14, 2018, https://www.washingtonpost.com/news/politics/wp/2018/05/14/half-of-evangelicals-support-israel-because-they-believe-it-is-important-for-fulfilling-end-times-prophecy/.

go to heaven at the end of the world.[21] Since Jewish control of the Holy Land can only be achieved by driving the Palestinians out, many American evangelicals support the anti-Palestinian politics of the Israeli government.[22]

Although Hagee had been known for making many anti-Semitic statements[23] in the past, at a certain point he made a U-turn and, with the help of the organization Christians United for Israel, started financially supporting Jewish settlers in their occupation of the Palestinian territories in the West Bank. The idea is that before Christ returns, Jews should control the whole Holy Land; however, when Christ comes, Jews will, in the beliefs of the evangelicals, need to accept the Christian religion or might end up in hell.[24]

Evangelicals waiting for the end of the world are quick to interpret any situation as a sign that Armageddon is coming. The COVID pandemic and the Russian invasion of Ukraine were such signs for them. Since the last major conflict predicted by fundamentalist evangelicals will take place in the Middle East, the war in Gaza was also seen as a sign that apocalyptic predictions are now coming true and that Christ

21   Sarah Posner, "The dispiriting truth about why many evangelical Christians support Israel," *MSNBC*, October 22, 2023, https://www.msnbc.com/opinion/msnbc-opinion/truth-many-evangelical-christians-support-israel-rcna121481.

22   Jaclyn Diaz, "Conservative Christians are lending support—and cash—to Israel at war," *NPR*, May 26, 2024, https://www.npr.org/2024/05/26/1244131702/conservative-christians-are-lending-support-and-cash-to-israel-at-war.

23   Emily Temkin, "Why televangelist John Hagee was a shocking March for Israel speaker," *MSNBC*, November, 15 2023, https://www.msnbc.com/opinion/msnbc-opinion/john-hagee-march-for-israel-antisemitism-rcna125291.

24   See the documentary "*Till Kingdom Come*," (2020) by Israeli filmmaker Maya Zinshtein. Also, David M. Halbfinger, "American Evangelicals, Israeli Settlers and a Skeptical Filmmaker," *New York Times*, February 26, 2021, https://www.nytimes.com/2021/02/26/movies/american-evangelicals-israeli-settlers-documentary.html.

is about to return. "The last days are coming," Texas pastor Jack Graham said in a sermon.[25]

One should also remember the political power of end-of-the-world stories. The late American professor of Islamic studies, Barbara Freyer Stowasser, in comparing the perceptions of the end of the world in Christianity, Judaism, and Islam, found that each religion likes to use end-of-the-world debates for secular political purposes.[26] At the same time, religions also have elements of superiority in their messages, which have also been strongly linked throughout history to the political interests of each country. Just as eschatological categories are often imposed on a particular political and social reality, this reality is also reflected in religious visions of the end of the world. Freyer Stowasser points out that this happens especially in situations of vulnerability and alienation when collective anxiety opens the door to privileging a particular religion and asserting its superiority over others.

COLLAPSOLOGY

Our life on Earth is truly changing. On top of a potential new pandemic, wars, and even possibly nuclear war, most countries are facing an increase in temperature, drought, and wildfires, and/or terrible storms and floods. The UK's Chatham House Institute[27] published an analysis predicting

25 Ruth Graham and Anna Betts, "For American Evangelicals Who Back Israel, 'Neutrality Isn't an Option'," *New York Times*, October 15, 2013, https://www.nytimes.com/2023/10/15/us/american-evangelicals-israel-hamas.html.

26 Barbara Freyer Stowasser, "The End is Near: Minor and Major Signs of the Hour in Islamic Texts and Contexts," https://www.files.ethz.ch/isn/46623/MESV6-3.pdf.

27 "Climate Change Risk Assessment 2021," Chatham House, updated November 4, 2021, https://www.chathamhouse.org/2021/09/climate-change-risk-assessment-2021.

that by 2050 the world will certainly need an increase in food, while extreme weather could reduce crop yields by as much as 30%. Much of the world might face famine, which can easily provoke new wars and civil strife.

Christian Parenti's study[28] predicts that climate change will radically change society in the coming decades. Drought and a two-meter rise in sea levels, and the resulting soil erosion and flooding, could unleash populations' extraordinary fury against their governments. The study also analyzes how people have reacted to natural disasters in the past and how they have expressed their anger at the failure of the authorities to act appropriately in the face of sudden and unpredictable crises. Often, major natural disasters have sparked religious fervor in society, and there has frequently been an increase in the number of people who have tried to explain a catastrophe in terms of oracles that speak of the end of the world. In crises, hostility and violence towards migrants and minorities have also consistently grown stronger. However, when fear and anxiety have increased in society, despair and numbness set in over time. In times of crisis, the door has thus often been wide open to autocratic political leaders and populists who offer people false hope.

Addressing what awaits our fragile world, a particular branch of future studies, called collapsology, is developing worldwide. These studies try to predict the likelihood of societal collapse due to climate change, pandemics, and similar catastrophes. Among the best-known authors in this field are the French agronomist Pablo Servigne and the Belgian researcher Raphaël Stevens.[29] Their thesis is that there is a difference between realists, who believe that immediate changes to socio-ecological systems are necessary to make

28 Christian Parenti, *Tropic of Chaos: Climate Change and the New Geography of Violence* (Nation Books, 2011).
29 Pablo Servigne and Raphaël Stevens, *How Everything Can Collapse: A Manual for Our Times*, trans. Andrew Brown (Polity, 2020).

Renata Salecl

them more resilient and to prevent catastrophic consequences, and utopians, who think we can carry on as we are.

Archaeologists are contributing to collapsology studies by looking at examples of the collapse of previous civilizations. Chris Begley[30] predicts that the collapse will occur unequally around the world and that, in addition to climate change, the critical factor will be how neoliberal capitalism operates based on increasing economic inequality. Begley also forecasts that future pandemics will spread rapidly due to high population densities and changes in the natural habitat, with an increasing possibility of viruses jumping from animals to humans.

Luke Kemp,[31] a researcher at the Centre for the Study of Existential Risk at the University of Cambridge, points out that the average lifespan of ancient civilizations was 336 years. The collapse of civilizations usually involves the rapid and permanent loss of the population, identity, and complexity of a society's socioeconomic organization. This is compounded by the breakdown of public structures because, in times of cataclysmic social change, governments lose control and no longer have a monopoly on the exercise of violence.

HOW TO FIGHT AGAINST A POSSIBLE CATASTROPHE?

Today, the fight against climate change is made much more difficult by social media, where skepticism about science is rampant, and deniers of ecological problems have a powerful influence on the public. Some political scientists speculate

30 Chris Begley, *The Next Apocalypse: The Art and Science of Survival* (Basic Books, 2021).
31 Luke Kemp, "Are we on the road to civilization collapse?" *BBC*, February 19, 2019, https://www.bbc.com/future/article/20190218 -are-we-on-the-road-to-civilisation-collapse.

whether a kind of enlightened populism could help mobilize people to fight to prevent the destruction of our environment and potentially the collapse of society. Indeed, movements such as Extinction Rebellion and Greta Thunberg's Fridays for Future have had some success in drawing attention to the threat of ecological catastrophe.

Let us also look at another form of sublimation, which is not linked to the creation of art but rather to its destruction. The destruction or defacement of art as part of climate activism often symbolizes the activists' perception of the climate crisis as an urgent, existential threat. By targeting cultural artefacts, activists aim to shock the public and policymakers out of complacency, highlighting the drastic consequences of inaction. Such actions challenge societal values, questioning why the preservation of the cultural heritage is often more fiercely protected than the natural environment. The activists' point is to provoke a re-evaluation of societal priorities, suggesting that the planet's destruction should be met with at least as much outrage as damage to inanimate objects.

The destruction of art raises ethical questions and often provokes criticism, even within the environmental movement. Critics argue that it can alienate potential allies, detract from the positive aspects of climate activism, and potentially overshadow the nuanced discussions necessary in order to address climate change. Some might also say that the destruction of art as protest deviates from the ideal of sublimation, which should foster creativity and constructive engagement. They may see it as a failure to find more constructive outlets for the underlying drives or as an act that risks alienating potential allies and undermining the cause it seeks to promote.

The challenge is to find ways to channel the same urgency, passion, and drive for change into forms of expression and activism that preserve the transformative potential of sublimation without resorting to destruction. This might

Renata Salecl

involve innovative art forms, participatory public installations, or other creative interventions highlighting the issues without erasing cultural artefacts.

One such endeavor was the action of the Greenpeace demonstrators who, in the summer of 2023, draped the country estate of Rishi Sunak, who was then the British Prime Minister, in black fabric to protest his plan to expand oil and gas drilling in the North Sea. This happened when Prime Minister Sunak announced that Britain planned to grant hundreds of new oil and gas licenses to gain energy independence.

A video posted by the group showed a crew dressed in bright red jumpsuits, helmets, and safety harnesses carrying ladders and climbing onto the roof of the Yorkshire house. They slowly unfurled long black sheets of fabric over the front of Sunak's home and held a yellow sign on the roof that read "No New Oil."

The activists did not damage the property, nor did they scare the Prime Minister's family since they were vacationing in California; however, alluding to the famous art practices of Christo, who used to wrap up public buildings, they were able in a creative way to sublimate the anxiety related to climate change and provoke public discussion thereon.

Franz Kaltenbeck, in his study on sublimation, pointed out that "the subject able to sublimate the drives is not obliged to renounce his satisfaction. So, the sublimated drive does not submit either to life or to death. The innovating artist works for the culture, helping to refine it, but at the same time, he works against culture and civilization, trying to revolutionize them." Kaltenbeck also warns that there is no reason to idealize this concept regarding sublimation: "Its triumphs are limited. It always has to struggle against anxiety, renunciation, and death, which are at work not only in the minds of individuals but also in the 'discontents' of civilization. The sublimated drive has to fight against despondency. 'I cannot go on; I will go on!" writes Samuel Beckett. One will never get a pure state of sublimated drive."[32]

When it comes to answering the real anxieties of the end of the world that we are facing today, the crucial political question is how to counter the answers to these anxieties that religious fundamentalists and authoritarian leaders offer. We might benefit from the reflection of the late Italian philosopher Antonio Gramsci, who said that in times of crisis, we need pessimism of the intellect and optimism of the will. The question, however, remains whether sublimation might help us sustain the optimism of the will.[33]

32   Franz Kaltenbeck, *De l'écriture mélancolique: Kleist, Stifter, Foster Wallace* (érès, 2020), 193–94.
33   The author acknowledges the financial support from the Slovenian Research Agency (research core funding No. P5-0221), supporting also the following projects: The Analysis of Emergency Measures: Protecting Human Rights and Preventing Social Harms in the Era of Perpetual Crises (J5-4588) and The Rise of Illiberal Democracies: A Criminological and Socio-legal Analysis (J5-50174).

Renata Salecl

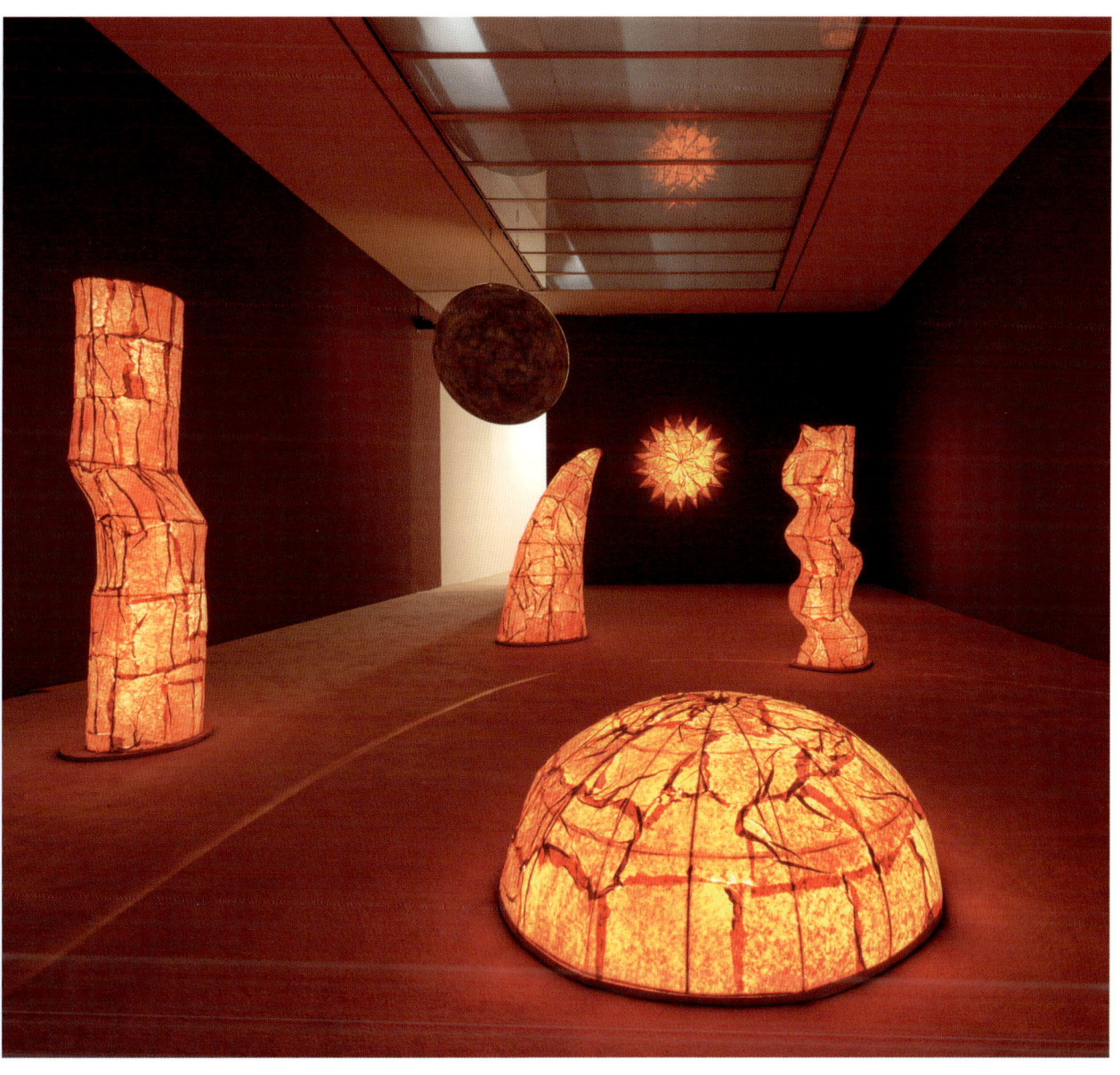

The following gallery continues to elaborate on our relationship with nature, this time in relation to fantasy. Made of rice paper, wire, and a projection, *Island in the Sun* by Derek Tumala shares with us a paradox: a cave illuminated by the sun. The underworld and a sun that illuminates it. He is interested in science, technology, nature, and speculative futures, but also in how science fiction literature imagines an environmental consciousness and alternative realities. Slovenia's stunning karst caves inspire a work that sees the cave as a portal, a way to connect the underworlds of both Slovenia and the Philippines. Additionally, Philippine sci-fi stories are inspired by the legend of Lemuria, a sunken continent believed to have left traces in Philippine caves. Lemuria represents an idealized past, a lost utopia. This is why the sun's presence is so important. In all of Derek Tumala's works, the sun embodies the promise of its energy becoming central to futuristic technologies. The sun manifests the non-binary possibility of spirituality and technology coexisting. The title is based on a 2001 song of the same title by Weezer, in which the lyrics go: "On an island in the sun / We'll be playing and having fun / And it makes me feel so fine / I can't control my brain." A metaphor for lucid dreaming to delirium, taking your time, from warm to cosy to extremely hot weather.

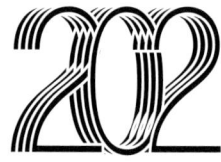

Walk-through of the Exhibition

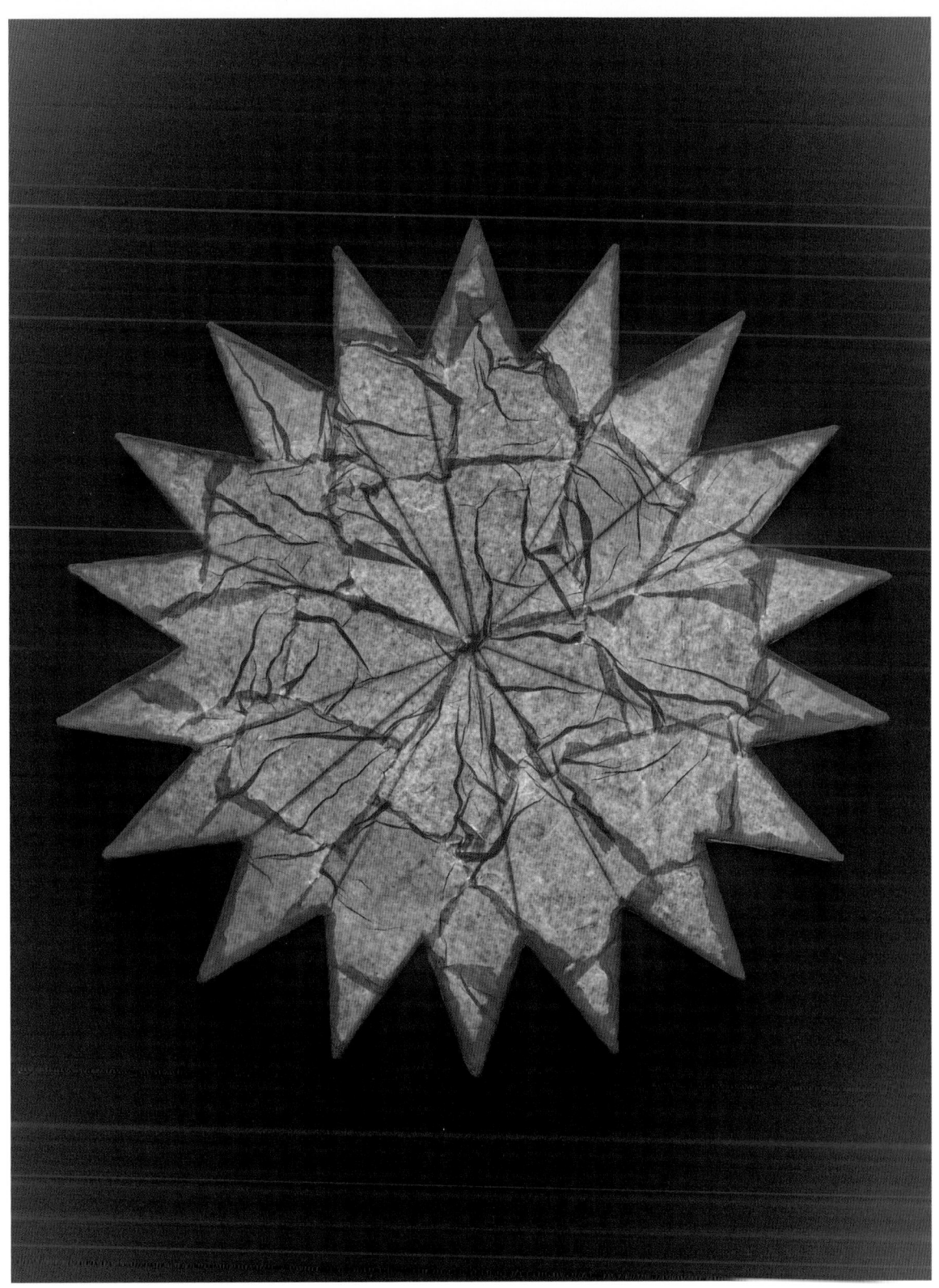

Derek Tumala, *Island in the Sun*, 2025

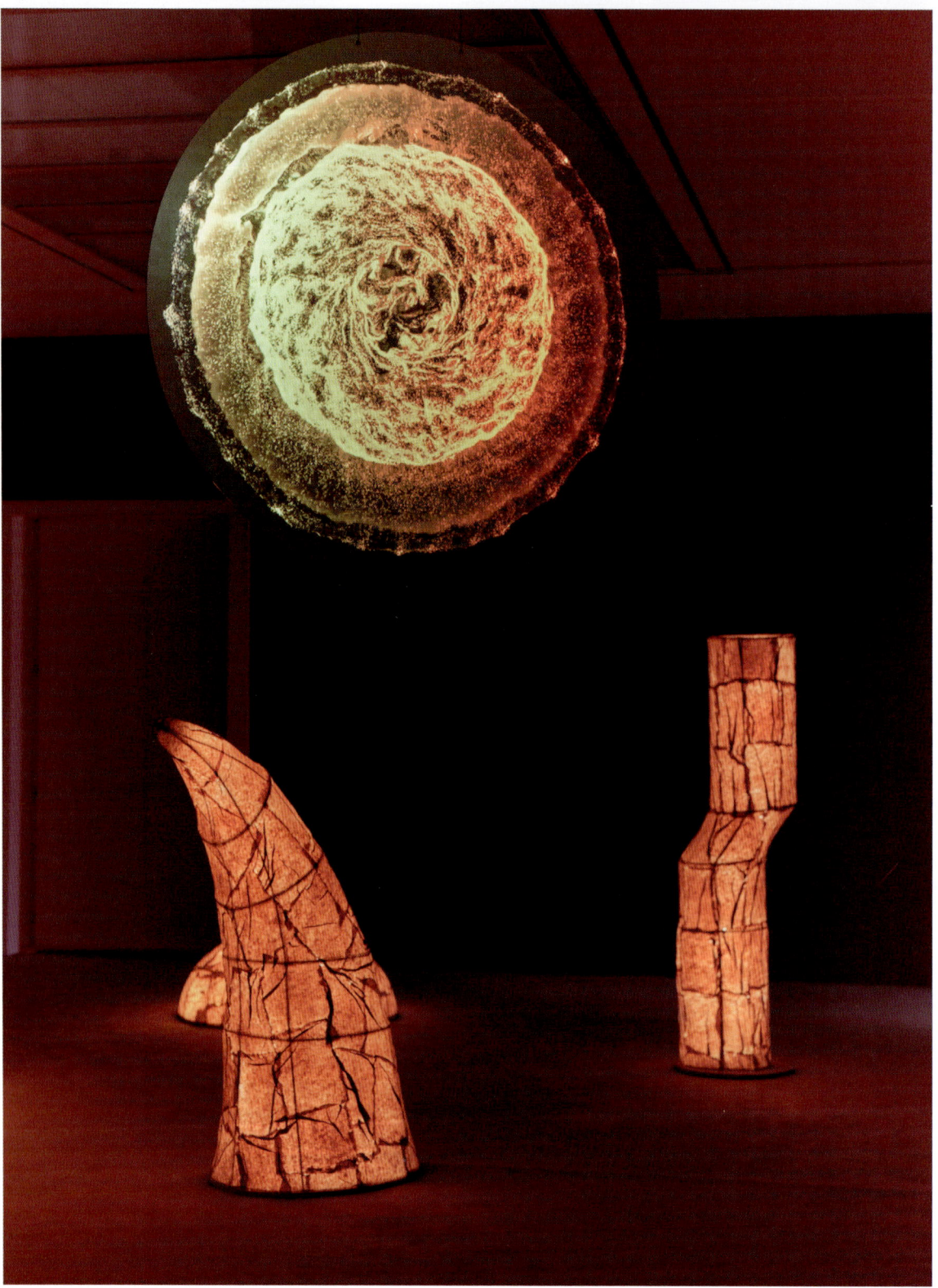

204   Derek Tumala, *Island in the Sun*, 2025

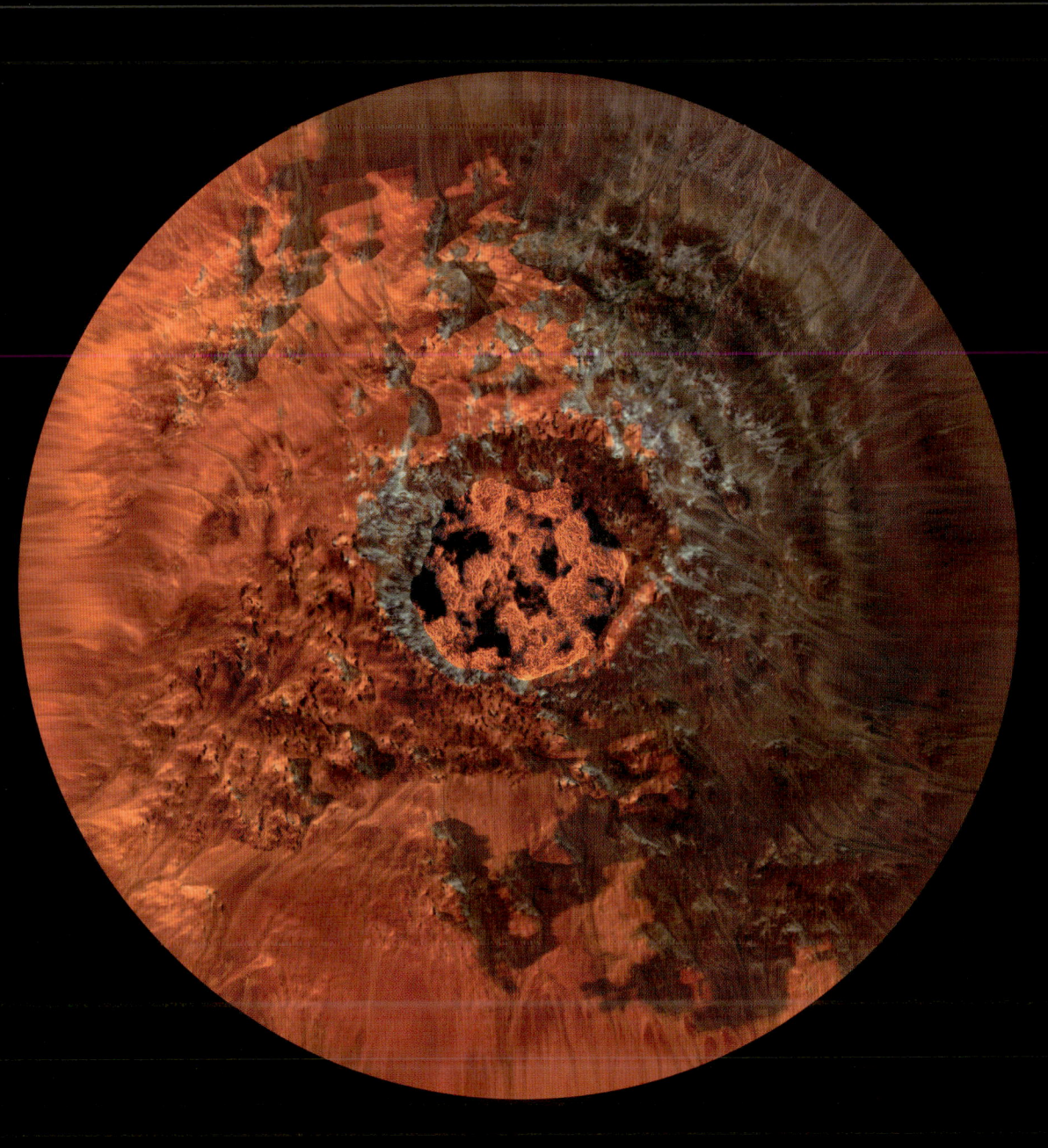

Derek Tumala, *Island Life* (video still), 2025

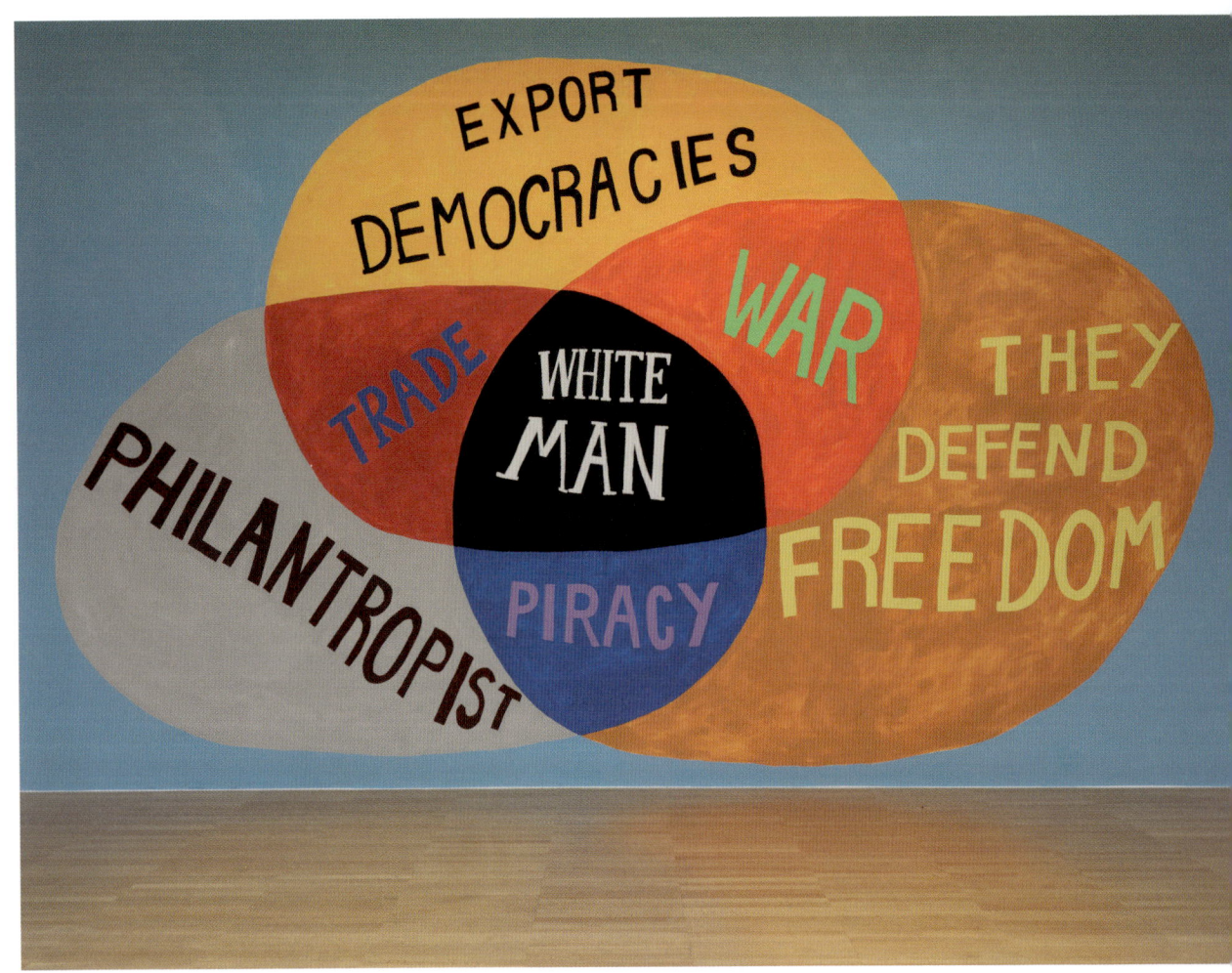

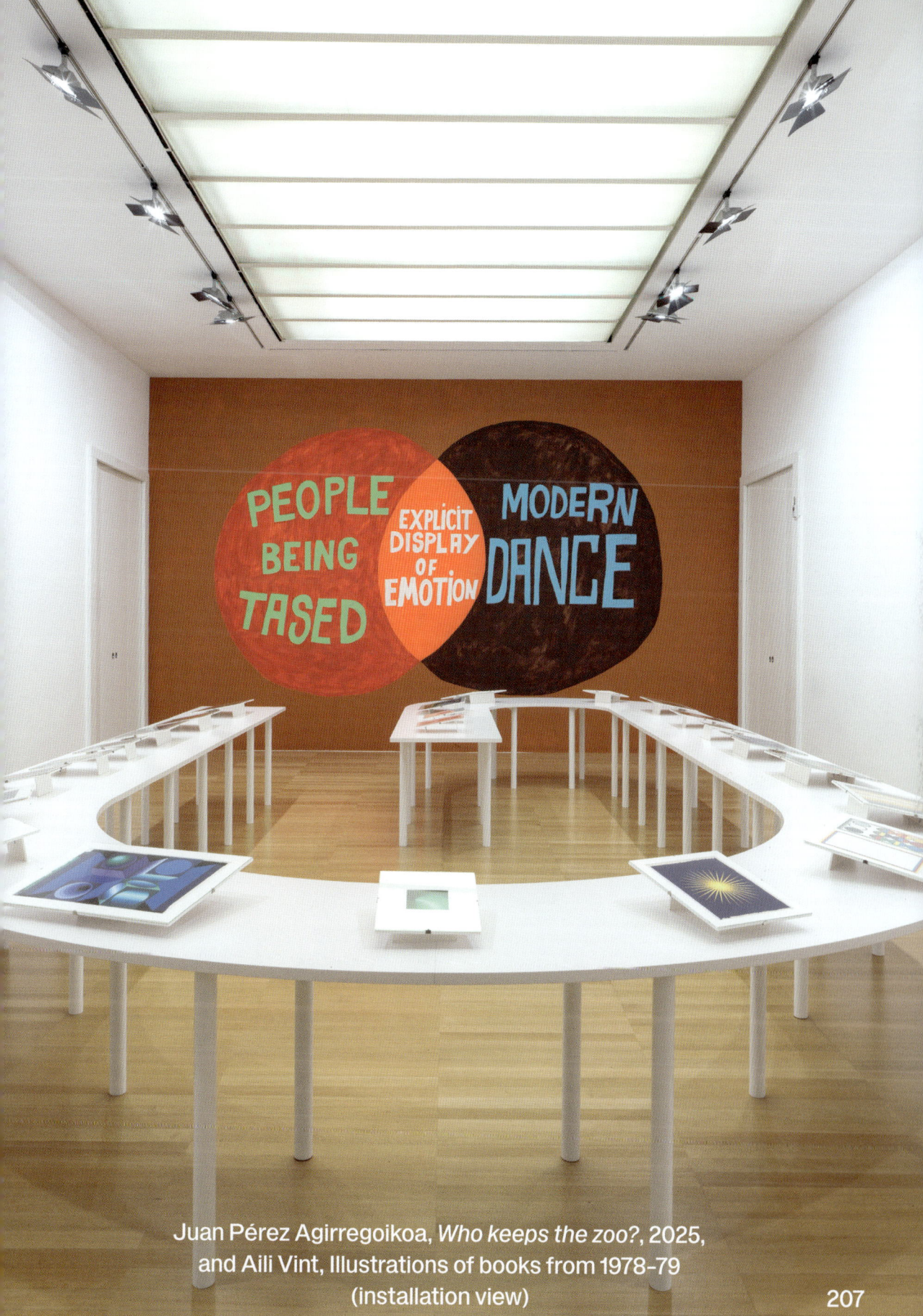

Juan Pérez Agirregoikoa, *Who keeps the zoo?*, 2025,
and Aili Vint, Illustrations of books from 1978-79
(installation view)

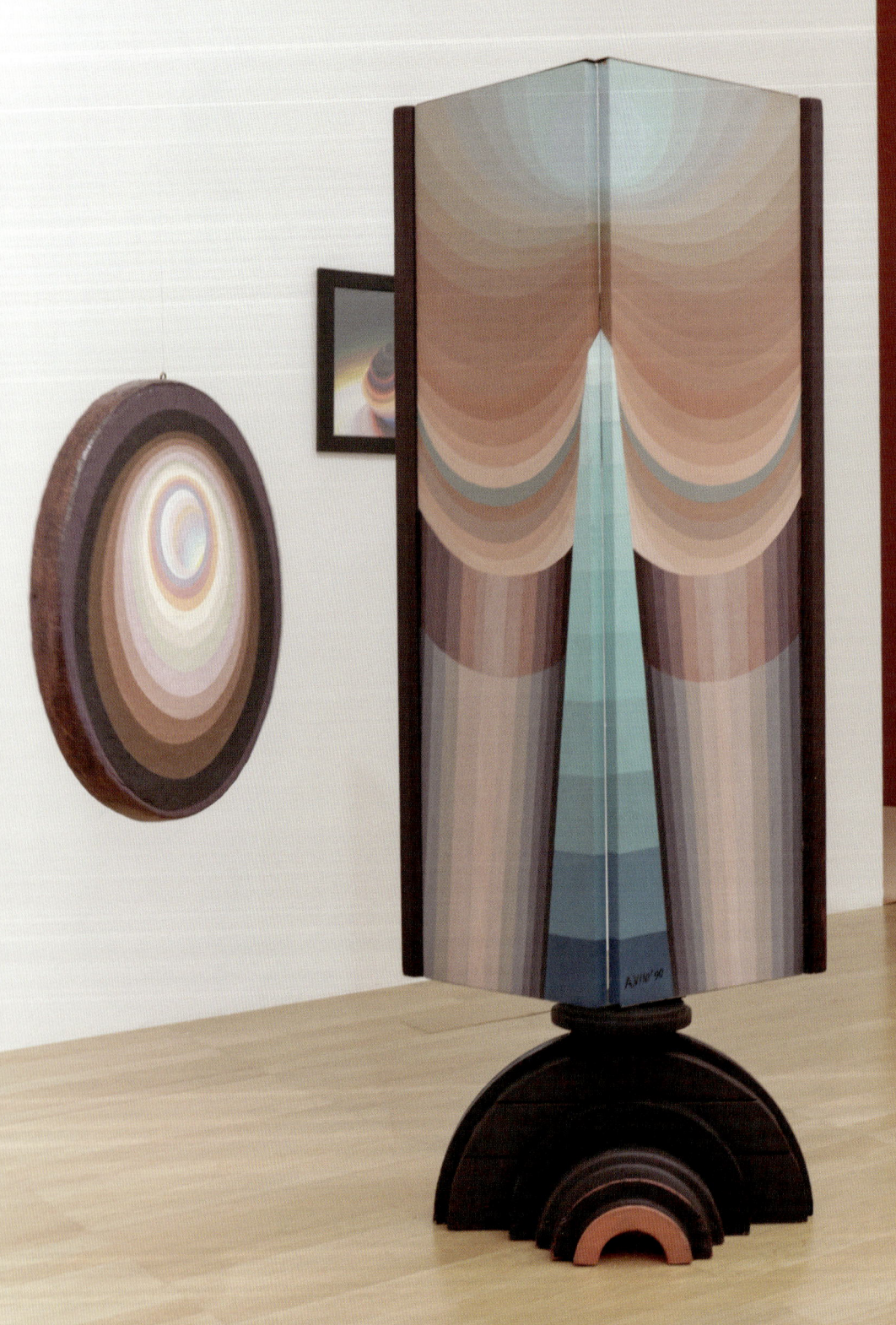

208   Aili Vint, *Installation detail No. 1* and *Meeting place*, 1990

In the contiguous room, there is the work of Aili Vint. Aili Vint's graphic work has revolved around cosmic cycles for decades, creating motifs that she repeats to refer to hope, renewal, and promise. Her work connects both with ancient Estonian mystical and spiritual traditions, deeply influenced by both their pagan roots and later Christian practices, as well as with the artist's own take on technology. Her work is like a handmade visual technology oriented towards the visualization of a new world, like the way Artificial Intelligence operates today. Her interest in immersive and dynamic visual experiences is technological. Do you remember the iconic rainbow Apple logo designed in 1977 by Rob Janoff? Similar to how rainbows serve as metaphors for crossing boundaries or reaching places beyond the ordinary in Estonian folklore, Vint's interest in speculative fantasy reflects the way mythological and cultural symbols can transcend time and place. This blend of folklore, speculative fantasy, and graphic art allows Aili Vint to both understand the past and imagine the future.

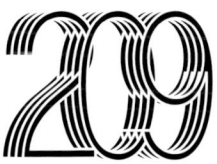

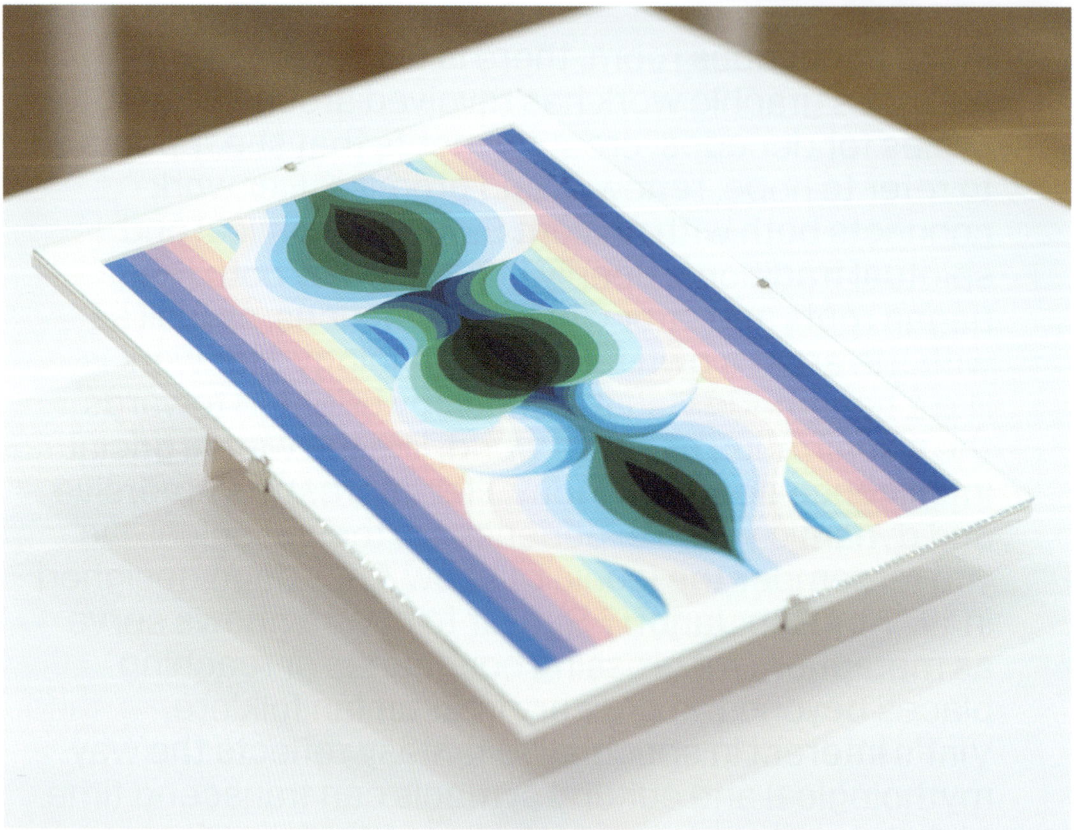

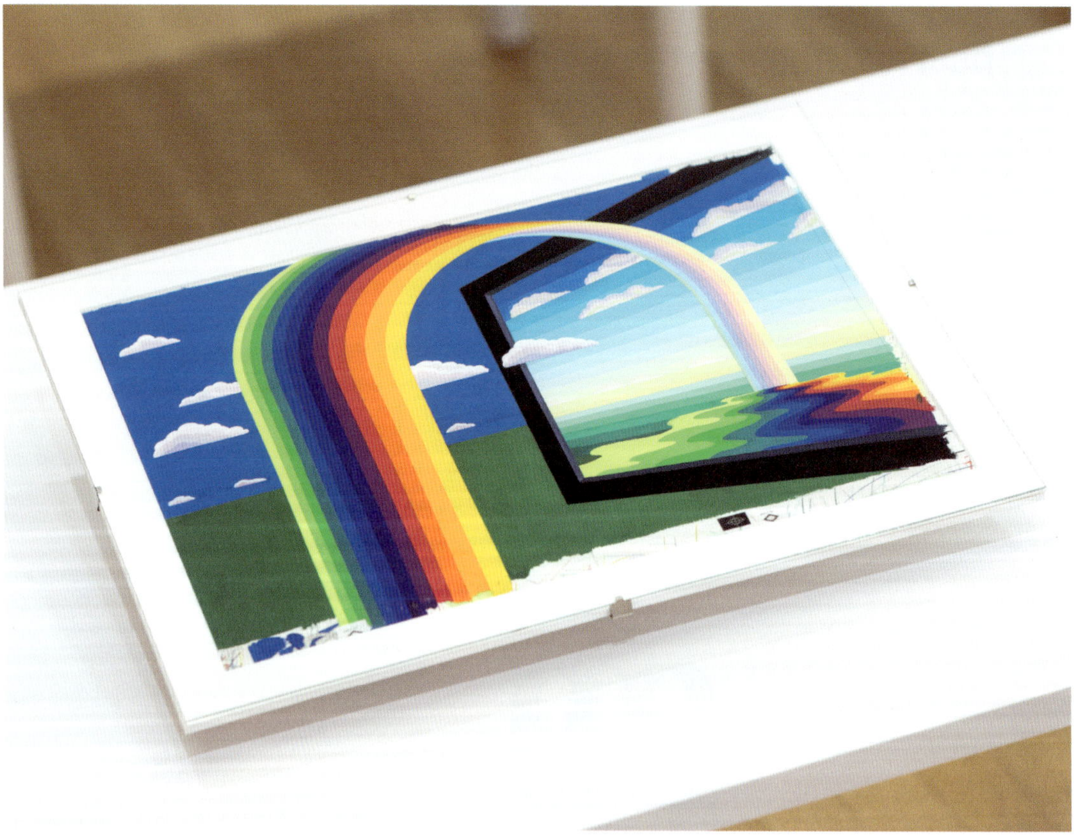

Aili Vint, *Detail of the Sea*, and *Rainbow*, 1979

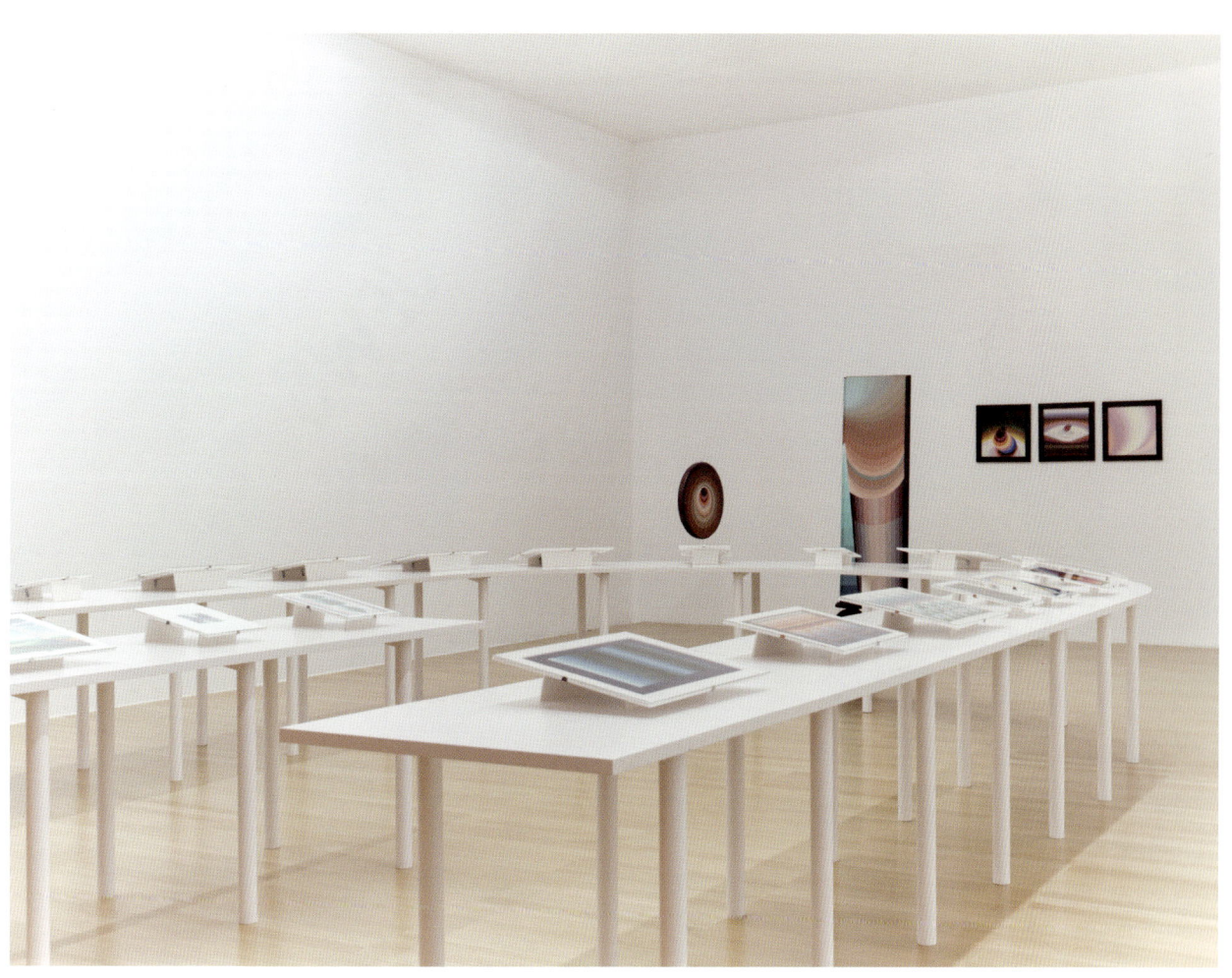

Aili Vint, selected works, 1978–90 (installation view) 211

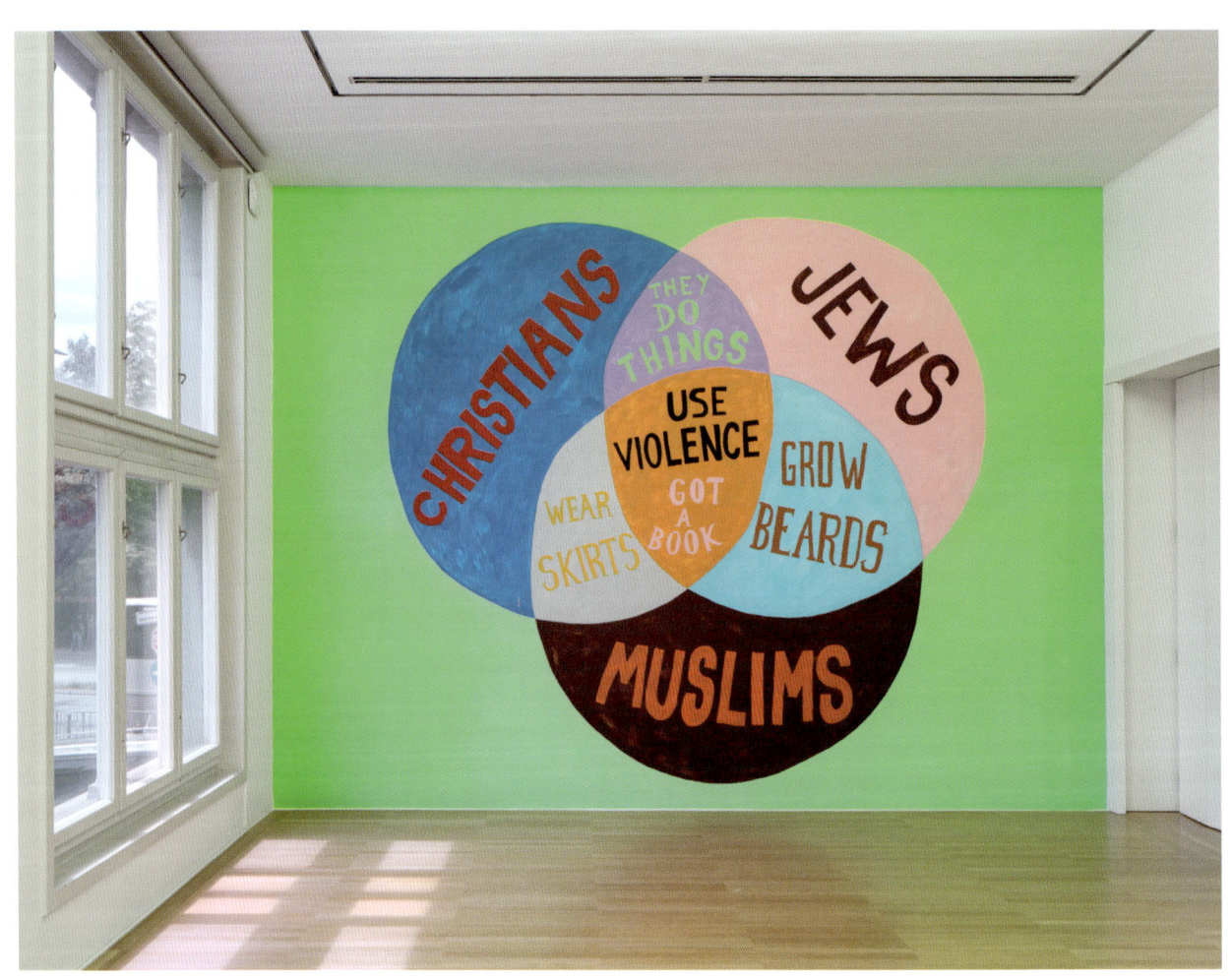

212　　Juan Pérez Agirregoikoa, *Who keeps the zoo?*, 2025

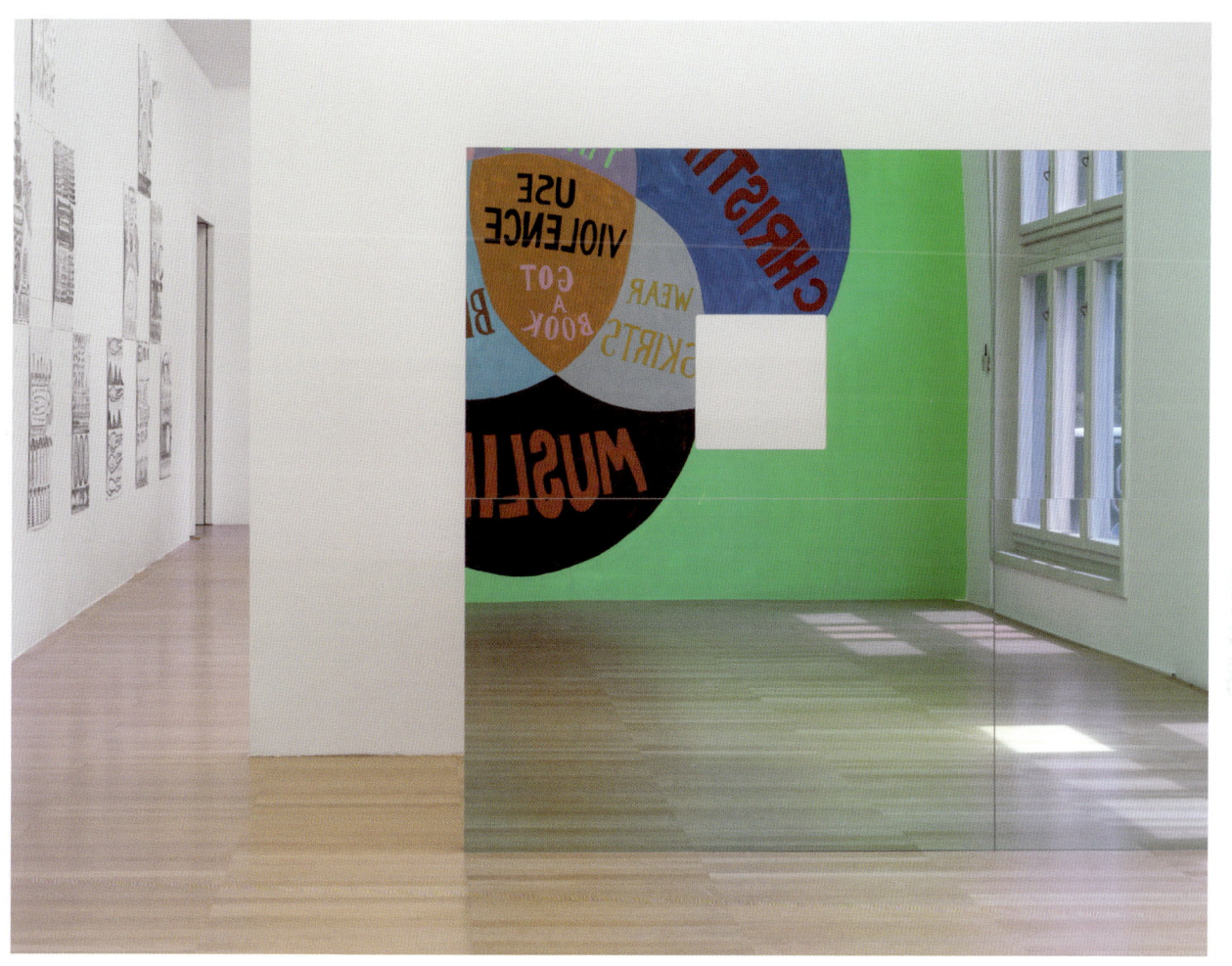

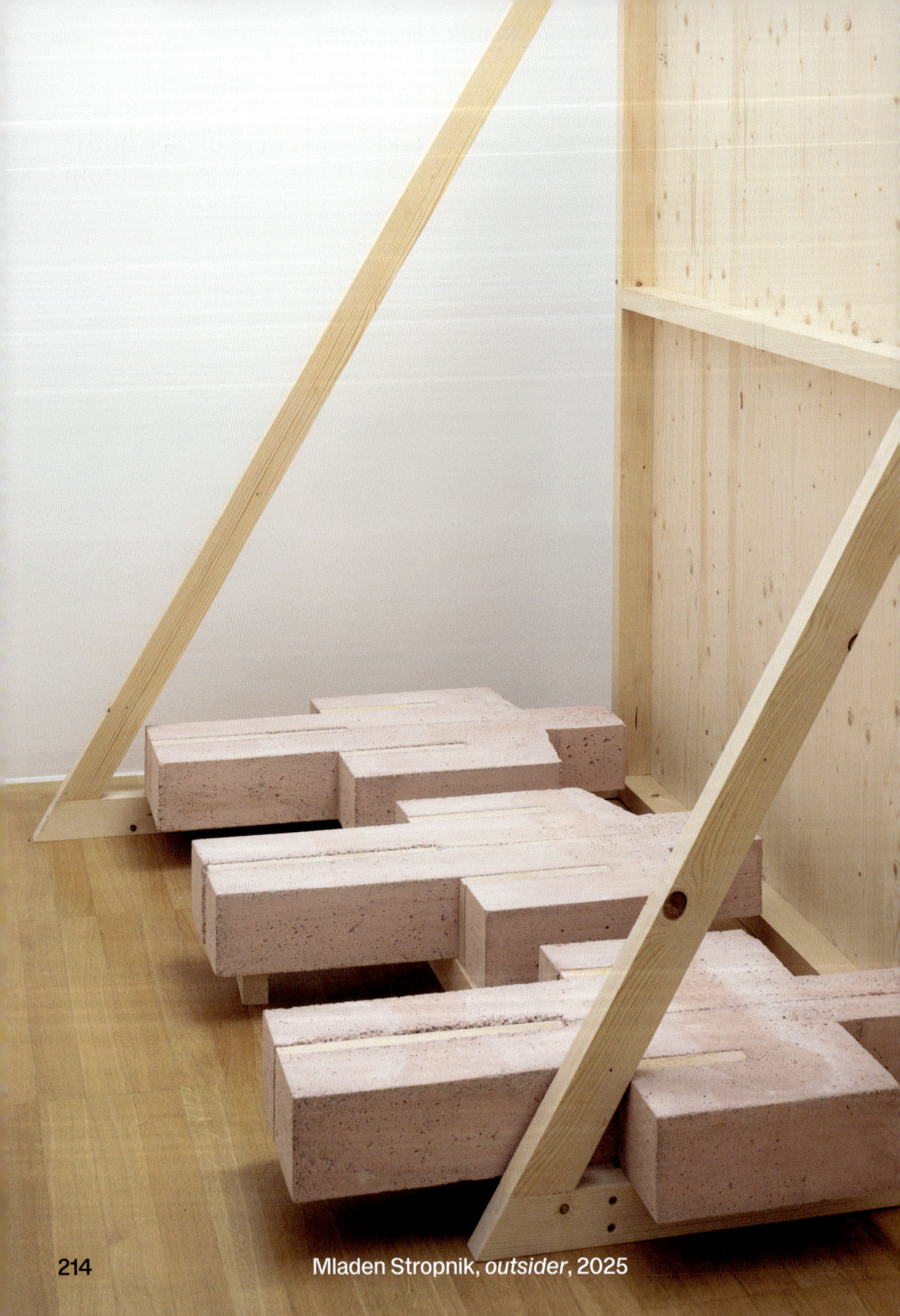

214 Mladen Stropnik, *outsider*, 2025

In the last gallery of this exhibition section, you will encounter the works of Mladen Stropnik and Eduardo Navarro. Mladen Stropnik's work has a deep existential dimension: the understanding of pain both metaphorically and physically. Using primarily painting and sculpture, he creates a "situation." There, our bodies coexist with the bodies he has created—three humans made of concrete, a spinning painting, and a mirror. His conceptual artistic language exists side by side with his interest in exploring energy healing and meditation. How? In a very particular way, like this wall-mirror that is, in fact, a head-in-hole as often seen at fairs, carnivals, and circuses. A large board with a cutout that people can stick their heads through, usually with a fun or funny scene painted around the hole, like a circus performer, a pirate, or a historical figure. But here, instead of a painting there is a reflection of the space and maybe other visitors. In this way, we all merge, sharing our worries and pain, creating a method to evoke empathy and solidarity among us all.

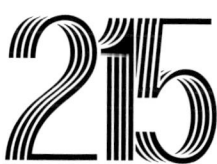

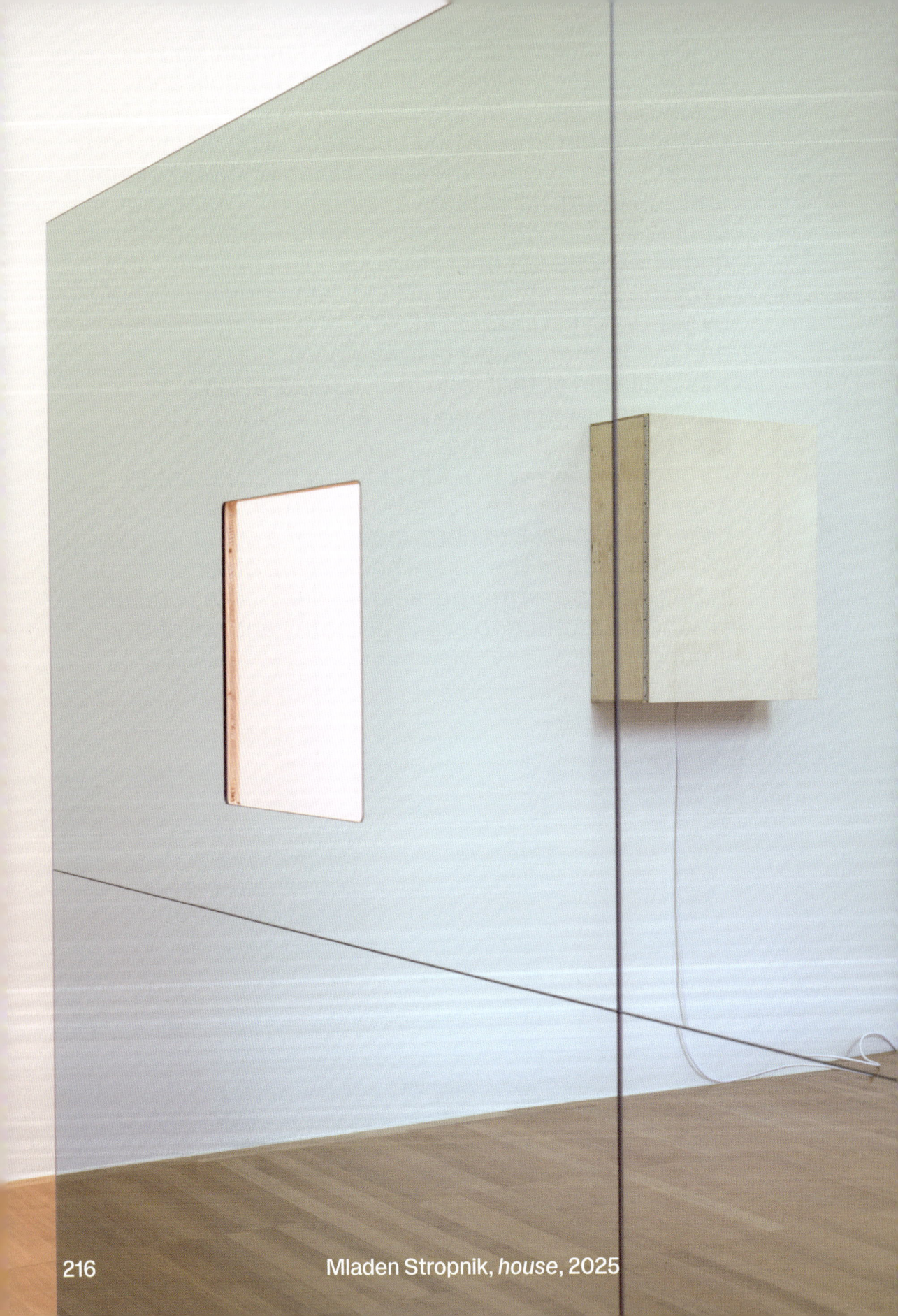

Mladen Stropnik, *house*, 2025

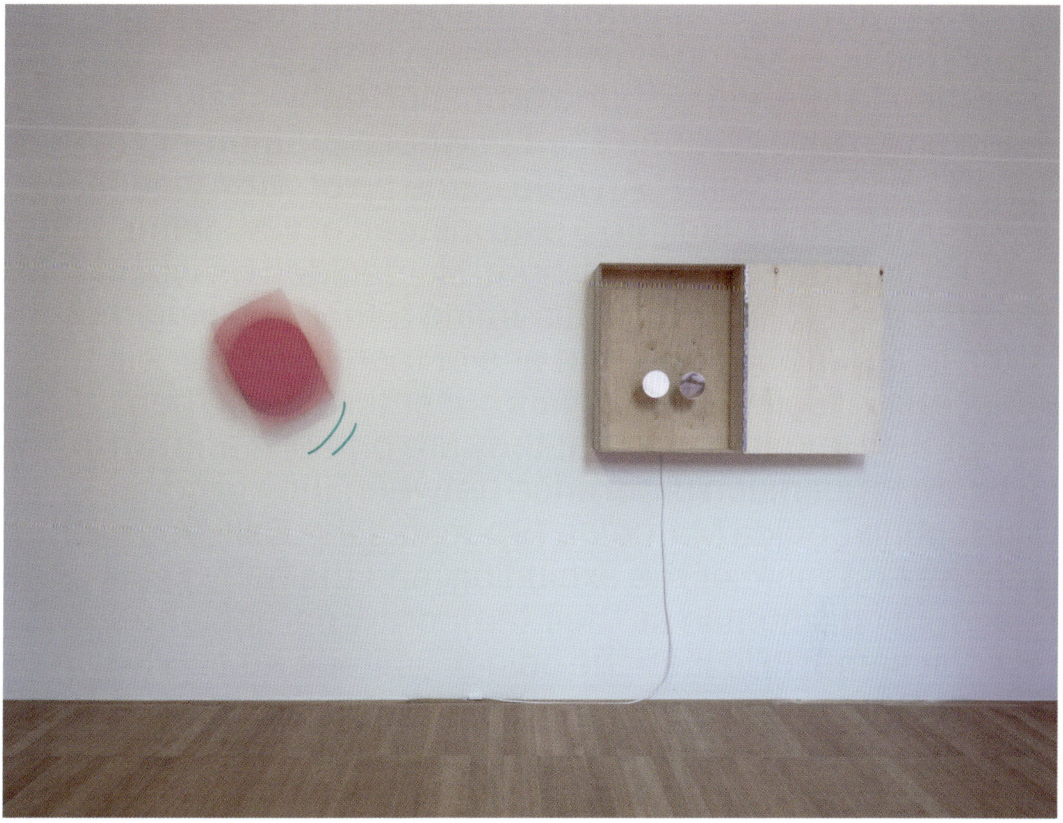

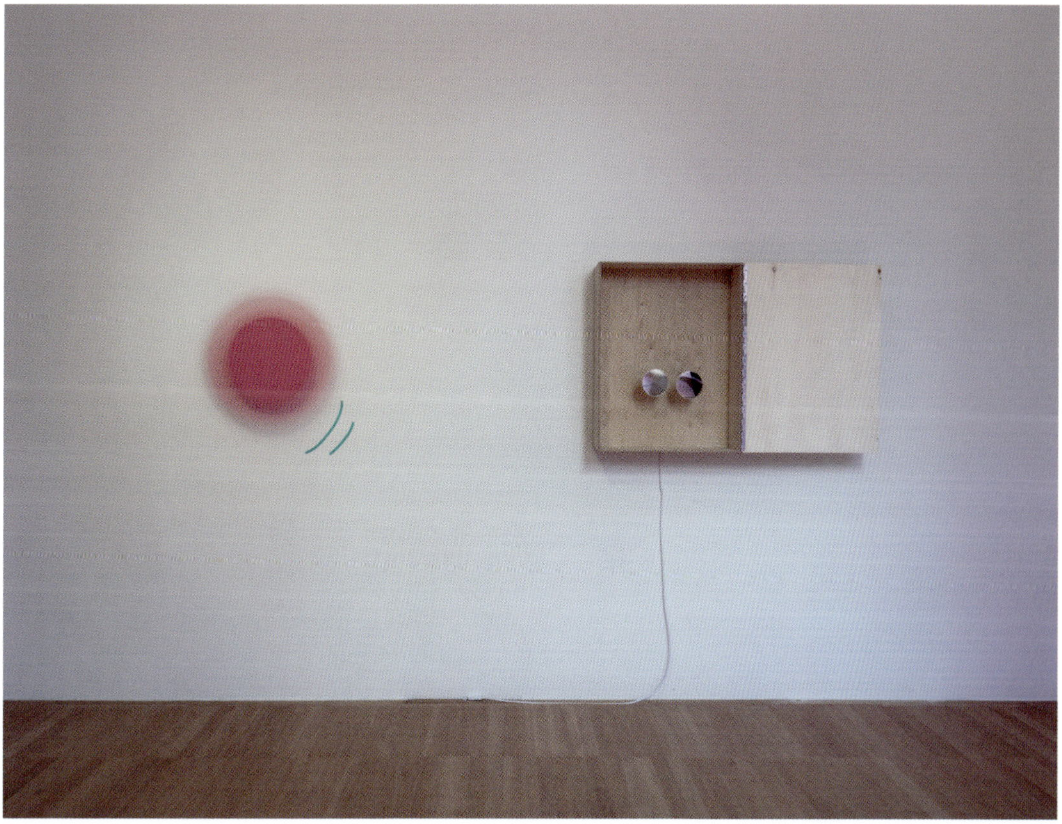

Eduardo Navarro's room continues this idea of merging with one another, the other, in this case, a seal. I am a seal, this work says. During the pandemic, Eduardo Navarro was in Uruguay and wished to interact with the orphaned baby seals at the emergency marine shelter, whose promoter he had known for years. An idea came up of what would happen if he turned into a seal instead of just going to the shelter to observe them. He decided he would visit them in a seal suit. Becoming a seal, knowing that the seals know you are not one of them. This work is not about fooling the animals but entertaining them so that they might forget that they are orphans and smile. There is not much difference between the old couple adopting Žogica Marogica (Speckles the Ball) you saw in the first room of the exhibition, and the baby seals accepting a human as their temporary parent. The aim is the same: to lessen the pain of solitude, to survive, to have hope.

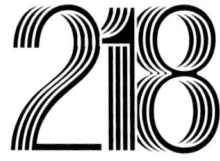

Walk-through of the Exhibition

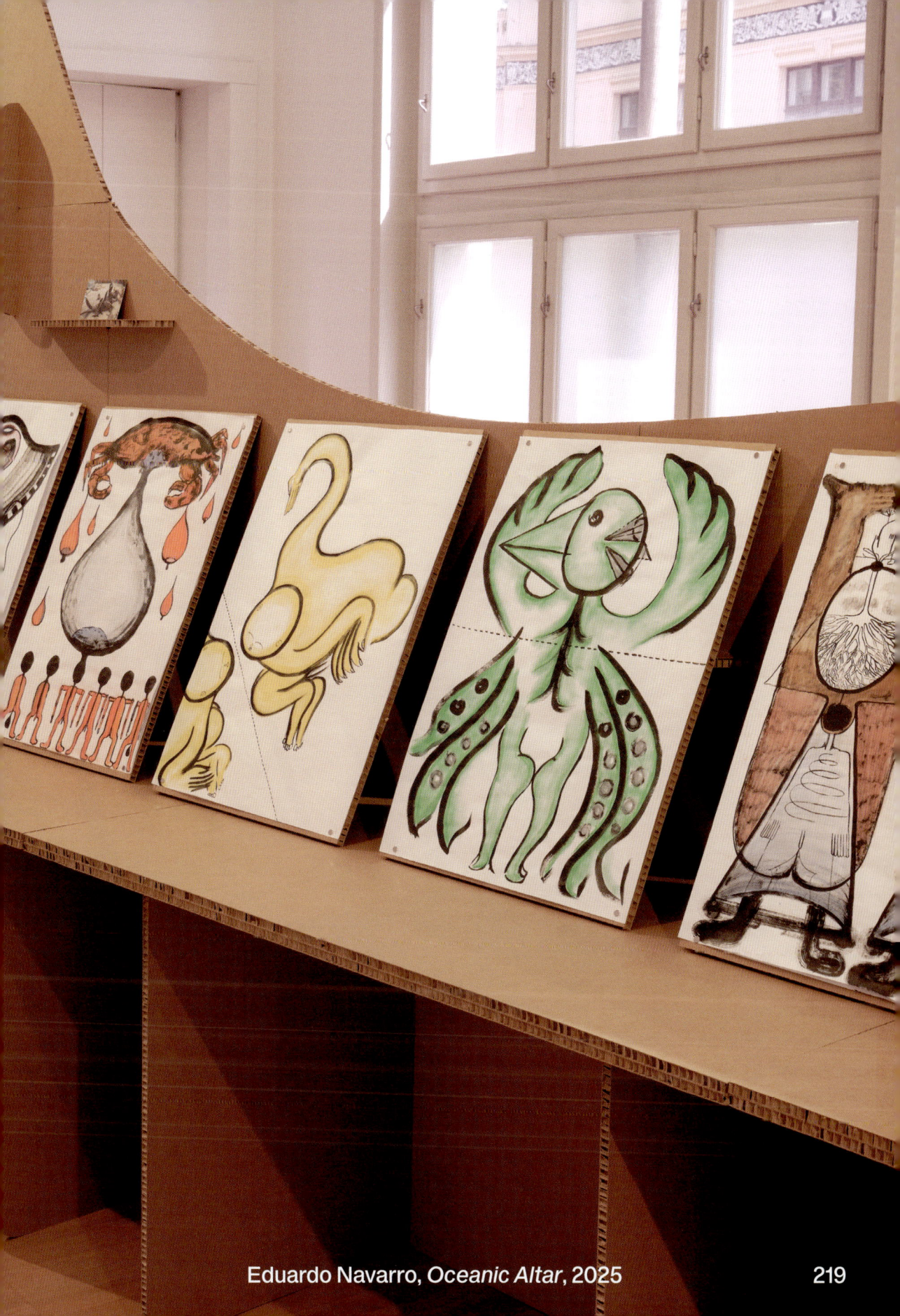

Eduardo Navarro, *Oceanic Altar*, 2025

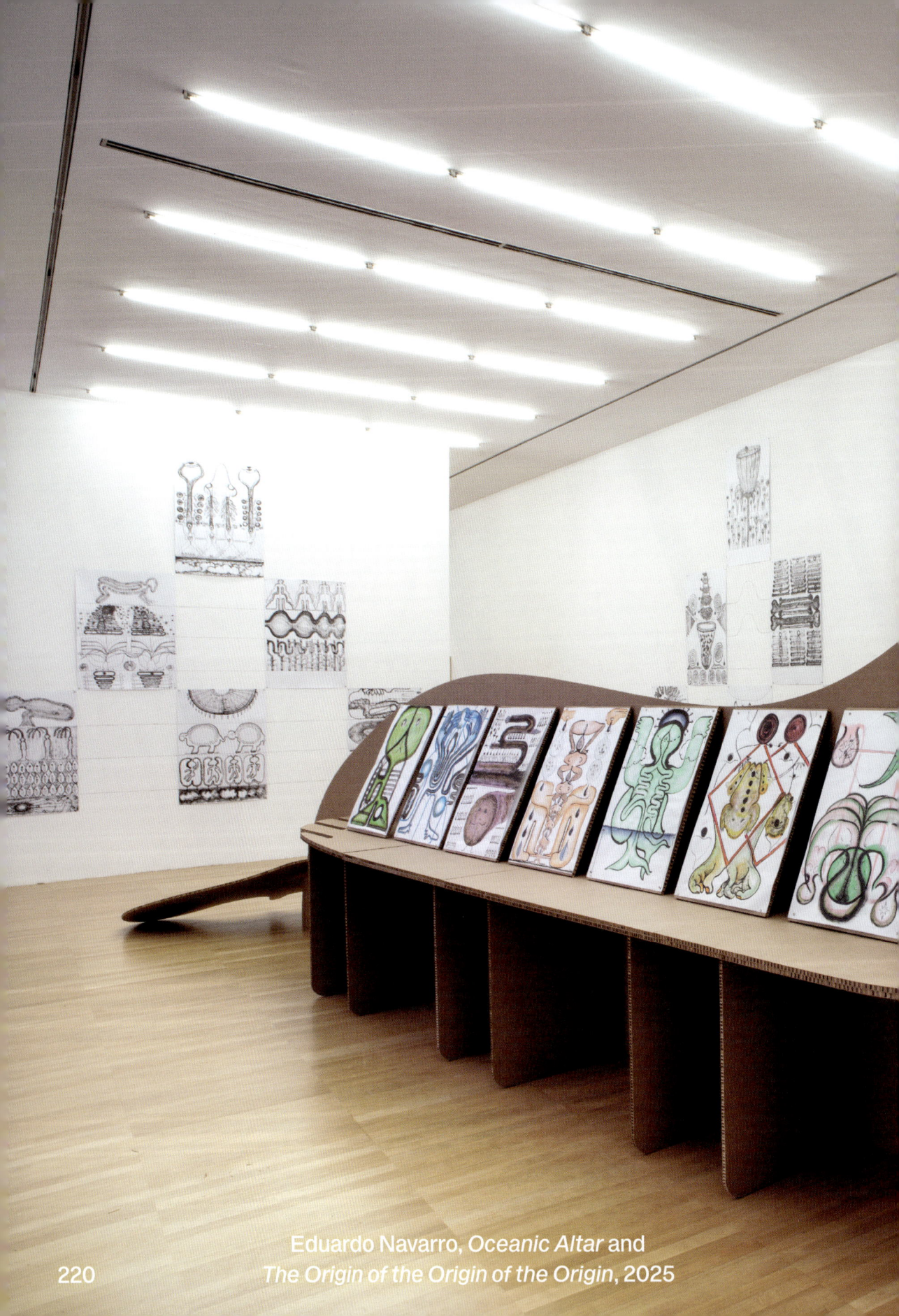

Eduardo Navarro, *Oceanic Altar* and
The Origin of the Origin of the Origin, 2025

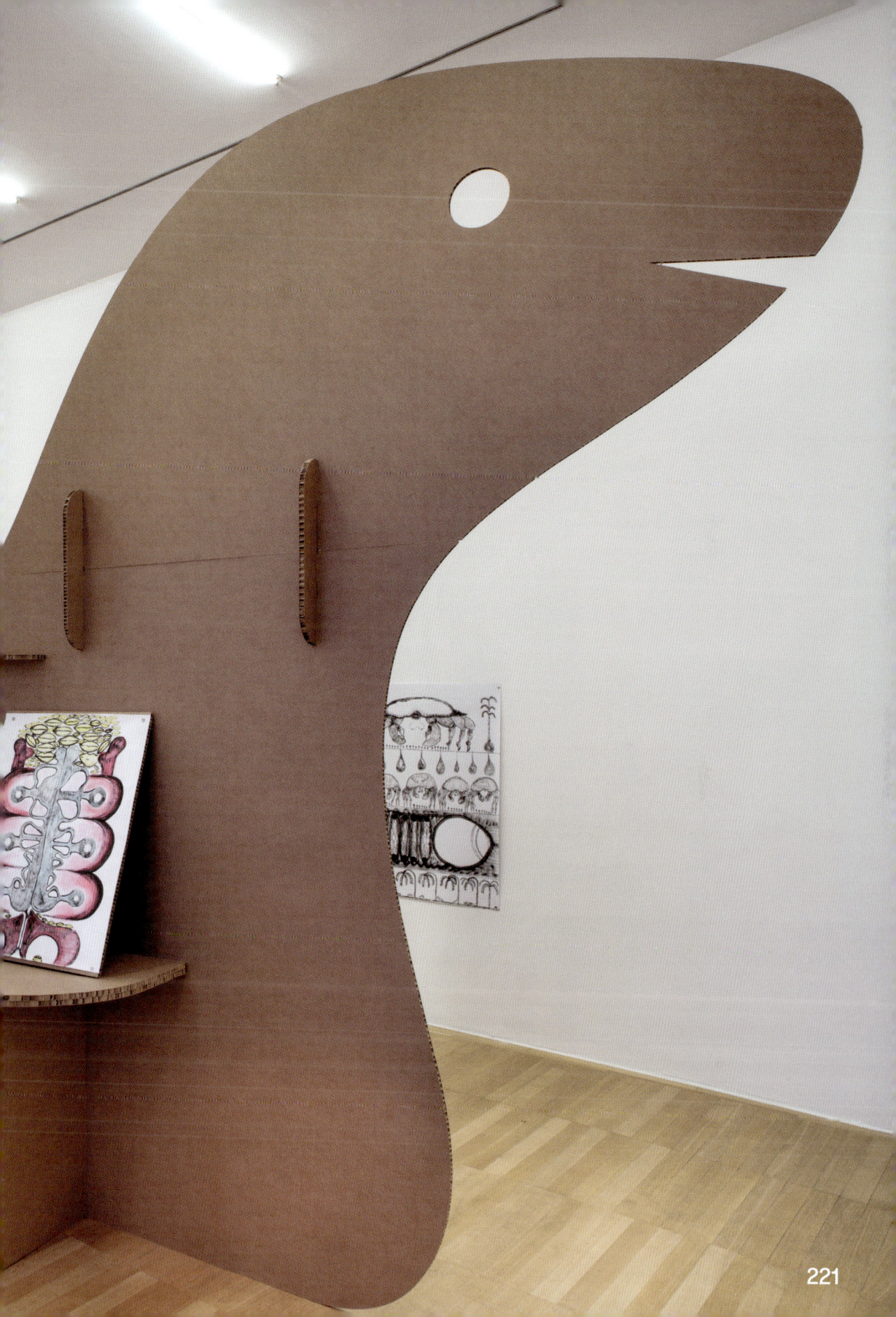

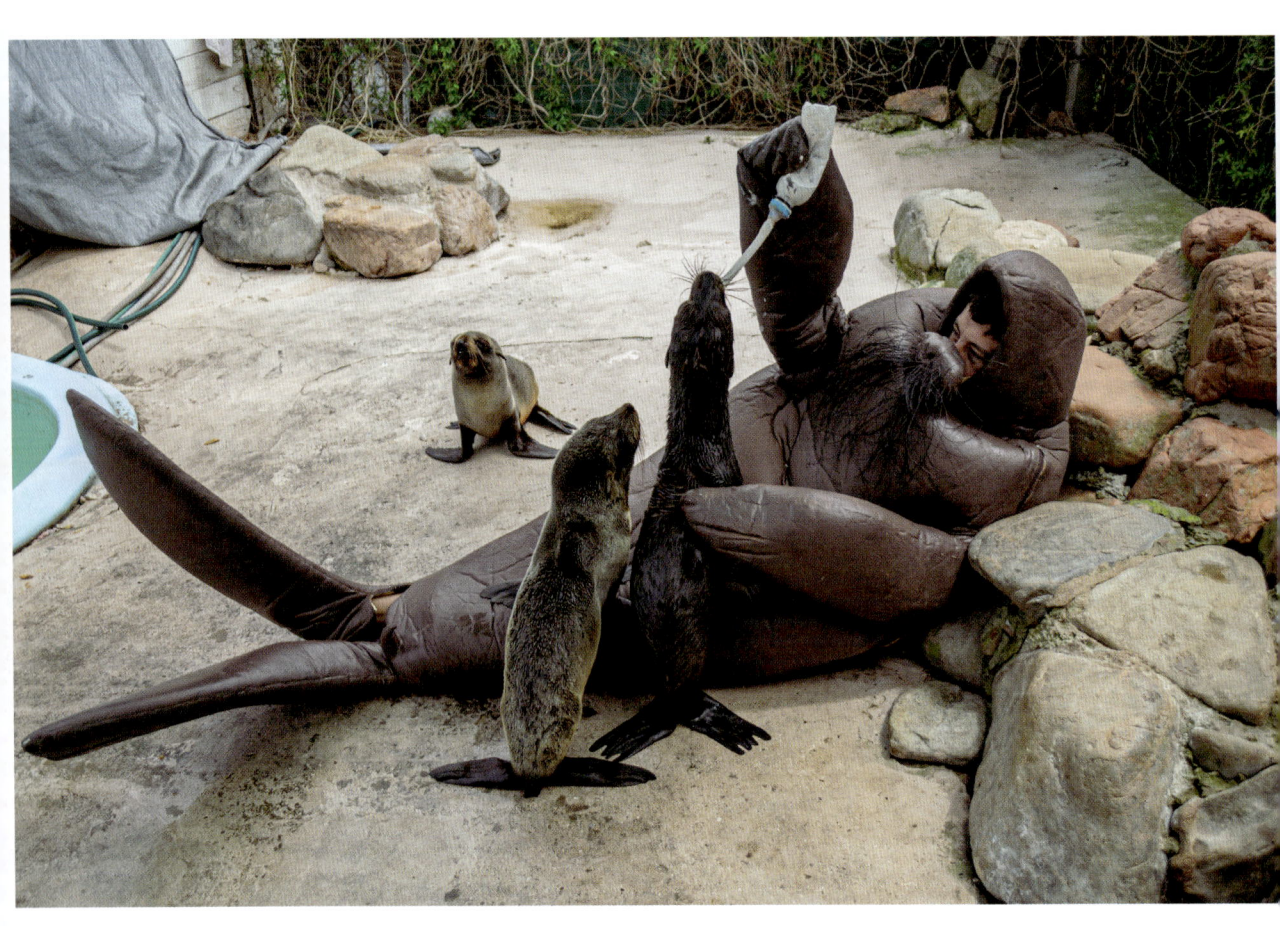

Eduardo Navarro, *F.O.C.A.*
(Foundation for the Oceanic Contemplation of Affection), 2022–25

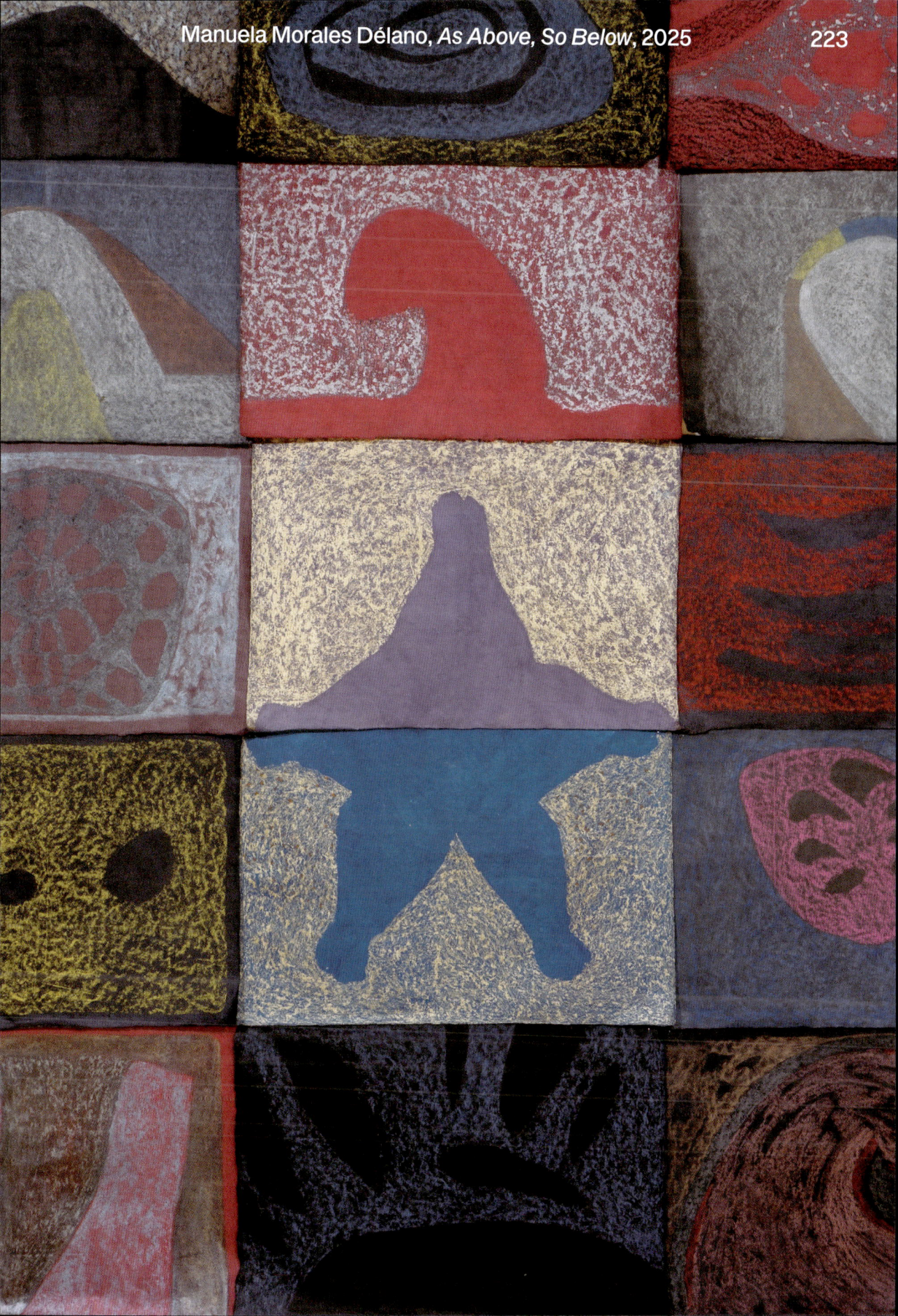

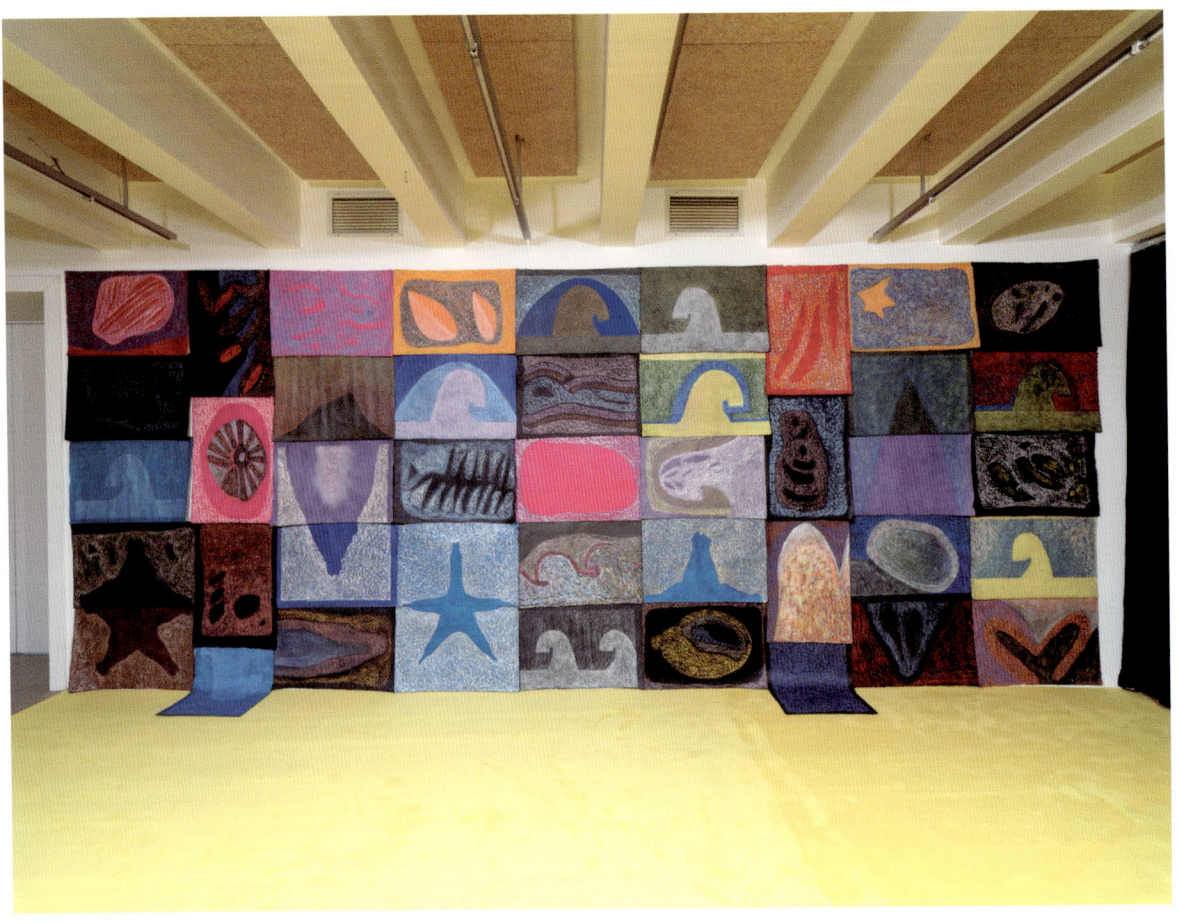

Downstairs, the exhibition continues with two more works in the auditorium: a film by Ema Kugler and a drawing installation by Manuela Morales Délano. The film collage by Kugler combines her signature experimental storytelling techniques to explore personal and collective memory. She invented a filmic universe where she could speak about identity and trauma, blending the boundaries between fiction and reality, challenging traditional storytelling methods. Her surrealism and dreamlike imagery are nourished by theater and performance art. Her images are bold, and her deep emotional explorations are wild. Wild is also her way of reminding us that we are all lost, longing, and, at the same time, searching for meaning.

Drawing has only recently appeared in the work of Manuela Morales Délano. She has mostly worked with performance or sculpture—her other work is on the first floor of the MGLC Grad Tivoli. These drawings, however, are very close to performance: the performance of nature. Made with pastels on soft paper, waves and volcanoes surface again and again. Waves and volcanoes, both symbols of nature's raw power, evoke transformation and the natural world's cyclical patterns. Repetition in drawing is like repetition in nature, the repetition of the seasons, eruptions, cyclones, earthquakes .... Humans and nature both have the power to cause massive and total destruction; only humans can decide not to do so.

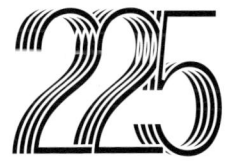

Walk-through of the Exhibition

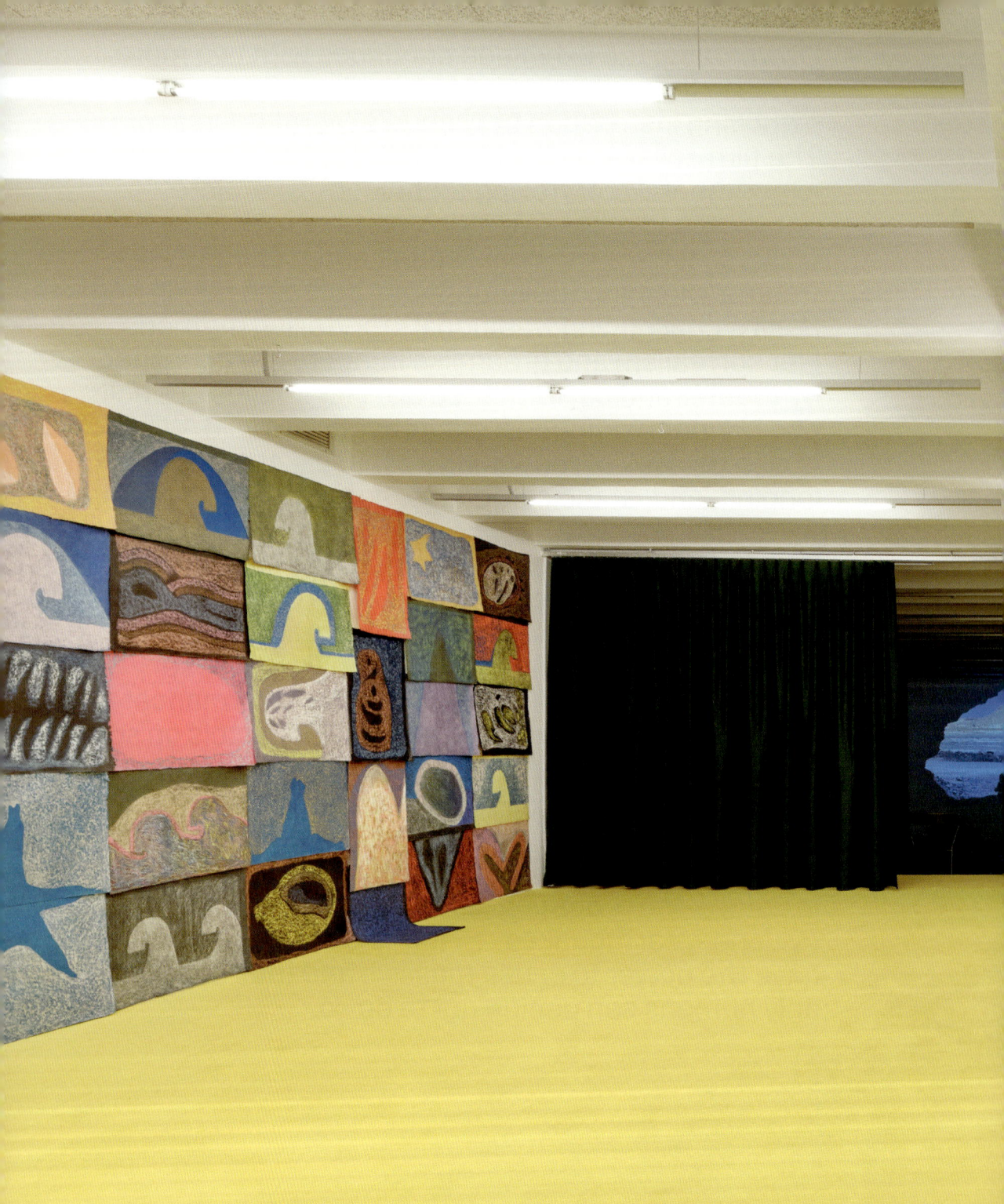

Manuela Morales Délano, *As Above, So Below*, 2025
and Ema Kugler, *Infinite Repetitions*, 2025 (installation view)

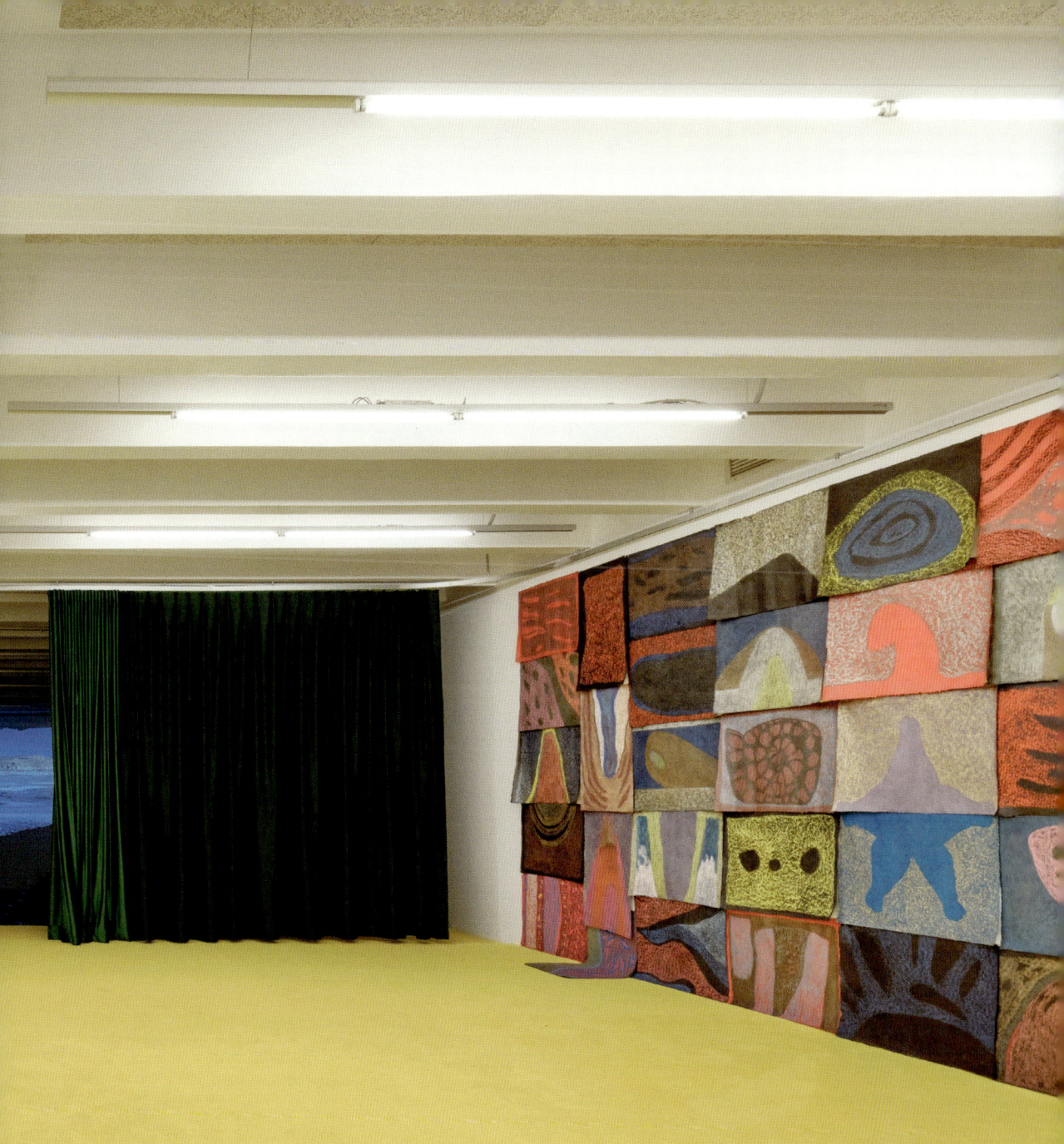

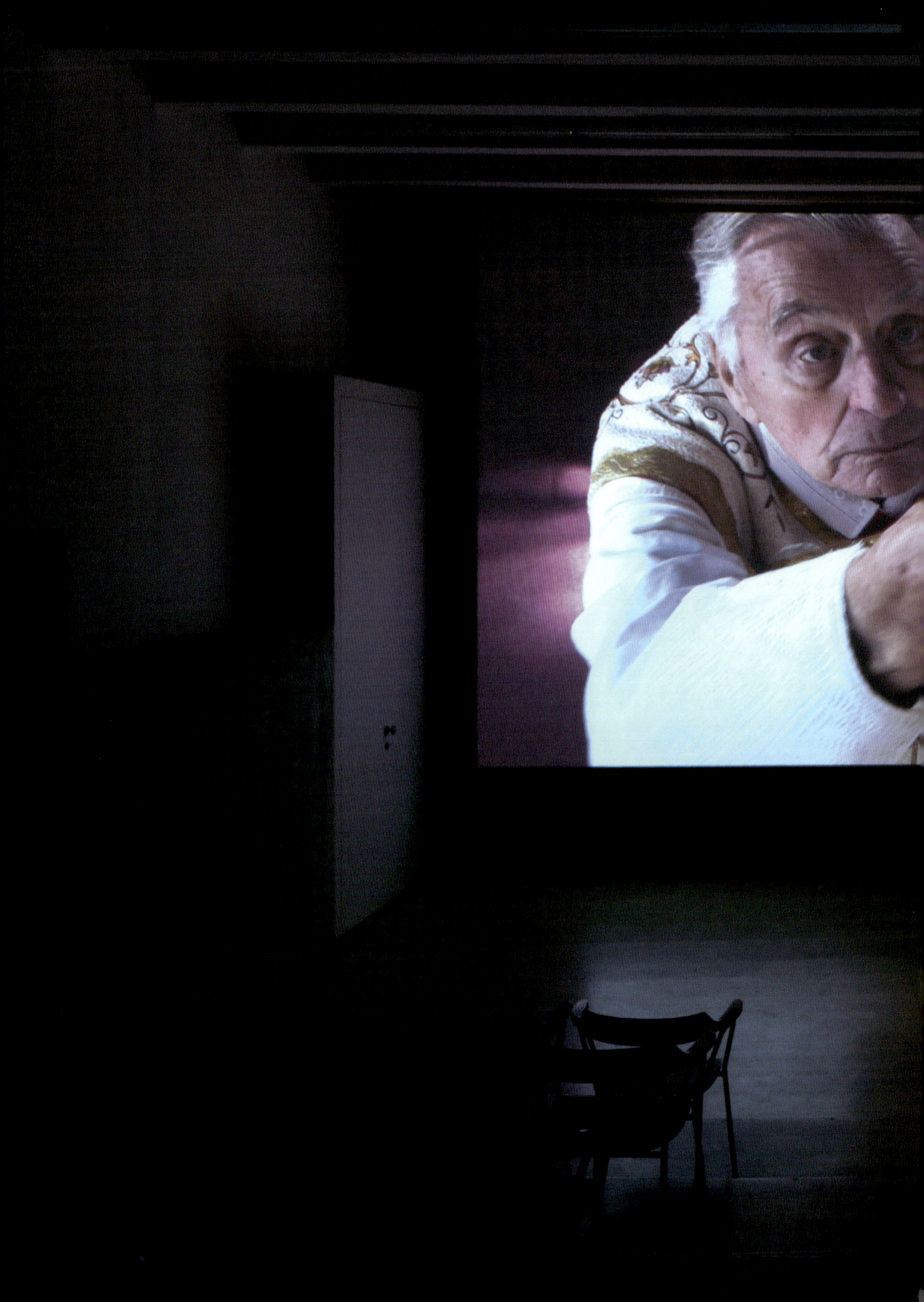

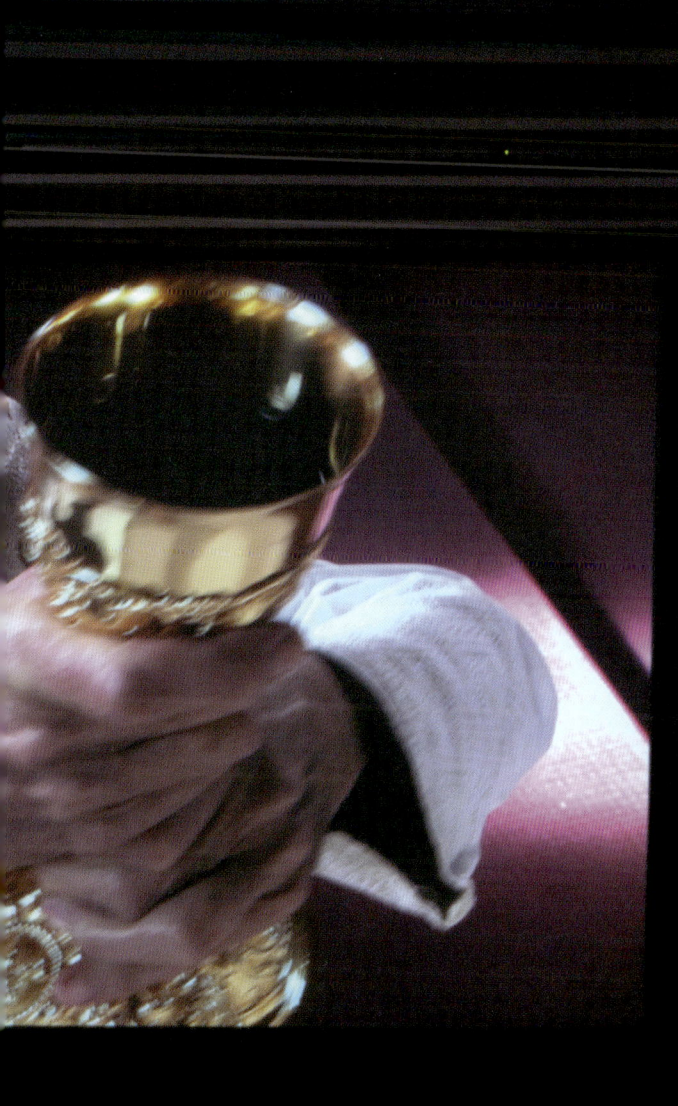

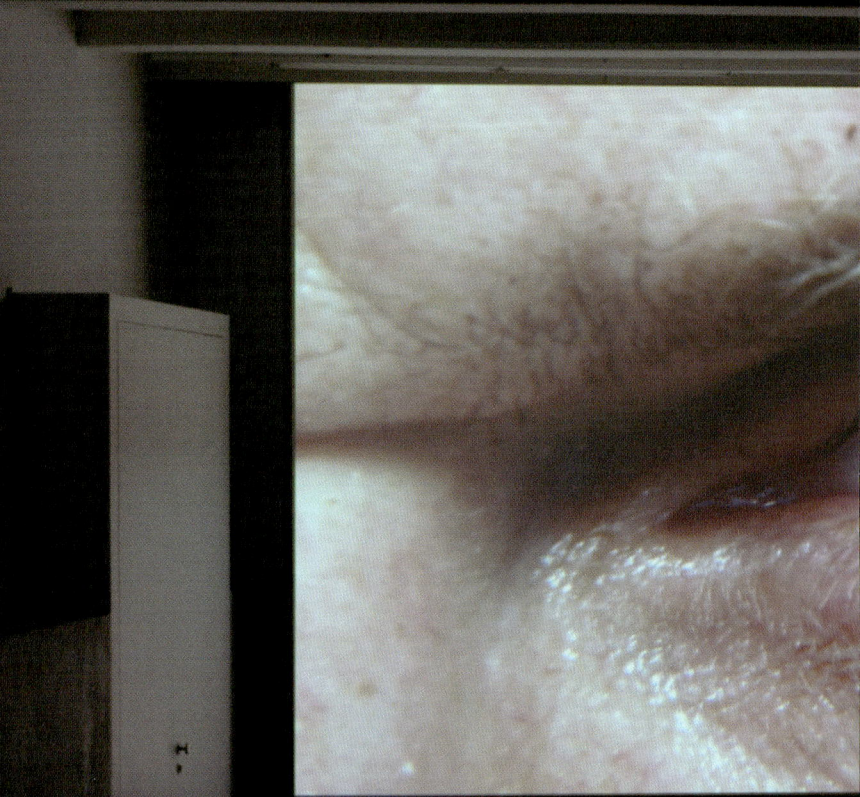

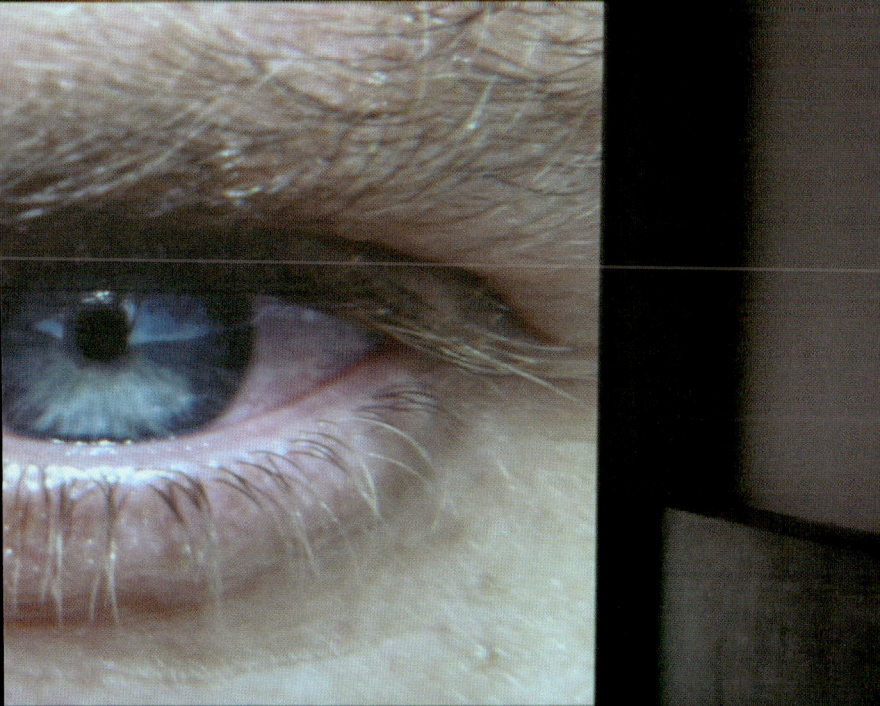

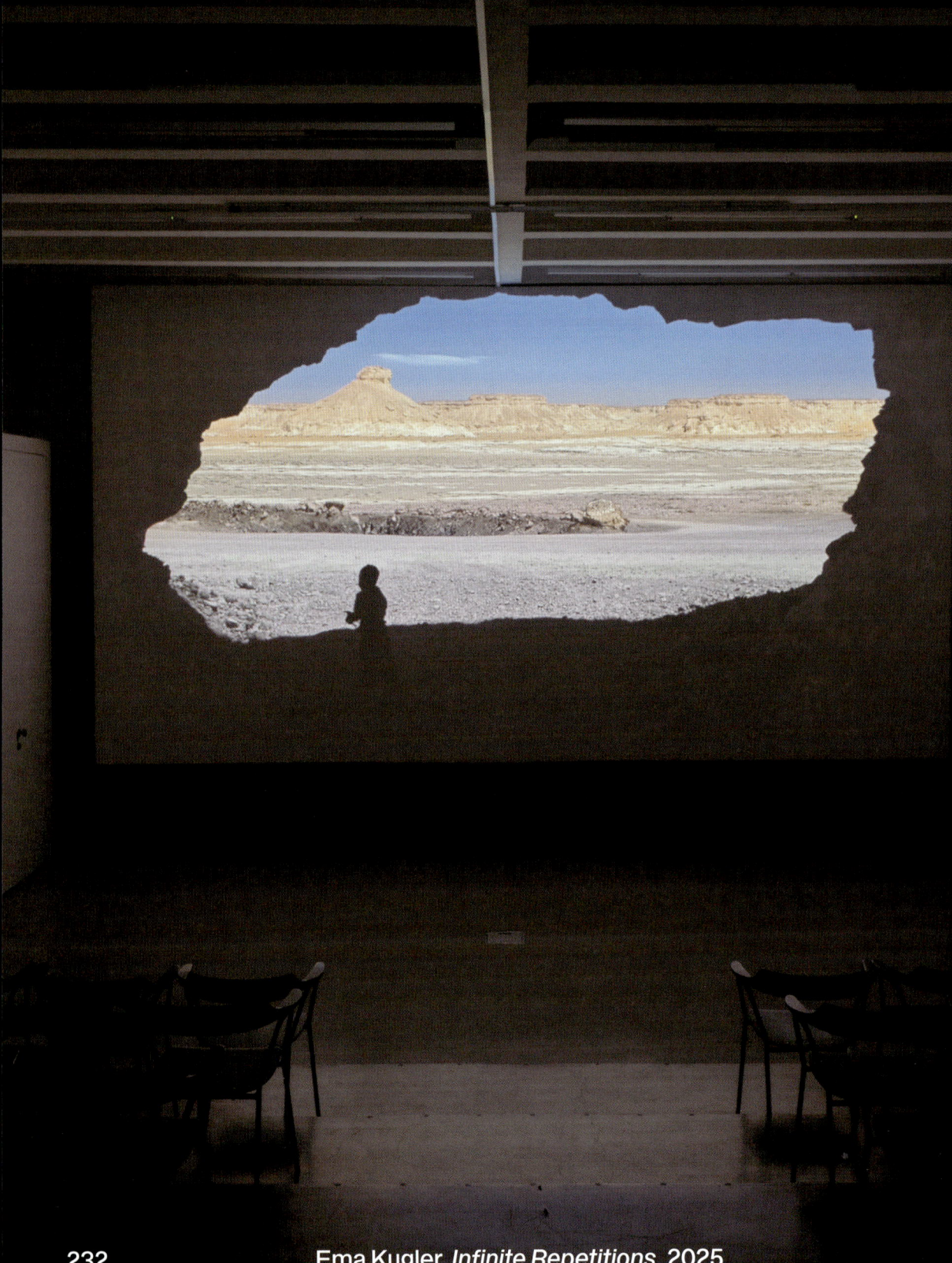

Ema Kugler, *Infinite Repetitions*, 2025

GRAPHING
GRAPHIC ART

Svetlana

Slapšak

Svetlana Slapšak

Here, I am using the word "graphing" with reference to the Greek word for "writing," reminiscent of the physicality of scratching the text onto a two-dimensional surface, in order to stress the etymological and genealogical link between writing and drawing/painting.

At the outset, I had the audacity to ask myself about the definition of art—or rather, I asked my AI support programs. ChatGPT produced a piece of scrambled jargon—if any student had presented the like of it to me while I was still teaching, they would have been a lost cause. Copilot, an AI tool that comes with the price of my new Apple AirBook, did slightly better, offering a collage of definitions and reflections based on the *Stanford Encyclopedia of Philosophy* online, which I quote here:

> Art is a multifaceted concept that encompasses a wide range of human activities, creations, and expressions. At its core, art involves the application of skill and imagination to produce objects, performances, or experiences that can be appreciated for their beauty or emotional power. It serves as a medium for individuals to convey their thoughts, emotions, and perceptions, often transcending conventional boundaries of language and culture.
>
> Throughout history, art has taken various forms, evolving with cultural, social, and technological changes. From ancient cave paintings to Renaissance masterpieces, from modernist abstractions to contemporary installations, art reflects and shapes the values and ideas of different eras and societies. It can celebrate, critique, and inspire, acting as a mirror to the human condition.
>
> Art serves multiple purposes, ranging from personal expression to societal influence. It can be a means of self- exploration, an avenue for social commentary, or a way to evoke aesthetic pleasure. The impact of art is profound, often challenging perceptions, evoking

emotions, and fostering a sense of connection among individuals and communities.

Ultimately, art is defined not just by its form or content, but by its ability to resonate with audiences, provoke thought, and enrich the human experience. It is a testament to the boundless creativity and imagination inherent in all of us.

I tried to summarize it and make it short, very short, and I came up with this: Art is the product of art. It follows a certain duality, which emerges from Stanfordian encyclopedic thinking, a duality between an obvious human need to produce art and the context, observations, and evaluations that define the product as art. Perhaps the term *artart* could be used to name this? Reduplication is a phenomenon in linguistic morphology that serves to make differences more expressive (for instance, past tense from aorist as in Ancient Greek or just repeating the same word, like hush-hush, so it sounds stronger).

At that point, I was struck by my lack of seriousness, and I decided to exercise humility by going through a process of disclosing and arguing, surely making mistakes on the way, but still hopefully keeping the traces of my irony under control.

* * *

I had just started to develop the basic structure, the triad art/nature/gender being constantly crushed by the merciless pressure of society, and was combining the meanings in different directions, looking for parallels/references, when it all exploded in my face, a joint blast from our recent past and crazy present. Allow me to explain:

A couple of weeks ago, there was a rally on the main square of Ljubljana, in front of the parliament. Since I live two steps from the location, it was very much acoustically present in my home. It was organized by a well-known provocateur/

mobster, former politician, and convicted criminal who now manipulates retired citizens and buses them to Ljubljana to protest whenever needed in support of the leader of the right-wing SDS party, Janez Janša. This time, besides the usual choice of populist topics such as immigration, LGBTQ+, low pensions, the left, and similar, the protest specifically targeted the recent amendment to the law on extraordinary pensions for artists who have received the highest state awards, which determined the criteria for being granted this privilege, concerning about a hundred potential recipients. The inflamed mob was shouting slogans against "parasites"—artists who "just fool around" instead of working and then take "our" money for doing so. Janša himself appeared at the rally, announcing the move by his party to organize a referendum against the amendment of the mentioned law. In the meantime, the referendum has passed all the required administrative demands and will take place on May 11, 2025. The government has openly suggested that citizens should refrain from participating in the hope that the minimum voter turnout would not be reached, and thus the amendment would not be rejected.

At the rally, two women artists, Simona Semenič and Maja Smrekar, were specifically singled out, named, and booed for being parasitic, degenerate, and disrespectful of art and the state. The former is an author, dramatist, director, and performer. In one of her installations, she presented a photo of herself wrapped in the Slovenian flag cut out around her pregnant belly. The latter is a bio- and hybrid artist who, in one of her performances, breastfed her dog. Both women were recipients of the Prešeren Fund award, the highest state award for artistic achievement, in 2018. Both artists are now in their late forties, they are well established abroad, often translated and recognized with awards, and struggling to survive and work at home.

A simple and easy interpretation of these two works of art under constant attack from the populist right, one graphic (a photo) and the other "graphic" in some lame transemic intervention, could be the following: a pregnant woman, this obvious sign of the continuation/victory of life, breaks through everything else—nation, narrative, symbols, frontiers, rules, patriarchy—just because she is more important than any and all of them. At the same time, this unbreakable bond between gender and nature is fragile and vulnerable, because it is art as well. Symmetry does not play any part in the number of bonding/bondage options: some may endanger the possible fourth in the nature/gender/art triad.

In these changes, the gaze and the reflection find an array of reactions, from horror to pleasure. This part is controlled solely by art. Art is the prism through which the gaze and the reflection are formed. The graphic work of art (a photo) in this case glorifies the nature/gender bond and deconstructs the symbolic shedding of human institutions in their historical passage.

The second case, the one that is "graphic" in terms of common sense, displays the nature/gender bond in a different way, not by glorifying it, but by pointing to survival, often marked by tragedy. Breastfeeding is an anthropological *longue durée*, from the Neolithic to practices today (e.g., in India), through many variations: not by mother, applied to grownups, by animals, and, as in this case, zootrophy, for the healing of mastitis, and so on. It marks one of the most widely expanded and longest-lasting belief systems related to the Great Mother Goddess. Thank you, Marija Gimbutas!

Zootrophy, as a bond between nature and gender, does not involve symbolic relations and does not care about human institutions: it is a warning about the threatening breaking of bonds. There can be no glory if death is close, and sometimes inter-species solidarity can temporarily prevent death. Art is a translator here, one of several possible translators, like science, among others. The importance of the message is related via both translations. The (technically) graphic and the "graphic" can, in fact, exchange places: the photo is "graphic" due to its provocative force, the performance is graphic because it follows a long line of zootrophic presentations. And they are both graphic and "graphic" when the notion of art is eliminated—that is, in the interpretation

Svetlana Slapšak

of the populist mob. This is relatively easy to disentangle and pulverize, but the criticism never reaches and hurts those who really deserve it. The question becomes increasingly unpleasant at this point: How do we shake off the label of exclusivism and elitism? How do we escape the disdain of the common people? How do we stop the social turmoil initiated by the hatred of art and artists? What if it is necessary and indeed inevitable to limit art to a restricted public that possesses the necessary knowledge and controls the many possibilities of expressing it? Society is spilling all of its dirt and poison over nature, gender, and art, and yet it is the only space in which art can be produced, gender constructed, and nature understood—and where all three may be enslaved and mutilated. But one thing remains clear: the interpretation defines the status of art in society, and this interpretation can amount to culture. The flow of social and cultural contexts, or history, does not allow the constant presence of any one cognitive system, but rather an arbitrary exchange of cognitive systems. And when art is in question, there are two competitive cognitive approaches, which may somewhat reflect the medieval controversy of realism and nominalism: either art is to be accepted or rejected without contextual knowledge, or art cannot be approached and understood/evaluated outside of culture. Neither of these approaches can be universal, that is, ungendered. And once gendered, they must be historical. Was art, then, ever spontaneous? Probably not. Psychology, one of the most conservative sciences today, still has a problem accepting that the human psyche, just like language, is historical, although not attuned to the phasing of human history. The historicity of the psyche can best be understood in the domain of the cognitive: for instance, the way ancient humans observed and understood the world consequently determined their behavior and their body. The change that occurred with the acceptance of Christianity in the Euro-Asian space is one of the most spectacular: silent, internal Christian praying changed the body, social relations, writing and reading, and all human communication, and all this happened in a relatively short time. But this understanding of the psyche is still not part of the widely accepted knowledge, because science has not popularized and scholarized it. So, what could be the way to introduce the historicity of the psyche to our understanding of the art? First of all, we should relate understanding to memory, and thus avoid any notion of "truth" which lingers around it. Memory is local, fixed in time, even when contaminated by the imaginary—and it almost always is.

SEMANTIC GENEALOGY

Help comes from linguistics, again, with the notion of semantic genealogy. This refers to a history of words which does not only follow the development of meanings, including branching, but sometimes follows those lost and arbitrary, or meanings not recorded in language, or just invented by humans. Logic does not count in semantic genealogy. For instance, the above horrible definition of art by ChatGPT does not use the admittedly obnoxious word "negotiating" from the academic jargon—it is now replaced by the foggier word "navigating." The *why* remains a mystery. Or not, if we think of the periodical reappearance of absurd, secret, crypto-ludic, and merrily reproductive artistic tendencies, movements, and schools such as *pataphysique*, the Voynich manuscript, or the drawings and paintings of Hilma af Klint. Semantic genealogy has answers to this kind of artwork: anthropological, social, and cultural, in addition to linguistic.

Almost forty years ago, I coined a word that recalls Bakhtin's *chronotopos*. My word was *chronospore*, and I used it as the title of my first book of essays. Its meaning, an example of a curve in semantic genealogy, is "a seed travelling through time, with no plan of when to root but looking for an occasion to do so."[1] The reason to stop and root

1   Svetlana Slapšak, *Hronospore* (Nezavisna izdanja, 1987).
     The book was awarded the Miloš Crnjanski Award for essays.

does not necessarily coincide with the flow of time (and thus with the context); it includes free will and some opposition to regulations and predictability. And above all, it does not exclude political engagement. At that time in Yugoslavia, mainstream theorizing in art and literature was very much opposed to the idea of (political) engagement. This was, quite paradoxically, a consequence of ideological pressure and real time/space repression. Engagement was considered vulgar and destructive for art, and it was a way to denounce those who not only engaged politically in 1968, but who continued to be engaged also after the happy hours (one week) of the revolution were over and the clemency of Tito was pronounced, thus becoming dissidents. Caring for the working class and social inequality in art, and all of that in a socialist country (however unique of its kind, and rather liberal) was considered bad, and compromising with the regime elegantly (read: with hypocrisy) was considered good! No wonder I was dreaming of a solitary seed that can float freely and choose the time and space for rooting ....

Semantic genealogy is thus inevitable in the creation and reception of art; it does (must?) participate or even direct the wish, intention, and will to engage, change, choose, and live a certain set of ideas open and critical to society. Semantic genealogy allows for fantasy, abstraction, negation, and madness to be present in the process. To put it into *pragma*, education, ethical stability, a state of peace, free gender orientation, and bodily comfort in/with nature are the closest examples of a co-understanding of the creation, seduction, reproduction, and pleasure in and with art. The two artists mentioned above, forcibly misinterpreted and made victims of mass hysteria, did just that, and are now attacked by people who were never exposed, not even on the level of general education, to any of these. What the artists did was graphing, which demasked such a system; they made art, which has to be rooted in a minefield in order to clean it for all others. Others now have to resist and defend them, because they were, in fact, saving their lives. That is how big in life their art became.

BEAUTY AS THE BEAST

The art-haters have their excuses, and none of them are pardonable. At their strongest, they are omnipresent and difficult to extinguish. There are some discursive signs which betray them immediately, and one of them is certainly the frequent return to the notion of beauty, so tricky that it tricked even Umberto Eco into drowning in controversies and choking on banalities. The concept of beauty in art, ruling both the upper and lowest sections of society from antiquity until the twentieth century, translates the class order of mostly Western societies and almost nothing more. The great change came with Christianity: still unclear and debated, contaminated with many later interventions and with sheer misunderstanding, the ancient concept of beauty was never limited to the body and rarely conveyed power. The beauty of ancient bodies, which we have been taught to admire, was based on technical and cultural conventions, slightly changing over time, testimonies of the artists' competition within their chronotopoi. In an ancient poem written by a woman, women in a city are invited to admire a statue of a hetaera, which she herself ordered and paid for, being rich and influential, and beautiful. In an anecdote, the painter Zeuxis painted an old woman, and while he was observing the finished work he started to laugh, and he laughed so hard that he died. Beauty was observed as pertaining to a small fraction of life, and the ugliness of old age was observed with laughter, the mightiest way to make demons, the souls of the dead, and death itself run away. While beauty demands admiration, which comes with the distance needed for observation, the ugliness demands intimacy, which comes with memory and closeness in the face of death. And there is a common core to both relations: sexuality. The gaze defines the change and graduation of desire, the touch and the sound of intimacy define the change and graduation of the fear of death. In ancient sexuality, which changed over time and across cultures, the

Svetlana Slapšak

counterbalance to male dominance, and sheer power over the physically and socially weaker, was the shortcomings of male sexuality in both sexual acts and life. The young man was metaphorically represented as a short-lived flower, quite contrary to the global (not only Western) representation of young women as flowers. During the exclusively women's festival of Adonia, celebrated in ancient Athens but also in other poleis in the midsummer, women would plant seeds in broken vessels, forcing them to grow; on the night of the festival, they would wear clothes and make-up in the sexiest possible way and take the sprouts, called "Adonis' gardens," to the terraces on the roofs, where they would indulge themselves in food and wine, and dance, accompanied by obscene jokes, and partied all night, while the poor sprouts were fading away. Adonis was a beautiful boy, sexually used by two powerful goddesses, Aphrodite and Persephone. An abandoned lover, husband, or jealous pretendent in love with Adonis sent a wild boar, who attacked and wounded him mortally. He died in Aphrodite's hands, and his blood turned into anemones. Aphrodite laid his body on lettuce or cabbage leaves (both symbolized sterility) and was devastated as long as she, as a goddess, could bear. Adonis really behaved like a plant, passing from one godly embrace to another, being a very clumsy hunter, and hunting was the most common ancient metaphor of sexuality. The festival does not have any wider religious meaning—on the contrary, it is rather an ironical replaying of events pointing to mas-culine sexual inadequacy, men's sexual efforts being short in time, and low in achievement; but it does not ironize only the story, together with goddesses—it ironizes men, who are excluded from the festival, who rule the world but not always the bed. This myth meets another, that of the prophet Teiresias, who was turned into a woman when he saw snakes copulating. The curse for breaking this taboo lasted for sev eral years, until he saw the same scene again. The goddess Hera then forbade the prophet from sharing with men the best-kept female secret, but he did anyway: women enjoy sex nine times more than men. Teiresias was punished by blindness, which just increased his prophetic capacities and boosted his career. The fear of women's sexuality remained noted among more obscure myths.

This excursus on the mythical production of antiquity was necessary to outline some neglected aspects of historical sexuality in art. The censorship of the Christian culture was eventually crushed by class change and cultural revolution in the Renaissance. The aristocracy and the rich social classes imposed their commodity—pleasure in the watching, presenting, evaluating, and marketing of ancient artworks, including all those naked bodies and sexual scenes. Helped by the rediscovery of ancient texts, the cultural *movida* finally overcame the strict rules imposed by the church, and even popes started ordering artworks that covered the walls and ceilings of the Vatican with naked bodies. Ancient art was the winner, with new regulations, and its owners distanced themselves further from the lower classes, also by insisting on new criteria of taste, sexual permissiveness, libertinage, etc. Different forms of democratic art and even the massive use of art in the monarchic and imperial periods of antiquity were forgotten. Through schooling and literacy, the new use of ancient art expanded enormously, creating a certain concept of beauty which, in its own terms, soon became conservative and limiting. Admittedly, it also became a hidden way to learn about sexuality in times when the censorship of sexuality became not only a church prerogative but also something mandated by the state. The ambivalent position of ancient art can still enable the same educative role in sexuality behind the excuse of worshiping beauty. Here is an example: in making yet another film version of Jane Austen's *Pride and Prejudice* in 2005, the director Joe Wright found a way to visually enhance the strong sexual tension, almost inexistant in the text of the novel. He did so with the help of artworks. Elizabeth Bennet finds herself in the very rich home of Mr. Darcy, and wanders alone in the glyptotheque. She faces the marble portrait of Mr. Darcy himself, and follows his petrified gaze directed at ancient sculptures (or copies

Svetlana Slapšak

thereof), which are mostly naked. This dual gaze quickly glimpses a wounded warrior and his genital parts, then pauses for a while on the perfect buttocks of a naked female body positioned horizontally. Elizabeth smiles shyly—she is beginning to understand Mr. Darcy's sexuality, his social clumsiness, his secret fantasies; in fact, his sexuality appears free here, grandiose and defined by culture. In other scenes in the film, burdened by despicable class hierarchy and the cruel superiority of Mr. Darcy's aunt, the walls of the room are covered with huge baroque paintings featuring naked nymphs and satyrs, even a scene of attempted rape. Thus sexuality, via ancient art and the commodity of the presence of naked bodies in a stiff society, is included in the plot and then "read into" the text of the novel. And all of this is done under the umbrella of "beauty."

The dark side of "beauty" comes from the same source—education, poor education, or no education at all, with just the shadow of its presence remaining under class pressure. The Palladian beautiful nudes do not affect the masses; their place is eventually taken by cheap and low culture and pornography, so finally, in the world of quick and global information with its final stage in the culture of lies, "beauty" is taken and ravaged at will by anybody. Maybe it deserved it. The vulgarity of "beauty" has become just one of the discursive ways to manipulate people and to direct their hate to yet another object—anything not beautiful according to the distorted ruling narratives. The use of ancient images, mostly from the Archaic and Early Classical periods in fascist, Nazi, and Stalinist official art is a startling example of possible abuses.

The lack of beauty or the denial of beauty in accompanying texts has stirred negative public reactions in modern times, and just a click is needed to manipulate public opinion such that it turns into violence. In the case of these two artists, Simona Semenič and Maja Smrekar, mixing the banality of beauty and the repressive notions of work has seen a new twist: the ethical capitalist condemnation of the parasitism of the poor "who do not work" (the upper classes are not even supposed to work), and political condemnation of parasitism, defined as an attack on collectivity, a notion originating in the former hardcore socialism—which was not the case in Yugoslavia. Capitalist condemnation is expected to be prevalent here, but it is not—the aggressive public openly demands a more equal and just distribution of money to all the retired! This populist mixture would confuse anyone vaguely acquainted with functional logic, but it works, and populist leaders resort to this confusion profusely. In doing so, they have a very restrained choice of tools, so they use "common sense" and "healthy peasant reasoning" to stifle any meaningful reasoning at all. After that, there is only one further logical step, and populists have already proposed it—to send parasitic artists to a work camp and make them cultivate potatoes and salad.

Both semantic genealogy and the beast named beauty have their role in the repression of art, and many artists still embrace both. A solution is not in view. One could deliberate on the greater openness of the art world, which would depend largely on education: the greater presence of artists in public life and more information on how artists work, on the benefits of loneliness, explanations of techniques, etc. But we live in a world that changed radically in a matter of months and weeks, and communication between artists and the public is now a lesser problem given the many and more dangerous threats. Commenting and criticizing such a world has become an intrinsic attitude of artists. Nature and gender are crucial parts of what we used to call engagement: there is no "engagement" after a declaration of war, just fighting.

Intimacy between art, nature, and gender has never been so strong and warm. A long way from the invention of Arcadia, through the fresh air in Barbizon, to the gas masks of WWI and those of the COVID age, and another long way from Lysistrata to Women in Black both end today, when the crowds are stopped by the last frontier, and intimacy is the only possible way to keep bodies alive. What kind of art can be produced now?

Svetlana Slapšak

PUPPETS IN THE CELLAR

My answer is one of modesty and madness, and I would
not dare to connect it to art or nature, but just slightly to
gender. Some fifteen years ago, I organized with a small
group of much younger friends, some of them my students, a
socio-cultural experiment based on something that I knew
well from my Greek experiences—the Karagiozis shadow
puppet theatre. We were helped by the Greek Embassy, and
we invited a well-known Greek Karagiozis puppet artist,
Spyropoulos (several generations of his family have been
in the same profession), who came to Ljubljana and taught
us how to draw, cut, color, and manipulate the puppets, and
how to perform. I drew the puppets, the father of one of my
students made handles to manipulate them, and a friend, a
puppeteer in a classical marionette theatre, constructed the
mobile set for us. I wrote five comic texts, putting Karagiozis
in local situations and in plots that could introduce this Greek
subculture to the Slovenian public. This play for children, in
which a rather clumsy Heracles, with the help of a stubborn
mule and under the ironic eye of the queen of the Amazons,
solves ecological problems, was a great success. After three
years of work, the group dissolved due to financial problems.
The puppets and the set are now in my cellar, waiting
to be used again. The two-dimensional world is patient.
The shadow theatre can be performed anywhere, anytime, by
anyone, even without electricity. The text, except for a couple
of formulae and songs, can be improvised. Today or tomorrow, in any case very soon, the waiting may be over. And
what is Karagiozis? It is poverty and famine fighting against
power. It is every day, today much more than yesterday.

This certainly is not a recommendation. It is just a thing
from down below, where motivation comes from when
needed. When institutions, such as exhibitions, museums,
and galleries, start to question themselves and art, when
many feel invited to defend art without directing it, when
intimacy is the fruit of protesting, when the need for laughing

Graphing Graphic Art

is stronger than ego, when everybody knows what art can make out of fear.

It looks like the graphic embraces graphing—the text, the meaning. The intimacy of the two helps art to survive and graphing to reject hopelessness. They may even try to question semantic genealogy and beauty itself, to deconstruct both, and to apply the experience of resisting and reconstructing them entirely.

Svetlana Slapšak

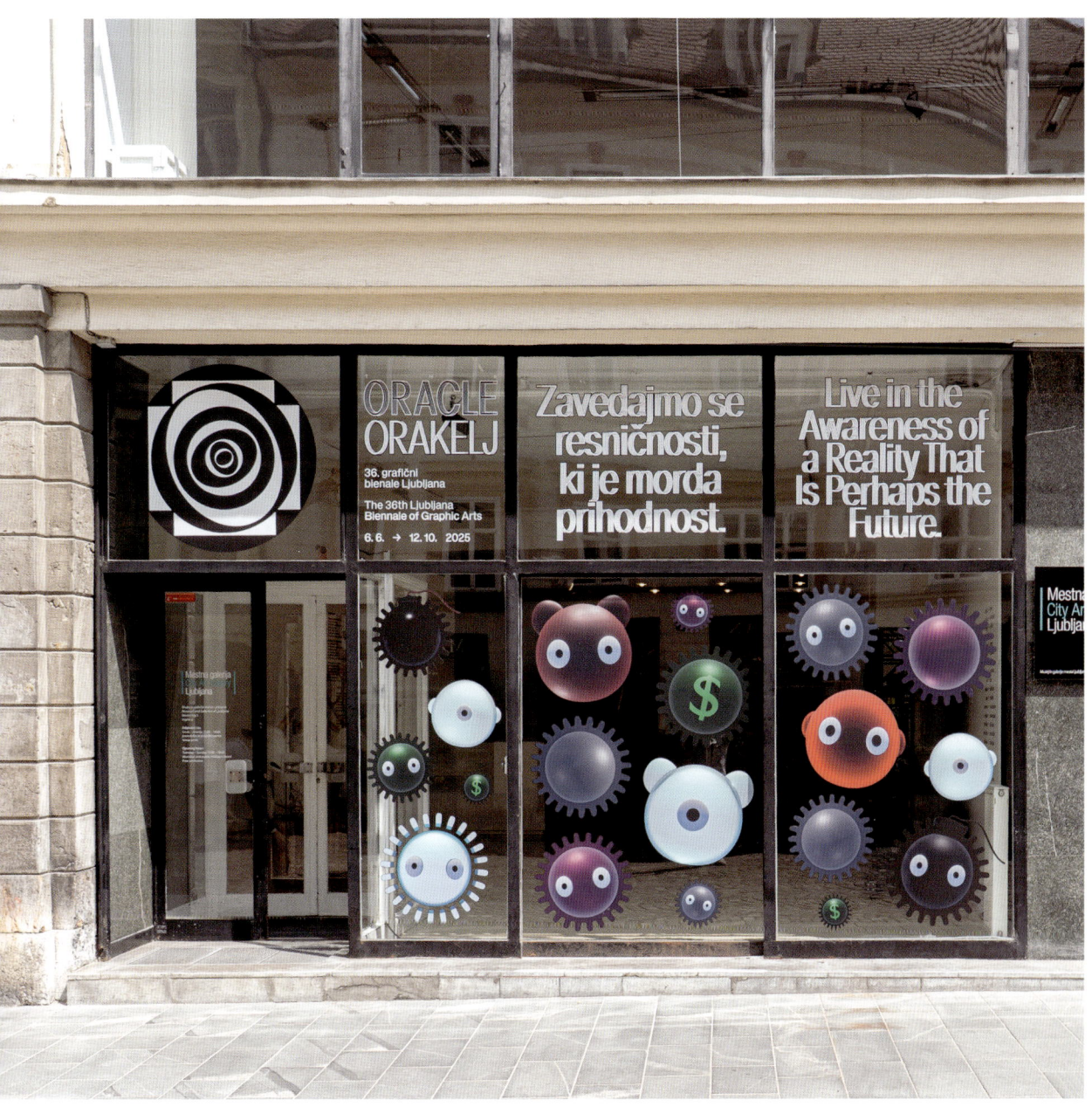

City Art Gallery Ljubljana:
Imagining for Real

Right at the window of the City Art Gallery Ljubljana, you will encounter the collaborative work of Mayte Gómez Molina and Ingo Niermann. *Hieroglyphs of the Monadic Age* is an animated catalogue of environmental, social, political, and emotional scenarios. It is a visual manual to help us think about what the world would be like if several—seemingly contradictory—post-liberal fantasies actually took place. Providing visualizations of probable worlds is fundamental to situate ourselves as citizens and consider to what extent we want to be part of these realities that are organized in completely new ways, today predominantly expressed as "impossibilities" or as "dangers." The work is based on Ingo Niermann's essay collection *The Monadic Age: Notes on the Coming Social Order* (MIT Press/Sternberg Press, 2024). Together with the poet, artist, and programmer Mayte Gómez Molina, they have created a strange visual dictionary of useful notions for a world-to-come.

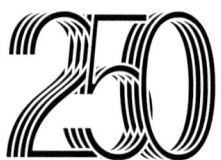

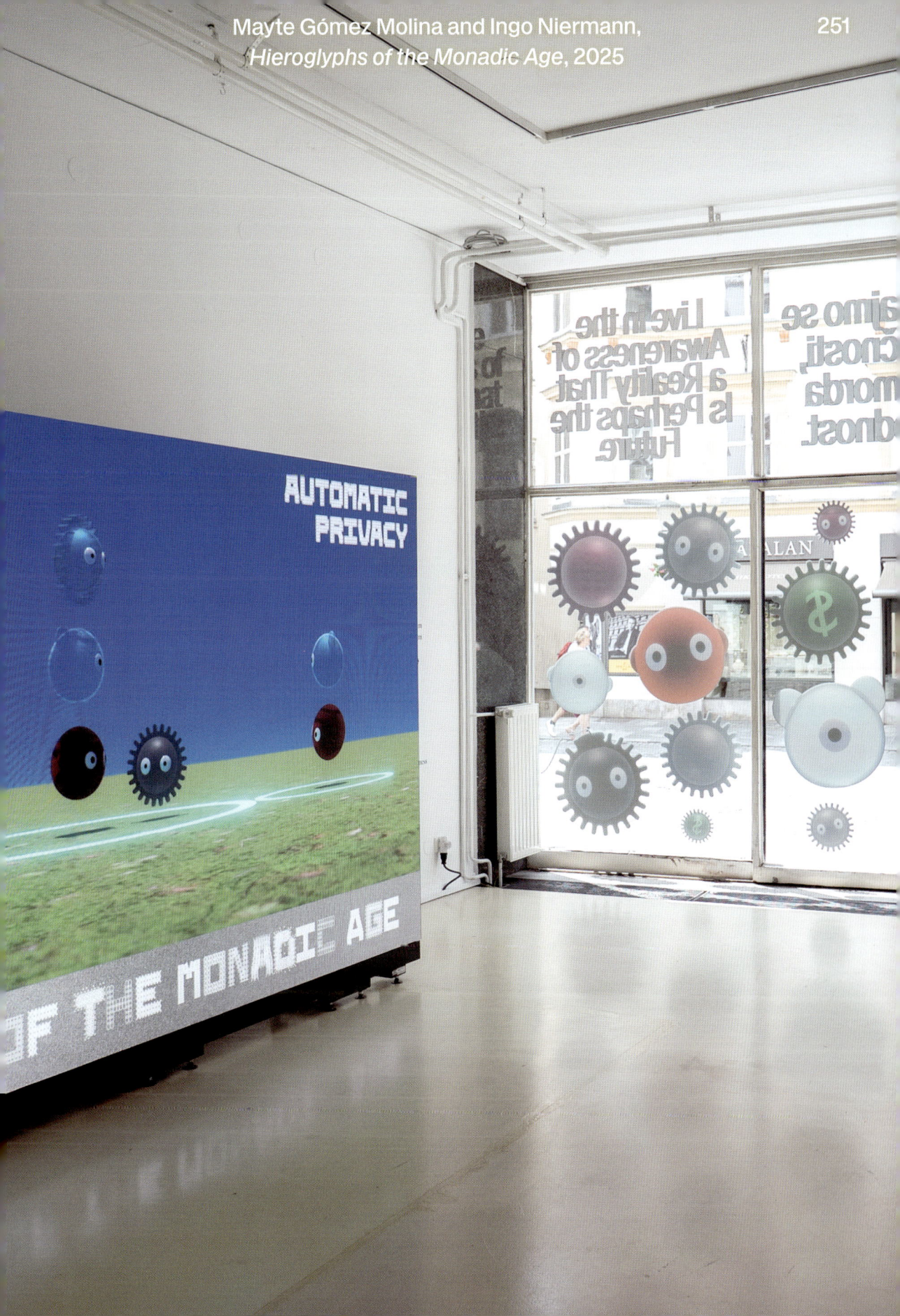

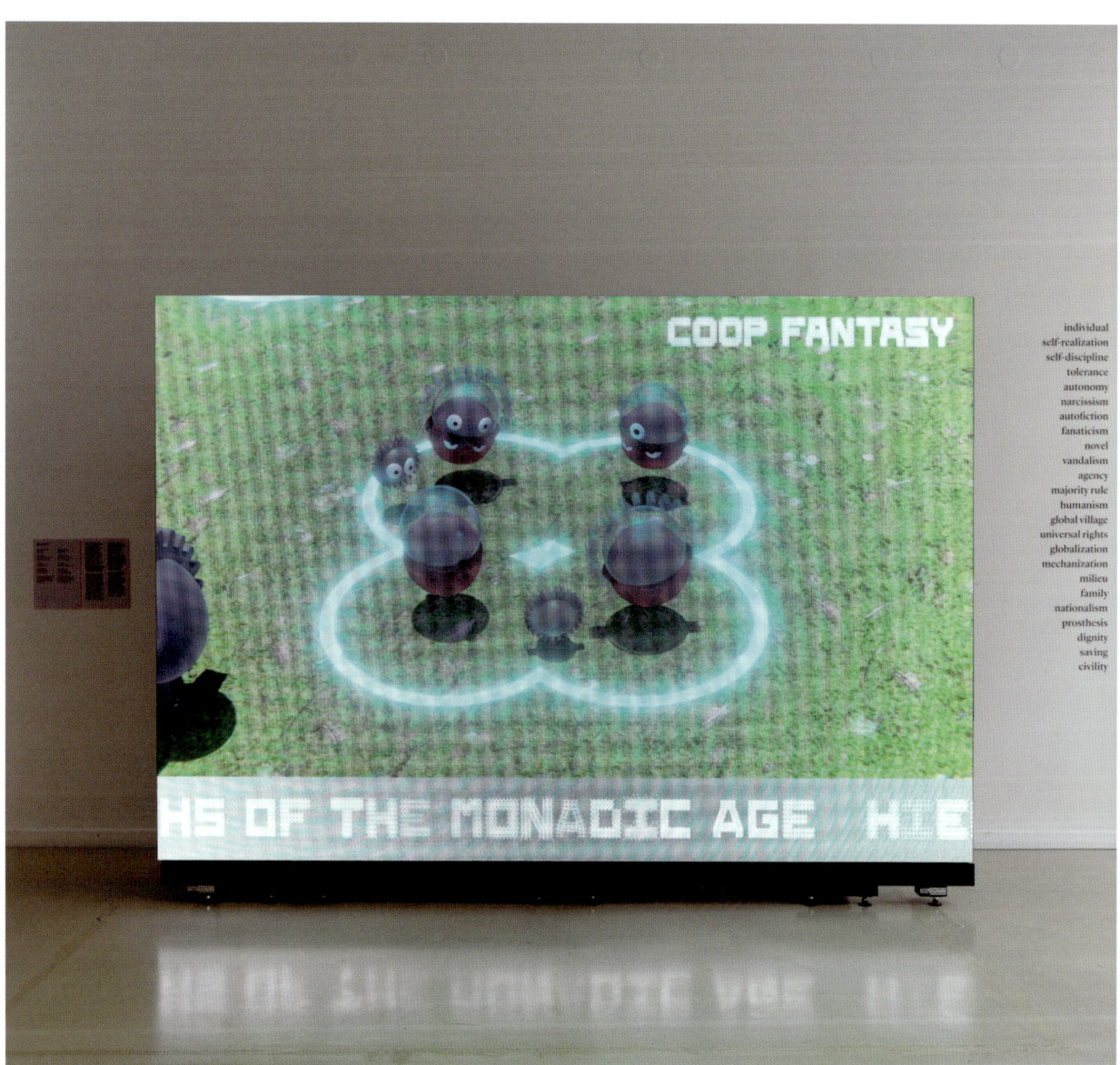

individual
self-realization
self-discipline
tolerance
autonomy
narcissism
autofiction
fanaticism
novel
vandalism
agency
majority rule
humanism
global village
universal rights
globalization
mechanization
milieu
family
nationalism
prosthesis
dignity
saving
civility

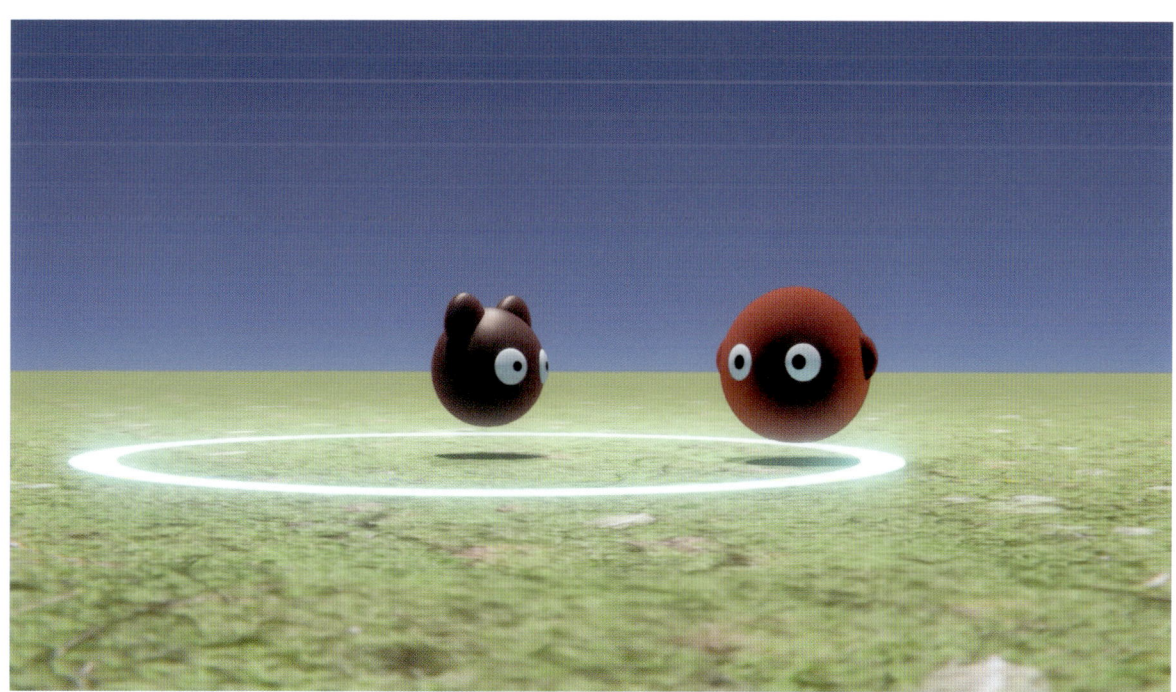

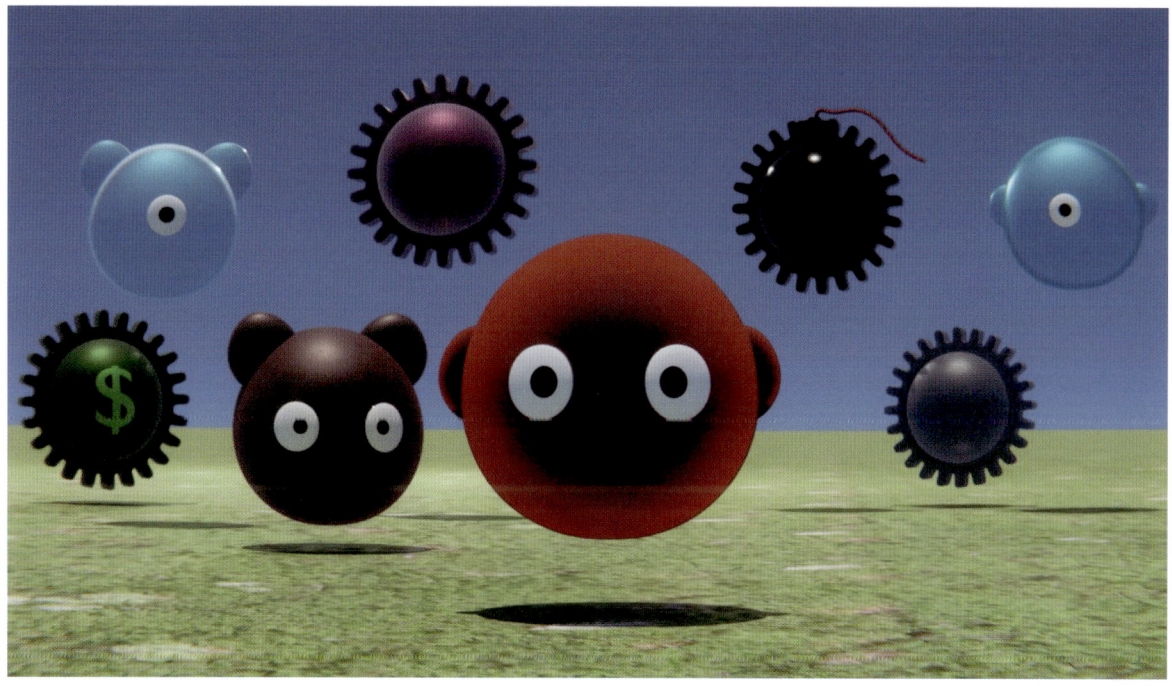

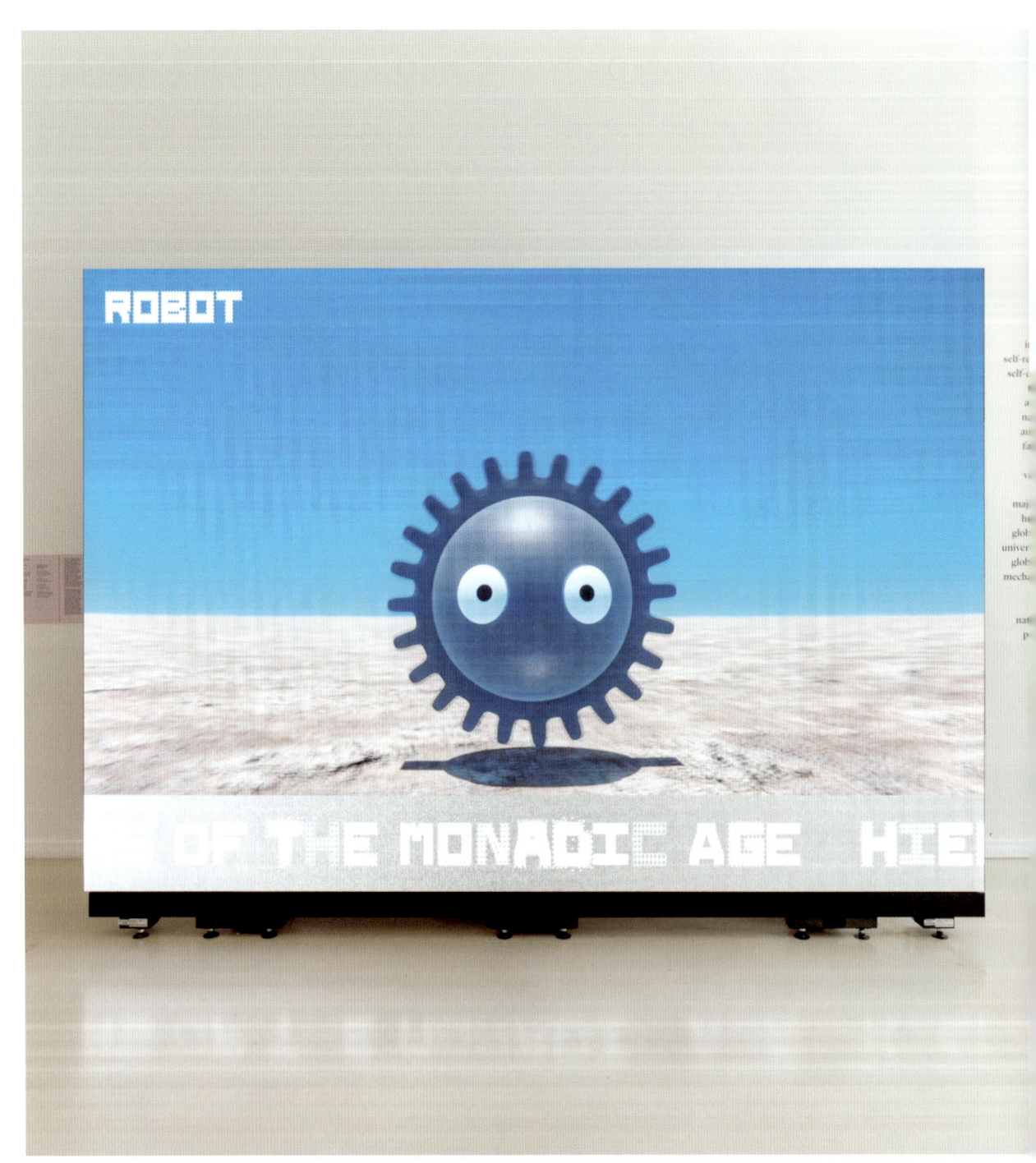

Mayte Gómez Molina and Ingo Niermann,
Hieroglyphs of the Monadic Age, 2025

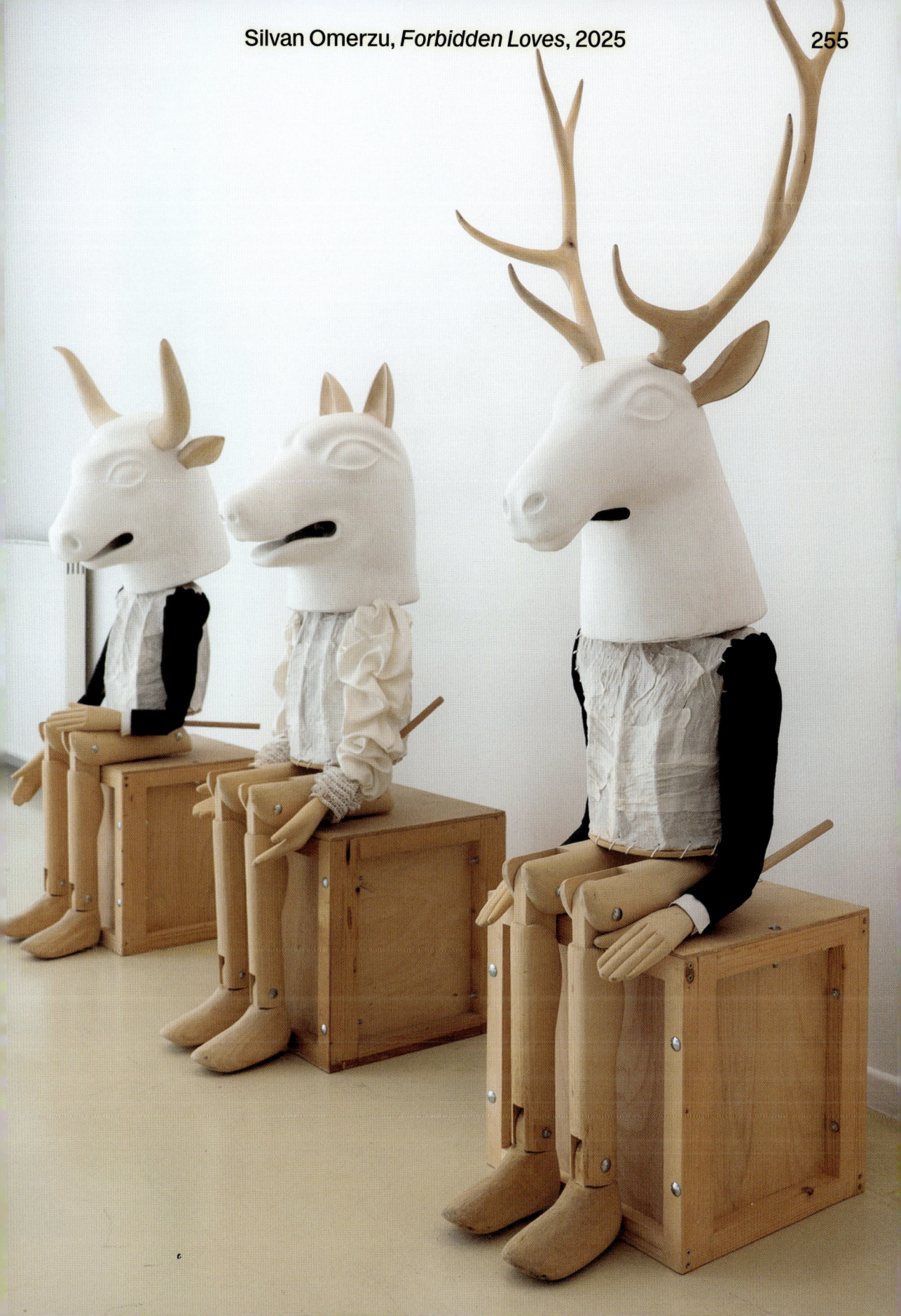

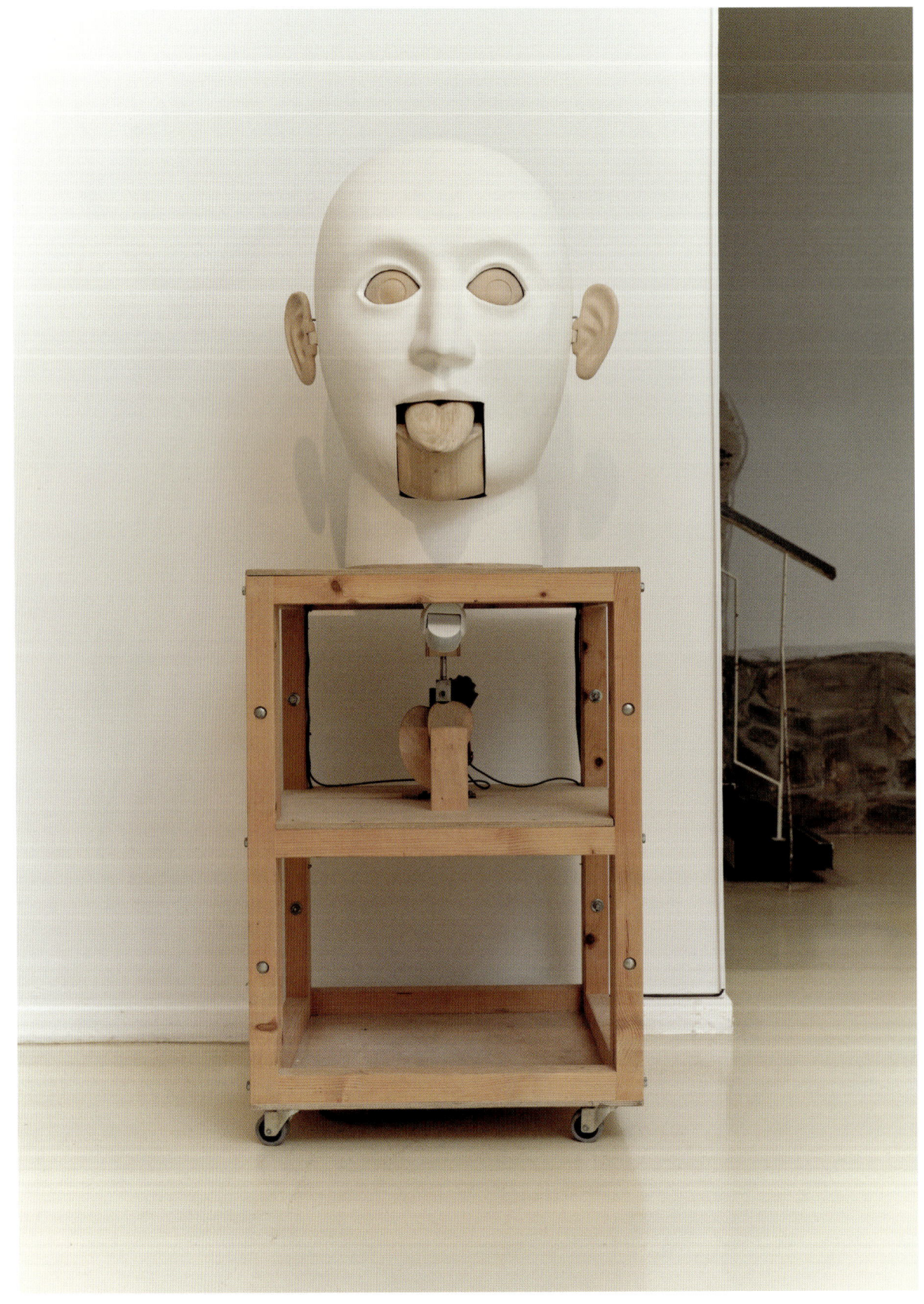

On opening the door, you will see an intervention by Silvan Omerzu. Legend has it that Ljubljana was founded by the mythical hero Jason, who stole the Golden Fleece from King Aeëtes and fled with the Argonauts aboard the ship Argo. Their journey led them across the Black Sea and further along the rivers Danube, Sava, and Ljubljanica. This installation draws inspiration from Greek mythology, particularly the myth of Daedalus, the ingenious inventor who created a mechanical cow in which Pasiphaë hid to deceive nature and conceive the Minotaur, a being caught between man and beast.

Upstairs, on the first floor, there are two installation works, *distilled* by Takeshi Yasura, right by the windows overlooking the City Square, and a drawing installation by Saelia Aparicio in the rooms that continue behind. Takeshi Yasura's work is a large surface of glass situated by the window. With light also being considered a part of the work, the piece reflects on the simplicity of water and the elements that create life and balance in this world. Regeneration sounds like an overwhelming endeavor, but in nature, it is a daily practice. The glass reflecting the light looks almost like a pond in the middle of the exhibition. A well, a source, a substance like water, able to blend with everything else and become fertile earth, a river, rain, and also tears. Deeply meditative and mathematical, the work requires our bodies to create a circle. Imagine forming a circle, holding hands, and going round and round together. This is what dynamic forces do in nature: aren't humans a part of natural dynamics as well? The work emphasizes the importance of direct engagement with materials and environments, believing that such interactions foster a deeper understanding and connection among everything that exists.

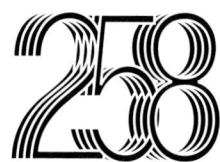

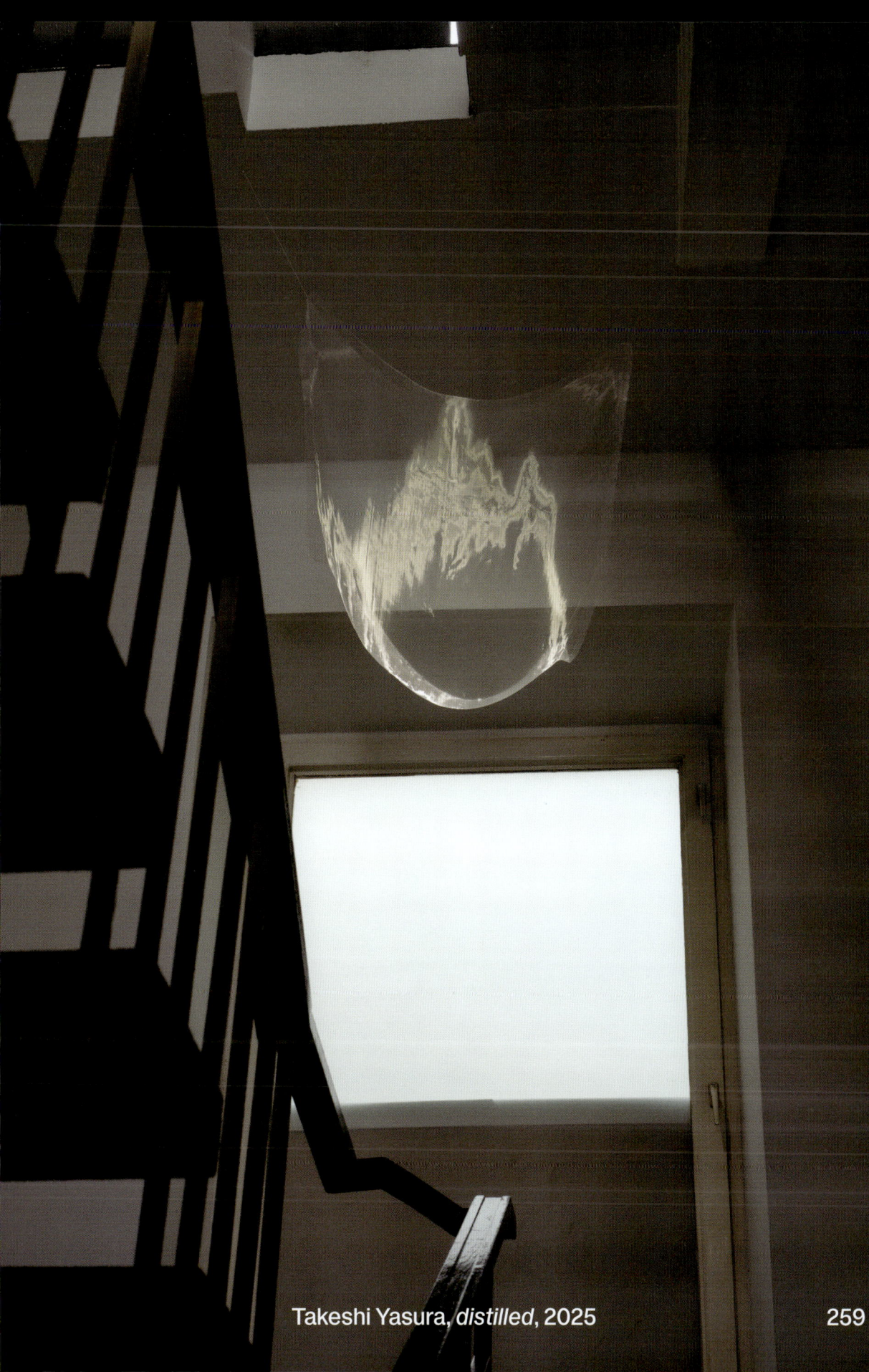

Takeshi Yasura, *distilled*, 2025

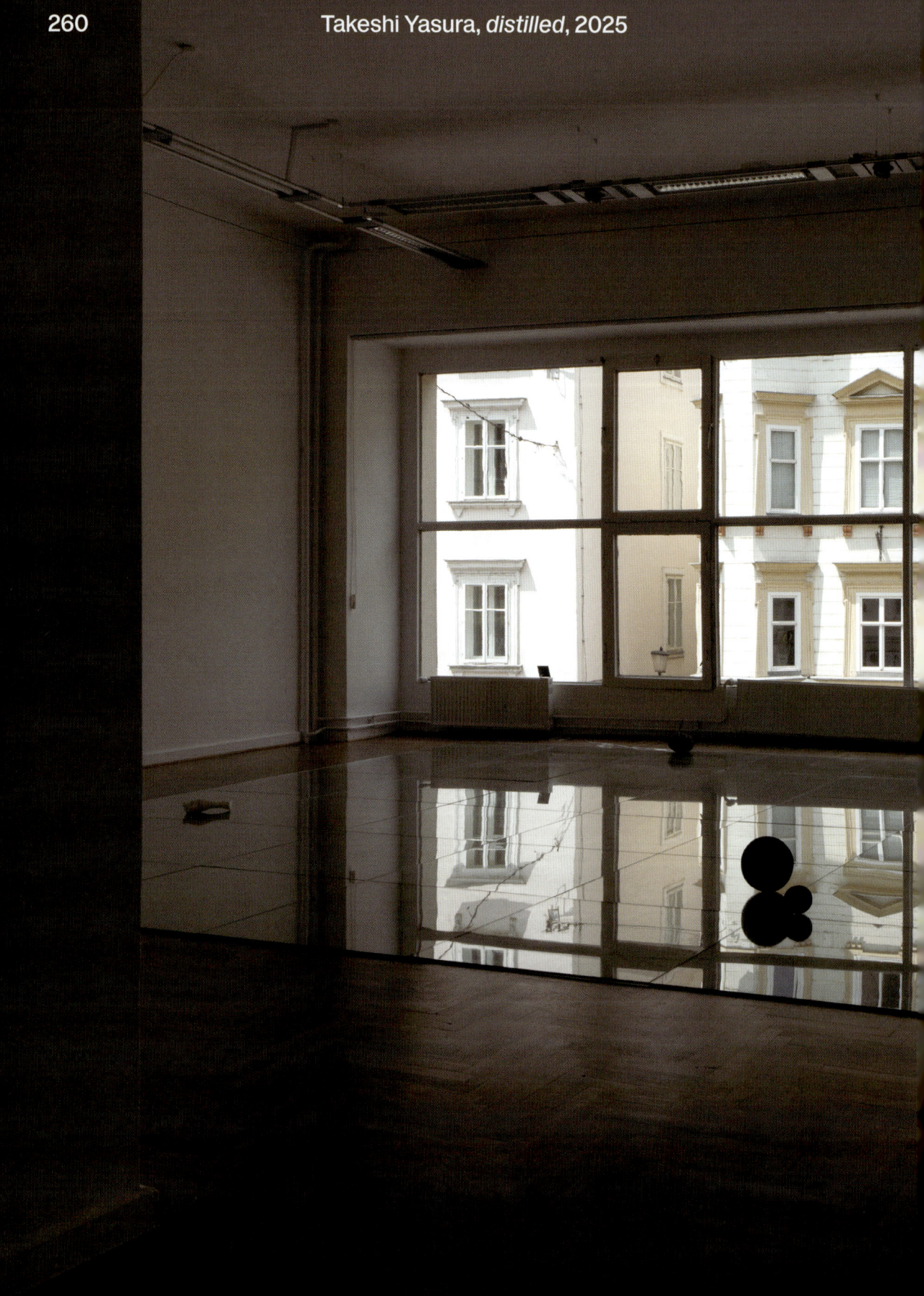

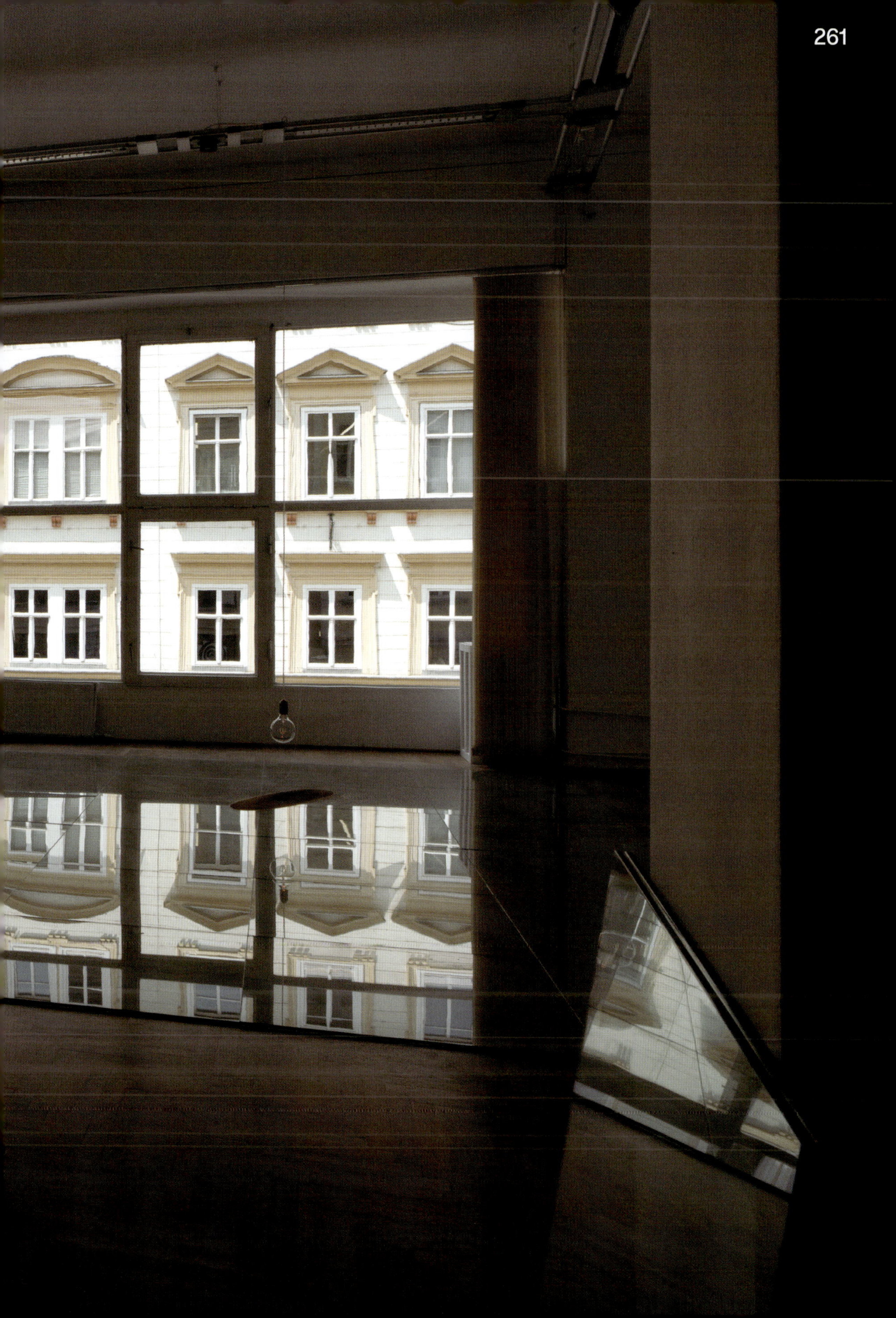

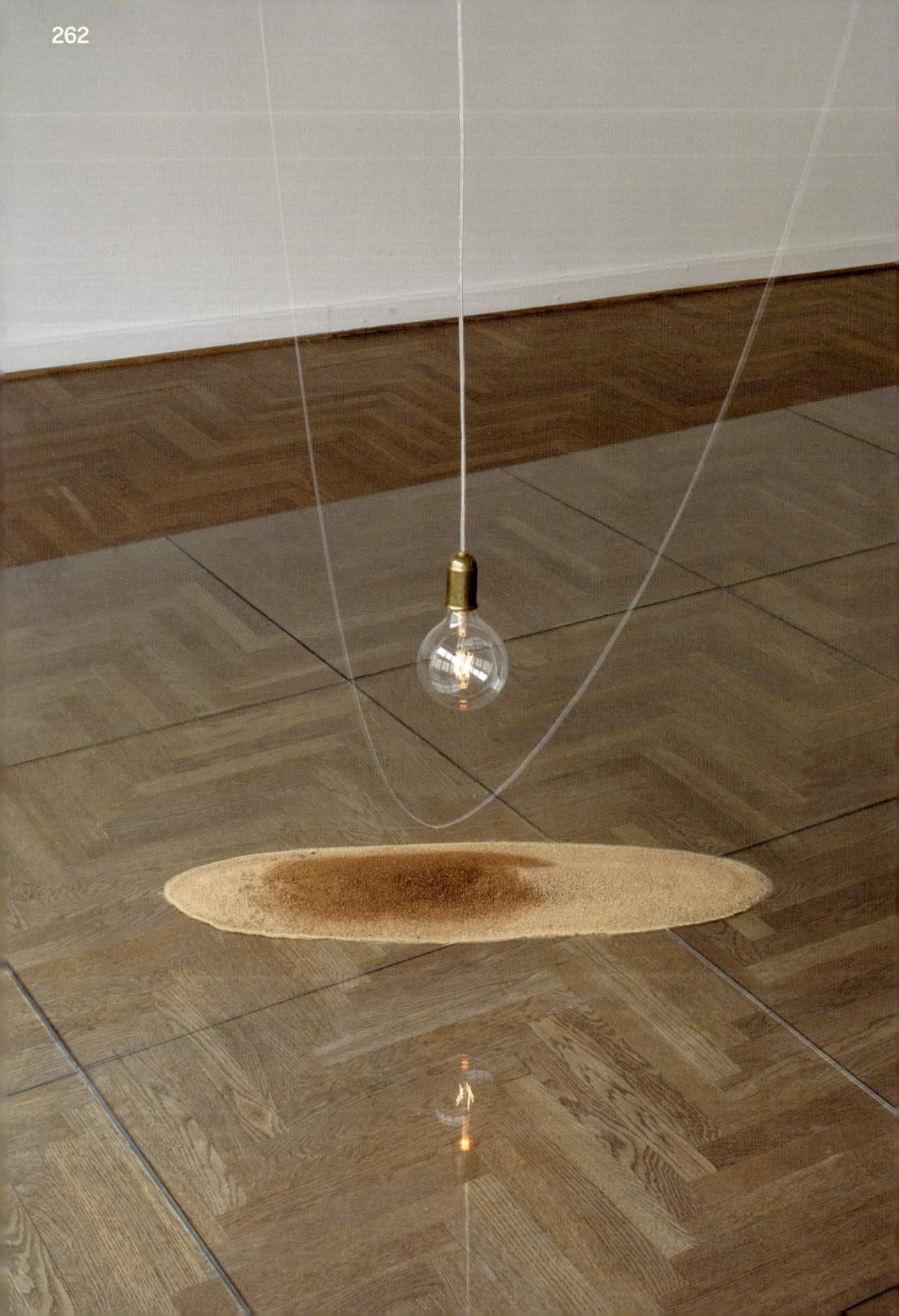

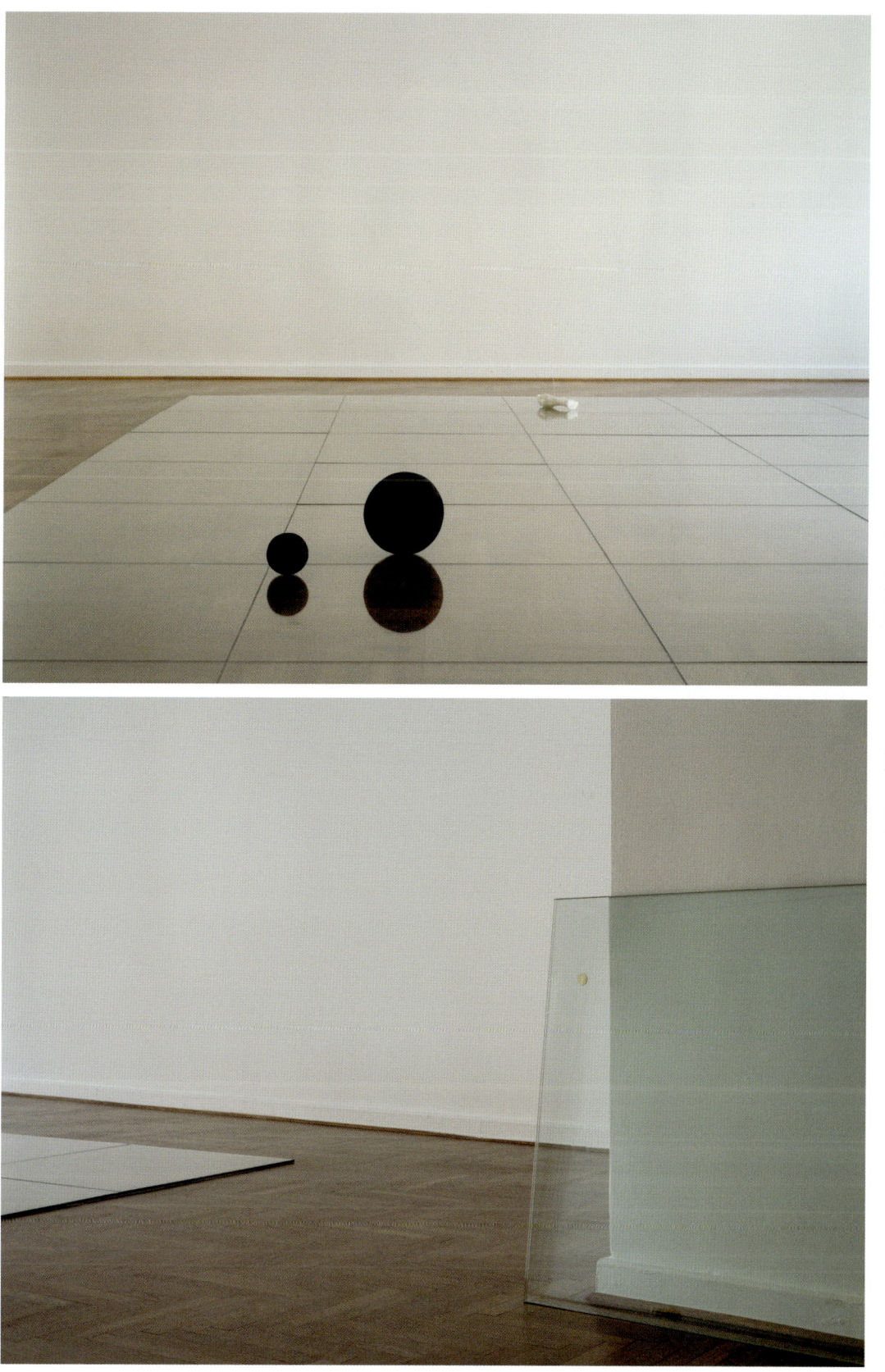

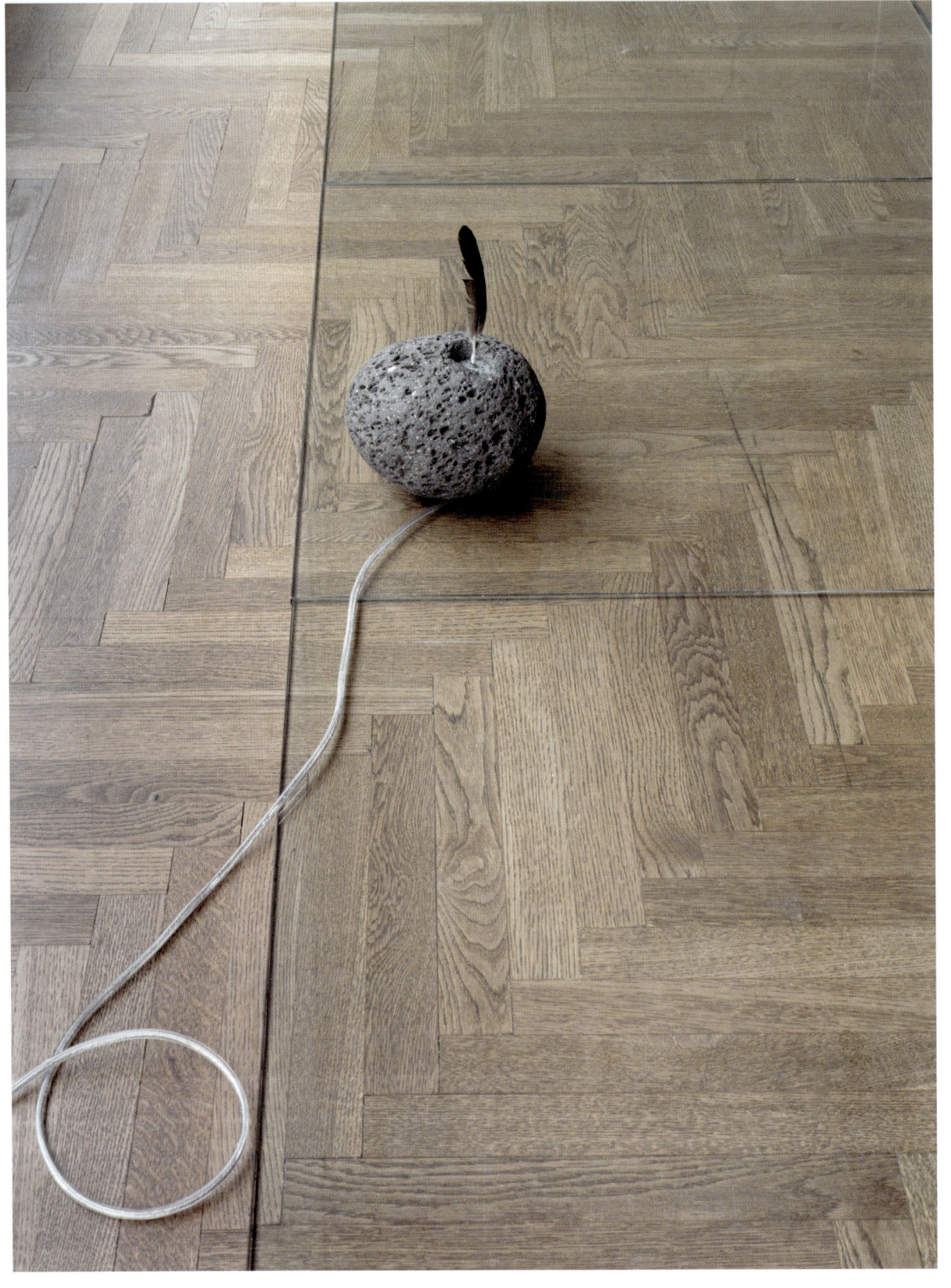

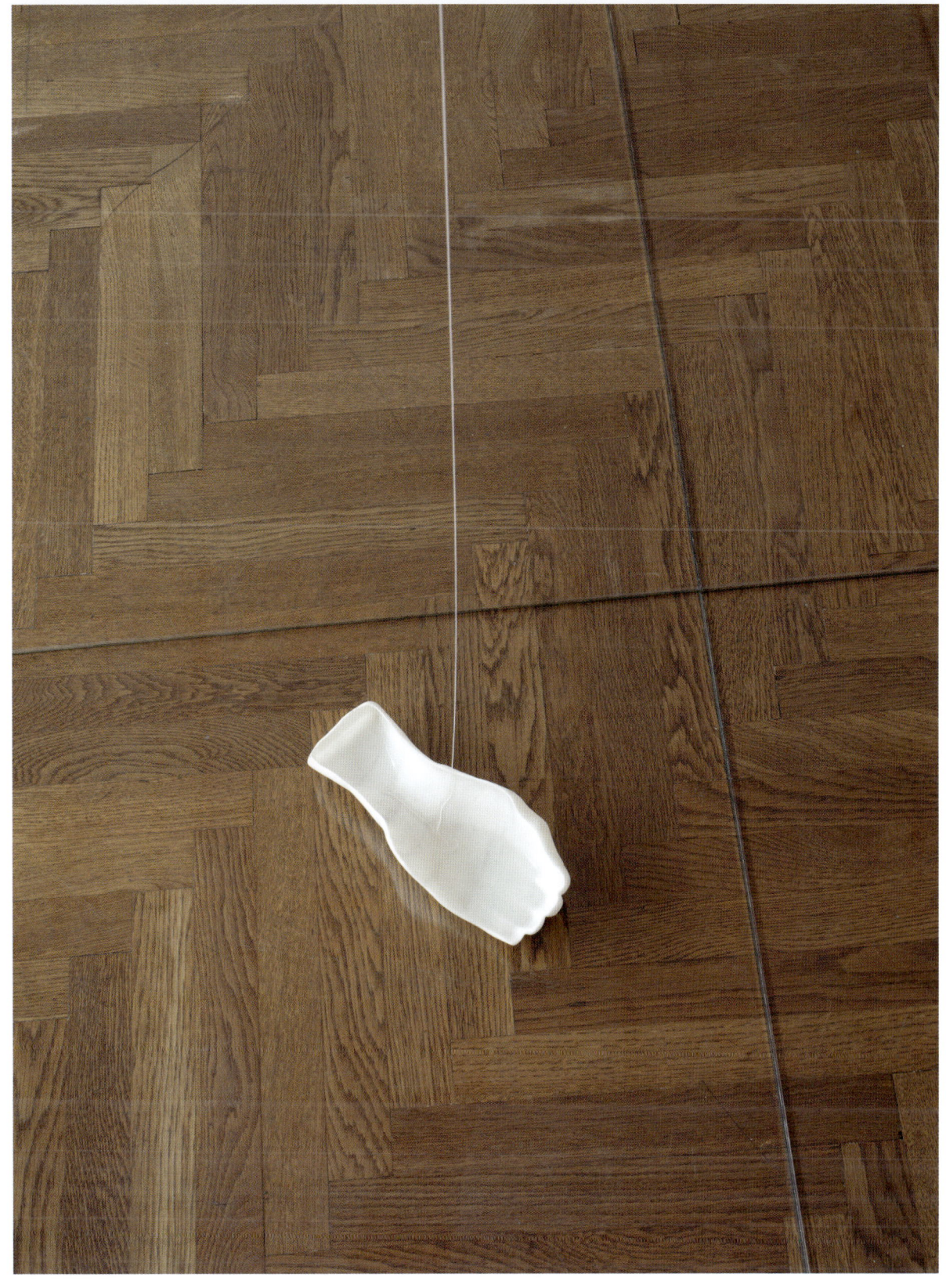

Takeshi Yasura, *distilled*, 2025

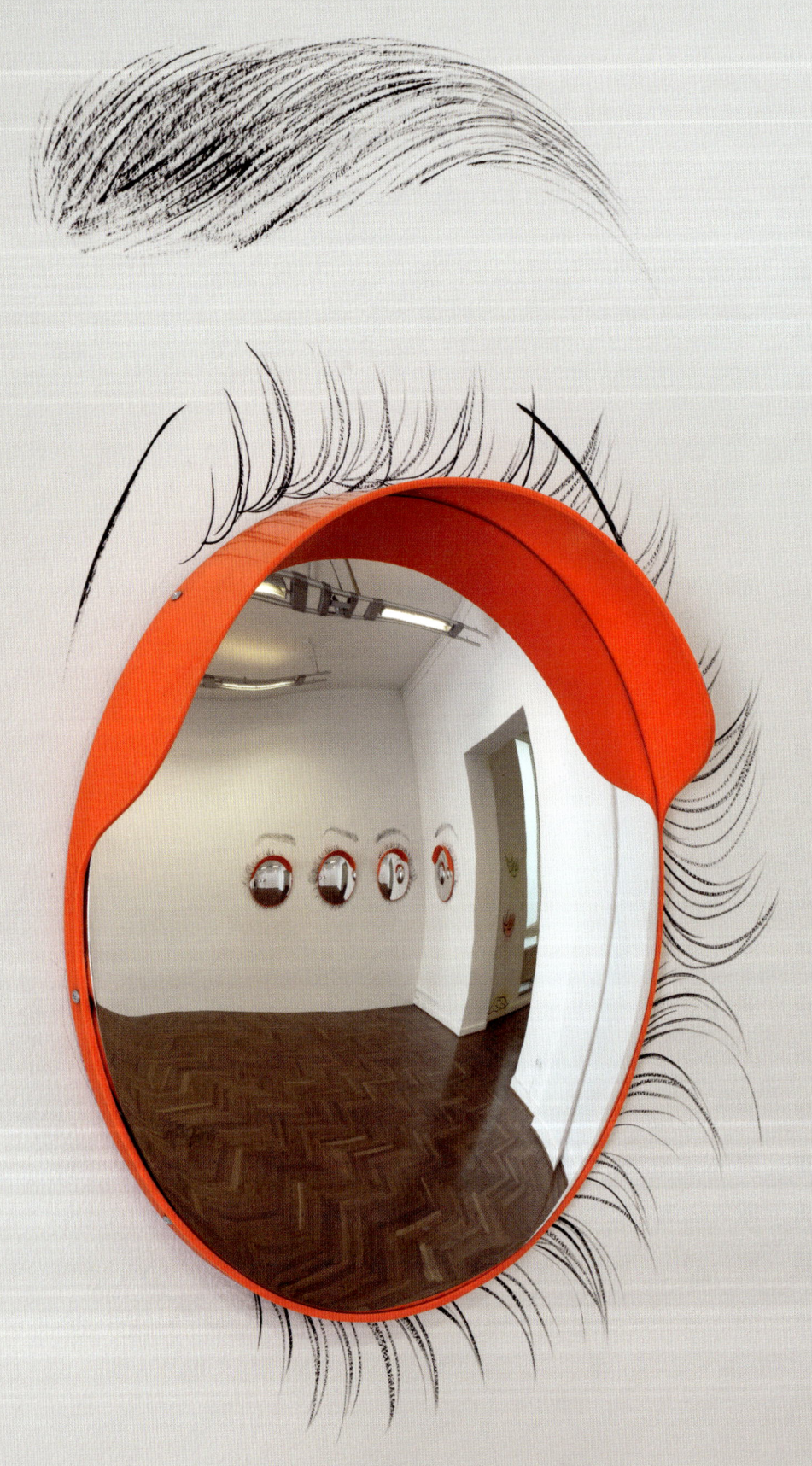

In the rooms located behind Takeshi Yasura's work, we encounter Saelia Aparicio's installation. If Yasura's work can be interpreted as a water well, it is from this well that the explosion of exuberance of Saelia Aparicio's work originates. Her work creates an imaginary line that connects the MGLC Grad Tivoli with the City Art Gallery. It is as if the Baroque interest in *trompe l'oeil* (a trick of the eye) and dramatic scenery to create ghostly or unreal atmospheres had migrated from the top of the park and landed in the middle of the city of Ljubljana. But the work is also nourished by the idols of ancient times, like those discovered at Tell Brak in ancient Mesopotamia. They are small figurines with oversized and beautifully circular eyes disproportionate to their small bodies, which serve as powerful symbols in early Mesopotamian religious and artistic traditions. From Mesopotamia to the emoji, as eyes developed in the late 1990s in Japan as digital emojis, eyes have a long history in culture, heightening awareness, curiosity, and emotion. Psychologists like Konrad Lorenz studied the "baby schema," showing that humans are instinctively drawn to large eyes (common in infants). In Japan, they call it *kawaii*, cuteness. Saelia Aparicio's work revives the Victorian Gothic interest in decay, in madness, and the uncanny in the supernatural. But it is always oriented towards a sort of pedagogical exorcism, the discovery of new ways of expelling fear and anxiety out of our bodies. Our individual bodies, but also and foremost, the social bodies.

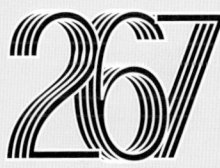

267

Walk-through of the Exhibition

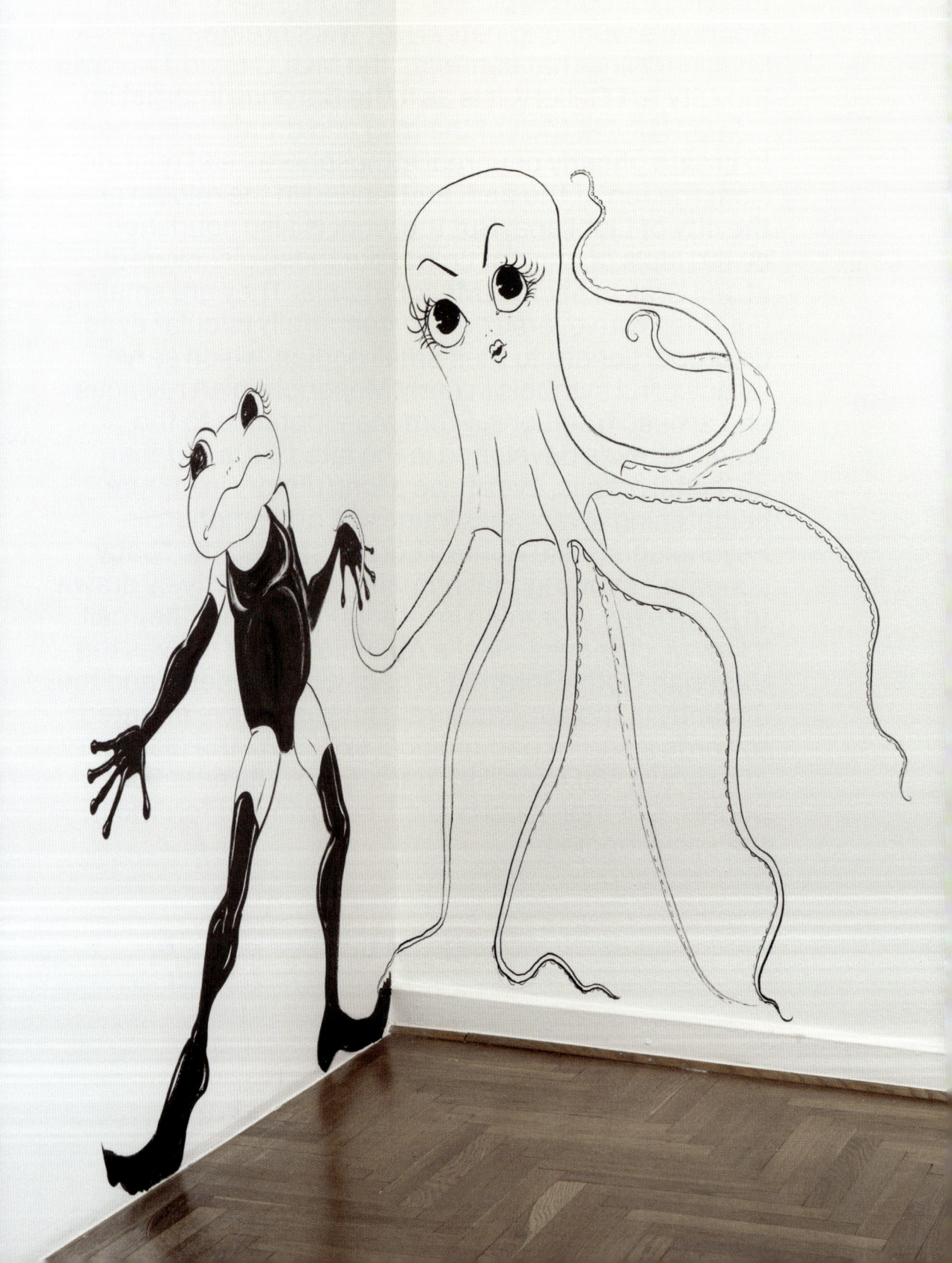

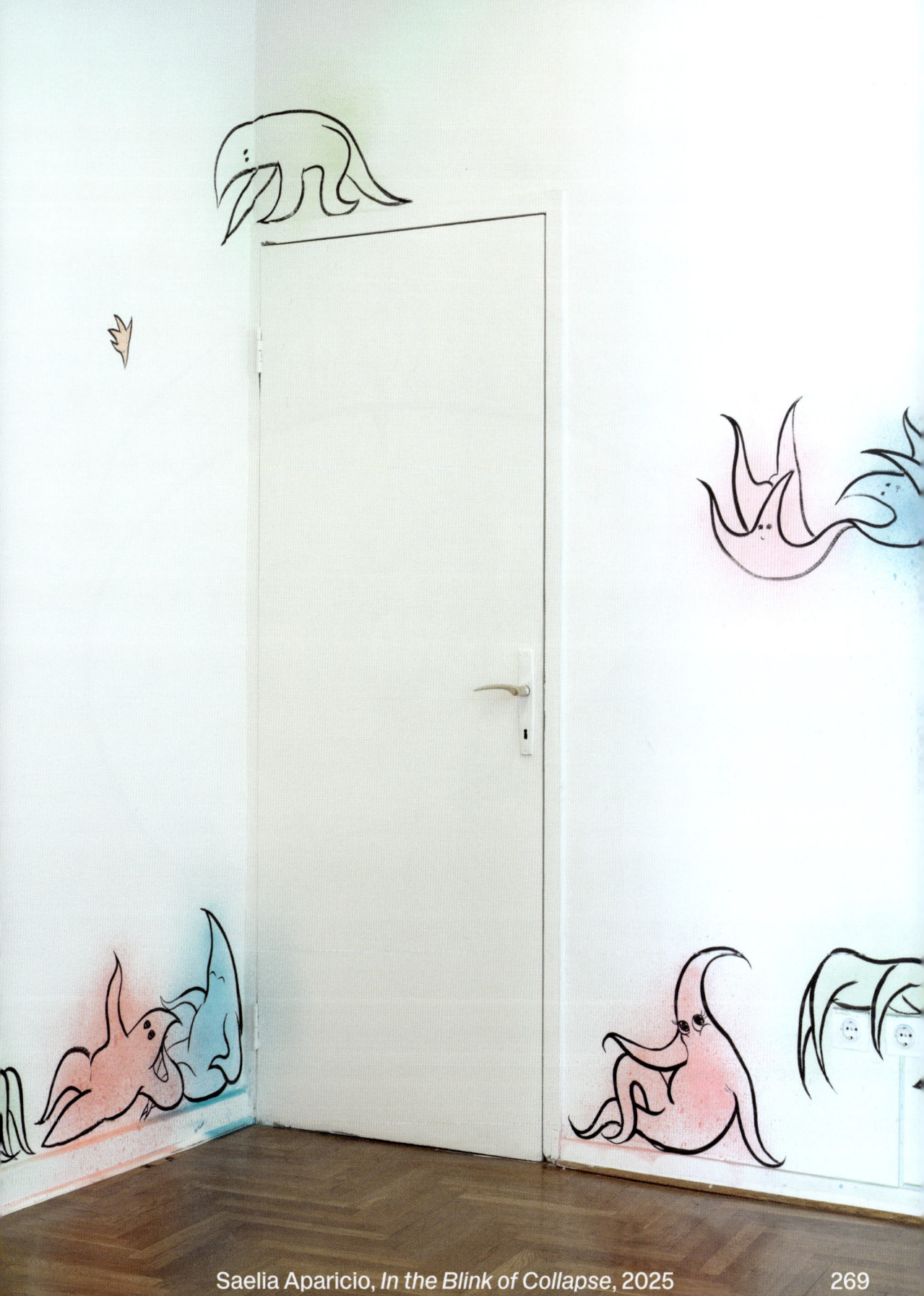

Saelia Aparicio, *In the Blink of Collapse*, 2025

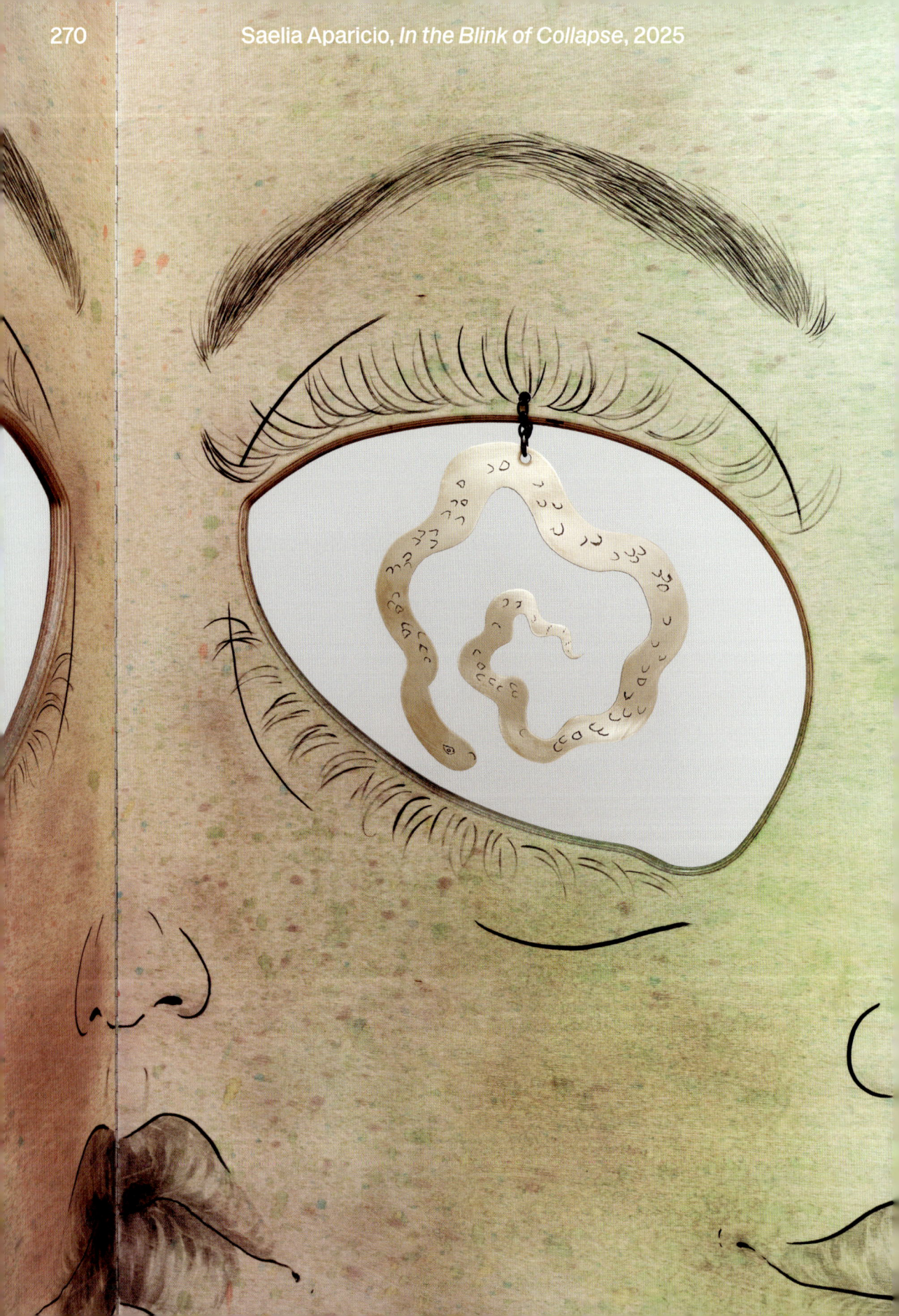

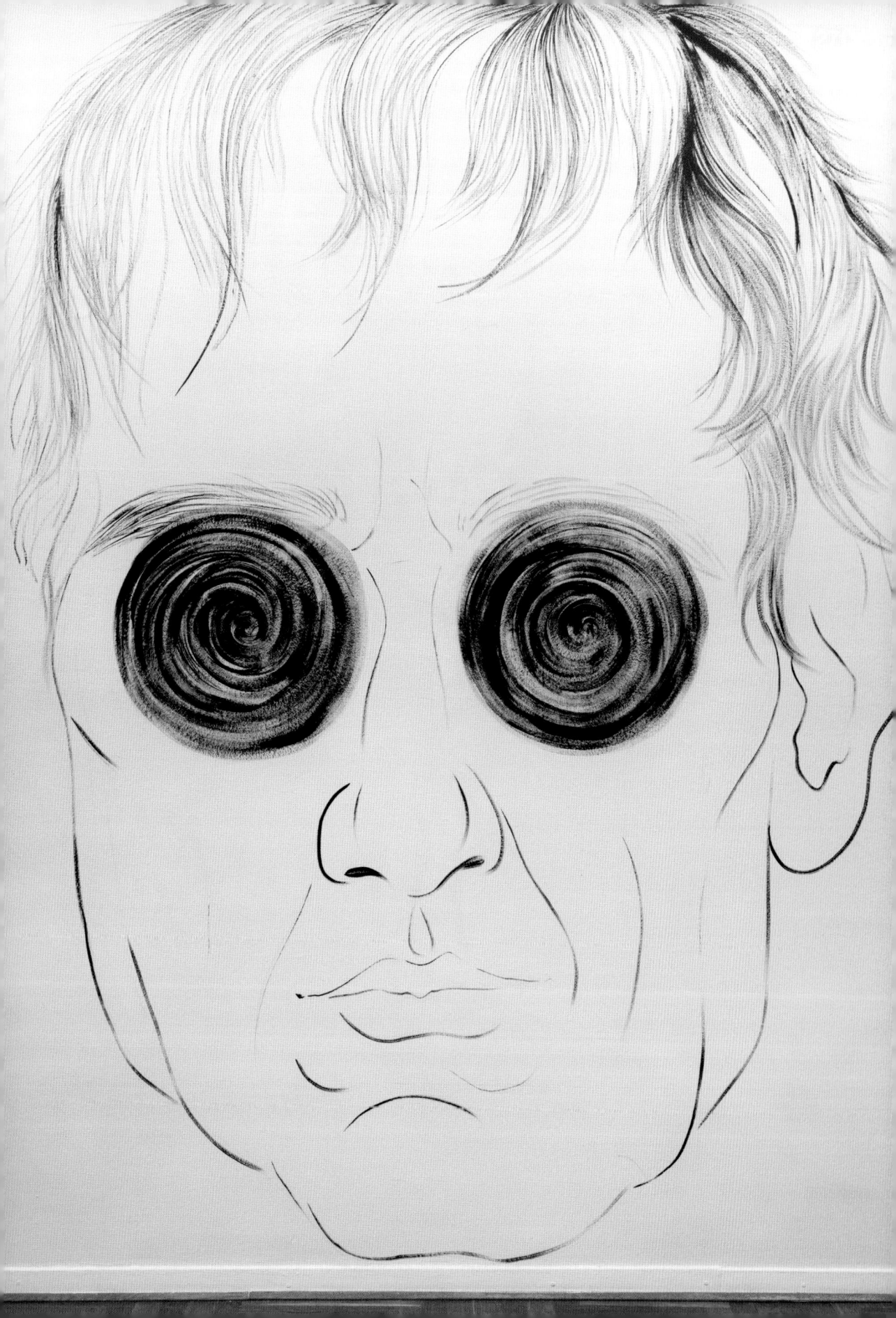

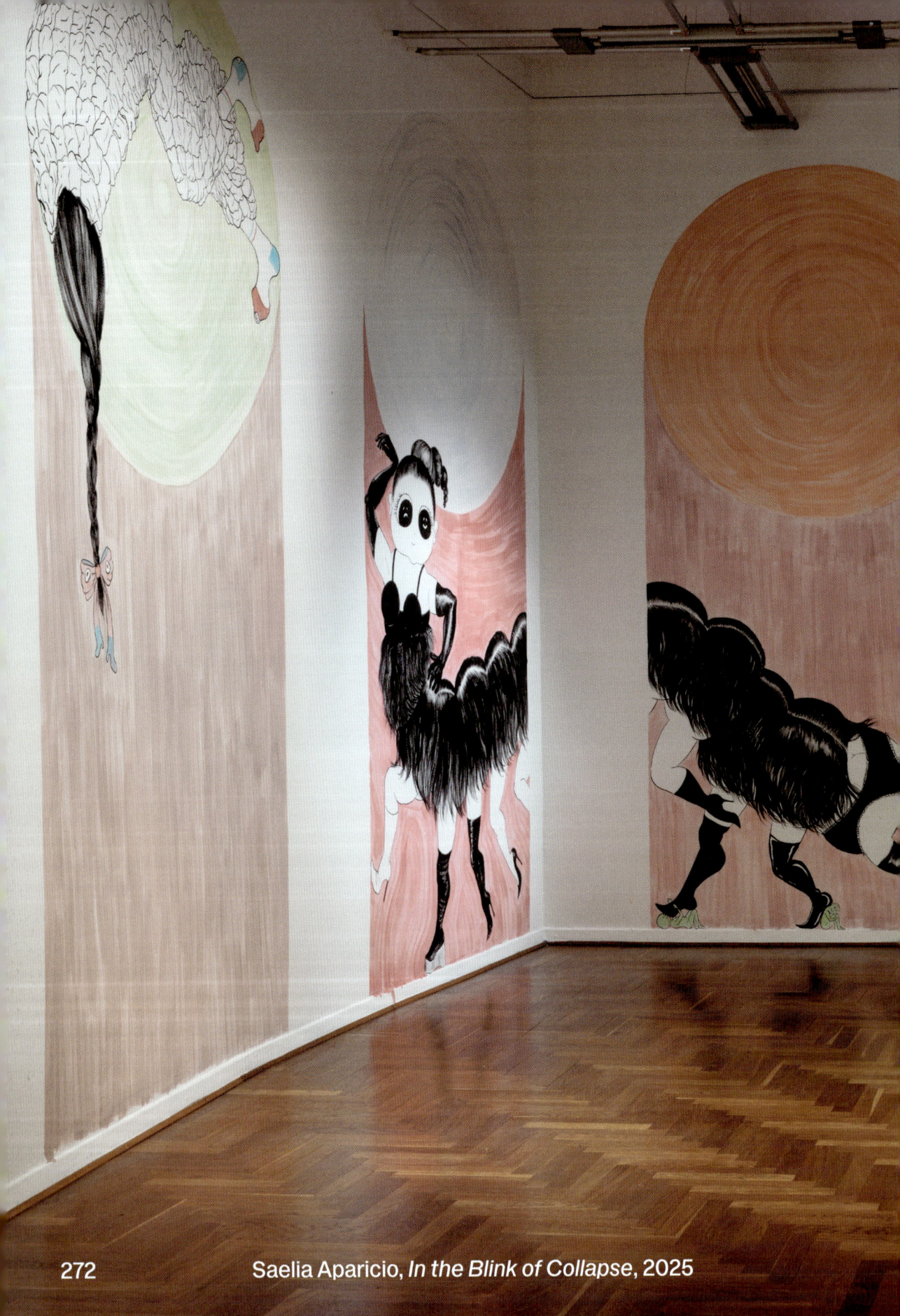

272   Saelia Aparicio, *In the Blink of Collapse*, 2025

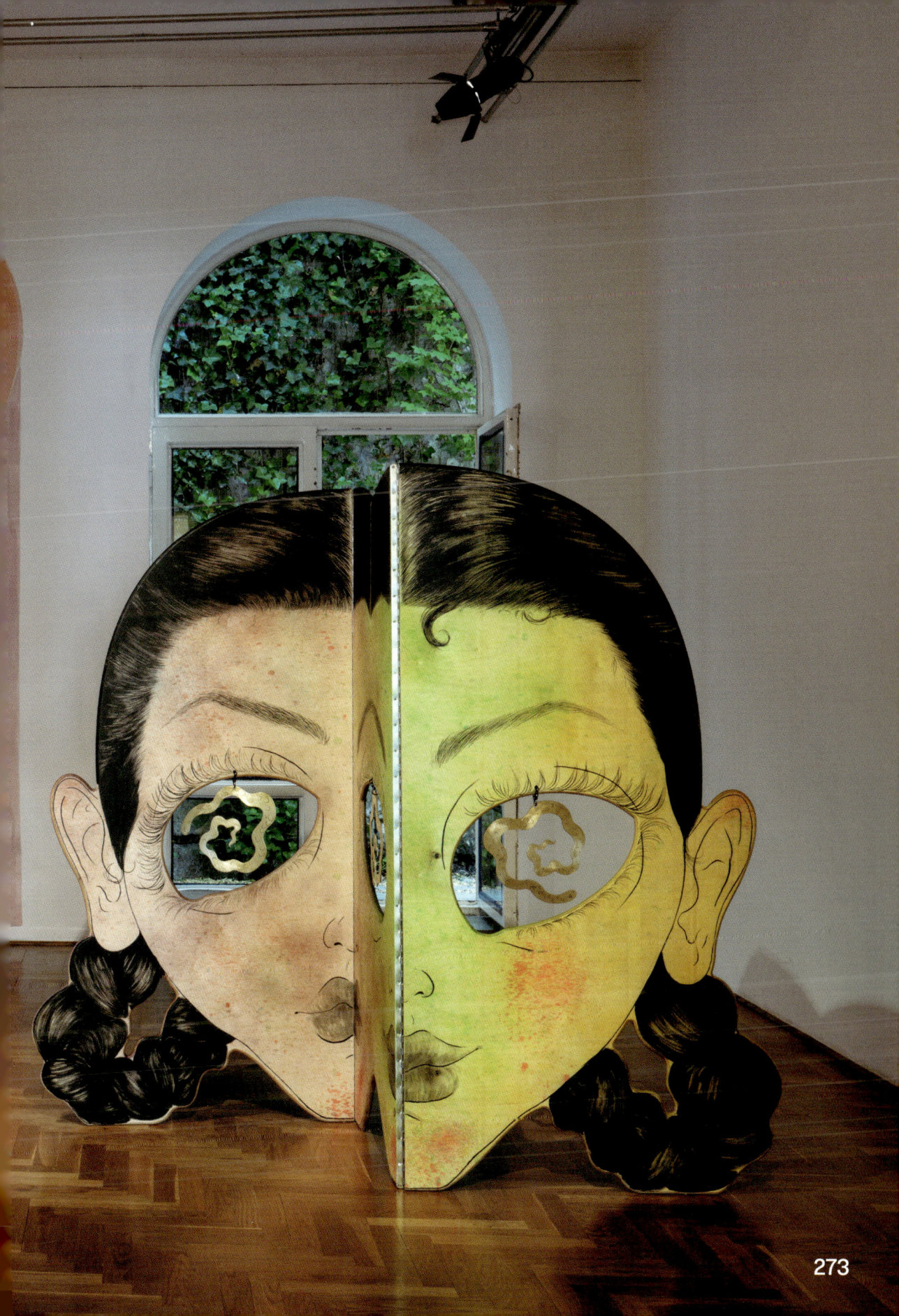

Exuberant and eternally interested in change, the work is both scholarly, nourished by plenty of past cultural materials, and boldly oriented towards the creation of new popular myths. One feels the energy and the release of tension that this work demands from all of us. With this energy, we go upstairs to the world of dreams and sounds by Nicole L'Huillier. The *Rehearsal Room* is a large installation developed in collaboration with Dr. Adam Haar Horowitz. He is a neuroscientist studying the relationship between certain sounds and dreams, working between the MIT Media Lab and the Harvard Medical School Center for Sleep and Cognition. Well-being, mental health, anxiety disorders, panic disorders, depression, and many other related diseases are affecting a very large percentage of the world's population. Sleep patterns have been heavily altered in the last two decades, with poor sleep at the core of subsequent illnesses. Poor sleep also causes an extreme sensitivity towards negative experiences, dark scenarios, sad moods, and an inclination to a light paranoid state of the mind. The emotional and mental handicaps associated with chronic sleep loss, as well as the highly hazardous situations that can be attributed to the lack of sleep, are serious concerns that we should be aware of. Sleep is a fundamental component of human life, which regulates our cognitive and behavioral functions, restoring and rejuvenating the brain for its optimal function. When we are sleep-deprived, the effects will become apparent in cognitive abilities, behavior, and judgment.

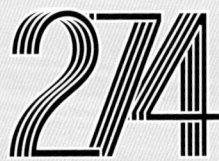

274

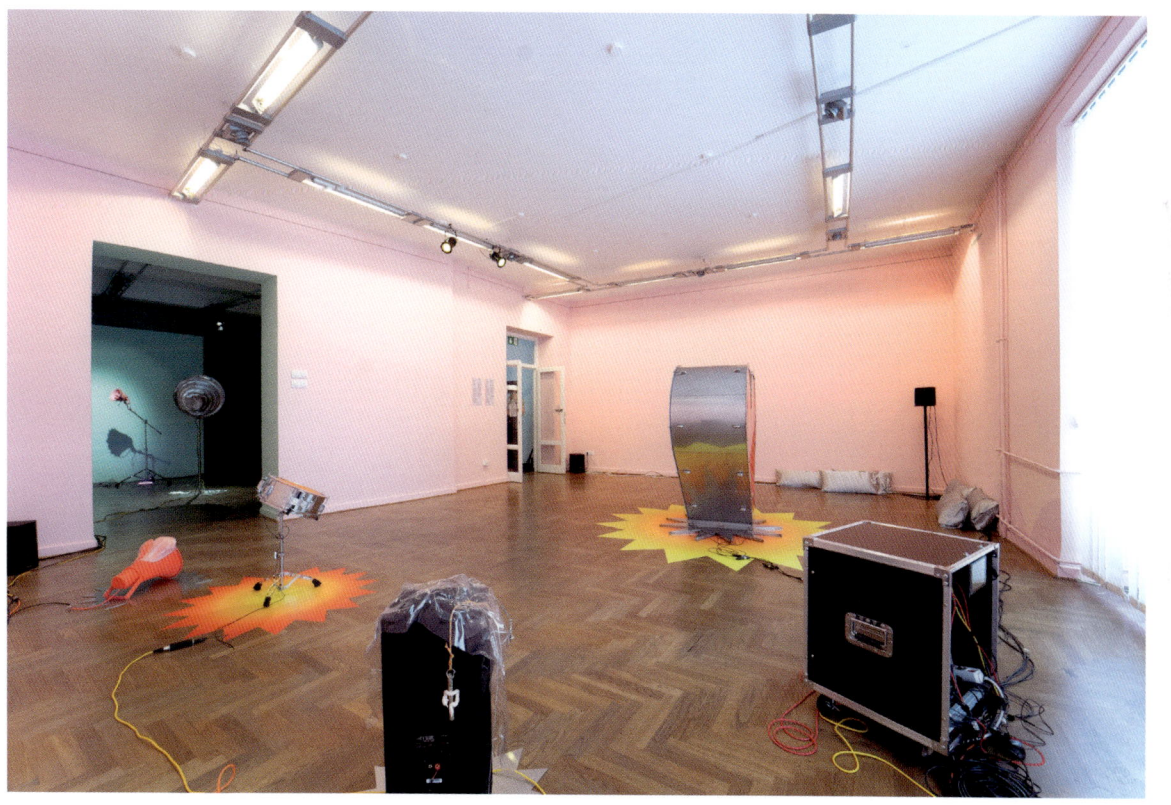

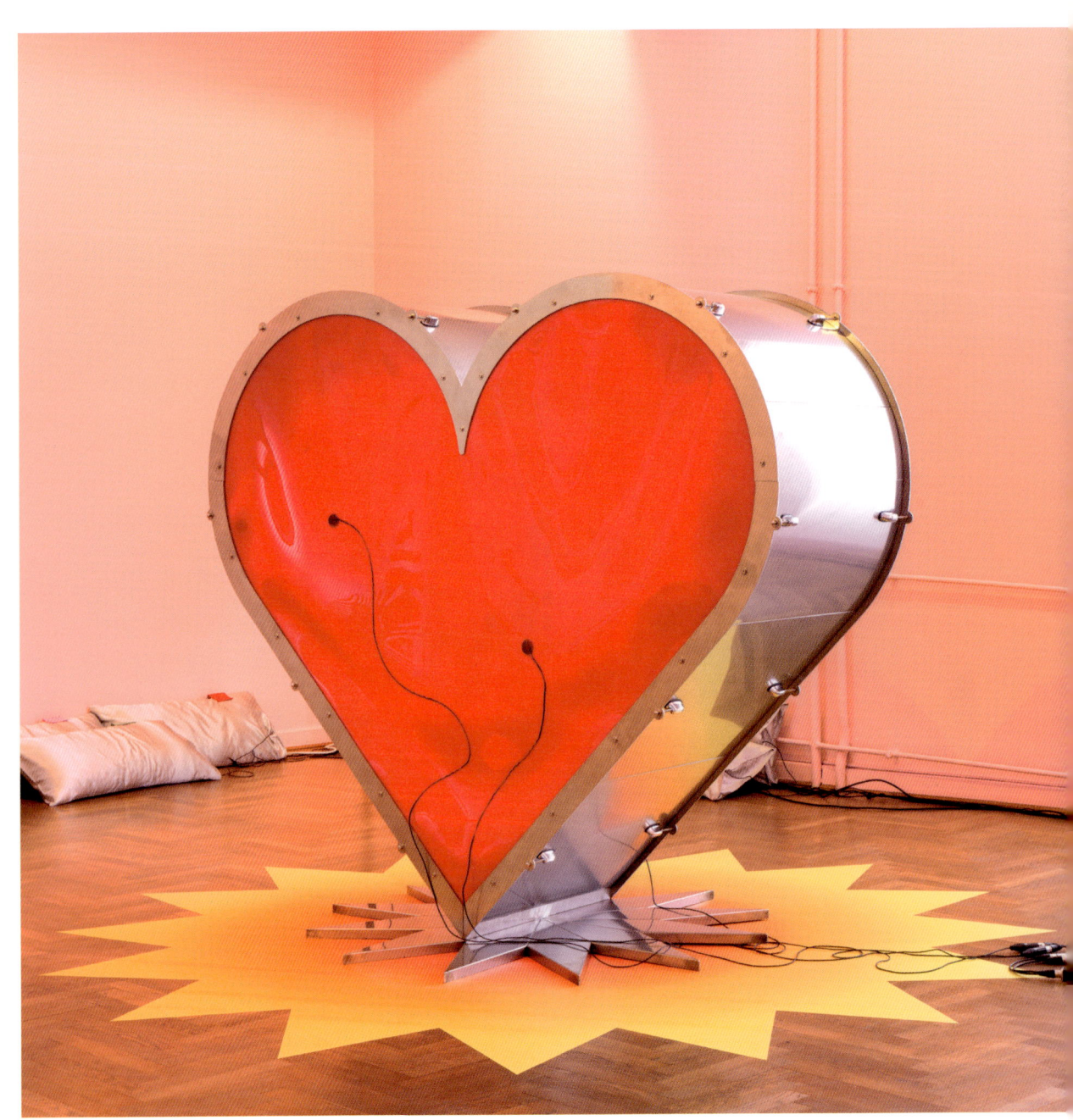

Nicole L'Huillier, *Rehearsal Room*, 2025

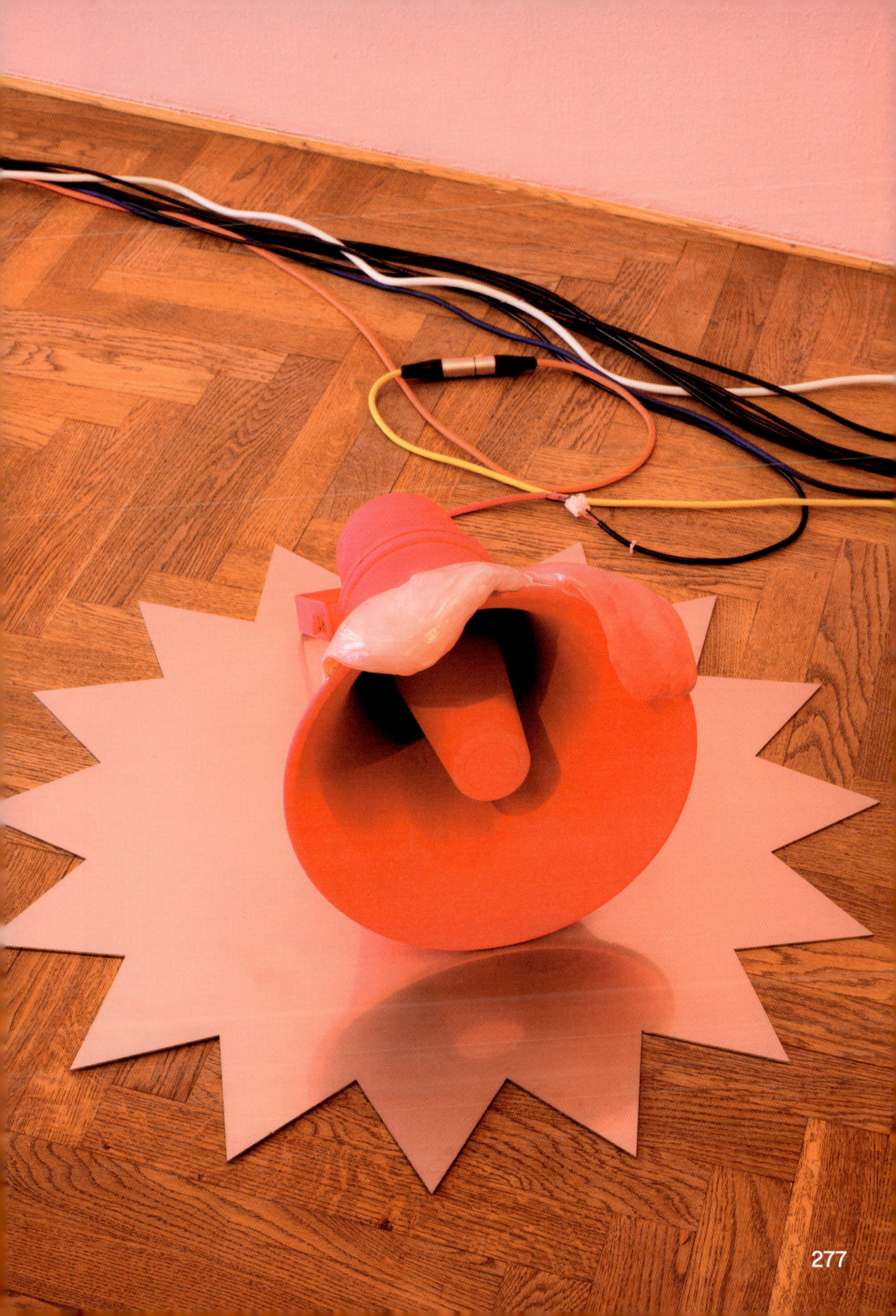

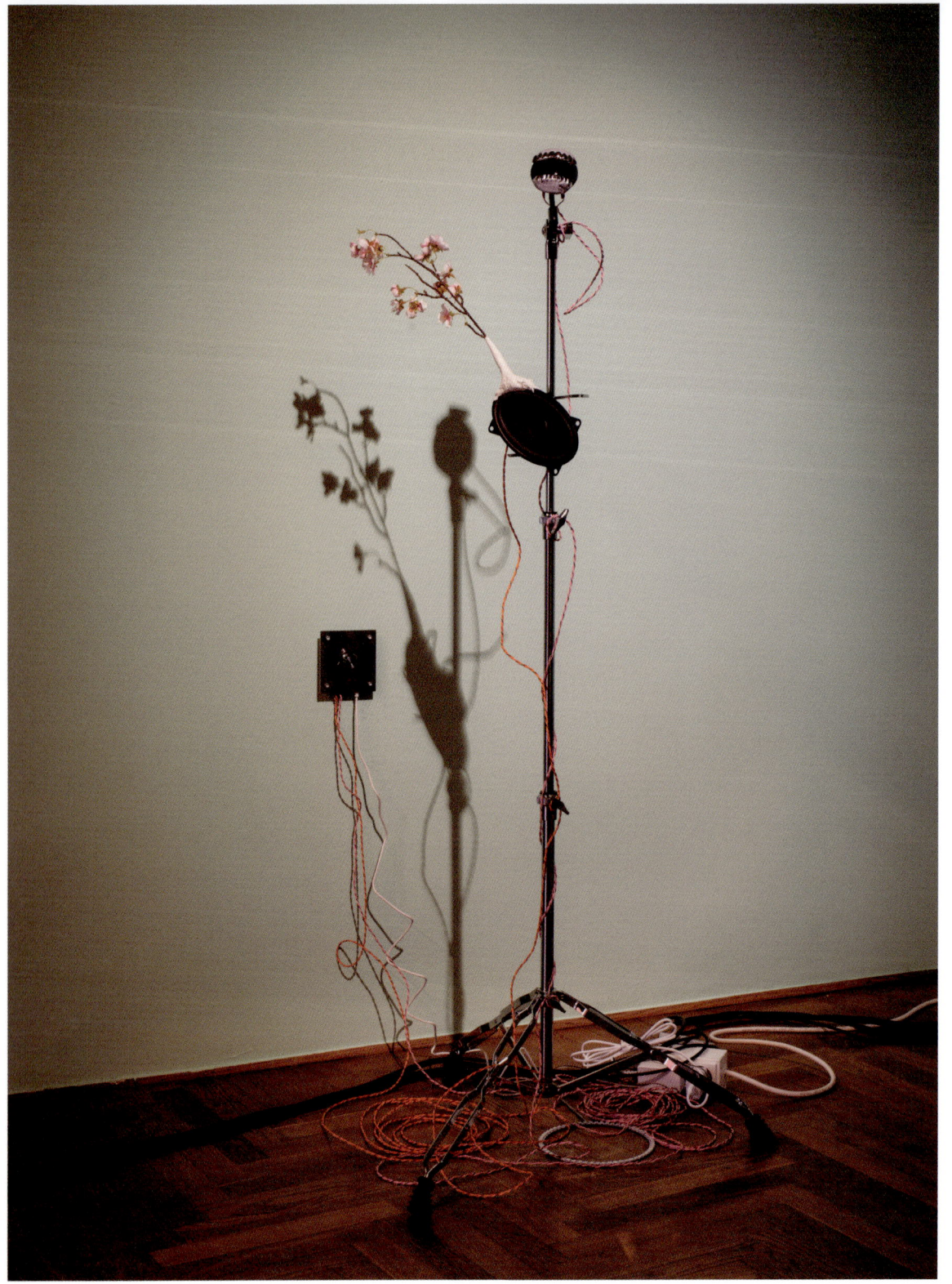

278 Nicole L'Huillier, *Rehearsal Room*, 2025

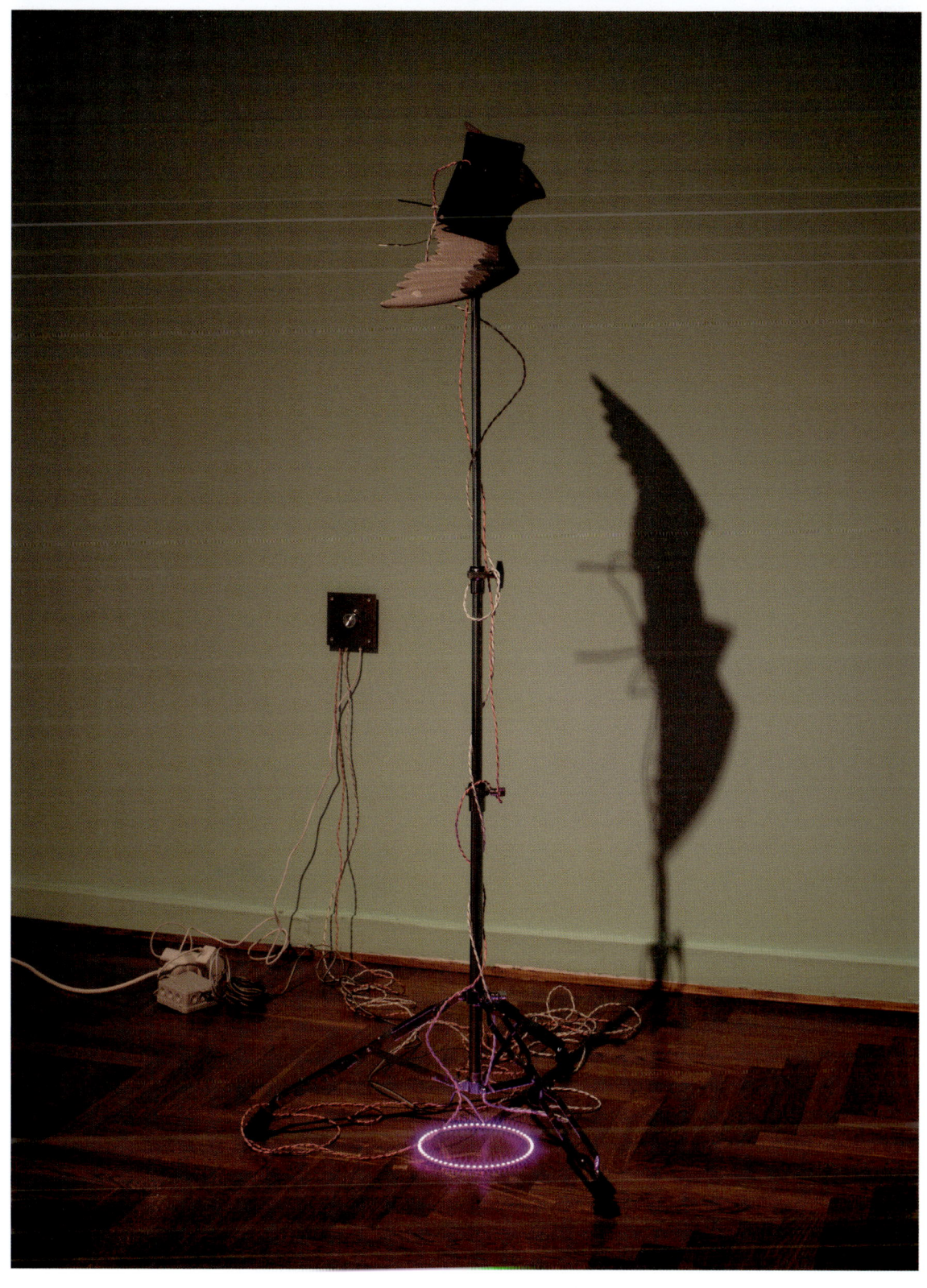

Nicole L'Huillier, *Rehearsal Room*, 2025

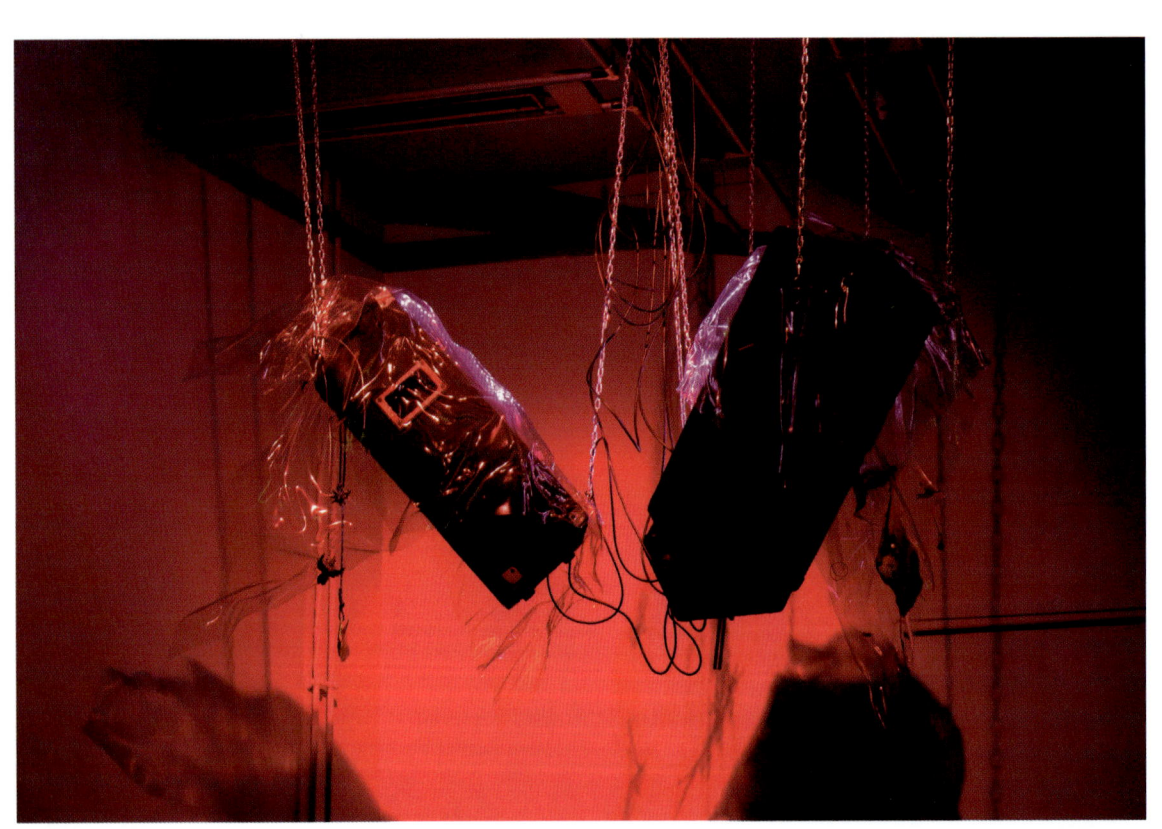

Nicole L'Huillier, *Rehearsal Room*, 2025

THE ORACLE:
A Curatorial Diary

Chus Martínez

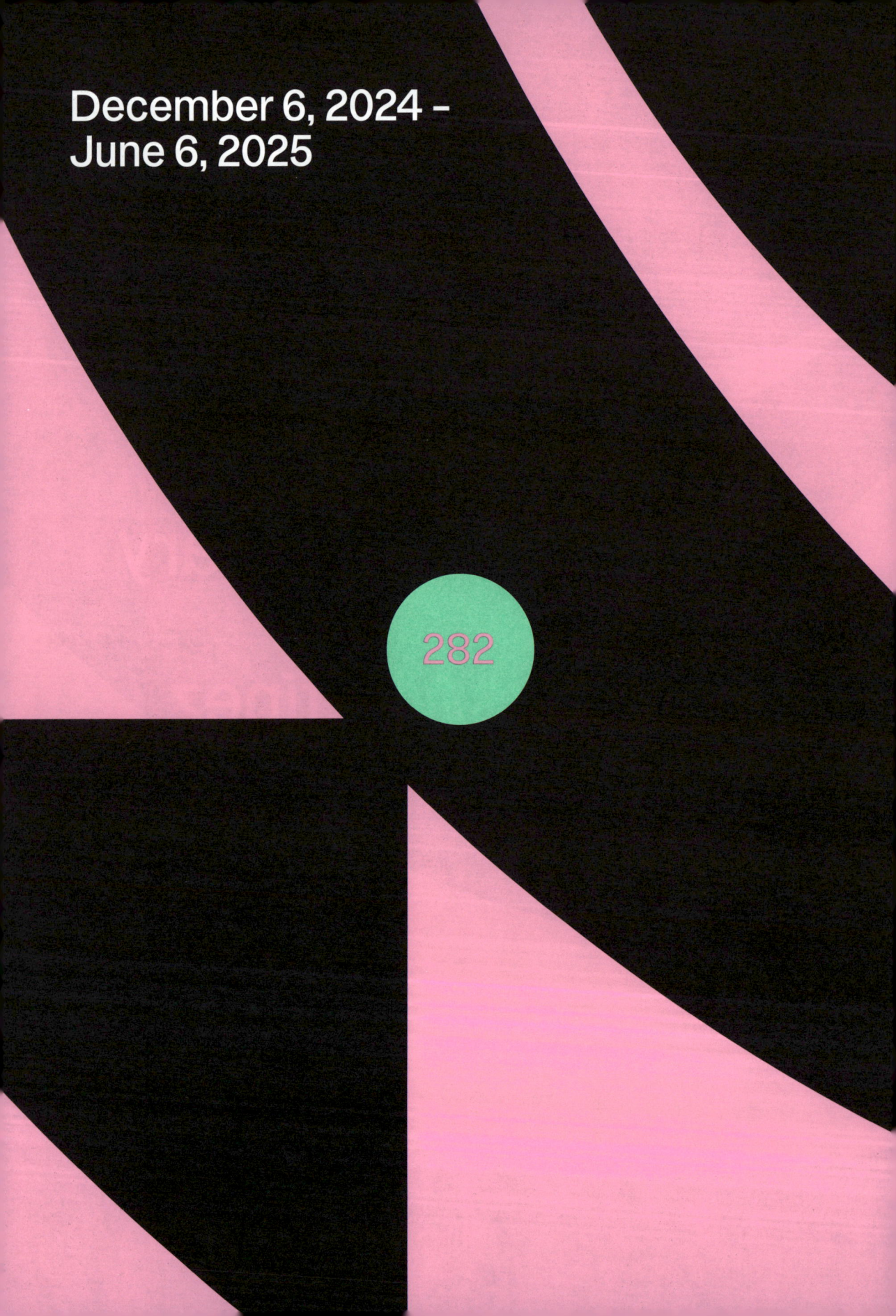

December 6, 2024 –
June 6, 2025

282

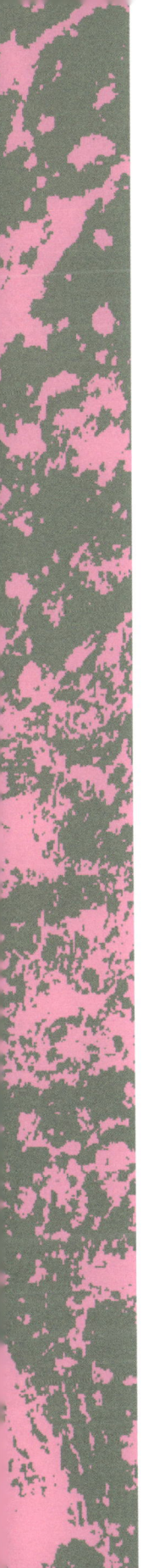

[December 6, 2024]

Today and here, I begin the adventure of telling about the process of making a biennale—the 36th Ljubljana Biennale of Graphic Arts—and sharing it with you. Last spring, artist William Kentridge and curator Carolyn Christov-Bakargiev invited me to be the Oracle in a late-night game conversation that took place in Venice. In facing the near future, we tend to rely on the basic structures of our concerns: HEALTH, because we want to live; LOVE, because we want to feel; and WEALTH, because we want to escape. This basic structure guides my journey.

Could we still dream of the health of democracy? Can we love those that we hate? Can we really escape? I read a sentence in a Korean book of poetry: "There is no paradise on the run." I would add that, if there is a paradise, we will not have access to it. We, the readers of these words; we, the people who work daily to maintain the structures of culture; we, the ones wishing that the wave of authoritarianism will lessen, will vanish, will go away. It will not. We are not very good at listening to each other. That is why I deeply believe in exhibitions. There, the talk and the listening do not happen between voices and ears. Listening, in an exhibition, is more like a swim in the ocean throughout the seasons—sometimes warm and pleasant, sometimes surprisingly cold. Yes .... I feel more and more passionate about the exhibition format over the years. The thing is that we don't dare to explore the fantastic potential of these spaces, the immense opportunities for social relations that they offer us. Don't be fooled, this potential can't simply be exposed by curators or artists. It must be re-lived by the reinvention of the structures that encourage encounters. Imagine thousands of conversationalists inhabiting the space. Don't you want to talk to strangers? My mother, shortly after we moved to Barcelona from the tiny village where she lived, would talk to people at bus stops, in front of children's shoe windows, in the market waiting for her turn. People ran away from her, thinking she was crazy. I want all of us to be like my mother and speak with strangers. Not metaphorically, but truly. That is the reason why I decided to include in this biennial many—almost all—artists I had never worked with before. I really want to know more, I want to speak with more, I want to engage with those who do not have an interest in me. Why? Because, to maintain my mental health, I need to trust coexistence.

I believe an exhibition is all about this.

[December 13, 2024]

Memory and the ability to comprehend the world are key elements of HEALTH.

A few days ago, at the CIMAM conference held in Los Angeles, I was mesmerized by the presence and the words of Zita Cobb, an economist born on Fogo Island who, in 2004, established with two of her siblings—Alan and Anthony Cobb—a program to catalyze a renaissance of traditional fishing, farming, and building techniques on the Islands. She spoke about her father, who used to explain how industrial fishing turned all the fish into money, and about her own desire to show that money could, in reverse, turn again into fish. How powerful—I thought—to remember how things can turn for the worse and then shift to make life possible again, to make nature alive again.

Lately, I have been obsessed with mnemonics, with the production of specific techniques and systems to enhance learning and memory. Since we humans are lazy animals, we believe we remember the past and are aware of what happened before

283

us. But actually, we both do and don't know. We only have a vague idea of the events that preceded the present; the essence and the texture of the past have faded away, leaving behind just a grey cloud full of vagueness and indistinct images that barely help our decision-making processes in the present. For this reason, I cannot stop thinking that, at the entrance of certain institutions and exhibitions, there should be a mnemonic map retracing similar events and institutions from the past, to help us connect the dots. I imagine a pedagogical plan that would allow us to create simple charts in our minds, so every time you mention a biennial you'll be reminded of its origin. For example, the Ljubljana Biennale of Graphic Arts was founded in 1955, the same year as documenta. These two events are symmetrical. Why? Because of the Iron Curtain. Germany and documenta represented the ground to play the binary capitalist versus communist world views. And, in this context, a format and a language appeared as having special significance: the graphic arts. In the years following the Second World War, under the shadow of the Iron Curtain, graphic arts biennials were of particular significance. From the middle of the 1950s until the beginning of the 1970s, international graphic arts biennials seemed to sprout like mushrooms. Why? For logistical reasons disguised as ideological: graphic arts travel easily, and graphic arts shows require fewer resources than other exhibitions. I think that creating these sorts of simple explanatory charts may help us to understand the times we are entering. Indeed, the binary of ideology and resources does resonate with our current situation. It is fundamental to understand where art, artists, and culture are situated in the current sociopolitical development. Forget the tourist logic of the past two decades: do not visit a biennial, do more than that, *read it!* Read the biennials and the contexts in which they are inscribed to try to interpret the current situation.

284

Only then can we figure out with how many to connect, and how to generate a strategy for the near future.

[December 20, 2024]

On LOVE and its counterpart in culture.

The process of making the Ljubljana Biennale is guided by the question of democracy today: Can we still regenerate the damaged tissue? Can we regenerate democracy?

I find myself echoing the words of the Spanish writer Rafael Sánchez Ferlosio, words I had almost forgotten: "Will we be able to survive without betraying?" It is with real horror and a growing sense of helplessness that I read how professionals—mostly in Germany but also, for instance, in Switzerland—in the arts and culture, who have not asked for or personally applied for a prize, are honored with an award and, minutes later, disgraced. It is publicly announced that they are receiving an award for who they are and what they have done, only to publicly and shamelessly dishonor them for who they are and what they have done. Their names are used as if they were examples of behavior that society should not follow, when in fact, the example we should not follow in any way is to allow those we would honor to be humiliated without the right to defend themselves and respond to a situation that they did not even seek.

I have the rare habit of jotting down phrases that are unkind to my ears or likely to create more problems than solutions. One such entry is "best practices" from October 30, 2017. I wrote it down during a meeting on the labor rights of non-EU artists. Adhering to ambiguous rules without studying the specific case and the human and personal conditions of the person concerned was justified as good practice.

I hardly read in the public opinion a deep reflection on what is allowed, on the consequences not only on the professional career of the artists who—if it were not for the interference of these "awards"—would not have been subjected to such negative campaigns that will undoubtedly deeply affect their mood, that of their loved ones, of their friends, and of those who may want to work with them in the future.

I do not read arguments explaining how the systems of protection of artists—the public authorities that we democratically elect to guarantee the public good—can leave professionals defenseless, without feeling an acute sense of betrayal of those independent and democratic processes. Juries that vehemently and unanimously want to honor someone are then disavowed.

This has never happened before, but it seems to be a best practice today. I must say that this time I am afraid. That is why there is only one topic in my mind: the possibility of creating democracy. From where? Let us try to explain to the public opinion that those who claim to protect us are weakening us to the point of becoming seriously ill.

The image of today's diary features the work of Nicole L'Huillier, who—in collaboration with Adam Haar—is researching sound and how it positively affects our dreams.

[January 2, 2025]

The World's WEALTH in a Cave: Part I

One of my research themes for the upcoming Ljubljana Biennale is fantasy. Fantasy—at least in my head—seems to be a new resource for reactivating our political logics. But it's not enough—as Ursula K. Le Guin demanded in her 1979 book *The Language of the Night: Essays on Fantasy and Science Fiction*—to write (or exhibit) a different kind of fantasy. Instead of offering it just for consumption (reading, watching, playing), we shall activate it as a force to create an alternative order. Fantasy is not illusion, nor is it imagination. But how to explain and materialize all these abstract ideas in an exhibition? In my desperate move to find a way to visualize my own thinking and find a way to explain it to others, I decided to look for answers in the dark. So, cave it is, and I decided to visit the Postojna Cave, about forty minutes away from Ljubljana. Since it was opened to the public in 1819, the cave has been a huge attraction for tourists. Even better, I thought. If the place, never mind the crowds, still manages to ring my neuronal bell, even more magic.

The visit begins by sitting on a train built in 1870, to then discovering that the whole environment is illuminated by colored lighting, added in 1884. After a few minutes of traveling through the already impressive passages, you begin to feel the magnitude of this Underworld. It is a system—a series of caverns, halls, and tunnels—about twenty-four kilometers long. But the immense strangeness and beauty of this two-million-year-old landscape can only be truly grasped after walking through it for a couple of hours.

Suddenly, I understood that before humans set out to colonize space, they were fascinated by the center of the Earth. Jules Verne published *Journey to the Center of the Earth* in 1864, one year after the scientist and writer Louis Figuier published *La Terre Avant le Déluge*, a very, very popular book on geology and paleontology. At one point, the guide said something I found incredible: "We have been walking down in a spiral. We have crossed the same river twice, as well as two bridges built by Russian prisoners of the First World War."

The World's
WEALTH
in a Cave:
Part II

In Jules Verne's *Journey to the Center of the Earth*, a group of travelers—similar to the group of tourists I was in—use a hollow volcanic conduit as a gateway to the Earth's interior. Verne depicts the trip of his explorers across amazingly large empty spaces formerly occupied by magma, truly fascinating chambers as deep as the aisles of cathedrals. And I was there! I was in the depths of the Postojna Cave, and I was also walking through the text written by Jules Verne! He describes an imaginary forest growing along the newly discovered "Lidenbrock Sea," and along the underground river in the Postojna Cave, I saw a forest of gigantic stalagmites, as gigantic as the oldest trees on earth, as tall as a one-hundred-and-fifty-thousand-year-old skyscraper. When you finally leave the bottom of the path spiraling downwards, you climb up again as if on a subterranean mountain. At the top, a chamber—like the ones imagined by Verne—opens in front of your eyes: the Calvary, formed from the collapse of the cave's ceiling. This breathtaking space is said to be as big as St. Paul's Cathedral in London. Just when I thought I had seen all the wonders imaginable, another one came into view: the Underworld glowed. Apparently, when a certain light hits these ancient mineral sculptures, the manganese molecules within them are activated, causing the calcite to emit a soft, beautiful white glow. In Verne's novel, there are colossal glowing quartz crystals, generated by the Earth's inner heat, a heat still preserved from the time before it cooled.

As I walk back and forth between the glowing stones of the Postojna Cave and the pyramid-like crystals of Jules Verne, I begin to wonder how it is that some people believe that a room full of synchronized projectors reproducing classical paintings can be considered "immersive." Wouldn't it be wild and beautiful if visiting an exhibition—an activity with only a limited range of effects—could arouse such curiosity in people that it inspires them to explore worlds closer than they think? Fantastically rich worlds, like those in Verne's book on my bedstand, or like reading the stars on a summer night.

Luka Čeč, a native of Postojna, disappeared for a while and suddenly reappeared from the top of a rock shouting: "Here is a new world, here is paradise!" I agree with him, but I also wish that we could bring this Underworld attitude of discovery into our way to experience art and culture and poetry and theater and dance ….

Puppet
LOVE.

It all started when an artist, set to participate in the Biennale this June, sent me a picture of a smiling ball. If you show this picture to anyone in Ljubljana, they will joyously shout: "Žogica Marogica!" The English name of this character is Speckles the Ball, but its original one is Žogica. It is the protagonist of a 1951 play written by Czech puppeteer, director, and playwright Jan Malík. The play was directed by Jože Pengov, the brother-in-law of Ajša Pengov, the puppet's designer.

The plot is simple: an elderly couple wishes for a child. Suddenly, a speaking ball flies in through the window: Žogica! The Ball is hungry, they hurry to give it some milk and let it stay home as their daughter. One day, when Žogica is home alone, an evil kite kidnaps it but with the help of all the children in town, the Ball is rescued and reunited with its parents.

Žogica is so present in Slovenian culture that—apart from telling the story—people still sing its song, composed much later, in the early 1990s, by Bojan Adamič for a radio play.

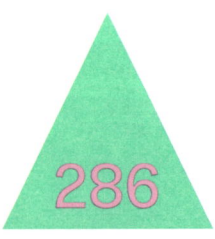

During a beautiful walk through Tivoli Park, the director and puppet artist Silvan Omerzu told me that Jože Pengov had hoped to become famous for classic theater, but something went wrong with his political curriculum. Ajša, on the other hand, wanted the marionettes to be so great that, in a letter, she even spoke of "indigenous puppets" with their own identity, autonomous from the hands of those who move them. It was Ajša's idea to make Žogica as small as a tennis ball, with strings over two meters long, allowing it to be free from people, yet always within the reach of their love.

I think of the Ball as a love ambassadress in the world of inorganic matter and inorganic intelligence. Indeed, we need LOVE to embrace them.

[January 24, 2025]

Puppet
HEALTH.

I have to admit I wasn't aware of the enormous importance of puppets in telling stories that people cannot tell because the pain of the world exceeds the capacity of actors and language.

In 2020, Carolina López, a friend and animation scholar, organized a magnificent exhibition at the Centre de Cultura Contemporània de Barcelona, where she juxtaposed the works of Ladislas Starevich (1882–1965), Jan Švankmajer (b. 1934), and the Quay Brothers (twins, b. 1947). Starevich's work left a deep impression on me. He is known for magnificent stop-motion films, populated by tiny puppets made of dead insects—he was an entomologist by training—that he used to stage his scientific and social observations. Recently, while talking to scholars and artists about the emergence of the Ljubljana puppet theater in the 1950s, I began to think about the relationship between deep crisis and collective claustrophobia, and the impulse to create animated proxies. In times of extreme conservatism and multiple

backlashes due to fear and economic constraints, it seems easier to create a surreal replica of living creatures. To exercise subversive energies, we need to believe that art is still relevant and use it to therapeutically animate a world otherwise full of terror, decay, and death, a world driven by an absurd spirit that lacks humor.

Discovering puppetry through the history of a particular community—that of Ljubljana—made me think about the reasons for the creation of simple mobile sets and stages, the reasons why many intellectuals were attracted to this genre, and also the ideological reasons for educating people to certain values and systems. Of course, puppets helped to propagate communism among children, but they were also chosen by the writers, playwrights, scenographers, and theater directors Federico García Lorca and Eduardo Ugarte, both members of the wandering Teatro La Barraca, which toured the villages of Spain during the Second Republic (1932). Since my stay and research for the Biennale in Ljubljana, the puppet seems to me a proper tool and language—and as a strange answer—to address today's stagnation.

[January 31, 2025]

Mind's
HEALTH.

An intriguing question while preparing a biennial is how not to do a catalogue but still create one, capable of documenting the work of every participant and—at the same time—adding reflexive textual parts to the whole process, to the artworks and the biennial as a genre. Today, few people are reading, and even fewer think that collecting the publications produced by biennials or other big-scale art events is important. At the same time, it still feels urgent to nurture our memory with past exhibitions and the questions that guided them. Are we the first to think this way about our current situation? Are the questions similar, but the angles and feelings different? What are the ideas and rhetorical arguments that can help us address the acute problems we are facing?

Since I'm not from Ljubljana, I tend to idealize it a bit (that is the role of an invited curator!) and perceive the place as particularly fertile when it comes to interesting thinkers. For this reason, the publication accompanying the Biennale is turning into a thinking companion to engage with the place where the exhibition is being produced. Historian Manca G. Renko, anthropologists Svetlana Slapšak and Maja Petrović-Šteger, and political philosopher Renata Salecl reflect on the transformations in our ways of thinking about democracy and on the collective forces that drive towards (and against) the common good.

Renko's research focused on women intellectuals in post-war transitions from a transnational perspective, covering Slovenia, Croatia, Austria, and Italy, and reflecting on the different concepts of work and intellectual labor in these countries. What I appreciate the most in her writing is her Olympic effort to demonstrate how extravagant comparisons sharpen our inventiveness and the way we think. In *Are We Having Fun Yet?*—an essay from her book *Živalsko mesto: Eseji o popularni kulturi, zgodovini in čustvih* (*Animal City: Essays on Popular Culture, History, and Emotions*)—published by Look Back and Laugh in 2024, she sheds new light on our perceptions of beauty and masculinity through a wide investigation spanning from the statue of Augustus of Prima Porta to Lenin. Comparing—and exercising it unceasingly—may offer a great alternative to our lack of reading and can be a catalyst to return to the texts, in the same manner that yoga made many return to vegetables and healthy food ….

Note on the image: Paolo Veronese, *Convito in casa di Levi* (*The Feast in the House of Levi*, 1573). This year, after many trips to Venice, I finally visited the Gallerie dell'Accademia for the first time. I went there intending to see Giorgione's *Tempesta* (1506–08), but as I navigated through the crowds, I stumbled upon Veronese's *Feast*. For the first time, I both literally understood and deeply felt the

concept of perspective. Unexpectedly, this painting transformed something within me—my fundamental relationship with art.

[February 7, 2025]

LOVE of life.

About ten years ago, I came across the name Svetlana Slapšak. Her name was written on the cover of a book called *How to Read Cabbage: Structuralism, Semiotics, Historical Anthropology*. As is often the case, the title was in English, but the book was not.

The words on the cover resonated in me, evoking the thinker's will to challenge identitarian nationalism in its most subtle forms—such as that of a food enjoyed by many, which, while being eaten, provokes the re-enactment of certain gender values and even affirms unquestioned sexual practices or behaviors.

Imagine my excitement when I found out that the Ljubljana Biennale could offer me the opportunity to get closer to this wonderful woman. Svetlana is a full-time professor of Ancient World Anthropology, Gender Studies, and Balkan Studies in Ljubljana, where she arrived after leaving Serbia in 1991. Most importantly, her life has been shaped by a lifelong involvement in human rights advocacy, activism, academic work, and fiction writing. She uses fiction to travel through history, exploring democracy in the history of ancient worlds and understanding the relationship between women and freedom across time. Thanks to this research, we are always provided with resources that inspire us and prevent us from surrendering to the belief that democracy is dead or nearly so.

Her novels—so eloquently written that they are regional bestsellers—embody an educational political mission: to understand the situation of women and their intellectual engagement through history. Listening to Svetlana in her apartment in Ljubljana is a revelation:

certain people have a therapeutic imaginary that enables them to convey their knowledge and studies of the past and make them relevant to the practices of the present.

I was hypnotized and deeply moved, but also saddened that this woman wouldn't be interviewed for eight hours a day by all sorts of media. I realized even more how much we need those magnificent minds capable of making us think, believe, and act in the interest of life.

[February 14, 2025]

WEALTH
of Imagination.

Ljubljana would not be the same without the architecture of Jože Plečnik (1872–1957) and, therefore, its cultural life, including the Biennale. Why? Because he had an unprecedented ambition and wanted to create something unique, something, so to speak, in non-alliance with Modern architecture. A friend of mine summarized Plečnik's style by saying that he mixed the Greek and Roman architectural orders in a blender, adding some fantastical touches to the result.

Fantasy is strongly present in Ljubljana, and one cannot thank Plečnik enough for that. Fantasy allows an alternative life beyond labor; that's why I agree with his dislike of rationalism and its views on form and function. Form should serve the mind and not follow function only. Form should not follow trends either. Forms should follow a path of entanglement with nature and the cosmos to create a true place, a *capital*.

Rationalism in architecture seems easy. It is much more difficult to Imagine a city where every building, square, and bridge is distinct. To encourage a spiral of building shaped by an imagination that defies canonical design. I admire the will to leave behind

a legacy of exceptional invention, where architecture works as a source of exuberance that inspires mental scenarios for daydreaming.

Interestingly, Plečnik himself was not particularly extravagant as a person. He was more often described as a monk. At first, this aspect surprised me, but then I started thinking of him as a gamer: as one of those individuals who play unending hours on Roblox, a solitary nerd who produced an entire universe with his pencils.

I'm glad that the Biennale takes place in a city with such a surreal atmosphere, unlike any other I have been to. I like that a biennial—no matter the scale— is intended to play on top of the million fantasies that were forecast for and from a community. Art exhibitions should happen, again and again, as ways to reactivate the exercise of thinking, within the parameters of fantasy, rather than the pragmatics of greed. The only way to stop political nonsense is to embrace wild fantasy, instead of relapsing into a rationality no one seems to relate to.

[February 21, 2025]

HEALTH of
Mind.

I always dreamt of exhibiting materials from congresses and summits that were historically motivated by the urge to transform the world: anarchists, Bolsheviks, socialists, communists, fascists, pacifists, Falangists, Stalinists, Cubists, Futurists, Dadaists, Surrealists, Suprematists, Constructivists, Destructivists, and Stridentists .... My dream was to show the bodies of all those citizens gathering to discuss what is next, what to do, what to say, how to claim, how to respond, and how to forge a new eloquent rhetoric capable of capturing the attention and appreciation of all people. There are tons of images of these historical meetings, but I never had the resources to properly research and exhibit such materials. This unfulfilled dream informs the making of the Ljubljana Biennale. How? By imagining a biennial as an opportunity to re-enact the dream of a society securing human rights, gender rights, labor rights, and equal opportunity rights.

We are entering a new era of fascism through the door of plutocracy—a government exclusively designed to assist the wealthy. Ingo Niermann describes it so well in his book *The Monadic Age* (2024).

I am recalling these congresses because, last week, I read about a far-right meeting—a big congress in Madrid—but I realized I hadn't heard anything about meetings from the left, in all their existing forms. Demonstrations and condemnations are not enough. It is time for powerful counter-messages, powerful

290

defenses of education, of culture, of art. We need a convincing response, not the exposure of evil as a response, nor righteous morality as a response, nor cancellation as a response, nor negation as a response. A response produced collectively: surprising, magical, seductive, easy to repeat. Yes! A response that people can repeat at home, at work, on the streets, when confronted with hideous daily headlines. The kind of response that grows in culture, in architecture, in literature, in philosophy, in the social sciences, in poetry, in theater, in art, in the classrooms, in the public health services, in cinema …. We need to form a body with all these cells, whose voice will be saying we want to live in freedom and peace. Naïve? Overflow the system with naïveté, provoke a tsunami of the obvious desires of having the right to live.

LOVE of the ORACLE.

One of the most magical and difficult aspects of an exhibition is its title. It is not equally important for everyone. However, it is fundamental to me. Titles are my way of bridging with others. I see them as a hand—therefore my obsession with hands—extended to others through a short sentence. A title—like the name of a baby—gives character and acts like a self-fulfilling prophecy. Once the exhibition knows its title, it starts forming according to it.

When I first received the invitation to curate this year's edition of the Biennale, I started thinking about what a biennial is and what it means today. The title revealed itself: *The Oracle.*

A biennial—a recurrent exhibition with a long history—embodies a place that appears and materializes from time to time in front of a community. *The Oracle* is the magical place from where we pose questions, daydream, and envision ways. Art and culture *are* that magical place.

Thinking happens in circles; it never follows consecutive steps. Art plays different functions at different times. At times, it made us hyper-aware of language; at times, of matter; at times, of gender; at times, of magic; at times, of space; at times, of the body; at times, of violence; at times, of ideology; and now, of the very form of thinking and intelligence. These notions are neither tools nor instruments to speed up greed and capital.

In my head, an exhibition is composed of a series of episodes that awaken our senses in ways that are not easy to control or suppress. Those episodes are formed by the presentation of works in a given space. Collective shows form clusters of energy that are strangely powerful and have a physical effect on the viewers. Exhibitions affect the way we remember the space, intermingling the real, the mental, and the emotional spaces, allowing us to visualize a new dimension. We lost the ability to aspire, through art and culture, to regenerate social trust. I believe there is no time to be cynical—we need to orient ourselves to create, to invent, and to transmit. *The Oracle* is our place.

[March 7, 2025]

HEALTH and the singing voice.

All my life, I have been dreaming of having songs for the spaces we relate to. A song for my home, a song for the office, a song for biennials. I never got why big sports events get songs—and even Olympic mascots—but biennials do not.

I know. It has to do with the political and industrial past of the biennials as very serious and intellectual matters, for presenting cultural developments as products of evolution in time, and indicators of the success of certain communities and societies. This, in turn, has determined how we transmit culture and ideas through these events and has shaped our expectations towards large-scale exhibitions. Politics and music, though, can go hand in hand.

These days, I keep reflecting on how to promote associationism. So I keep thinking about a Catalan master of it: Josep Anselm Clavé (1824–74). A musician and a writer, he was at the core of the formation of a huge movement in mid-nineteenth-century Barcelona. Amateur orchestras and choral societies flourished at the speed of light under his guidance. To be precise, his singing societies— each with its own uniforms and banners—were composed of workers. He created a movement around the act of singing together, transforming the sense of unity and belonging to a community.

As a teenager, I entered the Orfeó Català choir society. This prominent ensemble—inheritor of the workers' ones—has its home in a palace: the Palau de la Música Catalana (Palace of Catalan Music), one of the most beautiful buildings in the city center. At that time, singing in a choir was considered very uncool by my schoolmates. Despite this view, I continued because I loved it. Despite loving it, I never confessed to anyone that I was singing in choirs for twenty years.

However, now I am reflecting daily on simple ways of creating collective bonds. Singing is one way. I am also closer to my dream: a song for the Ljubljana Biennale to be performed collectively. We'll try to compose it this summer, from early June on. You can try as well: think about what would be your choir. And think about museums and art spaces as palaces to host its spirit.

[March 14, 2025]

WEALTH of Music.

In my last entry, I was reflecting on the immense importance of certain historical choirs.

Ensembles of workers and voices syncing together in unison. It is surprising how the whole wave of mindfulness, yoga, and meditation stresses the importance of becoming one—with nature, with our environment— but at the same time it reinforces a new wild tendency of individual-oriented experiences.

The togetherness arising from rooms where different people meditate on their own problems, anxieties, and worries is totally different from the bodily effort you need to connect when you sing, dance, or play music together. We have been slowly but surely erasing or undermining

291

these practices from our curricula, from our social lives, from our habits as a group.

Teenagers are forming fewer bands, no longer dreaming of making music together. The transition from the twentieth to the twenty-first century has been a long goodbye to participatory activities. We're losing the muscle that helped us connect easily. Easy talk is dying away—easy flirting, social flirting … everything is just impossible. It embodies too many dangers, too many "no-gos." Then the century topped this with a pandemic. Bang! People reacted to it all over the globe with a sense of uneasiness and anger mixed with a growing will to control, understand, and assess the possible risks of living.

We secretly dream of a rebellion or an avant-garde coming to the rescue of the values and manners of old culture. Yet, what we get is only the revolt of those who are suffering and seek political revenge from the left and its class-oriented way of sending promises into the air. The air? The air should actually be filled with songs. And daily concerts.

Perhaps this is one of the reasons why chanting is making a comeback in so many performances, and many musicians are returning to a voice that is not ashamed of singing a song. A voice that can recite, rehearse words, modulate verses, and merge with a machine.

A new family of singers is emerging from the arts, along with a completely new way of rethinking obsolete forms and genres. To me, it's particularly interesting in places like Catalonia, for instance, known for its national sentiment, where young musicians are detoxifying the sense of identity with a new repertoire of songs often rooted in ancient tunes, from times when the territory was organized differently and the national language was a mixture where Arabic, Hebrew, Castilian, and Catalan would come together.

292

HEALTH and control.

I have been re-reading Val Plumwood's work recently.

She was attacked by a crocodile, and she survived it. Her words have been guiding me to compose the concept around the exhibition in Ljubljana. How? While being in the jaws of the reptile, she realized that the crocodile did not know who she was. Animals are unaware of the fact that humans never consider themselves to be food for others—that this, actually, should not happen. She wrote: "It seems to me that in the human supremacist culture of the West, there is a strong effort to deny that we humans are also animals positioned in the food chain." But it was happening: the crocodile was not an alien or a vampire in a horror movie killing a fictional character, but a real entity with a real personality trying to eat her. After an exhausting fight, with her last bit of energy, Plumwood jabbed her thumbs into the crocodile's eyes and felt its jaws relax. She was free. She was alive.

After some decades in which Western countries have been free from wars in their own territories—even though the Balkans conflict is still so present—it seems that the idea of having a life outside the "food chain," a life above the dangers of violence, has once again become seductive to many. A life where weapons, defense, military talk, and technology are understood as instruments of gaining control. These notions are all over the daily press again.

What? Do I think that we can counteract this talk and this mentality shift with exhibitions and culture? Do I think there is a way to easily stop this bad energy from spreading? No. I don't think that this will be an easy task. But I think that we need to start regaining a sense of what we can say and do, a sense of control we have lost. Who is "we" here? "We," the ones that nourish and form the communities around arts and cultures? The communities form education? Yes. The Ljubljana Biennale is going to be based on methodologies to gain a sense of action, I would say control, simply and plainly. Enough control not to panic and to strategize a way of continuing with the task of living.

[March 28, 2025]

WEALTH
of dreams.

There is a story in my family that answers some questions on how to deal with anxiety.

After becoming an orphan at a very early age, my grandfather had the ambition of saving money to buy a cow. He migrated to Switzerland—working as a carpenter—and earned enough to afford a nice cow. The cow was living in a barn he had built himself. After lunch, especially on Sundays and holidays, he placed a makeshift camp bed next to the cow and took his siesta. That big body breathing gave him the feeling of safety and comfort he had lost with the death of his parents.

I often ask myself how to place a cow in everyone's life. Exhibitions have the potential of becoming this cow, I think. They should be open after dinner time, and promote special programs for meeting there to fall asleep—or to try entering a state of daydreaming. Capitalism penetrated our vital functions so deeply that we think that being asleep is being "off." Screens may seem like sources of entertainment but, if used after dark, they weaken our brains' capacity to dream properly. At night, we should go to a museum to sit and learn how to mentally wander around. Daydreaming should be an exercise that we all strive to perform, individually and collectively. Dreaming through space; inducing our mind to create scenarios we'd love to be in for a while; learning how to mix up fantasy encounters with places we like; rehearsing conversations that we'd love to have; and doing things we'd love

to do …. Spending time training the mind to create a sort of virtual world inside our head—one that we can partly control, yet still leads somewhere unexpected—is pleasurable. The combination of control and adventure would give us a sweet sense of possibility, capable of producing a feeling of fulfillment. There is so much right now that frustrates us, that the prospect of an effortless accomplishment seems like a present. We all dream of being surprised by something great, someone great. Dreaming properly is the key to a better future.

A pandemic of anxiety, self-doubt, and continuous disappointment is creating a society without goals, actions, and collective joy. Delusions and escapism are replacing this capacity to dream. We spend a great deal of time talking about cooking, or the many aspects of conviviality, yet we still have to re-conquer the public spaces as sites of fantasy, fiction, orality, and daydreaming. Open public spaces are difficult, they are too exposed. Museums are perfect. Art is perfect: It can bear our indifference while we try to practice how to dream better.

[April 4, 2025]

HEALTH.

Wells are important in exhibitions. I define the Oracle as the privileged place from where we wonder about the future. But the Oracle is also a well. In many tales, there is a hole, and from that hole emerges a wonder. The wonder is not something exceptional per se, but it's crucial to establish contact with another reality, with another dimension of the real.

As I have already mentioned, a book I always keep at hand is Jules Verne's *Journey to the Center of the Earth* (1864). By following the text of an ancient alchemist claiming to have discovered a passage to the center of the Earth, three men join forces and disappear through the mouth of a volcano.

Oracles, volcanoes, wells: they are all mouths

293

speaking about the inside of the world. Humans get a sense of scale and relevance from traveling mentally inside the Earth and far outside, into the immensity of the cosmos. Art has the same function. It operates as a regulative principle between reality and fantasy, sanity and insanity. Art can be seen as an amniotic fluid that allows us to breathe when there is no air, to see when our eyes are still closed, to understand when language is not there yet. Right now, art is really needed. We all feel the urge to escape; we all feel that nonsense is taking over, slowly but surely. No significant resistance seems to be in place—horrors and crimes are explained in reverse as if they were not happening, as the banality of suffering was meant to be.

I came to think that a big part of the problem is that people have stopped reading literature.

To restore an idea of the "common good" in politics, we need two things: the ability to be convinced by trustworthy emotions, and the ability to compare. If we doubt the news, the origin of images, and believe in the constant distortion of facts, then we need to train a mental muscle to compare situations and circumstances, and to make acceptable decisions. If we are unable to compare, it is difficult to see how things may affect our lives.

My husband's father—a slaughterer born in the German countryside—used to devour romantic novels. Through simple plots and patterns, one becomes familiar with the circumstances from where love emerges. One becomes aware of the signs humans send when they mean love, but talk hate. Since reading is difficult for many, we can propose exhibitions instead. A biennial as a literary introduction to the mind. As a way of experimenting with the transmission of forms and works, but also narrations and emotions. An exhibition as a literary journey to the center of the Earth. Earth as both a natural and social contract.

294

LOVE.

I once applied for a job at the Frankfurter Kunstverein, and it wasn't until I moved there that I realized I didn't know a single person in the city. My unconscious reaction was to dress quite extravagantly—as if I had my own kingdom of friends or fans—and the whole thing was not so terrifying. A few days into my new job, I received two letters: one from the artist Thomas Bayrle, and the other from the curator Jean-Christophe Ammann. Thomas sent me a letter—that is always with me, like my ID card—with his father's original membership to the Kunstverein, along with a note saying: "Let's be friends, dinner at ours," with a date, time, and address. Jean-Christophe's letter was a two-page manual of recommendations on what to do at work, with a telephone number at the bottom and a note saying "Call anytime."

I went to Thomas and Helke's—his wife, and also an artist—house for dinner, and that week he came by the office every day. He introduced me to two projects that left a profound trace in my life ever since: *Kinderplanet* and *Mortuarium für zwei Alphabete*, the immersive world of concrete poetry created by the German writer and artist Franz Mon for the 1970 Venice Biennale.

Kinderplanet was developed by Thomas Bayrle and Wolfgang Schmid with the students of the Offenbach University of Applied Arts, at the Messehalle Frankfurt, during the summer vacations of 1971. Around 45,000 children, who had nowhere else to go during the summer, participated. The images taken by Barbara Klemm on that occasion left me speechless. Is it that simple? In the photographs, you can see a constant flow of children and adults interacting as if the world makes sense to both groups equally. The other impressive project, by Franz Mon, was an octagonal structure with transparent panels, displaying progressive overlays of text and letters, symbolizing the gradual disappearance of language and script. In the images, the large-scale installation looked like a big technological display, but it was entirely made by hand, by using simply transparent plastic and letters.

At that time—I was in Frankfurt in the 2000s—contemporary art was supposed to carry the promise of societal change in the near future. We all secretly believed progress was inevitable and that we could never go back. I find it both sad and great to see the faces and smiles of all those enthusiastic artists who carried truly radical thinking in the past, and then look at the current present, so limited and narrow-minded. They were all positive, and happy to meet me, and willing to start again from scratch, as if these wonderful anarchic and powerful projects had never happened. They had, of course, but—already—no one seemed to remember them.

[April 18, 2025]

HEALTH.

Narratives of the past convinced us that certain formats—biennials, for example—aspire to a global appeal, while others are more oriented towards the local. We should forcefully contest this binary of "local versus international." This approach somehow reinforces the idea that there are two standards: the "local" is seen as less competitive and more endogamic, the "international" as greedy and elitist. Both paradigms are at risk nowadays. Perhaps it is time to acknowledge art and culture as an interdependent environment, in which all the messages artists convey must be seen in relation to one another.

We should never abandon the ambition to transform our communities and the thinking of our peers, even when our horizon is deeply local—and by this I mean deeply intimate, and deeply committed towards a specific context. Only then can we truly learn from the moments when locality opens itself, offering a threshold, a gateway to a bigger universe, that allows us to refresh and sync with the energies and practices of other equally specific and intimate communities. A biennial—and, even more, one that will turn seventy this summer—is exactly this: a portal, a membrane connecting worlds that would otherwise remain apart.

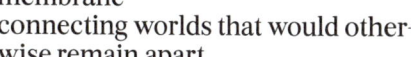

295

One big problem with the art world is the language it adopted long ago, and that gets repeated again and again: that a biennial is "an event," something big but empty, that happens in disconnection with the people and the place where it is hosted, leaving behind no traces when it ends. However, this disconnection is healthy. It is meant to carry messages, bodies, voices, and artistic languages that are not necessarily familiar. Why? To boost curiosity and avoid the natural entropy intrinsic to every locality. To break habits; to open eyes and hearts; to critically wonder about how many scenes one could be connected with; to dream of a bigger, open world. An open world? Yes, one that reflects on its own level of nationalism, self-protection, and narcissism. One that is curious about the others, that keeps asking questions. Now that worlds seem to be closing down, some may think it is about time to stop dreaming of anything but that which your home place already produces. And yet, no place produces anything without another, even one that cannot be physically reached. Myths and dreams have long been our ways for escaping the determinism of a place, a culture, a nation, a language, a race .... Biennials embody and collect this sentiment. But they—like any other cultural format—need us to exist. We need to feel responsible for sustaining and caring for these environments of exchange and hope.

It is always a matter of politics and never of taste to be where the artists are, where the art is, where the poets are, where the thinking is.

LOVE.

I never really cared much about puppets before. In my mind, they were placed in the past, and I never saw them as a potential language or substance carrying a message for the future. And yet, there is nothing that I love more than completely changing my opinion. When this happens, I feel full of hope, since I assume the same could occur to everyone. Changing opinion is a matter of feeling and revelatory experiential dimensions, rather than one of arguments.

I keep returning to Slovenian artist Ajša Pengov (1913–83); in a letter, she writes about her wish to free puppets from humans' hands, attaching them to long, invisible strings, as if those threads didn't exist at all. This reminds me of a book I read many years ago on the Czech marionette tradition, which started in the eighteenth century, often as part of itinerant performances. Another artist in it had caught my attention: Jan Švankmajer (b. 1934), a stop-motion animator who combined puppetry with live-action to create purely gothic, extravagant films.

All of a sudden, everything became clear: on the one hand, puppets are surrogates that act on our behalf, allowing us to observe ourselves with a strange mix of empathy and disgust; on the other, they embody the desire to tell stories and travel from home to home. Puppets and digital media are similar, then. They are driven by the ambition to turn you into a character, instead of just letting you be yourself. And they follow you all the way in, right at the center of your life. Once, that center was the main square or a bar, now it is the sofa. But the ambition to catch you is common to both the analog and the digital puppet. The difference is in the repertoire.

Marionettes—from small companies to national theaters—are committed to education. Corporate social media are not: they are invested in designing our behavior to standardize it, making it banal for living, and banal for voting. Puppets were crucial in developing language skills. They encouraged storytelling and speech, and were invested in telling folk and fairy tales, and fables, teaching ethics, empathy, and social values to their public. I am maybe idealizing here, but I can see a new puppet avant-garde emerging ....

HEALTH.

In a recent conversation we shared, an artist spoke about the importance of exploring the potential of avatars in dealing with all the pain she could not carry, and assisting her to readjust the perception of her own image—to see herself through the avatar. The connection between digital avatars and traditional puppets is fascinating, as both represent forms of virtual and physical fabrication of characters, made to expose certain behaviors and to tell stories. Humans are always interested in exploring how the expression of emotions and ideas—thinking, in a word—manifests itself and is represented.

I despise violence in all its forms and associate it with the implosion of thinking. But I assume that all those—politicians and other communities—who start a war and assist in the perpetuation of destruction and annihilation, or promote the rearming of all nations, have reflected on what comes afterwards. Like forgiveness.

Forgiveness is a very complex emotion that names the passage from acute and unbearable emotional pain, to peace. Of course, philosophers have written extensively about it, but how can we transform it into an experiential form? Lately, I have been reading the interviews and translated materials of Japanese animator, filmmaker, and manga artist Hayao Miyazaki (b. 1941), *Starting Point: 1979–1996*, translated by Frederik L. Schodt (VIZ Media, 2009), a co-founder of Studio Ghibli. Forgiveness is a profound and recurring theme in his writings and films. It is clear that he understood long ago how forgiveness—and war, too—cannot be experienced or understood by means

of abstract statements of any kind, but rather through the interpersonal relationships and inner growth of the characters involved in a story. In his view, understanding is the only way to avoid revenge. Healing is connected to understanding, and so is forgiveness. The ability to forgive is a vital part of the human experience. Without it, we would all turn into beings possessed by a very dangerous moral ambiguity that translates into simplistic views, like fake moral superiority.

How many millions of Totoros are we going to need to soak the world in empathy again? How many mystical creatures, avatars, puppets, artworks, poems, voices, performances, and tales, to regain a sense of wonder and innocence, and be able to face democracy again?

[May 9, 2025]

WEALTH.

All my life, I have defended quotas. And, all my life, I've been told that quotas are bad because you should look at the *quality* of things, events, works, and people. But I am both very pragmatic and stubborn, and I have insisted on quotas. To insist on a quota, in my view, is to insist on making certain regulatory decision-making principles clear to oneself. It is quite different from saying that the quota is the only thing we have to consider in making a decision.

One example. When I was a child, I hated white fish, especially when cooked. Not only does it have a certain smell, but it also has a very particular whiteness and texture that requires some kind of education. Enjoying this dish was a sign of respect for the elders in my family. As it seemed impossible for me as a kid to appreciate the quality of that recipe, my parents introduced it into my diet once a week for years. That's a quota. To eat cooked white fish more than once a week would mean breaking the quota.

Learning to educate our decision-making processes is important. If anything remains of the critical thinking ideals, it would be the revision of our choices and acquired tastes. And so,

to all the quotas already in place, I would add another: to include artists without major gallery representation in exhibitions and, particularly, in biennials. Indeed, to the question of gender and identity, I would add—again—the question of economy and class. I realize more and more that we (those mainly working in the public sector) are ashamed of being poor. There was a brief moment in history when politics seemed genuinely interested in culture. But that time has passed, replaced by a present where pleasing the wealthy seems not only important, but crucial. Cultural practitioners continue to insist on the values, on the principles, on the orders of social justice and equality. But the whole system is changing fast, and ignoring that won't make it disappear.

For a while, I have been hopeful that philanthropy would be refined and reorganized to preserve the common good. I got that idea from the growing interest in addressing the issue of rising sea levels, caused by natural inequalities and climate emergencies. But it seems much more difficult to merely protect education and public culture. And in the face of poverty, it would be better to stand with the poor than to merely sell to the rich. Otherwise, it should be like the cooked white fish, once a week.

[May 16, 2025]

HEALTH.

Many years ago, a very charismatic teacher and scientist from Iran guided us through the three most important pillars to build, in his opinion, a healthy future: universities, museums, and hospitals. He encouraged us to research the history of these institutions in different countries to discover who financed them: who the *stockholders* were. His idea was to turn us into—in his words—"sommeliers of funding."

I had never thought of looking at the world through that lens before. In my interpretation, the real world was divided into two imaginary hemispheres: one

297

was entirely publicly funded (Western Europe), and the other was privately operated (the US and a vast part of Asia, with the exception of Russia and China at the time). The complexities and entanglements of public and private funding were not transparent or easy to read. I discovered in shock, for example, that NASA had a publicly financed art program, created in 1962 by James Webb and active almost until the 2000s.

Thanks to this exercise of learning who pays for things that matter and are decisive in shaping collective views and values, I regularly keep doing these "funding checkups." For example, we now admire the "boom" in contemporary art in Korea. But behind a burgeoning community, there is always a huge investment. In the UK and US bookshops, 43% of the top forty translated fiction titles in 2024 were Korean and Japanese literature. The cultural fabric in Korea is up to 75% private. Together with the United States, it's the country with the largest number of private cultural initiatives—museums included—worldwide. In Europe, most museums are still public (only 1% are not).

From NASA to the Nobel Prize in Literature, the argument is the same: public funding is essential to create and support the idea of something remarkable happening. Although advertisements are very effective in communicating, when a message comes from a reliable source, the way we trust it is different. We want to believe that extraordinary things are still possible. But the magic behind the extraordinary comes from a coalition of public forces believing in it, which in the past was called "entente," from the French notion of understanding. We all need to push this understanding. An understanding of peace, an understanding of what nourishes a fertile society, one that is able to support equality and the idea of a life worth aspiring to. I am not an idealist. In the same way that people can agree on rearmament, they can agree on culture and peace.

LOVE.

Almost unconsciously, during the entire process of working out the ideas and artists for the Ljubljana Biennale, I had children in mind. From the aspirations of the incredible 1950s' puppeteers to reach a young public, to the incredible literature and poetry of Svetlana Makarovič, in the exhibition, there's a constant longing for genres and languages that have an appeal for kids. "Childhood" may mean many things, and different people, cultures, or communities interpret this concept differently. In some contexts, children are simply not yet grown people, while in others, they have an amazing status that touches epistemological questions and ethical conditions of humans in the social environment.

Moving mentally, day by day, through the different rooms and venues of the exhibition, I ask myself: How would children react? So, I started imagining the discussions we all could have. That's why one trait of the Biennale are special labels positioned in each space with the aim of inspiring all visitors—and especially the younger ones—to start a conversation.

Most children probably don't know that there was a time in history when puppet theater was booming, becoming a cornerstone of kids' cultural life in Slovenia, for example. Some of this culture still remains, of course, but in a different form. Children's literature could also be a political genre. Makarovič's stories possess a unique emotional depth, moral clarity, and a mix of darkness and tenderness that manages to capture the attention of the youngest without speaking down to them. What I like most is that Svetlana's prose and poetry can help children face their inner struggles and moral dilemmas.

The contemporary obsession with a dull version of safety—which is closer to repression than to the feeling of liberation that security is supposed to release—is producing a scared youth. Instead of revising, re-visiting, and reinventing the contents that we are creating for children, we started talking about the pros and cons of the digital.

In my native northern Spain, poor people are said to spend most of their income on children's clothes and accessories. Far from thinking that this is illogical or impractical, since they grow fast, I think the real problem lies in spending this cash on fast food, fast fashion, or fast culture. Treating children as the most important subjects of our world, without lazily spoiling them, would mean spending not just money, but time to talk properly with them about important subjects, like pain and joy. And, at the same time, of course, protecting them from any war and violence that adults have created. This might be a potential direction toward a different world.

[May 30, 2025]

LOVE.

Art, life, and work cross paths in so many ways while preparing an exhibition. When I last met Vesna Petrešin, not long ago, the last thing I could imagine was that illness would make it impossible for her to enjoy the reception of her work in the Ljubljana Biennale.

Vesna studied architecture at the Faculty of Architecture at the University of Ljubljana, where she graduated in the mid-1990s. Then she left for London, where she completed postgraduate studies in Art and Design at the Royal College of Art, specializing in areas connecting design, sound, and multimedia. She had been based abroad—London first, then Berlin for the last decade or so. Returning to Ljubljana and exhibiting in the Biennale was like a familiar but strange adventure she was truly willing to undertake. I completely relate to this feeling of returning to the place where you grew up with completely new eyes, and the hope

to connect and make friends with the younger generations.

Water has always been a passion and a subject in Vesna's work. She inherited this bond from her father, Eugen Petrešin, a scientist in the field of hydraulics and water management. In 2021, for example, she conceived a performance called *Immersio*, where she mixed underwater recordings of her soprano voice, transforming water into a percussive instrument. This work involved a live performance over video, featuring Vesna walking into the ocean. In *All Things Are Made of Water* (2023), she developed a multi-sensorial environment with wearable audio technology and VR to emphasize water's role in all biological processes.

For her, the divide between art, science, and technology did not exist. If we had enough passionate artists and mediators, people would understand that, indeed, the realms are connected and co-dependent. Science needs art, and technology finds in art its tongue, its organs. Like many other artists in the Biennale, she was a singer, a soprano. And as such, she saw synchronization as something we continuously seek as humans in order to transmit without words. Singing means vibration, air. And air flows like water, transmitting to an invisible world but also allowing us to capture the million signals the cosmos is sending to us.

She was truly visionary in seeing the human voice as a key element to conceive immersive environments. Voice over images. Water over bodies. Voice and water together are capable of an immense force, an immense expression. Expression is so important—because if we manage to express in the most forceful manner, if we could experience total expression, we might anni-hilate violence.

I am so deeply sad. I love you, Vesna.

299

HEALTH, WEALTH, AND LOVE.

I am writing the last entry of my diary about the Biennale in the lobby of one of its venues, while I am still installing the labels, the lighting, the poems that will greet you as you enter. I am possessed by a strange exhilaration. Writing kept me from being anxious, from overthinking every decision and thought. I was writing to you, to all of you, and this kept me connected with the receivers, with those I imagined coming and seeing the exhibition with me. Now this bond will change. When the doors would finally open, and everything that we

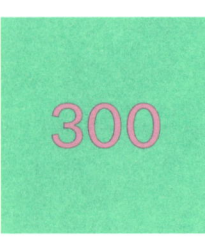

have collectively done would be shared. Producing new works entails engaging in millions of conversations: some are long and deep, some are just concise words shared after a sleepless night. Each room that you now see as finished had many forms. Till a work reaches its final "body," it wanders in the cosmic and mental space created by continuous exchange. It is magic to see these works materialize. It is probably the closest to *actual* magic.

Perhaps because we are not so many—twenty-five artists are participating—many elements and motifs resurface, conveying the impression of being somehow united: birds, eyes, elements that symbolize trespassing .... Aside from the will to interpret what is currently happening, the exhibition exudes a desire to see the current state of the world entering into another phase. "I have asked myself if there is hope," a student said while installing. "I know there is." These words acted as a balm while working these days.

We have all been deeply touched by the death of one of the artists, Vesna Petrešin. We know life does not know about happy endings. However, this exhibition is an act of collectively holding on to the possibility of living with hope. Only when I started installing the Biennale, I realized how strongly I had focused on the existential. I used to detest the prose of Jean-Paul Sartre. And yet I am doing an exhibition that embodies one of his most famous mottos: Existence precedes essence. Existence is understanding that life has no a priori meaning, and that we constitute the meaningful together.

I have also realized that biennials should be seeds for new cultural policies. Education and art are a matter of national defense. Exhibitions of this scale and significance are true sources of ideas and motivation for new ways of acting in the public space. Yes, I think this exhibition is all about courage. If we are alive, we need to be fearless in facing a fact: no one is going to reverse the wrong on our behalf; it is up to us. Take a deep breath, and go.

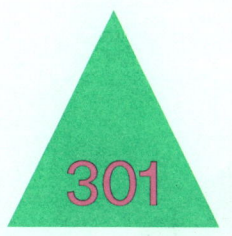

p. 6

Entrance to Museum of Modern Art Ljubljana with graphic design by Mina Fina and Ivian Kan Mujezinović / Grupa Ee, 2025. Photo: Klemen Ilovar. © International Centre of Graphic Arts (MGLC).

pp. 13, 14, 21, 22, 29, 30, 118, 119

Photos and graphic design by Mina Fina and Ivian Kan Mujezinović / Grupa Ee.

p. 38

MGLC Grad Tivoli with graphic design by Mina Fina and Ivian Kan Mujezinović / Grupa Ee, 2025. Photo: Klemen Ilovar. © International Centre of Graphic Arts (MGLC).

p. 41

Gabi Dao, *Uncharismatics*, 2023-24. Slip-cast ceramic and glazes, second-hand textiles, teddy bear shoes. Photo: Jaka Babnik. © International Centre of Graphic Arts (MGLC).

pp. 42 & 43

Gabi Dao, *Sweet Blood in Stagnant Waters*, 2025. Digital video, stereo sound, 30 min, stoneware ceramics, second-hand textiles, dried chunks of clay. Photo: Jaka Babnik. © International Centre of Graphic Arts (MGLC).

pp. 44 & 45

Gabi Dao, *Sweet Blood in Stagnant Waters*, 2025. Digital video, stereo sound, 30 min, stoneware ceramics, second-hand textiles, dried chunks of clay. Photo: Klemen Ilovar. © International Centre of Graphic Arts (MGLC).

p. 46

Silvan Omerzu, *Mr. Captain*, 2025. Puppet installation. Photo: Jaka Babnik. © International Centre of Graphic Arts (MGLC).

pp. 48–51

Silvan Omerzu, *Mr. Captain*, 2025. Puppet installation. Photo: Klemen Ilovar. © International Centre of Graphic Arts (MGLC).

pp. 52, 53, 55–57

CANAN, *Kıymeti Zatiyye* (*Intrinsic Value*), 2025. Installation. Photo: Klemen Ilovar. © International Centre of Graphic Arts (MGLC).

p. 58

Manuela Morales Délano, *Espantapájaro con ojo* (*Scarecrow with Eye*), 2025. Stone and pigeon spikes. Photo: Jaka Babnik. © International Centre of Graphic Arts (MGLC).

p. 60

Manuela Morales Délano, *Espantapájaro* (*Scarecrow*), 2025. Stone and pigeon spikes. Photo: Jaka Babnik. © International Centre of Graphic Arts (MGLC).

pp. 61–64

Gabriel Abrantes, *Bardo Loops*, 2024. Four-channel video installation, 2 min per channel. Photo: Jaka Babnik. © International Centre of Graphic Arts (MGLC).

pp. 81–84

Silvan Omerzu, *The House of Our Lady, Help of Christians*, 2025. Puppet installation. Photo: Klemen Ilovar. © International Centre of Graphic Arts (MGLC).

pp. 85, 87–90

Vesna Petrešin in collaboration with Prof. Dr. Eugen Petrešin, *Autonomous Energy Machine*, 2025. Acrylic glass, MDF, paint, soundscape. Photo: Klemen Ilovar. © International Centre of Graphic Arts (MGLC).

p. 92

Joan Jonas, *Ray* (detail), 2018. Watercolor on paper. Courtesy of the artist and Gladstone Gallery.

p. 93

Joan Joans, *Ray*, 2018, and *To Touch Sound*, 2024, video, 11'42" (installation view). Photo: Jaka Babnik. © International Centre of Graphic Arts (MGLC).

p. 95

Miles Howard-Wilks, selected works, 2014–24 (installation view). Photo: Jaka Babnik. © International Centre of Graphic Arts (MGLC).

p. 96

Miles Howard-Wilks, *Untitled*, 2022. Gouache, greylead pencil, 56 × 75.5 cm. Courtesy of the artist and Arts Project Australia.

Miles Howard-Wilks, *Untitled*, 2014. Gouache, 38 × 56 cm. Courtesy of the artist and Arts Project Australia.

pp. 121, 124 & 125

Sinzo Aanza, *The Irregular Line*, 2025. Drawing. Photo: Klemen Ilovar. © International Centre of Graphic Arts (MGLC).

pp. 123 & 128

Sinzo Aanza, *The Irregular Line*, 2025. Drawing. Courtesy of the artist.

pp. 126 & 127

Sinzo Aanza, *The Irregular Line*, 2025. Drawing. Photo: Jaka Babnik. © International Centre of Graphic Arts (MGLC).

pp. 131 & 136

Kathrin Siegrist, *A Shade We Share I*, 2025. Discarded, modified emergency parachutes (nylon ripstop), steel tubes (scaffolding elements). Photo: Jaka Babnik. © International Centre of Graphic Arts (MGLC).

pp. 133–35

Kathrin Siegrist, *A Shade We Share I*, 2025. Discarded, modified emergency parachutes (nylon ripstop), steel tubes (scaffolding elements). Photo: Klemen Ilovar. © International Centre of Graphic Arts (MGLC).

pp. 145 & 147

Kathrin Siegrist, *A Shade We Share II*, 2025. Discarded, modified emergency parachutes (nylon ripstop). Photo: Klemen Ilovar. © International Centre of Graphic Arts (MGLC).

p. 149

Ajša Pengov, *Žogica Marogica* (*Speckles the Ball*), 1951. Marionette. On loan from from the Museum of Puppetry (Ljubljana Puppet Theatre). Photo: Jaka Babnik. © International Centre of Graphic Arts (MGLC).

pp. 150 & 151

Ajša Pengov, Puppets from *Zlata Ribica* (*The Golden Fish*), 1953. Marionettes. On loan from from the Museum of Puppetry (Ljubljana Puppet Theatre). Photo: Jaka Babnik. © International Centre of Graphic Arts (MGLC).

pp. 152 & 156

Silvan Omerzu, *Table for a Poet*, 2025. Puppet installation. Photo: Klemen Ilovar. © International Centre of Graphic Arts (MGLC).

pp. 154 & 155

Silvan Omerzu, *Table for a Poet*, 2025. Puppet installation. Photo: Jaka Babnik. © International Centre of Graphic Arts (MGLC).

pp. 158 & 159

Noor Abed, *a study of a stick: movement notations and notes on defiance*, 2025. Film stills and sketches. Photo: Klemen Ilovar. © International Centre of Graphic Arts (MGLC).

pp. 160–63

Noor Abed, *a study of a stick: movement notations and notes on defiance*, 2025. Film stills and sketches. Photo: Jaka Babnik. © International Centre of Graphic Arts (MGLC).

p. 165

Juan Pérez Agirregoikoa, *Who keeps the zoo?*, 2025. Acrylic mural. Photo: Jaka Babnik. © International Centre of Graphic Arts (MGLC).

pp. 166 & 168

Yarema Malashchuk and Roman Khimei, *Open World*, 2025. Dual-channel video, color, sound, 13'42". Photo: Klemen Ilovar. © International Centre of Graphic Arts (MGLC).

p. 167

Yarema Malashchuk and Roman Khimei, *Open World* (video still), 2025. Dual-channel video, color, sound, 13'42". Courtesy of the artists.

pp. 170–72

Jane Jin Kaisen, *November*, 2025. Dual-channel video installation, 4K, color, stereo sound, 12 min, synchronized loop. Photo: Klemen Ilovar. © International Centre of Graphic Arts (MGLC).

pp. 174–76

Nohemí Pérez, *Guardians*, 2025. Charcoal and embroidery on canvas. Photo: Klemen Ilovar. © International Centre of Graphic Arts (MGLC).

p. 201

Derek Tumala, *Island in the Sun*, 2025. Video installation, composed of 6 light sculptures (abaca paper, metal, LED), round single-channel video, 3 min, loop. Photo: Jaka Babnik. © International Centre of Graphic Arts (MGLC).

pp. 203 & 204

Derek Tumala, *Island in the Sun*, 2025. Video installation, composed of 6 light sculptures (abaca paper, metal, LED), round single-channel video, 3 min, loop. Photo: Klemen Ilovar. © International Centre of Graphic Arts (MGLC).

p. 205

Derek Tumala, *Island Life* (video still), 2025. Round single-channel video, 3 min, loop. Courtesy of the artist.

p. 206

Juan Pérez Agirregoikoa, *Who keeps the zoo?*, 2025. Acrylic mural. Photo: Jaka Babnik. © International Centre of Graphic Arts (MGLC).

p. 207

Juan Pérez Agirregoikoa, *Who keeps the zoo?*, 2025, and Aili Vint, *Illustrations of the books from 1978-79* (installation view). Photo: Jaka Babnik. © International Centre of Graphic Arts (MGLC).

p. 208

Aili Vint, *Installation detail No. 1* and *Meeting place*, 1990. Sculpture, mixed materials. Photo: Klemen Ilovar. © International Centre of Graphic Arts (MGLC).

p. 210

Aili Vint, *Detail of the Sea*, 1979. Book illustration, gouache on paper, 28 × 21 cm. Photo: Jaka Babnik. © International Centre of Graphic Arts (MGLC).

Aili Vint, *Rainbow*, 1979. Book illustration, gouache on paper, 28 × 43 cm. Photo: Jaka Babnik. © International Centre of Graphic Arts (MGLC).

p. 211

Aili Vint, selected works, 1978-90 (installation view). Photo: Klemen Ilovar. © International Centre of Graphic Arts (MGLC).

p. 212

Juan Pérez Agirregoikoa, *Who keeps the zoo?*, 2025. Acrylic mural. Photo: Jaka Babnik. © International Centre of Graphic Arts (MGLC).

pp. 213 & 216

Mladen Stropnik, *house*, 2025. Mirror wall and wooden stand. Photo: Jaka Babnik. © International Centre of Graphic Arts (MGLC).

p. 214

Mladen Stropnik, *outsider*, 2025. Concrete sculptures. Photo: Jaka Babnik. © International Centre of Graphic Arts (MGLC).

p. 217

Mladen Stropnik, *sex*, 2025, rotating painting, and *toaleta*, 2025, painting with rotating mirrors. Photo: Jaka Babnik. © International Centre of Graphic Arts (MGLC).

p. 219

Eduardo Navarro, *Oceanic Altar*, 2025. Cardboard seal, 16 drawings, ink and pastel, 55 × 77 cm. Photo: Klemen Ilovar. © International Centre of Graphic Arts (MGLC).

pp. 220 & 221

Eduardo Navarro, *Oceanic Altar*, 2025, cardboard seal, 16 drawings, ink and pastel, 55 × 77 cm, and *The origin of the origin of the origin*, 2025, 20 drawings, ink on paper, 110 × 77 cm. Photo: Jaka Babnik. © International Centre of Graphic Arts (MGLC).

p. 222

Eduardo Navarro, *F.O.C.A.(Foundation for the Oceanic Contemplation of Affection)*, 2022-25. Courtesy of the artist.

pp. 223 & 224

Manuela Morales Délano, *As Above, So Below*, 2025. Kahari paper and pastel. Photo: Jaka Babnik. © International Centre of Graphic Arts (MGLC).

pp. 226 & 227

Manuela Morales Délano, *As Above, So Below*, 2025, and Ema Kugler, *Infinite Repetitions*, 2025 (installation view). Photo: Klemen Ilovar. © International Centre of Graphic Arts (MGLC).

pp. 228-32

Ema Kugler, *Infinite Repetitions*, 2025. Film, 22 min. Photo: Jaka Babnik. © International Centre of Graphic Arts (MGLC).

pp. 249 & 251

Mayte Gómez Molina and Ingo Niermann, *Hieroglyphs of the Monadic Age*, 2025. Video installation, 10 min. Photo: Gregor Gobec. © International Centre of Graphic Arts (MGLC).

p. 252

Mayte Gómez Molina and Ingo Niermann, *Hieroglyphs of the Monadic Age*, 2025. Video installation, 10 min. Photo: Jaka Babnik. © International Centre of Graphic Arts (MGLC).

p. 253

Mayte Gómez Molina and Ingo Niermann, *Hieroglyphs of the Monadic Age* (video still), 2025. Video installation, 10 min. Courtesy of the artists.

p. 254

Mayte Gómez Molina and Ingo Niermann, *Hieroglyphs of the Monadic Age*, 2025. Video installation, 10 min. Photo: Klemen Ilovar. © International Centre of Graphic Arts (MGLC).

p. 255

Silvan Omerzu, *Forbidden Loves*, 2025. Puppet installation. Photo: Gregor Gobec. © International Centre of Graphic Arts (MGLC).

p. 256

Silvan Omerzu, *Forbidden Loves*, 2025. Puppet installation. Photo: Klemen Ilovar. © International Centre of Graphic Arts (MGLC).

pp. 259-65

Takeshi Yasura, *distilled*, 2025. Water (Slovenia), silk thread (France), marble (Korea), soil extracted from 2,000-year-old strata (Japan), animal glue (Japan), found stones (Slovenia), indigo (Japan), amur cork tree bark (Japan), walnut hulls (Slovenia), spruce wood (Slovenia), lava stone from Mt. Fuji (Japan), bird feathers (Slovenia), coins (Slovenia), machine controlled by binary rhythm (using bird songs recorded in Ljubljana on May 24-25, 2025), solar panel, pump, speaker, LED bulb, 8mm glass pane, piano wire. Photo: Jaka Babnik. © International Centre of Graphic Arts (MGLC).

pp. 266-69 & 271-73

Saelia Aparicio, *In the Blink of Collapse*, 2025. Installation with plywood, stain dye, Chinese ink, mural, convex mirrors, found objects, mixed media. Photo: Jaka Babnik. © International Centre of Graphic Arts (MGLC).

p. 270

Saelia Aparicio, *In the Blink of Collapse*, 2025. Installation with plywood, stain dye, Chinese ink, mural, convex mirrors, found objects, mixed media. Photo: Klemen Ilovar. © International Centre of Graphic Arts (MGLC).

pp. 275 & 280

Nicole L'Huillier, *Rehearsal Room*, 2025. Sound installation. Photo: Gregor Gobec. © International Centre of Graphic Arts (MGLC).

pp. 276-80

Nicole L'Huillier, *Rehearsal Room*, 2025. Sound installation. Photo: Jaka Babnik. © International Centre of Graphic Arts (MGLC).

Biennale Publications:
Vesna Česen Rošker, Gregor Dražil, Sanja Kejžar Kladnik, Blažka Kirm, Ajda Ana Kocutar, Chus Martínez, Yasmín Martín Vodopivec, Nevenka Šivavec, Lili Šturm

Production Consultant:
Božidar Zrinski

MGLC Print Studio:
Jakob Puh

Accompanying and Educational Programmes:
Lili Šturm

Archival and Documentary Materials:
Karla Železnik

Public Relations:
Sanja Kejžar Kladnik

International Public Relations:
Nicola Jeffs

Marketing:
Petra Klučar

Fundraising:
Chus Martínez, Dušan Dovč, Petra Klučar

Logistics Coordination:
Dušan Dovč, Dijana Lukić, Boštjan Vidmar

Technical Support:
Borut Wenzel, Andrej Črepinšek, Borut Bučinel, Alen Đudarić, Jaka Erjavec, Maid Hadžihasanović, Jurij Hartman, Blaž Janko, Anastazija Pirnat, Vita Tušek, Simeon Cieslinski, Cezary Grabowski

Assistants to Juan Pérez Agirregoikoa:
Samra Buljić, Valentin Radulović, Isidora Todorić

Educational work:
Lucija Klauž, Katarina Marov, Klara Maček, Kaja Rožman, Jerca Šuštar, Isidora Todorić

Head of the MGLC Info Point and Museum Shop:
Isidora Todorić

Visitor Services and Reception:
Lana Hasić, Tinkara Kovačič, Klara Maček, Valentin Radulović, Tea Stepan, Isidora Todorić, Jan Toffolutti, Nika Žilavec

Participating galleries and venues:
City Art Gallery Ljubljana, Museum of Modern Art (MG+), Isis Gallery, "S" Gallery – Ljubljana Castle, National Museum of Contemporary History of Slovenia, Jakopič Promenade

Supported by:
National Center for Art Research, Japan; SAHA Association; Institute Art Gender Nature HGK Basel FHNW; Mondriaan Fund; Acción Cultural Española (AC/E); Embassy of Spain in Slovenia; Danish Arts Foundation; Pro Helvetia; James Howell Foundation; Institut Ramon Llull; Mousse; Gemeinde Riehen; Art Jameel; Fachausschuss Film und Medienkunst Basel-Stadt / Basel-Landschaft; Kunstkredit Basel-Stadt; Han Nefkens Foundation; Etxepare Euskal Institutua; Estonian Ministry of Culture; Estonian Centre for Contemporary Art; Arts Project Australia; Colección Oxenford; Pontevedra Art Biennial; The Vega Foundation; Pfyl Stiftung; Hitay Foundation; Batalha Centro de Cinema; Stiftung Erna und Curt Burgauer; Mercedes Vilardell; Gabriela Galcerán; Pieter and Marina Meijer-von Tscharner; and Nicoletta Fiorucci Foundation.

Published in conjunction
with the 36th Ljubljana
Biennale of Graphic Arts,
June 6 – October 12, 2025,
Ljubljana, Slovenia.

The Oracle:
On Fantasy and Freedom

Published by
Sternberg Press

Editors:
Chus Martínez,
Ajda Ana Kocutar

Contributors:
Manca G. Renko,
Maja Petrović-Šteger,
Sadie Plant,
Renata Salecl,
Svetlana Slapšak

Copyediting and
proofreading:
Dean J. DeVos

"Walk-through
of the Exhibition"
was first published in
The Oracle: On Fantasy and
Freedom; The Guidebook,
edited by Vesna Česen
Rošker, Ajda Ana Kocutar,
and Chus Martínez, and
proofread by Vida Jocif,
published by the
International Centre of
Graphic Arts (MGLC).

"THE ORACLE:
A Curatorial Diary"
was first published on
moussemagazine.it, edited
by Barbara Casavecchia
and Emma Passarella.

The text by Manca G. Renko
was translated from Slovene
into English by Vida Jocif.

Design:
Mina Fina, Ivian Kan
Mujezinović / Grupa Ee

Printing:
Matformat, Ljubljana

ISBN 978-1-915609-77-9

Co-published with the
International Centre for
Graphic Arts (MGLC).

With the support of the
City of Ljubljana and the
Ministry of Culture of the
Republic of Slovenia.

EU Authorised
Representative:
Easy Access System
Europe, Mustamäe tee 50,
10621 Tallinn, Estonia. gpsr.
request@easproject.com

Distributed by The MIT
Press, Art Data, Les presses
du réel, and Idea Books.

Printed in Slovenia.

Cover illustration:
Grupa Ee

Sternberg Press
71-75 Shelton Street
UK-London WC2H 9JQ
www.sternberg-press.com

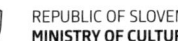

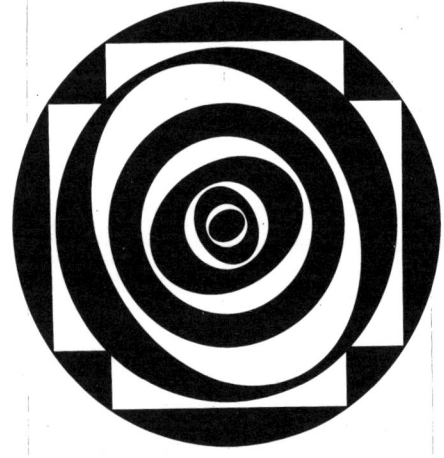